Strategies for Responsible Innovation

How can responsible business work in the highly competitive areas of innovation? Focusing on business opportunities and illustrating how Responsible Innovation can be successfully implemented in practice, this book captures experiences and insights from key decision-makers in business, politics, and academia, to answer this question. In addition to interviews with leading thinkers in the field, *Strategies for Responsible Innovation* describes the experiences of eight EU projects and provides tools for Responsible Innovation in the business sector.

The examples in this book illustrate how to move from a vague societal aspiration to a business case for Responsible Innovation, and provide a compelling argument for collaboration at the important intersection between government, business, and academia. In this way, Responsible Innovation transcends a singular market-based approach to deliver value at many levels, co-creating in a truly inclusive manner. The book sheds light on the strategic benefits of applying the concept of Responsible Innovation in practice and offers concrete tools for its implementation.

Aimed primarily at managers of innovation processes in organizations, and consultants and facilitators working on Responsible Innovation and sustainability management, the book also provides insight into the logic and principles of Responsible Innovation management for academics, policy-makers, and civil society organizations, helping them better communicate their requirements to business.

André Martinuzzi is founder and Director of the Institute for Managing Sustainability and Associate Professor at Vienna University of Economics and Business, Austria. For more than 20 years, he has co-ordinated EU projects on corporate social responsibility, sustainability management, Responsible Innovation, and the circular economy.

Florian Findler was a postdoctoral researcher and project manager at the Institute for Managing Sustainability at WU Vienna, Austria. His research focused on corporate sustainability, Responsible Innovation, and sustainability in higher education. He is currently manager at PricewaterhouseCoopers in Germany, focusing on sustainability in transactions.

Alexander Graf was a postdoctoral researcher and project manager at the Institute for Managing Sustainability at WU Vienna. His research focuses on responsible sourcing, mining policies, and the circular economy. He is currently senior consultant at Kumi Consulting Ltd., focusing on mandatory due diligence.

"This book offers a rich variety of experiences, insights, and tools to help organizations tackle societal challenges, engage multiple stakeholders, and strive for sustainable development."

Marcel Bogers, *Professor of Open and Collaborative Innovation, Eindhoven University of Technology*

"This book demonstrates the importance of making technology and innovation more responsible and sustainable, a necessity not only in the Global North but also in the Global South."

Payal Kumar, *Emerald Brand Ambassador and Principal Academic Advisor, Indian School of Hospitality*

"This book reframes responsible innovation from a societal expectation into an appealing business opportunity."

Rodrigo Lozano, *Founder and Director, Organisational Sustainability, Ltd; Visiting Professor, Central University of Technology, Bloemfontein, South Africa*

"Corporate responsibility is both a societal imperative and an attractive business case for multinational enterprises. This book offers guidance on its implementation in the area of innovation management."

Manfred Schekulin, *Long-term Chair, OECD Investment Committee*

"Co-creating the future we want, with a portfolio that enables a positive impact on our planet and society at scale. This is our ambition, therefore this book offers valuable tools and insights on how to successfully implement Responsible Innovation in a business context."

Judith Wiese, *Chief People and Sustainability Officer, Member of the Managing Board of Siemens AG*

Strategies for Responsible Innovation

Perspectives, Projects, and Tools for Co-creating the Future We Want

Edited by
André Martinuzzi, Florian Findler, and Alexander Graf

Routledge
Taylor & Francis Group
LONDON AND NEW YORK

Designed cover image: © Getty Images / ismagilov

First published 2025
by Routledge
4 Park Square, Milton Park, Abingdon, Oxon OX14 4RN

and by Routledge
605 Third Avenue, New York, NY 10158

Routledge is an imprint of the Taylor & Francis Group, an informa business

British Library Cataloguing-in-Publication Data
A catalogue record for this book is available from the British Library

Library of Congress Cataloging-in-Publication Data
Names: Martinuzzi, André, 1964-editor. | Findler, Florian, editor. | Graf, Alexander (Editor), editor.
Title: Strategies for responsible innovation : perspectives, projects, and tools for co-creating the future we want / edited by André Martinuzzi, Florian Findler, and Alexander Graf.
Description: Abingdon, Oxon ; New York, NY : Routledge, 2024. |
Includes bibliographical references and index.
Identifiers: LCCN 2024016943 (print) | LCCN 2024016944 (ebook) | ISBN 9781032333960 (hardback) | ISBN 9781032333977 (paperback) | ISBN 9781003319481 (ebook)
Subjects: LCSH: Organizational change—Moral and ethical aspects. | Sustainable development.
Classification: LCC HD58.8 .S7598 2024 (print) | LCC HD58.8 (ebook) |
DDC 658.4/063—dc23/eng/20240527
LC record available at https://lccn.loc.gov/2024016943
LC ebook record available at https://lccn.loc.gov/2024016944

ISBN: 978-1-032-33396-0 (hbk)
ISBN: 978-1-032-33397-7 (pbk)
ISBN: 978-1-003-31948-1 (ebk)

DOI: 10.4324/9781003319481

Typeset in Minion
by codeMantra

Contents

Contributors

Margot Bezzi (Agency for the Promotion of the European Research, Italy) holds a master's degree in communication science and media studies from the University of Bologna. She works on EU research and innovation policies with a focus on science-society relationship. This includes Responsible Research and Innovation, social innovation, open R&I models, the societal implications of technologies and of digital transformation.

Chiara Buongiovanni (Agency for the Promotion of the European Research, Italy) holds a master's degree in communication science from LUMSA University, Rome, and further specialization in Public Management, European policies, and Human Rights. Her work revolves around the intersections among communication, public engagement in policymaking and social innovation, with a focus on territorial ecosystems.

Alessandro Deserti (Politecnico di Milano, Italy) is full Professor and Head of the Department of Design at Politecnico di Milano, Italy. His research is focused on design-enabled innovation processes, methods, and tools, with particular reference to their introduction in new fields and to the ways in which their adoption can be combined with systemic and organizational change. He has been actively working as a researcher and coordinator for various EU-funded research projects.

Anne M. Dijkstra (University of Twente, the Netherlands) holds a PhD in Science Communication. She studies the changing relationship between science, technology, and society from a communication perspective, among others, in EU projects.

Jennifer Eckhardt (TU Dortmund, Germany) is a researcher in the Social Research Center of TU Dortmund, Germany, and her research focuses on the investigation of societal transformations in relation to the possibility of an inclusive society. She has researched social innovation and inclusion in national and European projects.

Florian Findler (PricewaterHouseCoopers Germany, Frankfurt, Germany) was a postdoctoral researcher and project manager at the Institute for Managing Sustainability at WU Vienna, Austria. His research focused on corporate sustainability, Responsible Innovation, and sustainability in higher education. He is currently manager at PricewaterhouseCoopers in Germany, focusing on sustainability in transactions.

Roxana Firth (Center for Computing and Social Responsibility, De Montfort University, Leicester, UK). She is a Design Anthropologist working across UX Research and Cultural Insights. She is the author of *An Ethnography of Household Energy Demand* in the UK (Palgrave Macmillan).

Malcolm Fisk (Center for Computing and Social Responsibility, De Montfort University. Leicester, UK) is a Professor of Ageing and Digital Health. He is an experienced project leader, and researcher with a demonstrated history of "making things happen" through his work on health and digital technologies. He is very active in the world of standards and the ethical foundations to underpin product and service design.

Catherine Flick (Centre for Computing and Social Responsibility, De Montfort University, Leicester, UK) is a Reader in Computing and Social Responsibility. Her areas of research have involved Responsible Research and Innovation in health technologies and cyber security, trusted computing, ethics and video games, and anonymous technologies. She is a Fellow of the Higher Education Academy and a member of the ACM's Committee on Professional Ethics.

Steven Flipse is an Assistant Professor in Communication Design for Innovation at the Science Education & Communication research group at the TU Delft, the Netherlands.

Alexander Graf was a postdoctoral researcher and project manager at the Institute for Managing Sustainability at WU Vienna. His research focuses on responsible sourcing, mining policies and circular economy. He is currently senior consultant at Kumi Consulting Ltd., focusing on mandatory due diligence.

Anja Grüll (Institute for Managing Sustainability, Vienna University of Economics and Business (WU), Austria) is a Teaching and Research Associate at the Institute for Managing Sustainability who specializes in circular economy, Responsible Innovation, and European Union project management.

Jens Ørding Hansen (Nordland Research Institute (NRI), Norway) is a Senior Researcher at the Nordland Research Institute. He holds a doctoral degree in International Management from the University of Agder, Norway. His research interests include corporate governance, corporate finance, regional development, Responsible Research and Innovation (RRI), and organization studies.

Marianne Hörlesberger (AIT Austrian Institute of Technology) has worked for AIT Center for Innovation Systems & Policy since 2001. She has applied various methodologies for detecting emerging technologies and science mapping (scientometrics and bibliometrics). She enlarged her field to applying foresight methodologies and engaging stakeholders for strategy development in innovation ecosystems.

Izaskun Jimenez Iturriza (TECNALIA, Basque Research and Technology Alliance (BRTA), Spain) has recently been involved in projects related to the engagement of society in research and innovation processes. She works in projects dealing with the societal aspects of energy, such as the integration of social science and humanities in energy policy-making and the role of collective initiatives in the energy transition.

Svetlana Ivanova (Institute for Managing Sustainability, Vienna University of Economics and Business (WU Vienna), Austria) is a Teaching and Research Assistant at the Institute for Managing Sustainability at the Vienna University of Economics and Business, Austria, focusing on business opportunities of Responsible Innovation. She studied public policy at the Central European University in Budapest and worked as a senior researcher at ISINNOVA, an Italian independent research institute, in the areas of Responsible Innovation and Foresight.

Christoph Kaletka (TU Dortmund, Germany) is Deputy Director at TU Dortmund University's Social Research Center (SFS), Germany. He is an innovation researcher and teaches social innovation, digital and societal participation at TU Dortmund's Faculty of Rehabilitation Sciences.

Pim Klaassen is an Assistant Professor Policy, Communication and Ethics in the Health and Life Sciences at Vrije Universiteit Amsterdam, the Netherlands.

Wilfried Konrad (DIALOGIK non-profit Research Institute, Stuttgart, Germany) studied business administration and sociology in Mainz and Frankfurt, and he received his doctorate from the University of Frankfurt in 1997. Since 2010, he has been a Project Manager and Research Associate at DIALOGIK in Stuttgart, Germany, with a focus on social science energy research, bioeconomy, and participation research.

Ursula Kopp (Institute for Managing Sustainability, Vienna University of Economics and Business, Austria) has been conducting research in Corporate Social Responsibility for more than 20 years, as well as in innovation over the past 10 years. She is a professional facilitator and mediator and has carried out several hundred design-thinking processes.

Brigitte Kriszt (Montanuniversität, Außeninstitut, Leoben, Austria) holds a PhD degree in material science. In 2004, she began working at the Institute for Industrial Liaison and was in charge of technology transfer and cooperation with Austrian and international partners. In 2015, she started working in additive manufacturing. From 2018 to 2021, she coordinated the I AM RRI project.

Daniel Krüger (TU Dortmund, Germany) is a Researcher at TU Dortmund University's Social Research Center (SFS), Germany. His work involves research on social innovation, social innovation ecosystems, and co-creation on the national and international level, with a special focus on digital inclusion. He holds an MA in Management and Regulation of Work, Economy and Organisation.

Rainer Kuhn (DIALOGIK non-profit Research Institute, Stuttgart, Germany) studied sociology and political science, and he has been a Research Associate at DIALOGIK Institute and the Centre for Interdisciplinary Risk and Innovation Research at the University of Stuttgart, Germany, since 2010. From 2020 to 2021, he was Coordinator of Communication at DIALOGIK, and he has been the Scientific Director of DIALOGIK since 2022. His research is centered on participation research and the development of qualitative methods, including consensus-building processes.

Zenlin Kwee is an Assistant Professor of Strategy and Innovation in the Department of Values, Technology & Innovation at TU Delft, the Netherlands.

Bianca Laue (Technology Accessibility Competence Center, Siemens AG) has been working for the Siemens Accessibility Competence Center in Paderborn, Germany, since 2014. Her expertise includes evaluating the accessibility of hardware and software, contributing to various accessibility standards, and participating in European research projects, such as the LIVING INNOVATION project.

Maria Maia is a Senior Researcher working on Technology Assessment in Health at KIT, Germany.

Elvio Mantovani is the former Scientific Director of Airi/Nanotec IT, the Committee for Nanotechnology and the other Key Enabling Technologies of Airi, Italy.

André Martinuzzi (Institute for Managing Sustainability, Vienna University of Economics and Business, Austria) is founder and Director of the Institute for Managing Sustainability and Associate Professor at Vienna University of Economics and Business, Austria. For more than 20 years he has co-ordinated EU projects on corporate social responsibility, sustainability management, Responsible Innovation, and the circular economy.

Elena Mocchio is Head of the Innovation and Development Unit in UNI, the Italian Standardization Body.

Nhien Nguyen (Norwegian University of Science and Technology (NTNU), Norway & Nordland Research Institute (NRI), Norway) is an Associate Professor at the Norwegian University of Science and Technology and a Senior Researcher at the Nordland Research Institute. She has led several EU projects focusing on innovation ecosystems and RRI. Her research interests include Responsible Innovation, organizational learning, artificial intelligence (AI), and digital strategy.

Adebowale Owoseni (Center for Computing and Social Responsibility, De Montfort University, Leicester, UK) is a Senior Lecturer in Information Systems (IS) with 13 years' industry practice, leading and assisting businesses to derive significant value from digital investments through digital transformation. At present, he leverages his industry experience and contributes to IS research, focusing on the societal impacts of digital technologies and digital transformation.

Daniela Pimponi is a Technology Analyst at Airi, the Italian Association for Industrial Research.

Andrea Porcari is a Project Manager at Airi, Italian Association for Industrial Research, Italy.

Francesca Rizzo (Politecnico di Milano, Italy) is a Full Professor at Politecnico di Milano, Department of Design, Italy, where she teaches User Centred Innovation and Digital Design. She is an expert in Participatory Design applied in the fields of Service Design, Interaction Design, Social Innovation and Public Sector Innovation. She has been working as a researcher for various EU- funded research projects and is the author of many international publications relating to design research.

Felicitas Schmittinger (Politecnico di Milano, Italy) is a Service Designer, Research Fellow, and Teaching Assistant at Politecnico di Milano in the Department of Design, Italy, with a special interest in the introduction of design techniques and tools in organizations. She has worked on projects in various sectors exploring the influence and impact of design.

Norma Schönherr (GMI, Gregor Mendel Institute for Molecular Plant Biology, Austria) was formerly a Senior Scientist at the Institute for Managing Sustainability at WU Vienna. In this capacity, she participated in several EU-funded projects on Responsible Innovation, including the COMPASS project. She has since joined the Gregor Mendel Institute for Molecular Plant Biology as a Grants Manager and currently leads efforts to develop an Equity, Diversity & Inclusion Plan.

Bernd Stahl (Centre for Computing and Social Responsibility, De Montfort University, Leicester, UK) is a Professor of Critical Research in Technology and Director of the Centre for Computing and Social Responsibility at De Montfort University, Leicester, UK (www.dmu.ac.uk/ccsr). His interests cover philosophical issues arising from the intersections of business, technology, and information.

Klaus-Peter Wegge (Technology Accessibility Competence Center, Siemens AG, Germany) is head of the Siemens Accessibility Competence Center. He is a blind computer scientist and has worked as an accessibility engineer for more than 25 years. He specializes in ICT accessibility and product evaluation with older persons or persons with disabilities and actively contributes to international standardization and European accessibility research.

Sarah-Kristina Wist (DIALOGIK non-profit Research Institute, Stuttgart, Germany) obtained her BA in sociology and political science from the University of Mannheim. She received her master's degree in empirical political and social research from the University of Stuttgart. Since 2012, she has been working as a Research Associate at DIALOGIK and she is the Head of the Communication Department. Her research centers on participation procedures and democratic innovations.

Bianca Witzel (DIALOGIK non-profit Research Institute, Stuttgart, Germany) obtained her BA in cultural sciences from the University of Koblenz-Landau. She completed her MA in media studies at the University of Bonn and obtained a BSc in psychology from the University of Erlangen-Nuremberg. She is currently pursuing an MSc in psychology at the Technical University of Chemnitz. Since 2021, she has been working as a Research Associate at DIALOGIK, with a focus on energy transition, acceptance, and participation.

Emad Yaghmaei is a Senior Research Fellow in Responsible Innovation at the Department Values, Technology & Innovation at TU Delft, the Netherlands. His research interests cover governance of organisations and processes with focus on their ethical, social, and governmental impacts. He is specially interested in designing and developing necessary policies and methods for implementation and evaluation of Responsible Innovation within industrial context. He is founder and partner of YAGHMA B.V., a consultancy specialized in materiality assessment and monitoring of non-financial values.

Foreword

Research and innovation are key drivers for overcoming challenges and paving the way toward a sustainable, competitive, and resilient future.

The European Commission is fully engaged to provide the best conditions for innovation to flourish and to give it direction so that our society benefits, that no one is left behind and that we respect the boundaries of the planet. Our policies and programs require strong collaboration with Member States to foster a fit for purpose, inclusive and connected European innovation eco-system that helps Europe to capitalize on its scientific excellence, its collective intelligence and creativity. At the same time, we put our common European values, freedom, ethical, societal, and fundamental rights at the heart of our policies.

European industry is key in achieving prosperity, competitiveness and leadership in the transition towards a resilient, green and digital economy. Many companies already embedded responsibility and sustainability into their strategies and core business functions.

I welcome the timely reflections and new perspective presented in this book on Responsible Innovation as a source of multiple business opportunities. It will help putting both concepts high on the agenda of entrepreneurial management, as innovations are subject to strong international competition, resulting in responsibility and sustainability often being misperceived as an additional burden.

The book presents insights, outcomes, and experiences of a series of projects supported by the EU Programme for Research and Innovation. Hands-on tools, provided in this book, can support companies to innovate for positive impact, to co-create innovations in a truly inclusive manner and to become industry game-changers. Following such strategic approaches, innovators from all business sectors can turn knowledge into tangible solutions, take into account the wellbeing of all people and co-create the future we want.

Mariya Gabriel

European Commissioner for Innovation, Research, Culture, Education and Youth

Introduction

André Martinuzzi, Florian Findler, and Alexander Graf

MAJOR TRENDS IN INNOVATION POLICY

The last several years have been marked by major disruptions, including the COVID-19 pandemic, escalating global conflicts, and the first effects of climate change. These disruptions have not only created challenges but will also persist in generating challenges in global supply chains, with the potential to trigger a global recession and re-shape innovation policy and management. While innovation areas such as digitalization, health, nanotechnology, and biotechnology have maintained their status as key drivers of competition and global success, new areas have started to gain attention from policymakers and businesses. On the one hand, these emerging areas include de-carbonization and the circular economy, while, on the other, they encompass specific aspects of digitalization, such as artificial intelligence (AI), cyber security, and chip manufacturing. At the same time, there has been a noticeable shift in the overarching perspective of innovation policy, moving from a previous emphasis on openness and collaboration to focusing more strongly on competitiveness. In addition, the notion of technology sovereignty has gained prominence in national and international debates as an additional rationale for innovation policy and as a strategy to mitigate dependencies in key technologies and critical raw materials. Consequently, the years ahead will be shaped by intensified global technology-based competition, geopolitical antagonism, and open disagreements regarding value systems (Edler *et al.*, 2023).

The World Economic Forum (Schwab & Zahidi, 2020) has highlighted that achieving long-term economic transformation hinges on strategic investments in the right type of products, services, and technologies to generate economic growth and prosperity while also safeguarding the planet, empowering individuals, and strengthening communities and institutions. Increasing diversity, equity, and inclusion across the entire innovation chain will be fundamental to broadening the pool of potential talent, improving the capacity of new solutions to reflect the needs of society, and ensuring that all segments of society benefit equally from the economic advantages of innovation. Without explicitly calling it "Responsible Innovation," the World Economic Forum highlighted some of its main principles, such as collaborative and participatory innovation processes, on the one hand, and the impacts of innovation outcomes on people, the planet, and profits on the other.

DOI: 10.4324/9781003319481-1

Responsibility, sustainability, and solidarity have long been the guiding principles of Europe's innovation policy, and are perceived as Europe's unique proposition on global markets. The European Union has developed several initiatives and frameworks to ensure responsible and sustainable innovation. One such concept is "Responsible Research and Innovation" (RRI), which aims to integrate societal values and ethical considerations into the research and innovation process; promotes the inclusion and deliberation of citizens, civil society organizations, and end-users in innovation processes; and encourages the anticipation of the social, environmental, and ethical impacts of innovations. The European Framework Programme "Horizon 2020" has provided support for approximately 180 projects by investing more than 360 million euros in an effort to develop tools for RRI, encourage research funding and research organizations to implement it, and thus foster the institutionalization of responsibility in innovation processes and organizations (Ivanova *et al.*, 2023). However, only a few projects have focused on the business sector or involved companies as partners in their activities. Consequently, strategies for successful Responsible Innovation in the business sector are still scarce.

A BUSINESS PERSPECTIVE ON RESPONSIBLE INNOVATION

The business sector is a key player in research and development (R&D): in 2021, around two-thirds of the R&D activities in Europe were performed by companies, while 58% of the total R&D expenditure in Europe was funded by companies (Eurostat, 2023). Directing these R&D processes and outcomes toward social responsibility and sustainability is vital to addressing grand societal challenges, safeguarding the public acceptance of technologies, and increasing competitiveness. The societal responsibility of research and innovation must therefore consider the acceptability, societal desirability, and sustainability of innovation processes and outcomes (von Schomberg, 2012). In science, the discourse on the societal responsibility of research and innovation is diverse and framed by different concepts:

- *Responsible Innovation* is rooted in scholarly debates on science and technology studies, anticipatory governance, and technology assessment, which gained prominence in the 1970s (Barben *et al.*, 2008; Lubberink *et al.*, 2017). Moreover, it emphasizes the future-oriented notion of responsibility, care, and responsiveness. Finally, it acknowledges the power of innovation to shape the future and actively seeks to engage with society (Stilgoe *et al.*, 2013; Owen & Pansera, 2019).
- *Sustainability-Oriented Innovation* which emerged in the early 2000s (Gallego-Álvarez *et al.*, 2011), highlights the need to integrate aspects of sustainability into innovation management as a source of business opportunities and as a promising means for addressing societal and environmental challenges (Bouglet *et al.*, 2012). However, the ethical limitations and potential negative impacts of innovations are rarely discussed.
- *Responsible Research and Innovation* originates from a public policy dialogue initiated within the European Union in the late 2000s. It was put forward by a

dedicated funding stream in the EU Framework Programme Horizon 2020 (von Schomberg & Hankins, 2019) and operationalized by themes such as gender equality, public engagement, science education, open access and data, governance and ethics, and science education.

Several scientific studies have linked Responsible Innovation to business practices. Iatridis and Schroeder (2016) demonstrated the usability of several corporate social responsibility (CSR) tools for Responsible Innovation, arguing that to be practically relevant to companies, Responsible Innovation needs to take companies' interests and incentives into account. Dreyer *et al.* (2017) presented a consensus view on Responsible Innovation from a group of industry practitioners who shared the view that the existing concepts, tools, and methodologies are not sufficiently aligned with current industrial practices. Van de Poel *et al.* (2017) developed a conceptual model of RRI for the business sector and a comprehensive set of RRI-related key performance indicators (KPIs) in order to integrate responsibility aspects into innovation standards. Martinuzzi *et al.* (2018) explored a wide range of positive outcomes associated with Responsible Innovation, including a better understanding of consumer needs, prevention of innovation failure, greater trust in stakeholders, safeguarding the license to operate, and alignment with regulatory expectation. However, they also highlighted that the direct and indirect impacts of innovation are difficult to quantify, that economic returns frequently depend on the behavior of external stakeholders, and that the transformative potential of innovation can be highly unpredictable. Brand and Blok (2019) identified potential tensions between competitive markets and between the social and ethical requirements of innovation processes. Scherer and Voegtlin (2020) developed a framework for Responsible Innovation based on reflexive and participative corporate governance and highlighted that current practices fail to set the right incentive structures for businesses. Gurzawska (2021) found that most companies engaging in Responsible Innovation either assess their compliance with laws and regulations or carry out environmental, social, human rights, or health impact assessments. Lukovics *et al.* (2023) proposed the implementation of a certification scheme for Responsible Innovation for consumers in order to reduce information asymmetry and to allow companies engaged in Responsible Innovation to command higher product prices. Ivanova *et al.* (2023) demonstrated that Responsible Innovation in industry addresses different discursive frames, considers potential conflicting interests, and requires different incentive mechanisms, depending on the context (i.e., if Responsible Innovation is approached in a regional context, in a specific company, or within a particular innovation process).

Despite these diverse findings, a strategic approach that highlights the business opportunities associated with Responsible Innovation is still missing. With this book, then, we intend to fill this gap and thereby support a wider uptake of Responsible Innovation in the business sector. In Part A of the book, we present insights from ten key decision-makers in business, politics, and academia, all of them dealing with the question "How can responsible business work in the highly competitive areas of innovation?" In Part B, we present the results and experiences of eight EU projects that focused specifically on involving and engaging the business sector in Responsible Innovation. In the final part, Part C, we provide hands-on tools that can be used across five distinct areas of Responsible Innovation. Altogether, this book illustrates how to move from a vague societal aspiration to a business case for Responsible Innovation.

PART A: INSIGHTS AND CHALLENGES

Part A of the book explores the insights and challenges related to the application of Responsible Innovation in the business sector. Our panel of ten high-level experts represents a diverse set of stakeholders, including top executives from the private sector, former Director Generals of the European Union, senior researchers, and one best-selling author. Together, they identify and address various strategic challenges related to Responsible Innovation.

The first aspect concerns the importance of Responsible Innovation for safeguarding the European Union's strategic positioning, both with regard to European values and global competitiveness. Sabine Herlitschka (Chapter A1) sees a mutual impact between innovation and technology and social value systems. For Europe, the adequate control of key technologies, including their innovation, is therefore a question of protecting and strengthening its deep roots in democracy, equality, sustainability, and other areas. This perspective calls for proactive measures and presents a business opportunity to foster Responsible Innovation while reinforcing European values. Robert-Jan Smits (Chapter A2) similarly advocates for a value-driven approach to sustainable innovation to ensure long-term success, while at the same time acknowledging the challenge of not falling behind in the digitalization wave, particularly in Europe's automotive, pharmaceutical, and food industries. Achieving this requires combined efforts from both the public and private sectors, including increased venture capital and mentoring, training of soft skills, partnerships, and the promotion of an innovation system that enables responsibility without overregulation. Meanwhile, Robert Madelin (Chapter A3) argues that a "social culture of innovation" with a positive view of opportunities rather than mere risk aversion is required to unlock Europe's full innovation potential. This depends on securing the right funding mechanisms and framework conditions from EU administrative bodies. Companies are asked to realign their purpose toward an economics of mutuality for maximum net positive outcomes in terms of the Sustainable Development Goals (SDGs) across all relevant actors.

The second aspect involves the connection between Responsible Innovation and collaboration, particularly within the context of systems innovation. Robert-Jan Smits (Chapter A2) strongly advocates for innovation collaborations, such as the Eindhoven Brainport, which is collaborative and competitive at the same time. In such a setting, frictions caused by conflicting interests can drive Responsible Innovation by challenging all participants to create win-win situations and design systemic solutions for the future. René von Schomberg (Chapter A4) makes the case for openness and cooperation not only for Responsible Innovation but also as important balancing mechanisms to increase the efficiency of public and private innovation ecosystems that are overstrained by competition. He proposes a shift in innovation priorities, moving from technological potential to the more systemic view of societal challenges in order to achieve a sustainable impact. In this context, the role of public authorities should be strengthened to guide innovation management and partnerships. Tima Bansal (Chapter A5) explains how successful collaboration between academia and business starts with both sides having the freedom to pose their questions. For public and private organizations to achieve sustainable innovation, sustainability has to be understood as a means by which to solve problems with a long-term perspective. This entails organizations seeing themselves as part of a larger system and embedding sustainability sufficiently deep into their innovation functions so that they are not affected by personnel changes over time.

A third important theme regards the implementation of Responsible Innovation by companies in terms of challenges, needs, benefits, and possibilities. Richard Owen (Chapter A6) sees the benefit of their pioneering four dimensions of RRI (see Stilgoe *et al.*, 2013) in the reorientation toward the power to shape new technologies rather than as a mere risk mitigation tool (cf. also Robert Madelin, Chapter A3). However, he acknowledges that the integration of Responsible Innovation into organizational structures and practices remains a key challenge for the future due to the ongoing paradigm of productivity growth and competition based on confidentiality. Successful and responsible private sector innovation harmonizes in the view of Sandra Kolleth (Chapter A7) by combining customer-led innovation with business-to-business cooperation, strong company values, and long-term planning. Scenario-based product development is one tool to explore and exploit the synergies between social and environmental sustainability and economic viability. However, this also requires the "courageous realization of ideas" in which profitability does not always represent the top priority of innovation. Harald Leitenmüller (Chapter A8) observes that innovation is increasingly shifting toward a more holistic approach to solution design. Co-creation and interdisciplinary collaboration across industries and stakeholders rapidly open up new possibilities for innovation, but the establishment of a common language is necessary to produce positive results.

A fourth theme concerns the potential impact and risks of technological innovations currently employed in our societies, particularly AI and augmented/virtual reality (AR/VR). Harald Leitenmüller (Chapter A8) recognizes that striking the right balance between human and autonomous decision-making in concrete use cases remains a key issue. He stresses that it is imperative for companies to apply clear ethical frameworks and procedures to select use cases for AI and design responsible solutions based on local contexts and values. Marc Elsberg (Chapter A9), similarly, addresses some of the key concerns associated with AI and big data, including personal data. By taking control of certain decision-making processes, AI has the power to define our values without users having any awareness of how such values were formulated. If misused, AI may lead to higher dependency, surveillance, and manipulation, ultimately eroding our competency and diversity, which are crucial for innovation. Security and convenience should not restrict our freedom, Elsberg argues; rather, we should be able to seek security and convenience through freedom. In a similar fashion, AR/VR poses huge risks, as noted by Armen Ovanessoff (Chapter A10). Concerns include the (mis-)use of personal data and the unknown mental health impacts of using AR/VR. Due to these unknown elements and our limited understanding of how such technology might affect the human brain, Ovanessoff calls for the integration of proper Responsible Innovation into design and innovation processes from the outset, rather than addressing issues retrospectively. This would not only reduce any negative impacts but also save time and costs.

PART B: PROJECTS AND EXPERIENCES

Part B of this book provides insights from eight RRI projects that were funded by the European Union and that are perceived as being among the first attempts to deal with RRI in the business sector. They had a project duration of between two and three years and were carried out between 2014 and 2022. On average, each project had an EU contribution of 2.21 million euros, amounting to an overall contribution of 2.26 million euros. In total, 89 organizations from 22 countries participated in these projects. The eight projects are categorized based on their different focus areas as follows:

- Four projects focus on the *company level*. RESPONSIBLE INDUSTRY served as a pilot project for RRI for companies in the previous FP7 EU Framework Program. PRISMA and COMPASS targeted small and medium-sized enterprises (SMEs), while I AM RRI concentrated on value chains within additive manufacturing. All projects were Coordination and Support Actions (CSAs) coordinated by higher education institutions.
- One project focuses on *innovation processes*, namely SISCODE. This project pursued the idea of co-creation by involving citizens and business representatives and developing methods for co-creation. It was a Research and Innovation Action (RIA) coordinated by higher education institutions.
- Three projects focus on the *territory level* and cover multiple highly developed regions in Western Europe. These projects integrated RRI principles into regional development. The projects, namely DigiTeRRI, SeeRRI, and RRI2SCALE, were Coordination and Support Actions (CSAs) coordinated by research organizations. They involved local and regional authorities as well as businesses in their initiatives.

Chapter B1 presents the RESPONSIBLE-INDUSTRY project, the first project funded by the European Union to address RRI in industrial contexts. It explores how practices in commercial research and innovation environments can be applied to the RRI debate and addresses the transfer of RRI funding principles to the private sector. The chapter also introduces RRI as a concept of meta-responsibility and highlights the significant role it plays in ensuring Responsible Innovation in industry.

Chapter B2 describes the COMPASS project, which aimed to make RRI accessible to SMEs. It recognizes that entrepreneurs need to understand the value of RRI thinking to ensure its mainstream adoption. The chapter focuses on the methods and tools developed and tested in the project to empower SME decision-makers to create their own RI visions and roadmaps.

Chapter B3 focuses on the PRISMA project, discussing the principles, framework conditions, and implementation of RRI in industrial practice. It introduces a guideline developed in the project to assist in the implementation of long-term strategies (roadmaps) for Responsible Innovation. This guideline builds upon existing standards and strategies for corporate social responsibility (CSR), quality, risk, and innovation management. Moreover, it provides support to corporate decision-makers in implementing structural changes that foster forward-looking, inclusive, and Responsible Innovation practices.

Chapter B4 introduces the project I AM RRI that focuses on the integration of key aspects of RRI, known as the RRI Keys, into the system of innovation value chains, with additive manufacturing (AM) serving as an example. More specifically, it considers the distinct characteristics and significance of six RRI Keys for effective innovation management and presents a guideline to assist decision-makers in companies in their efforts to integrate RRI principles into their innovation processes.

Chapter B5 describes the SISCODE (Society in Innovation and Science through CO-DEsign) project, which examined co-creation ecosystems at the micro, meso, and macro levels. The project conducted a comprehensive analysis of the dynamics and relationships within these systems to identify effective co-creation tools, practices, and approaches. Based on the findings, the chapter derives guidelines and tips for corporate decision-makers to leverage RRI through co-creation strategies in order to foster innovation development.

Chapter B6 presents findings from the SeeRRI project in an attempt to bridge the gap between RRI and the field of environmental economics. It demonstrates how RRI can effectively address current environmental and economic challenges and contribute to increased economic efficiency by reducing asymmetric information among industry, policy-makers, academia, and citizens. The chapter includes a case study of the plastics industry in Lower Austria, highlighting the long-term benefits of RRI for corporate decision-makers.

After that, Chapter B7 introduces the RRI2SCALE project, which focused on integrating RRI principles into regional research and innovation policies, strategies, and ecosystems. The chapter specifically explores experiments conducted across four regions to enhance stakeholder engagement and test co-design methodologies. The approach and results of RRI2SCALE provide companies with a better understanding of future societal developments and market opportunities.

Chapter B8 then looks at the EU project DigiTeRRI, which focused on transforming traditional industry regions into digital ecosystems and emphasized the role of different stakeholders. The chapter presents a case study of the Styrian innovation ecosystem and provides a roadmap for establishing sustainable digitalized innovation ecosystems based on the RRI approach.

For further information on the projects covered in each chapter, see Table I.1.

Table I.1
Overview of the RRI projects presented in Part B

<table>
<tr><th>Project</th><th>Focus</th><th>Start date</th><th>End date</th><th>Total costs (million euro)</th><th>EC contrib. (million euro)</th><th>No. of partners</th></tr>
<tr><td>RESPONSIBLE-INDUSTRY</td><td>Company</td><td>February 2014</td><td>July 2017</td><td>1.9</td><td>1.5</td><td>10</td></tr>
<tr><td colspan="7">RESPONSIBLE-INDUSTRY developed and tested a benchmarking method for RRI maturity and published a guideline for the information and communication (ICT) industry</td></tr>
<tr><td>COMPASS</td><td>Company</td><td>May 2016</td><td>April 2019</td><td>1.5</td><td>1.5</td><td>7</td></tr>
<tr><td colspan="7">COMPASS developed an interactive online platform for small and medium-sized enterprises (SMEs), a self-check tool, and a variety of online resources</td></tr>
<tr><td>PRISMA</td><td>Company</td><td>August 2016</td><td>July 2019</td><td>1.7</td><td>1.7</td><td>5</td></tr>
<tr><td colspan="7">PRISMA developed an RRI-related management standard and key performance indicators (KPIs) as well as guidelines for how to develop RRI-based long-term strategies</td></tr>
<tr><td>I AM RRI</td><td>Company</td><td>May 2018</td><td>October 2021</td><td>3.0</td><td>3.0</td><td>14</td></tr>
<tr><td colspan="7">I AM RRI investigated so-called “webs of innovation value chains” in additive manufacturing, identified openings for RRI, and developed a complex network model of additive manufacturing innovation chains</td></tr>
<tr><td>SISCODE</td><td>Process</td><td>May 2018</td><td>April 2021</td><td>4.0</td><td>4.0</td><td>18</td></tr>
<tr><td colspan="7">SISCODE experimented in ten co-creation labs with a broad variety of topics and delivered a virtual learning hub with a wide range of tools, a platform for interested actors, and an interactive guidebook for practitioners</td></tr>
<tr><td>SeeRRI</td><td>Territorial</td><td>January 2019</td><td>October 2021</td><td>2.0</td><td>2.0</td><td>12</td></tr>
<tr><td colspan="7">SeeRRI focused on developing a framework for integrating RRI principles into regional smart specialization strategies, developed a process model and policy recommendations, and shared the results through webinars, a final conference, and a network of other regions</td></tr>
<tr><td>RRI2SCALE</td><td>Territorial</td><td>January 2020</td><td>December 2022</td><td>2.0</td><td>2.0</td><td>11</td></tr>
<tr><td colspan="7">RRI2SCALE explored how RRI can be integrated into regional research and innovation ecosystems based on four pilot regions, delivered roadmaps for them, and designed implementation processes beyond the pilot regions through a series of stakeholder dialogues</td></tr>
<tr><td>DigiTeRRI</td><td>Territorial</td><td>January 2020</td><td>December 2022</td><td>2.0</td><td>2.0</td><td>12</td></tr>
<tr><td colspan="7">DigiTeRRI developed RRI-based roadmaps for responsible digitalization in three exemplary industry regions, delivered regional visions, objectives, and implementation measures, and disseminated them through an International Incubator Exchange, and a final conference</td></tr>
<tr><td>TOTAL</td><td></td><td></td><td></td><td>18.1</td><td>17.7</td><td>89</td></tr>
</table>

PART C: TOOLS AND METHODS

Part C of the book highlights the tools and methods designed to facilitate the implementation of RRI in business practices. These tools and methods were developed, implemented, and tested as part of the LIVING INNOVATION project. The project spanned from 2018 to 2021 and received a total budget and EU funding of 3.5 million euro. The Institute for Managing Sustainability at the Vienna University of Economics and Business (WU Vienna) coordinated the project, which involved 17 participants, including 10 companies. The features, outcomes, and learnings of the project are presented in Chapter C1.

Chapter C2 introduces co-creation as an approach that enables businesses to translate the concept of RRI into practical business practices. It highlights how co-creation aligns innovation practices with societal challenges, allowing businesses to discover new opportunities. Drawing from the results of six co-creation labs, the chapter identifies essential quality criteria for co-creation and presents suitable methods for its implementation in practice.

Chapter C3 addresses the lack of effective methods for Responsible Innovation management in industry and presents an innovative approach for integrating sustainability and responsibility into design thinking. The chapter then describes the tools used to facilitate this integration by serving as valuable add-ons in specific phases of the design thinking process, thereby guiding innovations toward responsibility and sustainability.

Chapter C4 presents an innovative, collaborative, and asynchronous workshop approach to generate innovative ideas for future digital technologies that can benefit households. Notably, this workshop focused on the specific challenges faced by parents and children living in disadvantaged regions. The chapter showcases the unique features of this workshop approach, emphasizing its focus on inclusivity and addressing real-world problems.

Chapter C5 presents an innovative toolkit designed to challenge the prevailing design of innovation workshops by incorporating the needs and desires of individuals suffering from blindness or other visual impairments. The chapter emphasizes that existing tools have often overlooked this particular group, thereby wasting its considerable untapped potential from a significant customer segment.

ACKNOWLEDGMENTS

We would like to express our gratitude to all the authors and interview partners who have dedicated their time and effort to contribute to this book. Their valuable insights and expertise have greatly enriched its content. We would also like to thank Susan Dunsmore for the highly professional and efficient proofreading and copy-editing.

REFERENCES

Barben, D., Fisher, E., Selin, C., & Guston, D. H. (2008). Anticipatory governance of nanotechnology: foresight, engagement, and integration. In E. J. Hackett, O. Amsterdamska, M. Lynch, & J. Wajcman (Eds.), *The handbook of science and technology studies* (3rd ed., pp. 979–1000). Cambridge, MA: MIT Press.

Bouglet, J., Joffre, O., & Simon, E. (2012). How to reconcile business with Sustainable Development: An innovation approach. *Society and Business Review*, 7(3), 212–222.
Brand, T., & Blok, V. (2019). Responsible innovation in business: A critical reflection on deliberative engagement as a central governance mechanism. *Journal of Responsible Innovation*, 6(1), 4–24. https://doi.org/10.1080/23299460.2019.1575681
Dreyer, M., Chefneux, L., Goldberg, A., von Heimburg, J., Patrignani, N., Schofield, M., & Shilling, C. (2017). Responsible innovation: A complementary view from industry with proposals for bridging different perspectives. *Sustainability*, 9(10), 1719. https://doi.org/10.3390/su9101719
Edler, J., Blind, K., Kroll, H., & Schubert, T. (2023). Technology sovereignty as an emerging frame for innovation policy. Defining rationales, ends and means. *Research Policy*, 52(6). 104765.
Eurostat (2023). R&D expenditure. Available at: https://ec.europa.eu/eurostat/statistics-explained/index.php?title=R%26D_expenditure&stable=1 (accessed April 11, 2023).
Gallego-Álvarez, I., Manuel Prado-Lorenzo, J., & García-Sánchez, I. (2011). Corporate social responsibility and innovation: A resource-based theory. *Management Decision*, 49(10), 1709–1727. https://doi.org/10.1108/00251741111183843
Gurzawska, A. (2021). Responsible innovation in business: Perceptions, evaluation practices and lessons learnt. *Sustainability*, 13(4), 1826.
Iatridis, K., & Schroeder, D. (2016). *Responsible research and innovation in industry*. SpringerBriefs in Research and Innovation Governance. Cham: Springer International Publishing, https://doi.org/10.1007/978-3-319-21693-5
Ivanova, S., Reichetzer, C., Martinuzzi, A., Findler, F., & Miko-Schefzig, K. (2023). Frames, interests, and incentives: A typology for institutionalizing RRI in the business sector derived from ten pioneering projects. *Journal of Responsible Innovation*, 10(1). https://doi.org/10.1080/23299460.2023.2267736
Lubberink, R., Blok, V., van Ophem, J., & Omta, O. (2017). A framework for responsible innovation in the business context: Lessons from responsible-, social- and sustainable innovation. In L. Asveld, R. van Dam-Mieras, T. Swierstra, S. Lavrijssen, K. Linse, & J. van den Hoven (Eds.), *Responsible Innovation 3: A European agenda?* (pp. 181–207). Cham: Springer.
Lukovics, M., Nagy, B., Kwee, Z., & Yaghmaei, E. (2023). Facilitating adoption of responsible innovation in business through certification. *Journal of Responsible Innovation*, 10(1). https://doi.org/10.1080/23299460.2023.2211810
Martinuzzi, A, Blok, V., Brem, A., Stahl, B., & Schönherr, N. (2018). Responsible research and innovation in industry: Challenges, insights and perspectives. *Sustainability*, 10(3), 702.
Owen, R., & Pansera, M. (2019). Responsible innovation and responsible research and innovation. In D, Simon, S. Kuhlmann, J. Stamm, & W. Canzler (Eds.), *Handbook on science and public policy* (pp. 26–48). Cheltenham: Edward Elgar. https://doi.org/10.4337/9781784715946.00010
Scherer, A. G., & Voegtlin, C. (2020). Corporate governance for responsible innovation: Approaches to corporate governance and their implications for sustainable development. *Academy of Management Perspectives*, 34(2), 182–208.
Schwab, K., & Zahidi, S. (2020). *Global competitiveness report: Special edition 2020*. Davos: World Economic Forum.
Stilgoe, J., Owen, R., & Macnaghten, P. (2013). Developing a framework for responsible innovation. *Research Policy*, 42(9), 1568–1580. https://doi.org/10.1016/j.respol.2013.05.008
van de Poel, I., Asveld, L., Flipse, S., Klaassen, P., Scholten, V., & Yaghmaei, E. (2017). Company strategies for Responsible Research and Innovation (RRI): A conceptual model. *Sustainability*, 9(11), 2045. https://doi.org/10.3390/su9112045
von Schomberg, R. (2012). Prospects for technology assessment in a framework of responsible research and innovation. In M. Dusseldorp & R. Beecroft (Eds.), *Technikfolgen abschätzen lehren: Bildungspotenziale transdisziplinärer Methoden* (pp. 39–61). Berlin: Springer.
von Schomberg, R., & Hankins, J. (Eds.). (2019). *International handbook on responsible innovation: A global resource*. Cheltenham: Edward Elgar Publishing.

Part A
Insights and challenges

Part A contains ten interviews with top managers, policy-makers, and experts on different aspects of Responsible Innovation in the business sector:

- **Sabine Herlitschka**, CEO Infineon Technologies Austria, discusses European values and the global race for innovation.
- **Robert-Jan Smits**, former Director General of DG Research and Innovation, describes the need for system-wide innovations in Europe.
- **Robert Madelin**, former Director General of EU DG for Communications Networks, Content and Technology, proposes a social culture for innovation for Europe's business sector.
- **René von Schomberg**, Science and Technology Policy specialist at the European Commission, shares his experiences in responsibility and transformational change in innovation systems.
- **Tima Bansal**, Professor of Strategy at Western Ontario University, Canada, and Executive Director of the Network for Business Sustainability, gives insights into sustainability innovations in industry-academy collaborations.
- **Richard Owen**, Professor of Innovation Management at the University of Bristol, UK, discusses the development of Responsible Research and Innovation within the last decade.
- **Sandra Kolleth**, CEO of Miele Austria, Croatia, and Slovenia, discusses the meaning of Responsible Innovation for our future homes.
- **Harald Leitenmüller**, CTO of Microsoft Austria, Responsible Innovation and Artificial Intelligence, emphasizes the need for companies to apply clear ethical frameworks and procedures when engaging with AI.
- **Marc Elsberg**, best-selling author, shares his experiences on the most important concerns related to AI and big data.
- **Armen Ovanessoff**, Principal Director at Accenture Research, provides insights into the potentials and risks of Virtual Reality.

A1

European values and the global race for innovation

AN INTERVIEW WITH SABINE HERLITSCHKA

Sabine Herlitschka is Chief Executive Officer and Chief Technology Officer of Infineon Technologies Austria AG. Under her direction, the Germany-based semiconductor company invested 1.6 billion euros in a new high-tech-chip factory in Austria, further strengthening Infineon Austria's effective combination of research and development, production, and global business responsibility. She is Vice-Chair of the Austrian Council for Research and Technology Development and Vice-President of the Federation of Austrian Industries. Her professional career includes industrial biotechnology research, international cooperation and financing in technology and innovation, as well as being founding Vice-Rector at the Medical University of Graz, Austria. For almost 25 years, she has frequently been involved in European Research as advisor, project coordinator, and evaluator, as well as participant and chairperson in strategic European and international expert groups. From 2018–2021, she was elected Chair of the Governing Board of the 5-billion euro European Public Private Partnership Programme ECSEL – now officially renamed KDT, Key Digital Technologies.

Companies are already facing shorter technology life cycles and increased time pressure. On top of this, demands for higher responsibility and sustainability are becoming more and more crucial. How does this affect companies' innovation management?

Sabine Herlitschka: Companies are expected to compete on the market and improve continuously through innovation at various levels. On the product and technology side, innovation means realizing ideas that successfully perform in the

DOI: 10.4324/9781003319481-3

market. This requires a set of different skills and organizational settings, for example sufficient opportunities for experimentation and, at the same time, a clear framework for structured development of incremental innovation, as well as the close observation of current and future trends, combined with the agility to adjust to changing ecosystems and different product life cycles across sectors. Overall, we need what has been called a multi-stakeholder cross-sectoral systemic approach and collaboration for holistic solutions in terms of the 3Ps: Planet, People, and Profit. This is decisive in order to remain competitive in the short-to-long term, as well as globally and locally. What becomes more and more obvious, however, is the fact that any innovation and technology is based on a set of social values, which, in return, influences them in different ways. Therefore, in the changing global dynamic and technology race in many sectors, for Europe, adequate control of key technologies becomes a question of strategic sovereignty, thus protecting and strengthening its deep roots in democracy, equality, autonomy, and, more generally, in sustainability. On the side of European companies, it is both a call for action as well as a business opportunity to innovate responsibly and strengthen these values.

The European Union has strongly promoted the notion of Responsible Innovation in the past few years. How does Infineon understand this concept?

SH: Our approach is that any innovation has to be a responsible innovation. The question is how or in which way it should be. Innovation as a realized idea successfully performing on the market means that responsibility has to be shared among all market stakeholders, consumers, and producers alike. On the company side, corporate social responsibility and transparency have become a standard for many years. One example is Infineon's rating under the Dow Jones Sustainability Index for the past 12 years, thus demonstrating that Infineon is among the top 15% of the most sustainable companies worldwide. However, it is more and more difficult to decide what is ethically acceptable and what is not. For example, in the context of data protection, tracking technology in mobile phones might be used to counteract theft and loss of personal data. The trade-off could be more data collection about individuals in the first place. Particularly in contexts where the advantages of data usage lead to clear and increased user benefits and convenience, ethical aspects will become more difficult to evaluate with no categorical or global answers. A clear understanding of the ethical framework criteria, as well as a constructive societal discourse, are required, instead of setting top-down ethical guidelines. In addition, proper knowledge about a certain technology and its features, together with the possibility to opt out and decide independently how to use it, are important. Unfortunately, these are often insufficiently provided. On the side of consumers, responsible usage requires awareness about the trade-offs of digital devices, such as Amazon's Alexa privacy settings and subsequent proper decision-making about their use. It is understandable and has to be respected if individuals or groups of people do not want their data to be collected in certain areas. At the same time, users also bear the responsibility for what and how they share information on digital platforms. However, proper education and awareness-raising are prerequisites for users in order for them to make informed and responsible decisions.

Responsible and successful innovation is not only about new technologies, but also the co-design of entire systems in which multiple companies have to cooperate. What does your collaboration with other companies look like in the context of research and innovation? What are the particular challenges you are facing?

SH: The question of systems development is one of the major questions of our time. For companies, this concerns their competitiveness as well as their responsibility – both issues converge. Irrespective of the sector, we are dealing with increasingly complex systems and global challenges, such as climate change, energy efficiency, environmentally-friendly mobility, smart homes, secure data transfer, and other areas in an increasingly connected world. At Infineon, we cooperate with suppliers and customers, as well as universities and R&D institutions, and engage in partnerships. We see active and continuous cooperation as a vital element to embrace and to initiate innovation. Together, we can develop knowledge-based answers for future issues, such as digitalization or achieving the climate targets and, above all, implementing them in products and solutions. Thinking in systems is a societal challenge that needs to be considered along the entire value chain. This exceeds simple supplier-customer relationships and requires collaboration in a wider context. Digitalization and smart technologies, such as microelectronics, can make major contributions in creating a more digital and sustainable future. However, such a systemic approach and collaboration have both technical and organizational challenges. On the technical side, Infineon has committed itself to grand societal challenges and opportunities, such as energy efficiency, future trends of mobility (e.g., electric and autonomous cars, car safety), and data security. Each of these areas includes its own questions of how to make our future easier, safer, and greener and these only increase the complexity, urgency, and the pace at which they have to be addressed. On the organizational side, the diversity within Infineon's team, with over 50,000 employees from over 70 different countries, is a great resource to tackle complex issues, but also requires significant coordination and intercultural skills. The same applies to collaboration with partners in a global context.

How much are companies cooperating and not competing on the market? Is collaboration only happening in those areas where companies are linked through the value chain, otherwise companies are competitors, irrespective of systemic requirements?

SH: In many cases today, companies are in "co-opetition" with multiple other companies and stakeholders. While collaborating in one area, you may compete in another with the same entity. For example, in the European context, Infineon collaborates with competitors in EU-funded projects that are often addressing systemic questions, such as emission-free cities, etc., even more so in the current mission-oriented Horizon Europe programme. Such cooperation with competitors is easier as long as the respective innovation is still in an early stage and thus far from the market. It is important to act strategically regarding which research questions are relevant in the short, medium or long term. It requires joint efforts on which questions you work and allow collaboration due to market competition. Although competition is important and healthy to avoid monopolies, in particular for grand challenges, collaboration seems to be a more mature approach, yet with due consideration of the specific questions and context at hand. Moreover, creative systemic thinking allows for the consideration of business opportunities to complement each other in existing ecosystems and markets by understanding where and how to fit best, and, thus, going beyond mere competitive approaches. In this way, both sides can benefit from systemic cooperation.

What is the role of civil society and consumers within the collaboration for and holistic co-design of systems?

SH: Ultimately, every company has to be successful on the market with its innovations and this means that they need to have a sufficient customer base. It is critical to include considerations about consumers and end-users during innovation processes. The importance of customers in this regard is still underestimated even by themselves, in particular, the decision-making power of every single person when purchasing products. This is how consumers indirectly affect companies in their future orientation. Products are not just made of certain technologies, they are linked to philosophies and values that we as consumers either promote or reject through our decisions. Key technologies, such as microelectronics, play a special role here. Today, we find ourselves in a situation where only three of the world's 20 largest semiconductor manufacturers are based in Europe. However, microelectronics have a crucial strategic value for European society, and their functionality and usage models directly affect our democratic values.

At the European level, the discussion about technology policy is mostly governed by competitiveness and growth. How is technology linked to values, and is this a third important theme?

SH: Historically, military and economic power have been the central means to achieve dominance and autonomy. Today, technology is becoming more and more a decisive geopolitical factor. This is particularly true for digital technologies. The starting point of most new digital technologies is the ever-increasing accumulation of data as the twenty-first century's oil. It is crucial to understand that in many processes much more data is produced and collected on a daily basis compared to the time before digitalization. Thus, important questions arise, like what is happening with the data, who owns it and how to handle it responsibly.? Each of these questions is answered differently in Europe compared to the US or China, for example. Most of the large data companies are located in the US with only 4% of existing data platforms from Europe. Therefore, it is mostly outside Europe where data analytics and AI are developed that set critical framework conditions for governing values, such as democracy, freedom, and ultimately also our behavior. Consequently, the entire data business within the EU becomes dominated by US value systems regarding data privacy, protection of identity, etc. Another more drastic example is China's AI-based social credit system. It is intended to capture all citizens in one big database, including facial recognition and other identification methods in order to measure social performance against do's and don't's that are linked to certain values. Technology, in this case, AI, is enabling the implementation of such systems. Therefore, technological dominance translates into dominance over value systems and consequently societal models. This also has implications for Responsible Innovation. It is not just ethics which dictates innovation management systems to comply with certain values. Innovation is also required to stabilize and preserve the desired value systems. It is important to note in this regard that Europe's priority on topics, such as data privacy and protection, is not enough. In order to play an active role in the data economy, Europe needs data access and data sovereignty.

Could the strengthening of European values through a systems approach be a business case for Responsible Innovation in European start-ups and companies? Is there a competitive advantage over non-European players?

SH: Yes, indeed, but this will require further action at the European level. Europe has a huge potential of diversity but we have to collaborate with a joint Europe in mind, instead of various Member States. Europe has strong strategies and theoretical frameworks, but it needs to go beyond these and become much more determined in the straightforward implementation of its goals. What is urgently needed is speed in implementation. An important reason for this issue is connected to the diverse interests of European stakeholders and the missing commitment to a united European continent that is competing globally with, for example, the US or China. This is mirrored in legal frameworks, such as the European law on competition and state aid that is still from the 1950s and thus addressing more inner-European competition between Member States rather than reflecting the much more globalized situation. What is needed in our globalized world and economy is a level playing field.

Despite being a political and economic union, the EU has hardly arrived at a common language and approach regarding industrial policy. In the area of science and technology, Europe, indeed, has come up with strategies and has set up – decades ago – what is nowadays the largest cooperative and competitive research and technology program worldwide, the so-called Framework Programmes. They are intended to set the basis for European competitiveness. A strategy for technology and technological competencies is urgently needed in order to protect and strengthen Europe's technological potential, interests, and values. The recently implemented Chip Act will pave the way in this direction. In the context of mergers and acquisitions by non-EU entities, individual Member States need to provide approval under pre-defined conditions. Yet, decisions seem to be taken much less strategically in terms of European interests and, therefore, are leading to a loss of key technological competencies. Building on a European framework, some Member States, including Austria, have created a tightened basis with its Investment Control Act. In contrast, countries like the US and China act in a more protective and strategic way regarding acquisitions of domestic businesses by foreign actors, maybe for security or other reasons.

Given the fast advances in data collection, AI, e-mobility, smartification, etc., how will we live in 2030?

SH: Looking back to the first iPhone presentation in 2007 and how much has changed over the years, it is simply impossible to predict how the world will look like in another 10–15 years. Today we have the opportunity to use the new framework conditions for a sustainable change on many levels – especially for smart digitalization and climate protection. We need to be aware – as users and consumers – that we have a clear impact on our future in terms of sustainability, convenience, product usability, and simplification. The environment humans live in will likely become more smart and interactive, offering more options for our individualizing our homes, work environments, etc. These systems will operate responsibly only if they are combined with appropriate security technologies, otherwise the risk of misuse will become a major entry barrier. At the same time, smarter environments based on sensors and data analytics offer great opportunities for disadvantaged population groups, as well as higher user convenience, more efficient and personalized health care systems, and generally more informed decisions, behavior, and lifestyles. Besides that, already today, technology can make a significant contribution to energy efficiency, reducing energy consumption and, thus, minimizing the carbon footprint in many applications and, as such, achieving our climate goals.

Technology is a driving force in our daily lives. In order to develop our society toward a responsible future, adequate technology is required that needs to be understood sufficiently by society, i.e., producers, users, and lawmakers alike, regarding its impact on our environment and value systems. This is an ongoing, mutual process of continuous change that has never been as fast as today and will never be again as slow as it is now. Yet, it is also a call for action and business opportunity for European companies to shape the future in a smart and sustainable way.

A2

Why Europe needs system-wide innovations

AN INTERVIEW WITH ROBERT-JAN SMITS

Robert-Jan Smits has been the President of the Eindhoven University of Technology in the Netherlands since May 2019. From 2010 to 2018, he was Director-General of Research and Innovation at the European Commission. In this capacity, he was one of the main architects of Horizon 2020, the 80 billion euros European Union program for science and innovation, which ran from 2014 to 2020. He also worked on the design of the successor program, Horizon Europe. Smits is also known for his key role in the field of Open Access, where he developed "Plan S," an initiative that requires scientists and researchers who benefit from state-funded research organizations and institutions to publish their work in open repositories or in open access journals.

Among the many strong values Europe has to offer, which are most fundamental to innovation regarding global competitiveness as well as sustainability?

Robert-Jan Smits: Like the European science model, the European innovation model is based on fundamental European values, such as human rights, freedom, democracy, rule of law, respect, dignity, etc. In addition to these, cooperation and partnership are crucial components of this model. There are other innovation models at the global level, some of which are more state-driven and top-down. I am of the opinion that these models succeed in the short run, but often fail in the long term, because they undervalue the importance of cooperation based on a win-win situation, openness, and transparency. Therefore, the strength of the European model lies especially in its emphasis on open innovation based on cooperation and inclusiveness, allowing, besides industry and academia, also public authorities and citizens to join in.

DOI: 10.4324/9781003319481-4

An impressive example of open innovation is the high-tech campus in Eindhoven. It started as an internal R&D center of Philips until it opened the gates to other innovative companies in 2003. By now, the campus comprises more than 200 companies and hosts more than 12,000 innovators to develop new technologies jointly to solve societal problems and bring them to the market.

Cooperation and openness are big brands of the European Union and are well reflected in its research and innovation programs, primarily the Horizon Europe program. Nonetheless, strong competition and competitiveness play a major role in innovation. How can this tension between cooperation and competitiveness be reconciled?

R-JS: Cooperation and competition are both important and the European Commission has developed in Horizon Europe specific instruments for these purposes. The grants of the European Research Council (ERC) allow for very strong competition of Europe's top-notch researchers on frontier research in order to break new ground and extend the very frontiers of knowledge. In other fields, where the objective is to find solutions for the grand societal challenges, cooperative research and innovation are promoted in order to combine the strengths of the very best partners.

You mentioned society and citizens as important actors of the win-win partnership for innovation. What is their exact role and how can they have a real impact on innovation networks that are often dominated by industry leaders and strong business interests?

R-JS: I strongly believe that the role of citizens as co-designers in innovation is becoming increasingly important on multiple levels: co-designers of the innovation system, of the innovation agenda, and of concrete solutions. As such, innovation is no longer a matter of industry or universities conducting research and development, rather, it is about an all-inclusive process whereby partners from the quadruple helix sit together, work together, and co-develop long-term strategies and roadmaps in order to deliver successful innovations. This model is already emerging more and more. I see it especially in the region of Eindhoven. An important organization that fosters this multi stakeholder partnership is Brainport Development, which brings together citizens, municipalities, companies, and the university to develop and implement innovation agendas in the region. Through this partnership, innovative ideas are given free room. An example of this is Brabant Smart District (BSD), a new-to-develop district fully based on the principles of energy-neutrality, circularity, eco-innovation, and innovative mobility systems, in which different stakeholders are involved on an equal footing. This ensures that everyone's needs, those concerning society, the environment, and the economy, are adequately heard and incorporated.

Do you see a business case for companies in open and collaborative innovation that is more based on partnership than competition?

R-JS: Absolutely, and again the larger region of Eindhoven is a beautiful example of this. The region was facing enormous problems in the aftermath of the global economic crisis of 2000–2003. Companies, such as DAF and Philips, struggled severely or even went close to bankruptcy. It was due to this crisis that the different stakeholders started to sit together and develop a common innovation strategy based on partnership and cooperation that resulted in a real success story for the region. Today, Eindhoven is the fastest-growing economic area in the Netherlands and one of the fastest in Europe. The annual turnover of companies in the city of Eindhoven is amazing and their investments in research and innovation are the highest in the Netherlands. Unfortunately, however, it is often a crisis that is needed to stimulate change and start thinking more inclusively with a view to disrupting entire established systems. However, Eindhoven is very eager to spread and share the best practices it has developed over the last decade in the region with the rest of the world.

What mechanisms or tools does one need to bring the different actors together on an equal footing? How does one deal with tensions and conflict of interests between them?

R-JS: It is all about trust and respect: Trust that cooperation will take you further and respect that even the smallest player can bring you added value. It does require a solid governance structure, in which all stakeholders are represented on an equal footing.

However, frictions are a normal part of the game. In the mentioned housing developing project, BSD, conflicting interests include companies' expectations about growth, shareholder value and competitiveness, citizens' desire for cheap housing and affordable transport, and the university's ambition to maximize its contribution to the Sustainable Development Goals (SDGs). Having a common agenda based on a clear governance structure sets the framework to bring the different requests to the table and reconcile them. If citizens say that they want affordable housing due to limited income and the university adds that this should be energy-neutral and recyclable, then this requires that all parties team up to sort this out. With a constructive and positive attitude based on a strong governance framework, problems can be solved.

What is Responsible Innovation, based on this model, and is there a difference between companies' and universities' innovation management in this regard?

R-JS: Responsible Research and Innovation (RRI) is a concept that aims to increase inclusiveness and sustainability in research and innovation by assessing, in an early phase, potential implications for society. The major principles of RRI are collaboration and co-design, engaging society, ethical standards, gender equality, and the anticipation of impact. These principles apply to companies and academia alike. For collaborative research projects, it is crucial to apply the principles of RRI fully from the very start to anticipate impact and understand the ways in which a new technology or other potential outcome of a project may affect the planet and the people.

Where do you see the biggest challenge of RRI based on cooperation and partnership?

R-JS: The biggest challenge of an RRI-based approach is to avoid that things will become very complex and bureaucratic and, as such, will impede productivity, interaction, and output rather than enabling them.

Another challenge concerns the involvement of so-called "soft skills" that are still often underestimated in the context of innovation. Our experience at the Eindhoven Brainport region showed that technological skills and knowledge are necessary, but not sufficient and cannot produce the best possible outcomes on their own. Creativity, multi disciplinarity, teamwork, the ability to challenge each other, and co-design, which I would like to call "enabling skills," are utterly important in order to achieve systemic solutions that can be sustainable, inclusive, and successful at the same time. Here at the Eindhoven University of Technology, one way of teaching these skills is challenge-based learning. Students are assigned, or assign themselves, a certain challenge, such as the participation in the Australian solar race by building a solar-powered car. This requires students to work together and think across different disciplines and, most importantly, respect each other in order to achieve a common goal.

Apart from strong collaboration with clear governance structures and proper training of enabling skills, what else is needed for Europe to achieve its ambition of RRI and succeed economically with it?

R-JS: We need more cooperation at the level of the 27 Member States of the EU. Wherever Europe is able to unite and work together, it is highly successful and competitive on a global scale. This is the case with CERN regarding basic research, or the Airbus in the field of aeronautics. Such collaboration should be further strengthened across Europe through instruments, such as the "Projects of European Interests." It will require a review of Europe's competition policy and support structures for entrepreneurs to scale up. The fact that almost 40 percent of entrepreneurs and start-ups in Silicon Valley are from Europe is a sign of Europe's potential, but also of our inability to offer our most dynamic entrepreneurs an environment in which they can flourish. Europe has a relatively small venture capital market and it often has the tendency to overregulate new disruptive technologies. Europe has a different mindset regarding regulation compared to other parts of the world with the right intention of responsibility and sustainability, but with the unfavorable outcome of losing out on opportunities. One particular area, in which Europe needs to invest big time, is digitalization, since this affects all sectors of the economy, from automotive to food and pharma. The "smartification" of these areas results in important future growth markets, such as smart homes, smart health, or smart transportation. In order to remain competitive in these areas, Europe needs to catch up on digital technologies while staying true to its values.

A3

An innovation vision for Europe's business sector

AN INTERVIEW WITH ROBERT MADELIN

Robert Madelin is Chairman and Chief Strategist at Fipra International, as well as a policy thinker with four decades of public policy experience in the UK administration and the EU. From 1997 to 2003, he was a trade and investment Director in the General Directorate for Commerce. In January 2004, he was appointed Director General in the General Directorate for Health and Consumer Affairs. In 2010, Madelin took over the management of the Information Society and Media Directorate General, then re-named DG CONNECT. In 2016, he concluded his Commission career with the publication of an innovation strategy review, "Opportunity Now: Europe's Mission to Innovate."

How do you assess Europe's current position in the global race for innovation and what role does Responsible Innovation play in it?

Robert Madelin: Europe can be a leading innovative continent in the global innovation game, but we have not exploited all our potential. In order to change this, we need a social culture of Responsible Innovation that is not just about risk aversion, but also about opportunities and the readiness to try something new. It is about an innovation culture that believes that human society can make things better by trying out new ideas. On a deeper level, this is intimately connected to better collaboration between different actors. We need, in particular, a much stronger inclusion of citizens and academia, who are still often siloed away from innovation spaces and processes. We also need innovation education, including soft skills, starting from primary school.

DOI: 10.4324/9781003319481-5

Is there a specific European approach to global competitiveness?

RM: Despite the common fear of new technology killing traditional values, be they European or other, the development of new technologies and, thus, innovation, is a central part of a society. Inevitably, societies make use of technology and, by definition, our technologies will stay true to our values as long as we stay true to them. The ideas that technology is either above society or that there is an intrinsic conflict between the two are both misrepresentations of the real situation, because, per se, there is no technology or innovation that is value-free, yet specific values depend on the value system at hand. Even a seemingly neutral, next-generation aircraft engine, for example, may raise questions about energy efficiency and resource consumption, which can be very important in value systems based on the Sustainable Development Goals (SDGs).

Staying true to values is, thus, decisive for a positive social culture of Responsible Innovation, capable of looking at opportunities rather than risks. As an extreme illustration of this point, facial recognition is very easily understood as a technology which gives rise to a series of innovations, all of which go to the heart of important values around privacy, security of personal identities, and integrity. Instead of seeing the threat to European values, we need to believe in Europe's strong values and aim to embrace this technology by making it do what Europe wants and needs it to do. This requires a clear understanding of, and commitment to, our values in combination with the right public funding mechanisms, and open, Responsible Innovation, including co-creation with all relevant actors beyond the innovators themselves. In this way, a social culture of innovation can bear significant potential for European innovations to be exported, not just in terms of technology, but also in terms of values. If Europe stays true to strong ambitions, such as high data privacy, transparency, and trustworthiness, as well as general sustainability, it will satisfy specific consumer demands and gain a global competitive advantage over other technological solutions that may be cheaper, but less trusted.

A culture of innovation requires a more open, positive, and entrepreneurial attitude of society toward innovation. How can we foster such an attitude and, accordingly, how can we stimulate society to participate and become engaged in innovation?

RM: First, we need an open and positive public discourse that is not centered around fears and risks often intensified by targeted misinformation, as has been the case in topics, such as national elections or vaccine hesitancy. Misinformation is not only problematic on the political level, but also stifles science and innovation by impacting society's perception, both in terms of the innovation process and its outcomes. Second, and related to this, innovators need to demonstrate the positive power of their innovations for sustainably solving the problems society cares about and needs solved the most.

On the European level, what would be the right mechanisms to promote a more positive culture of Responsible Innovation with a view of opportunities rather than risks? How does this relate to the Horizon Europe Program that offers more than 90 billion euros for public and private research and innovation?

RM: The European Commission's mission-oriented approach to research and innovation seems to be the right direction that also well reflects the complexity of the systemic challenges we are facing. The main question, however, is how to manage the proper execution of this approach, in order to achieve its major objectives, namely to tackle climate change, support the SDGs, and boost competitiveness? My report "Opportunity Now" back in 2016 already dedicated a chapter to the necessity of modernizing EU institutions. In general terms, a more open administration and organizational innovation within public institutions are required to deliver increased participation and citizen engagement in innovation.

As for Europe's research and innovation programs, including the Horizon Europe program, it is the Commission, together with Member States, that decide the overall priority topics. Specific research or innovation proposal, however, are assessed by independent experts. Diversity and interdisciplinarity of experts are as important as concrete expertise in sustainability for the assessment of project proposals. Interdisciplinarity is the keyword not only in assessing proposals, but also for actual research and innovation in and outside programs, such as Horizon Europe. Intense innovation requires societies to involve different perspectives for them to know what they want. Likewise, I would argue that innovators need to involve more perspectives to achieve what society needs most efficiently. As a generalist, I was always critical of the idea of specific calls for e.g., social sciences, engineering, etc., which all get their separate piece of the pie. Rather, different disciplines should be incentivized to collaborate on societal challenges as a prerequisite to receive funding and support. This type of change agenda is required across academia, business research laboratories, etc., and this is also how mechanisms, such as Horizon Europe, are to be designed and executed to deliver its vision and promote a culture of Responsible Innovation.

You have already addressed two key elements of Responsible Innovation: one is the participation of citizens, the other is caring about future impacts. How can we translate these two elements and, more generally, Responsible Innovation for the private sector so that it can see a business case in it?

RM: This issue goes to the concept of Economics of Mutuality (EOM), now the growing baby of a Geneva-based Foundation (http://eom.org). EOM thinking first developed in late-2006 as a product of the Mars Inc. internal think tank, and then led to the creation of the Economics of Mutuality Laboratory at the Saïd Business School (University of Oxford) in 2014. The EOM school of thought starts from the question of what the right level of profit for companies should be and, consequently, the purpose of the firm if it is not simply to maximize profit. It is about mutuality of benefits among all stakeholders to meet the critical needs of the ecosystems we live in, by connecting businesses with society and the environment. I would argue that this purpose is closely related to SDG positivity.

The EOM mind-map focuses on a balanced portfolio of impact goals, covering not only financial, but also natural, individual, and social community capital. The major insight is how best businesses can create the incentives, governance structures, goals, and KPIs that drive their business units to hit all four goals with a maximum net positive outcome in terms of the SDGs, instead of merely maximum economic growth.

With regards to innovation, this requires development teams to include the SDGs in their objectives of innovation and, in turn, this requires the right experts and broader society to be involved. Talking to the development team of a European self-driving concept car, the most surprising experience in their view was the amount of time needed to think about people's needs. The team leader not only understood that the technology's sustainability depends on these needs, but also that the commercial success depends on the popular acceptance in an urban setting. Initiatives, such as the Economics of Mutuality. are already developing methodologies and tools for this fundamental reorientation through rigorous testing with leading universities and top multinational companies.

Engaging with people and involving them in innovation processes is the ambition of open innovation. How does Responsible Innovation differ from this approach, or is it only open innovation 2.0?

RM: One may say that open innovation 2.0 would be the full inclusion of the so-called quadruple helix (government, business, academia, and civil society) in the innovation process. Responsible Innovation goes one step further and is open innovation with a purpose. In other words, mere engagement with people, businesses, governments, and academia during innovation processes still may not provide sufficient answers that lead to the desired impact. On top of a responsible and open innovation process, clear goals as a shared ex-ante purpose are required. By default, my view would be to derive this purpose from the SDGs as a globally established benchmark. Underneath the 17 SDGs we still have a multitude of intermingling targets and indicators revealing that the SDGs are – quite understandably – and necessarily – a work in progress. Nonetheless, it would be a tremendous step ahead, if the SDGs became the starting point of innovations such that new technology, products, and services are evaluated both with regards to positive and negative impact on them. To emphasize this point further, innovations are usually intended to fix certain problems and improve the present state of affairs. The SDGs should be the very basis for which problems to solve.

Many companies already incorporate the SDGs as a strategic orientation. They figure frequently in sustainability reporting, management systems, and general policy documents of companies, but less so with regards to innovation. How can the SDGs be better linked to innovation in companies, and vice versa?

RM: Even for the best-in-class companies, sustainability reporting often tends to be centered on philanthropy, compliance, and public relations. This remains siloed away from the core business, and therefore from innovation. This gap can be bridged by the Economics of Mutuality approach, since it will align all the firm's business unit metrics and incentives, including those for innovation, with the SDGs. At a stroke, the core business, as such, directly delivers on sustainability. Businesses therefore need to learn how to build and implement strategic understanding of the SDGs within their internal governance structures and management hierarchies from top to bottom. In such a way, sustainability is integrated into innovation activities as a guide to create maximum net positive outcome.

What would be concrete sectors and key technologies for Europe to realize this proposition, given the fierce global competition in areas such as big data, artificial intelligence, or robotics?

RM: Indeed, one has to acknowledge global competition, particularly in digitalization across all industries, remains dominated by US and Chinese companies. However, it remains uncertain whether the big players of today will be the same in a decade, and Europe, in the current push for strategic autonomy, does have a lot of disruptive potential in this regard. For example, in artificial intelligence, we continue to have some of the best universities in the world. Here, the issue is more that insufficient investment leads to new innovations and start-ups being bought out too early by non-European competitors. Other potential technologies would include quantum cryptography and energy-efficient computer chips. More generally, Europe can be especially strong in those areas where systemic, social, and technological innovation come together. The provision of systems services, such as smart health, etc., would be a good example, because it requires trust and is more sensitive to values. European national health systems are a global asset that is deemed trustworthy and exports well internationally. If used as demonstration platforms for innovation in health technology, this would be a win for patients, taxpayers, and innovators alike. Despite global competition, Europe should not see itself as opposed to the rest of the world. Rather, Europe should be ready to play and partner with others, if it wants to follow the proposition of a society of innovation, even more so of Responsible Innovation geared toward true sustainability.

Could sustainability and responsibility be Europe's narrative for the future?

RM: Both sustainability and responsibility are Europe's way ahead if it wants to continue to prosper. It seems that prosperity was a good paradigm for getting better at a time when resources were ample, technologies were limited, our perspectives regarding social and environmental ecosystems were much more local and short-term, and poverty levels in Europe were significantly higher. Although short-term prosperity is still the preferred goal of many actors, I would argue that they have not sufficiently understood the fact that for society, what we now call sustainability is real prosperity and what we used to call prosperity has a short shelf life.

A4

Responsibility and transformational change in innovation systems

AN INTERVIEW WITH RENÉ VON SCHOMBERG

René von Schomberg is a philosopher, a Science and Technology Policy specialist, and guest Professor at the Technical University of Darmstadt in Germany. For two decades he shaped Responsible Research and Innovation (RRI) policy at the European Commission. He is the author and editor of 15 books that have appeared in half a dozen languages. He is currently running one of the most influential blogs on Responsible Innovation, ethics, emerging technologies, sustainable development, and open science.

As a major authority in the field of RRI, what is your understanding of RRI and what was your ambition during your time at the European Commission?

René von Schomberg: My initial definition of RRI consists of two major components: One is the mutual responsiveness of innovators, citizens, politicians, and other societal actors and the other one is the focus on societally desirable outcomes in the process of responding to each other. On a global scale, it stands to reason that the latter is closely linked to the grand societal challenges and the Sustainable Development Goals (SDGs) as globally agreed agendas. This approach to RRI was, and still is, geared to achieve change on four levels:

1. It started with the ambition to address the deficits of previous science and society programs across Europe – not only of the European Commission – over the last decades. These include the focus on risk management and assessment to avoid negative impact without a positive view on what research and innovation should achieve in terms of desired societal outcomes. Likewise, the missing participation

DOI: 10.4324/9781003319481-6

of companies and innovators as indispensable actors of Responsible Innovation was an important constraint of many programs.

2. Driving innovation towards societally desirable outcomes requires concrete mechanisms in order to be successful. The establishment of such mechanisms is intimately related to institutional changes, including roles and interaction of different stakeholders. Notably, overall efforts toward RRI should be more concerned with public authorities taking on a stronger role.
3. Another important point concerns the ambition to advance the conceptual work for Responsible Innovation, particularly with regards to ethics. Ethics was predominantly a field of ex-post evaluation that constrains innovation efforts rather than a more constructive, process- and results-oriented approach to technology design and innovation management.
4. Lastly, understandings and operationalization of Responsible Innovation differ significantly across the globe and there is a strong need to address the field's global dimension collectively. Interestingly, having initiated activities to connect different understandings and communities outside the EU in the US and China, the latter, especially, responded very positively.

You mentioned the need for companies' participation in public science and society programs in order to drive RRI. Where do you see the difference between public-sector responsible research and private-sector Responsible Innovation?

RvS: The term RRI indicates that the two are obviously connected and yet they follow a different dynamic. A previous director of the U.S. National Science Foundation once said that good science anywhere is good for science everywhere. While this is true to certain extents, it cannot be applied in the same way to innovation, since a good innovation anywhere may or may not be beneficial for some, somewhere, or sometime. Obviously, the predictability and allocation of impacts have a very different dynamic. Next, there is also a significant difference in terms of competition within science and innovation. By definition, private-sector innovation is seen as competitive between companies, trading blocs, and countries. From that perspective, it may be counterintuitive to say that innovation needs more openness and collaboration. Yet, cooperation is exactly what is required on local and global levels from both research and innovation in order to increase responsibility toward desired outcomes. Likewise, researchers typically spend significant time applying for grants, while private companies follow the rules of short- to long-term profitability. Interestingly, large companies arrive more and more at the insight that they can only be sustainable if they include a long-term perspective on innovation and investment, which is an important prerequisite for sustainable outcomes. As for SMEs, I would argue that collaboration is all the more important in order to compete on the market responsibly, because they are not able to make the same long-term investments as the big players.

Speaking about competition and profitability in the private sector, is there a business case for Responsible Innovation?

RvS: The answer to this question directly connects to key parts of the previous question. First and foremost, perhaps the strongest business case lies precisely in the mentioned long-term perspective that Responsible Innovation with sustainable outcomes is becoming a necessity in order to be sustainable as an organization 20 years from now and beyond. It is then more a strategic question of when to follow this transition and, I would argue, time pressure is ever increasing on companies, both regarding their own business continuity, and regarding broader sustainability. In addition, openness and cooperation are not only a matter of RRI, but they are also important balancing mechanisms to increase the efficiency of public and private innovation ecosystems that are overstrained by competition. In many areas, research and innovation have become too closed up due to competition and business interests and, therefore, self-destructive. Closed science and innovation lead to bad results, often without innovation at all, because knowledge and data are insufficient or even flawed. In medical science, 90% of second-phase clinical trials fail, because of flawed or not reproducible data. A brilliant counterexample would be the genome consortium at Oxford, which really applied open science by sharing data globally and instantly prior to publication and by establishing a public-private partnership with industry. This allowed it to reduce the timeline for more than 20 medical products from an average of 20 to less than 2 years. They did so by focusing on those enzymes under-researched by the big companies that restricted themselves to only a small number they deemed most profitable. The collaboration to produce outputs and their sharing prior to publication both proved decisive in increasing efficiency. This holds particularly true in the context of the grand societal challenges that require collaboration on an unprecedented global scale. However, open collaboration does not mean that public and private organizations cannot compete any more in terms of patents, IPR, etc. The point is that the traditional argument of injecting big investments into the innovation system leads to faster results and makes Europe, as a whole, more competitive may be flawed. In my view, a more nuanced approach with a better balance between openness and competition will likely prove to be more effective for the European economy and sustainability.

You also mentioned the need for institutional changes, including a stronger role for public authorities to drive innovation toward desirable impacts. Why do you think we need it?

RvS: Unfortunately, in my experience, it was precisely the public authorities including the European Commission that were most hesitant when introducing the concept of RRI at the beginning. Public authorities retreated from their role of steering science and innovation due to increasing market orientation and privatization to boost the economy. The economy's drive for short-term profits has tremendously intensified compared to the 1960s and 1970s, where long-term investments were much more common, whether state-driven, by companies, pension funds, etc. As has become clear over the last decades, this exaggerated focus on a competition-driven market economy is not commensurate to produce societally desirable outcomes on many fronts. I would argue that public authorities need to acknowledge that privatization has gone too far in certain areas and, therefore, they need to regain some ground to counterbalance short-term profits with open collaboration on long-term perspectives and sustainable outcomes. This not only concerns companies as such, but also the rules within which they operate, such as publishing and intellectual property rights, patenting, etc., which are – to certain extents – not conducive to open collaboration with a view on long-term perspectives. Successes, such as the Ebola and Zika vaccines – as few as they are, unfortunately – have shown the tremendous potential of such an approach that was only allowed because of the urgency to find a treatment and by lifting constraining publishing rules. I strongly believe it to be a fundamental mistake of our society if we allow a much more efficient and effective approach to research and innovation only to happen in cases of utmost immediacy and danger.

How do you see this role of public authorities in more detail?

RvS: To start with, we may distinguish between three innovation paradigms. The first is full state control, as we see it, for example, with technologies, such as nuclear energy. The second one is the well-known market-driven innovation based on supply and demand. The third pillar, as I argue, would then be Responsible Innovation with yet another dynamic. Most importantly, although the current imbalance due to private sector dominance needs to be reversed, all three paradigms can co-exist to a certain extent and in certain ways. For example, innovation for energy efficiency needs fewer incentives from public authorities, because there is a business case regarding cheaper prices. Here, market-driven innovation, indeed, leads in the right direction. Nonetheless, all actors have to come together to work toward sustainable impact and avoid overconsumption that would offset efficiency gains. In other areas, market dynamics fail to identify needed impact as is the case with the malaria disease. Although it is among the deadliest diseases and top 10 causes of death worldwide, research and innovation to fight malaria depend on the goodwill of philanthropists, such as Bill Gates, who invest more in it than the entire European Union. This is where public authorities need to step up much stronger to redirect public and private research and innovation toward grand societal challenges and desired impacts. The middle ground between full state control and uncontrolled market dynamics establishes the space in which RRI operates based on the concerted collaboration of all actors. However, the role of public authorities should be different from simply dictating agendas. It is much more about convening all the relevant actors and reallocating responsibilities based on time and context in an open and collaborative manner under their guidance. This will lead to the production of new instruments to guide innovation management, e.g., codes of conduct agreements and, most importantly, public-private and other partnerships, without which the aforementioned successes, such as the Genome Project or also the development of the Ebola vaccine under the compassionate use protocol.

In your *International Handbook of Responsible Innovation*, you provide a global perspective of the concept. Is RRI a genuinely European concept and if not, are there important differences in terms of culture, etc.?

RvS: Responsible Research and Innovation are not exclusive to the European agenda despite the fact that in my conception of the term I also linked it to core values or anchor points in the European Treaty. Values, such as solidarity, may not necessarily be shared unanimously across the globe, but we do find multilateralism and cooperation as important international principles institutionalized on platforms like the United Nations. If not universal, most of these values are, therefore, transferable and there is no reason why they should not be promoted beyond Europe. Perhaps even more important than the values is that we do share the grand societal challenges as a common starting point and, therefore, different manifestations of responsible research and innovation in- and outside Europe.

The differences in RRI approaches are less connected to culture per se as the primary determinant, but more to existing institutions, as well as internal challenges that countries are facing. For example, Germany and the Netherlands have technology assessment enshrined in their public institutions and even linked to the parliament. Therefore, RRI may have a stronger role compared to other countries. At the same time, China's socio-economic organization, including innovation, is much more state-driven, for which reason it cannot be said in the same way that government retreated too far from the field compared to most western nations. Likewise, countries' roles to tackle grand societal challenges and, therefore, their responsibility, are strongly intertwined with their internal situation. India, for example, is a major actor that bears significant responsibility for our shared future, yet it has to address issues, such as massive income gaps within their vast population at the same time. This will affect decisions on, and approaches to, future development, including innovation, and, one may argue, quite rightfully so. Most interestingly, India has an impressive record of frugal innovation, which comes close to the concept of RRI in many ways and is aimed at meeting poor people's needs with sustainable and affordable solutions. This is one example of an approach from which Europe may want to learn.

Looking at the current state and future of RRI, why is global cooperation for more Responsible Innovation so important, in your view?

RvS: As I argued throughout this interview, Responsible Innovation is aimed at desirable societal outcomes and this is closely linked to the grand societal challenges and international agendas, first and foremost, the SDGs. Since these challenges are shared across the globe, it makes sense that they can only be tackled collectively and through global cooperation. This requires a global paradigm shift of innovation from a goal in itself to a more normative approach based on shared values. In Europe, for example, science and technology policy is not subsumed under the same normative frameworks and values as environmental policies, since it is driven by a macro-economic logic, in which outcomes are good as long as they lead to European growth. The same issue manifests itself in other countries, with national interests mostly in terms of economic outcomes dominating public innovation policy and agendas. This is a major inhibitor for RRI to achieve the desired impact with regards to global challenges.

To take the example of nanotechnology, at the beginnings of the twenty-first century, there has been a large program between the US and Europe to collaborate on the risks of future technologies in this field, including general risks, legal and social aspects. Although international cooperation for the development of an international code of conduct failed in the end, there was still some progress to steer this field into desirable outcomes for the global society. In contrast, current efforts in the area of artificial intelligence are without any cooperation from public authorities at all, because it is left to self-regulatory market dynamics. Effectively, this means that this technology will be shaped by a handful of singular market players, such as Google, Facebook, Apple, and Alibaba – Europe only investing minor sums in comparison through local programs – without an open and mutually responsive collaboration of all relevant actors on questions, such as who owns the data and who can access it, etc. Therefore, international cooperation is urgently required on, and between, the public and private levels in order to achieve truly sustainable impact of key technologies within, and across, national borders.

A5

Sustainability innovations in industry-academy collaborations

AN INTERVIEW WITH TIMA BANSAL

Pratima (Tima) Bansal is a Professor of Sustainability Strategy at the Ivey Business School, Ontario, Canada, with previous visiting appointments at, and affiliated with, the University of Cambridge, MIT, and Monash University. She is the Executive Director and Founder of the Network for Business Sustainability, a growing network of over 35,000 followers from management research and practice. The network is committed to advancing sustainable business, and Innovation North, a collaboration of researchers and managers seeking to innovate the corporate innovation process to embrace systems thinking. She also heads the Ivey Innovation Learning Lab, which helps businesses create value for themselves and society simultaneously over the long term. She chairs the Canadian Council of Academies Expert Panel on the Circular Economy, vice-chairs and sits on the Boards of the United Nation's Principles for Responsible Education, and sits on the Board of Governors and of the Academy of Management.

We frequently see that innovation and corporate social and environmental responsibility are quite separate issues in companies. Where do you see the linkages between those in organizations?

Tima Bansal: Since the late 1980s and early 1990s when the term sustainable development gained traction through the World Commission on Environment and Development (WCED), sustainability really has significantly evolved, particularly in recent years. New challenges caused by rapid changes in our natural, social, institutional, and technological environment are rendering innovation more important than ever in order to move in a direction commensurate with intergenerational equity. Therefore, there is certainly a need for innovation in sustainability, yet equally the need for more sustainability and responsibility in corporate innovation.

DOI: 10.4324/9781003319481-7

However, I fully agree that sustainability and responsibility are typically separated from innovation in organizations. While the former may be integrated through strong auditing functions to cover compliance requirements or also be part of public relations, innovation tends to be a core business function closely connected to profitability and business continuity. It is very rare that companies anchor their innovation strategy in sustainability. Having said that, I think many companies are receptive to embedding sustainability and social-environmental responsibility into the core of their innovation processes to achieve better corporate and societal outcomes. Sustainability has historically been seen as risk management and auditing, which constrain the organization. Innovation, on the other hand, unlocks creativity and potential.

A fundamental re-thinking of sustainability and responsibility is required – not of innovation – such that sustainability is about systems and solving systems problems. Sustainability then becomes an opportunity for organizations to see themselves as part of a larger, multi-layered system and the problems they try to solve as problems nested within other problems. This allows for more innovative and inclusive solutions and widens the time horizon from short to medium and long term. If innovation becomes innovation of and for systems, especially systems of and for different actors, then sustainability and responsibility become deeply rooted in the innovation function. Such innovation encompasses both aspects, achieving desired outcomes, and doing so in an inclusive way through co-design.

Do you have a concrete example where a more systemic approach to innovation can help organizations straddle between core business interests and sustainability?

TB: The Canadian oil sands in the northern parts of Alberta may serve as a good example, because they are arguably among the most polluting sectors in Canada, yet an important one for the economy, with hundreds of millions of dollars of investments annually. Canada's oil sands are environmentally toxic for several reasons. There is the obvious impact of the extraction of fossil fuels, which is in itself the release of carbon sequestered in the ground, but also the high amounts of energy needed to extract oil from the oil sands. In addition, the process involves significant amounts of water and releases other toxins into the land. The size of the projects not only stresses water, land, and air systems, they also have a large impact on Indigenous communities and on local ecosystems. Likewise, local labor, various industrial ecosystems services, etc., are important factors adding to the complexity of the industry next to companies' own business interests.

Seeing the problem as systemic enables the industry's companies to distinguish between their current needs from their long-term ones. In the short run, people need energy to survive and we depend on oil. Canada's oil sands operators need to move the oil to market in the most cost-efficient, most environmentally benign way possible. However, in the long term, these companies need to think about closing the mines and moving to different forms of energy production. This transition to renewable energies requires changes to numerous systems. Sustainability and systems become inseparable. Once these companies see themselves as part of the system, they will see that the future requires them to innovate in order to shift their business and succeed in the long term.

Taking sustainability and systemic thinking that are closely connected together, what can innovation managers learn from them?

TB: I think most people find systems thinking either fuzzy and unclear or simply terrifying, as it is complex and unpredictable. They are afraid they will be asked to map complex systems, which is inherently impossible. However, there is nothing scary about systems thinking and it requires only a few basic principles.

First, it is important to understand that change, even more so systemic change, materializes over certain periods of time. Bigger systems take longer; smaller systems are faster. One needs to determine the basic temporal patterns and simply bound the space over which they observe. Modeling tornadoes over years is pointless, yet modeling climate change over days is also pointless. Therefore, companies need to see their innovations as both small, rapid events (e.g., incremental improvements in energy or water use) as well as major radical transformations (e.g., transformations to renewable energy).

A second principle concerns the fact that it is not about the size or number of partnerships and/or adopters of a technology, but rather the right system of partners and adopters is required for an innovation to become successful. Starting in a small, controlled system and then expanding and exploring how the results fit with other nested systems is an approach that allows innovations to grow organically through adaptation and "contagion" rather than the attempt to hit the whole field at once.

A third principle is the notion of a tipping point. Established systems tend to be inherently stable, as indicated by the fact that they have persisted. They can be nudged into changing, but it is hard. Yet, at some point, they get nudged too far and they transform completely, as we are seeing with the move to electric vehicles.

These are only three examples, scratching the surface of systems thinking's principles. In sum, the application of systems principles in innovation means a real shift toward a better understanding of the dynamics in an industry's ecosystem in terms of stability, dynamics, and tipping points. Insights into these can tremendously support your research and development for business interests and sustainability that are converging more and more in such an approach. Naturally, it also extends the time horizon innovators and managers think about.

For large companies, innovation is a joint effort in which they have to open up, acquire knowledge from different sources, and collaborate with various actors. You have been at the forefront for many years in making academic knowledge more accessible to managers. How did you do this?

TB: About 20 years ago, I founded the Network for Business Sustainability (NBS), which was born out of the notion that academics did not really have a place to put their knowledge into practice. In Canada, as in many other parts of the world, most universities are publicly funded and one may expect that the resulting research also has a real impact on the researched organizations. This requires organizations to have a more active role in what universities research. NBS offers a platform for academia and business to come together mainly in two ways. One is the distribution of knowledge with the focus on translating academic outcomes into a language that is accessible to managers. In addition, the network convenes managers across sectors to discern the research questions jointly that are most valuable to them, two of which are then researched by the network through collaboration between academia and industry.

Based on your experience with NBS, what do you see as the do's and don'ts of successful industry-academia collaboration, especially in the context of sustainability?

TB: One concrete experience we made was that the translation of academic research into business language was much more challenging than expected. As a consequence, NBS went through an evolutionary process, in which we realized that it was less about finding the right language to make academic research more accessible and more about finding the right questions. While academics are often very much focusing on the why, managers are much more interested in the how. Typical issues, such as why should firms be environmentally responsible or integrate sustainability into innovation, are driving many academics in search of a viable business case. However, managers do not need to know so much about the why, but rather much more the how, in order to see the business case. Furthermore, no generic-theoretical approaches, but rather concrete methods, tools, and next steps of how to re-organize the business, including implications on management systems, leadership, or cultural implications are needed more. This is why we moved to the second approach to have managers asking the questions that are then answered through co-creation of concrete frameworks by businesses and academia. A second important learning regarding business-academia collaboration is about interaction. There exist many strong collaboration tools that support interaction and exchange. However, we realized that real success depends less on the tools we use and more on the meetings in which people meet and talk to each other. It is crucial to create room for exchange, much more so than simple knowledge production. It is in these rooms that real change occurs. This is why the NBS is not only still active in the field of knowledge translation and co-creation, but also elevated its ambition to provide tools and guidance for other schools to create these necessary spaces.

How do you balance the ambition of all the parties in these rooms and develop a constructive and collaborative process?

TB: Collaborative spaces between multiple companies and academia require a high degree of trust. This is also one of the most challenging aspects of collaboration, especially in the context of innovation, because, ideally, these collaborations create a lot of intellectual property and value. In addition, at NBS, we foster collaboration by using knowledge as the lubricant and motivation to be in the room. This includes a structured process, in which we start meetings with a certain baseline knowledge shared among participants and then challenge the meeting with a problem. We then move on to create an environment of co-dependency, in which we break down the initially large-scale problem into a very concrete one and everyone needs to share their knowledge in order to arrive at feasible solutions. This process requires competent facilitation of the conversation, which is not fundamentally different from case study teaching using whiteboards, sticky notes, and other tools to keep students engaged and connected. In that sense, it is very refreshing to see how university teaching techniques become instrumental in board rooms and innovation labs.

Did the NBS apply this collaborative approach in the context of the afore-mentioned Canadian oil sands example, and how did it work?

TB: One concrete collaboration was conducted between oil sands companies, researchers from the Universities of Edmonton, two government departments, and an industry collaborative. There was big commitment and enthusiasm from all sides on the project that started from the industry's question on how to accelerate innovation and make it more agile. There was a strong sense that the oil industry moved very slowly compared to other sectors, such as ICT and places like Silicon Valley. We conducted multiple interviews, collected data based on defined non-disclosure agreements, and brought all relevant materials together to engage participants in a collaborative process along the lines described above. These results were collected into a framework that is both academically rigorous and empirically relevant, covering leadership issues, organizational structure and governance, types of innovation, and resource expenditures. The project turned out as a remarkable success, because all participants gained deep insights into the functioning of their organizations and innovation processes. This not only helped in identifying concrete ways of how to accelerate innovation along the innovation process chain, but also helped in recognizing that the speed of innovation is interlinked with the ambition of, and investment in, an innovation project. Smaller, incremental amounts of resources are much easier to accelerate compared to the hundreds of millions of dollar investments I mentioned earlier in the context of the oil sands industry. A lot of innovation, therefore, cannot be conducted by the large oil companies themselves. They have to rely on a network of SMEs.

What challenges did you encounter during this collaboration?

TB: Every success story also has its fair share of failures. In the context of this particular project, we did not anticipate the high turnover of personnel in organizations. During the 12-month project, every single one of the six major partners changed their main point of contact with us. One company was sold to another, with the new chief technology officer having had less commitment. In another case, the responsible person retired, and in the case of government institutions, we experienced a generally high movement of personnel through the system. This type of turnover makes long-term commitment in industry-academia collaboration very difficult, as the two move at different rates and are not easily matched. The lesson learned, therefore, was to embed such projects deep within the innovation functions of organizations as such, to reduce the dependency on individual commitment, including having more people involved in the project by each of the organizations, which reduces the risk of default and increases the likelihood of successful outcomes.

Based on the vast experiences you have had in the field of sustainability and with the NBS over the last decades, what will sustainability innovation contribute and change until 2030?

TB: The sustainability movement has undergone a significant evolution since the term was coined in 1987. It moved from a typically isolated compliance, philanthropic, or marketing orientation that was decoupled from the core business to now being integrated into many corporate strategies. I think that people are now increasingly seeing sustainability as a macro issue that requires multi-business and multi-sectoral collaboration. Looking into the future, it is critical to remember that sustainability is first and foremost about intergenerational equity, namely that we want to ensure and protect the prosperity of future generations. One of the biggest barriers to this is natural resources and the issue of how to sustain them. A major contribution of sustainability and Responsible Innovation in the near to mid future needs to be ensuring maximum efficient use and reuse of natural resources, including the use of renewable energy. This is the major ambition of the Circular Economy that will hopefully bring us to the point where all organizations work in an industrial ecosystem that mirrors the temporality and synchronicity of our planet's natural cycles. I strongly believe that this is possible and that humanity can arrive at this point through Responsible Innovation. I guess the biggest question in my mind is whether they can do so fast enough – before we reach the tipping point.

A6

A decade of Responsible Research and Innovation

AN INTERVIEW WITH RICHARD OWEN

Richard Owen is Professor in Innovation Management at the School of Management at Bristol University, UK. He is one of the most-cited authors and a world-renowned thought leader on Responsible Research and Innovation. His research interests are in politics, risks, ethics, and governance of innovation and new technologies in society, from big data in financial services and planetary climate engineering to innovation for development. His research sits at the intersection of innovation governance and science and technology studies as he is a critical, interdisciplinary scholar.

You are one of the authors of the ground-breaking publication "Developing a Framework for Responsible Innovation," in which you introduced the foundational four dimensions of RRI. How can they best be explained to someone who has never heard about RRI before?

Richard Owen: The four dimensions of RRI start from the basic understanding that innovation is a so-called "future creating phenomenon." We tend to think of innovation as creating value from novel ideas (e.g., innovative products and services). It is that, but my departure point for innovation is different: it is innovation's profound ability to create futures through our imagination, and if innovation is about creating futures, this brings the responsibility with it to care for our future and ask the question what kind of future we, as a society, want innovation to create. Next comes the insight that the future remains uncertain and unpredictable and, therefore, we need to understand how we conduct research, create knowledge, innovate, and take decisions under conditions of great uncertainty. In response to these insights, we developed these four fancy terms, the fourfold dimensions that sit under a framework of

DOI: 10.4324/9781003319481-8

RRI. Anticipation as the first dimension helps us to articulate and explore the futures we may be creating during innovation by asking about impacts, for example, their future costs and benefits, intended and unintended consequences, etc. Reflection, as the second dimension, consists of two parts. On the one hand, it literally means for the innovator to look in the mirror and ask the question why (s)he is doing this in terms of purpose, values, and motivations. Second-order reflexivity adds the aspect of understanding the political contexts, social norms, etc., in which a certain researcher or innovator is embedded. The third dimension is inclusion of all relevant actors in the conversation about the sorts of futures we want to create through innovation, as well as a discussion about their potential social, ethical, environmental, and political entanglements. This ensures not only that innovators understand what matters to those impacted by an innovation, but also that affected stakeholders are empowered to help shape the agendas and trajectories of innovations toward desired outcomes. The fourth and final dimension is responsiveness, which is all about implementing the knowledge from the previous three dimensions to design innovation agendas, management systems, and ultimately innovations for a desirable future under conditions of uncertainty.

The four dimensions describe a strongly process-oriented approach to RRI. Was this deliberate and why did you not add a more results-oriented perspective in terms of climate, societal, or other goals?

RO: Responsible Innovation is normative by definition and, at the same time, we are facing a climate change crisis, major geopolitical challenges, and even the consequences of a pandemic. In fact, looking back at the original publication of the framework,[1] you will read we were asked by the UK Engineering and Physical Sciences Research Council to embed it in a very contentious area of science and technology funded by them, namely geoengineering, which is about the intentional engineering of the planetary climate. I started my academic career as an environmental scientist and, thus, it would have been incredibly tempting for me (and perhaps my colleagues) to embed our own values into the framework, of which sustainability would be a core one. We could have added specific goals to that end. Nonetheless, we remained adamant in the view that any definition of RRI outcomes has to be the product of an inclusive, deliberative process, rather than being defined by ourselves, and that is why we focused on the process rather than outcomes per se. Neither academics, such as ourselves, nor any other narrow group of actors should define what is right or wrong for our common future on their own. Of course, we hope that an inclusive and democratic process will result in a vision of the kind of future humanity needs and wants.

Over time, while I still adhere to this principle, I have come to the view that sustainability and addressing climate change are so important that they need to be part of any framework for RRI and that the planet's long-term sustainability must be at the center of all our attention and that includes innovation. I think now I would make this more explicit as a goal in the RRI framework, along with social justice.

Would you differentiate between Responsible Research (RR) and Responsible Innovation (RI), given that they are often pursued by different actors with different interests and for different purposes?

RO: The four dimensions have been designed for both contexts (RR and RI), despite the fact that there are important differences. We might distinguish between two modes of knowledge production: "basic" (or "fundamental") research vs. more "strategic"[2] or "applied" research and innovation in this regard. The first is about research, with the primary aim of producing new knowledge that contributes to our understanding of the natural and social worlds, but it also includes critical scholarship in, for example, the social sciences and humanities. It is less about real-world applications and societal impact. The institutionalization of this research in universities, for example, through codes of conduct, specified norms, and ethics approval processes has been incredibly important and may even be arguably seen as sufficient for this sort of fundamental research and scholarship. They concern issues, such as plagiarizing, intentional selection or misrepresentation of data, attention to researching vulnerable groups, etc. As soon as we move to strategic research and innovation, however, be it motivated by profitability, productivity, meeting social challenges, or other reasons, the importance of real-world impact increases decisively in terms of creating and shaping the future, rendering such existing norms and processes as still important but insufficient. For this type of knowledge production, I think these four dimensions of Responsible Innovation are tremendously important and extend beyond existing codes of ethics and isolated examples of public engagement, etc. For example, the unprecedented wave of digitalization research and innovation driven by some of the big tech companies and the state in the aftermath of the dot-com bubble in the early 2000s brought real change regarding digital surveillance by companies and states that we are now living with as part of our present. Going back to that time, could an RRI-based approach have helped us better anticipate and open up to debate those futures being imagined and created through these technological innovation processes and by which actors? Second, could it have helped us critically engage as a society with these futures in the making to help shape the future of digitalization in responsible, equitable, and just ways? Waiting for regulation to catch up, as we know from history, is not enough. There needs to be something else, enacted earlier on in the innovation process. Some people may ask. what does this have to do with universities as actors?: it is worth noting that a lot of strategic research and innovation happens in universities, and that the boundaries between universities and the private sector are increasingly entwined. We in universities have an important role to play.

Applying the idea of RRI's inclusiveness and openness to the context of the corporate sector, is there an inherent tension between RRI and competition of market actors?

RO: Indeed, it is important to understand that companies operate in a competitive market economy that is becoming more and more globalized. This includes the fact that competition and competitiveness are built on knowledge asymmetries as a source of profits and, therefore, naturally constrain openness and collaboration. Even more so, if responsibility and sustainability, as such, are viable business opportunities, companies may have the interest of monopolizing them rather than seeking collaboration. However, at its core, RRI is the responsibility toward ourselves, others, and the planet with a view of our shared future. In that sense, RRI is also empowering us and fostering our creativity to innovate. Fortunately, especially since the 2008 financial crisis, we can see growing consent among younger generations to test alternative approaches to business and innovation in line with this understanding. The four RRI dimensions, including openness and collaboration, are powerful and necessary means for suchlike innovation to succeed, even more so in complex value chains, in which innovation systems, comprising multiple actors, are essential. I would see this as an encouraging vision of innovation with a certain pinch of idealism to challenge the status quo, yet without the naivety to ignore the reality of currently fierce competitive markets.

The four dimensions of Responsible Innovation are one of the best-known and most-cited conceptual frameworks in the field. Why do you think this framework has been so successful?

RO: The four dimensions build on narratives and critiques in the context of science, technology, innovation, and society that have been well established for several decades. They stand on the shoulders of giants, for example, co-productionist and anticipatory perspectives. They extend back to debates on responsible nanotechnology development (e.g., in the US and the EU) which was a big driver for, and precursor of, Responsible Innovation. Our framework, therefore, did not emerge out of a vacuum, but further developed and continued important conversations about society's relation with technology, science, public and private research and, ultimately, our future. It seems to have resonated, but it is important to note it is part of a bigger story, in which many have made important contributions. Next to this, another success factor was likely the idea of responsibility and being responsible as being a central feature. We were keen to explicitly locate our framework in concepts of future-oriented responsibility, of which care and responsiveness are central. Rather than accountability or risk management that have typically constraining connotations, our framework promotes a collective and constructive approach to innovation that emphasizes responsibility, which differs from previous risk- and assessment-based approaches in the past. These ideas of what being responsible means in the context of innovation, underpin the four dimensions, which, in total, I think, have not lost relevance since the publication of the framework in 2013. However, at the end of the day, these are words and what matters as much is what it means in real-world practice and how to best apply it. That is where the real challenges begin.

As a major authority in this field, what are generally the achievements of RRI and what are its major challenges for the future, in your view?

RO: A major achievement is certainly the establishment of an RRI community including scholars, politicians, and practitioners from industry and beyond. Such a community of practitioners is important to build a common understanding of the issues connected to Responsible Innovation despite having different backgrounds, views, and interests. The European Commission has been instrumental in this regard over more than a decade. A second achievement regards the ongoing and rising experimentation in terms of putting RRI into practice. As mentioned above, a major challenge is the application of RRI theories in real-world conditions and, therefore, it is crucial to nurture experimentation for the translation of these profound concepts into practicable strategies, processes, tools, and mechanisms. I frequently receive messages, in which individuals or organizations are informing us about successful new ways of how to practice RRI and are interested in further collaboration. This is something I would like to encourage everyone to do. Both a living community of practice and experimentation are important complements to advance RRI in theory and practice.

On the side of challenges, three major areas require close attention by the RRI community. The first concerns policy and the fact that Responsible Innovation connects to a certain idea of deliberative and direct democracy that includes a critique of the market-technology dyad and the role of the state in it. These political dimensions cannot be ignored. Second, adoption of RRI in the corporate sector is increasing, yet still lagging behind, especially in the area of innovation systems and how different actors combine knowledge within them. A systemic approach to RRI is as important, but this also needs to challenge the status quo and how innovation systems are configured, their normative context, power dynamics, and vested interests. In addition, practitioners and researchers need to better understand the profound organizational challenges for companies in order to adopt RRI. We need to better understand the contribution that organizational studies and institutional theory can make to help us in this respect. The third challenge relates to the global context and how the concept of RRI as a strong European one translates into different cultures. Concepts usually are re-interpreted and re-shaped as they travel across contexts and this requires carefulness and sensitivity when "introducing" RRI to other regions. This includes questions about applicability, but is also about being sensitive to situated context and open to incorporating new ideas into the theory and practice of RRI from other non-European parts of the globe.

Which actors are most needed with regards to the implementation and practice of RRI?

RO: Rather than directly addressing this crucial question from the perspective of actors, I would start with thinking about those forces and norms that are legitimizing our practices, institutions, etc., and consequently configuring our behavior in terms of innovation. These tend to become stable and habitual over time to create a status quo that may offer resistance to RRI implementation. The COVID-19 crisis created a multitude of questions about the legitimacy of social practices and institutions, such as established forms of office work or the use of surveillance. One may say that such crises hold tremendous potential, as many pieces of our society's organization go up in the air, but might not fall back to their original place. We have a window of opportunity. These are decisive moments for a discussion about re-imagining norms and institutions and the kind of innovation we want to follow in the wake of the current crisis, supported by an RRI process. We need to engage with and open up innovation being undertaken in the wake of COVID-19 and in its name, but not only that, take this opportunity to shape this innovation in ways that help us create a future that is more sustainable, just and flourishing for all. Actors have an important role to play, but for me this about institutional change, which includes, but goes a lot further than, actors.

What would be your vision and outlook of RRI for the future?

RO: The faith in progress and the faith in innovation to deliver more productivity, jobs, and economic growth are no less than they have ever been. Having tested and integrated RRI in different public and private settings, it became clear that if it does not speak to this narrative of growth and driving productivity, RRI is seen as a real hindrance. At the same time, we also observe that the EU as a main driver of RRI moved away from its vision that was inspired to a large extent by those such as René von Schomberg and had a lot in common with the ideas proposed in this interview. The European Commission's so-called five RRI keys (ethics, societal engagement, gender equality, open access/science, and science education) are important entry points, but risk losing the bigger picture and the integrated and even transformational approach that constitutes RRI at its core.

Against the background of these two developments, I would argue it is crucial to maintain momentum toward things, such as gender equality and open access in science, but equally important to return RRI to its original, more ambitious vision. In that sense, this includes an important debate about innovation and its intimate connection to progress and growth, our relationship with the future and how innovation can go beyond growth and blind progress to foster a future that is more sustainable and equitable. RRI, both as a community and process-oriented approach, is instrumental for this vision. Building the RRI community was mentioned as one of the field's big achievements and it will be critical to nurture, further diversify, and enrich this community as a critical counterbalance to the hegemonic framing of innovation we currently see. However, critique and scholarship alone will not be enough. Any vision for RRI in the future has to extend beyond these to foster change, which will require activism.

NOTES

1. Stilgoe, J., Owen, R., & Macnaghten, P. (2013). Developing a framework for responsible innovation. *Research Policy*, 42(9), 1568–1580. https://doi.org/10.1016/j.respol.2013.05.008
2. An example of a strategic research (policy) objective might be "net zero."

A7

Responsible Innovation in our future homes

AN INTERVIEW WITH SANDRA KOLLETH

Sandra Kolleth is the Managing Director of Miele Austria and was awarded the Silver Medal of Honor of the Republic of Austria for her services. In 1995, she started working in quality management at Xerox Austria and switched two years later to sales. She was soon promoted to several management and leadership positions. In 2008, she took over the management of Xerox Global Services, the service subsidiary of Xerox Austria. In 2013, she was appointed General Manager of Xerox. She joined Miele in 2018, where she is currently responsible for the Austrian Market, as well as for the company's activities in Slovenia and Croatia.

The COVID-19 pandemic dominated much of our social and economic lives globally. How did Miele Austria adjust to this situation and what challenges did you experience?

Sandra Kolleth: For Miele, COVID-19 was challenging, because more than 90% of our sales channels needed to close because of lockdowns across Europe. As a premium brand, we are strongly relying on in-person contacts with our retailers and consumers. Therefore, we were really worried about the impact on our business. However, we found that local relationships between specialists and their customers remained strong in the electronics sector, whether online or via telephone. Consumers' orientation toward local purchasing and, therefore, local retailers, turned out to be an advantage in our experience. In fact, Miele experienced a global increase in demand that was even stronger than the general demand increase the industry experienced.

Facing a situation that none of us has experienced before, it was particularly important that we could rely on our longstanding corporate values as a privately owned business. One such value that we also included in our mission statement is "to take care of each

DOI: 10.4324/9781003319481-9

other," which we strongly highlighted in our internal communication. Likewise, Miele focused on reliability both in its relationship with B2B partners and customers. More generally, a big challenge was the unpredictability of the situation and the impossibility of long-term planning. Previous decisions had to be changed frequently and on short notice. The resulting uncertainty required significant flexibility from our side and that of our employees. Therefore, clear, proactive, and honest communication cannot be overemphasized, even more so in situations where previous decisions had to be reversed on short notice. For example, frequent status updates – even simple notifications that there are no urgent matters for a day – provided Miele and its employees with the necessary dependability and reassurance for continued collaboration during the COVID-19 pandemic.

Did you also experience challenges regarding supply chain continuity?

SK: Miele Austria shifted early from reactive risk mitigation to a more proactive approach focused on opportunities. The strong focus on the life at home due to the pandemic next to the generally strong sector of electronic home appliances represented a chance for Miele. Housekeeping activities, such as cooking and cleaning, even gained traction. In addition, the COVID-19 pandemic has shown that customers value high-quality and sustainable products. This development is positive both for important sustainability goals, including climate targets, and for us as a premium brand. We experienced an unexpectedly strong growth in demand – while at the same time facing supply chain issues that grew during the duration of the pandemic. Although Miele has a high depth of producing parts and materials in our own factories, mainly in Europe, to fulfill our quality expectations, we are dependent on electronic parts like microchips and base materials as well as logistic services. We were able to produce more in 2019 and 2020 than in the years before. Still, with the strong demand, we were facing long delivery times to our trade partners and consumers, as well as predictability issues.

Responsible Innovation has gained traction at the European level in the last few years in the context of broader sustainability. For Miele Austria, what does responsibility mean in the context of innovation?

SK: Miele does not differentiate between responsibility in one or the other business area. In simple terms, responsibility for us means following the company's values throughout our operations, including innovation. We share Europe's emphasis on sustainability since the company's inception more than 120 years ago, by striving to innovate longer-lasting products, higher reparability, higher energy-efficiency, and caring for our employees, communities, and the markets in which we operate. As a privately owned premium brand, this is Miele's philosophy of "*Immer Besser*." This means that we will do all that we can to be forever better than our competitors and forever better than we already are. That does not refer to ever faster, ever more, ever bigger, but rather to simpler, higher-quality and more sustainability in everything we do and products that have true value and usability for our customers. Clarity about a company's values is, thus, the basis of Responsible Innovation in order to know which goals to achieve and how.

The inclusion of stakeholders represents an important aspect of Responsible Innovation, both in terms of product design for socially disadvantaged and excluded groups, as well as participation in innovation processes. For example, Miele's experience from collaborating with visually impaired persons helped us realize that Braille on home appliances is not the ultimate solution, since eyesight deteriorates more often at an older age when people lack the finger sensitivity to learn reading the script. Instead, we followed a different approach, in which we strongly simplified the use of a new washing machine that we named "Guideline." This simplification attracted a variety of other target groups as well and, at the same time, led to the development of our first touch display for visually impaired persons. In this case, responsibility lies in the participation of marginalized groups during the innovation process and in providing equal access to products through better usability. In addition, another important aspect of accessibility regards the purchasing power of customers and the need to provide sustainable and responsible products, such as energy-efficient dishwashers that require fewer resources than handwashing, also in the entry-level segment without compromises on quality.

For innovation to succeed, is the real challenge more on the side of creativity to develop new ideas or on the side of the ability to identify the right idea among the many others?

SK: The real challenge is to identify the right idea, because there are always many of them. In addition, it is the courage to realize new ideas that goes beyond considerations of mere profitability. Economic viability is important to have a business case, but exclusive focus on it would not have allowed us to develop products, such as the "Dialog oven" ("Dialoggarer"), a new dimension in the culinary world. The appliance maintains a constant dialog with the ingredients to cook dishes in their entirety – instead of from outside in – until achieving the desired result. Cooking a fish in ice or veal tenderloin in beeswax without melting the ice or wax, separating browning from baking, preparing different dishes and ingredients simultaneously. We knew that this product would not be profitable in the short term. However, Miele's long-term planning horizon opened the door for the mentioned courage to realize ideas and make an investment in this product as the basis for further technological development. Generally speaking, innovation management requires strong focus on the selection of ideas and the right balance between innovative courage and economic factors. This is even more important in the context of Responsible Innovation and sustainability that add aspects, such as inclusiveness and impact.

What does long-term planning look like at Miele and how do you identify and prioritize ideas based on it?

SK: As mentioned before, it is extremely difficult to know the future and predict the long-term impact of megatrends, for example, of the COVID-19 pandemic. Therefore, we use scenario-based planning in order to better understand possible trajectories for future developments, based on which we can prioritize innovation projects and new investments. These scenarios analyze trends, for example, what societies may look like in 2030, including social, environmental, and economic factors. Of course, we are not able to build representative scenarios on our own and, therefore, cooperate with other organizations through initiatives, such as Universal Home, that help us to develop scenarios for the future in a human-centered approach that includes important considerations about sustainability, such as the reduction of resources and risks.

At Miele, scenarios are mapped against three different time horizons, two, five to seven and above ten years, respectively. For the horizon of five to seven years, in particular, Miele strongly engages in customer-led innovation through various projects. One of these is accompanying people at home around the globe, cooking together and having a glass of wine, joining them during shopping and much more. This very direct engagement on an informal and personal level produces important lessons about the needs and fears of our customers, which then feed into the social scenarios. In contrast, typical crowdsourcing did not prove as successful, because it usually produces fairly predictable or unfeasible results in Miele's experience. In total, the scenario-based planning is focused on a holistic view of societies and combines strong networking with customer-led innovation.

Looking at the time horizon until 2030, what will change in the ways we live at home and what does this mean in terms of sustainability? In which direction will technologies evolve, and will they only become "smarter" or will there be a more fundamental transformation?

SK: This will depend on the specific scenarios and which of these will manifest. From a present perspective, despite having a general sense of current and upcoming trends, the probability of the different scenarios is difficult to predict due to the long-term horizon. Quite likely, it will not be just one scenario, but an amalgam that will come to real life. However, an inclination toward a society of solidarity, in which quality, sustainability, etc. play a strong role, will have a different impact on how we live compared to a scenario in which technological advances and dominance by big tech-players are the major driving factors. Stronger sustainability, including product quality, reparability, and technological advance, especially in terms of digitalization and ecological benefits, will very likely be strongly growing trends in the future that open opportunities for companies and a better future alike.

Home appliances will certainly become smarter and more integrated to address questions of health, among many others. In addition, issues, such as reparability and sustainable life-cycle optimization are getting more and more into focus, which requires us to go far beyond the production phase as such. In terms of a washing machine's energy and resource use, only 20% are part of production and disposal, 80% occur during actual usage. This bears great responsibility on the side of product innovation not only to design more economical and energy-efficient products, but also to ensure their usability. It is interesting to see that energy-efficiency is an important criterion in our customers' purchasing decisions. However, only about 5% regularly use the eco programs in daily life. This means that trade-offs between sustainability, on the one hand, and convenience (like duration of washing programs), on the other, are decisive factors to be considered in Responsible Innovation to achieve the desired impact. In other words, it is not just about designing more sustainable products, but also about how to ensure the desired use of a new product by customers. This requires a more integrated approach to innovation, likely supported by smarter technologies and AI.

How do you envisage a life in ever smarter homes? Which are the most important target groups and markets for smart homes?

SK: Currently, smart homes have already reached a stage beyond that of technology enthusiasts, but remain strongly dependent on the purchasing power of the customers. We envisage a point at which most people will use so-called smart technology for different purposes. The more functionality we are able to add to our products that is useful to our customers, the more we can see the adoption of smart technology and the willingness to connect appliances.

A strong trend that we expect to pick up speed is a significantly increased responsiveness and decision-making capacity of household equipment with the ability to adapt to different contexts. Artificial intelligence is important in this regard to recognize behavioral patterns and user preferences in specific situations. One example is coffee machines that adjust to personal taste and distinguish between morning and afternoon. In 2016, Miele published a study on the so-called "invisible kitchen" with an integrated cooking guide that adapts to the knowledge of the cook and only intervenes when necessary. Contextualization, personalization, higher integration of data from other areas, like health, are developing very fast. This goes hand in hand with more advanced sensor technology, cameras, and acoustic systems to produce the input for smarter and more automated machines. Technologies, such as voice-control, will likely lose some of their importance in this regard, because artificial intelligence will automate many processes that then do not require direct human intervention any more.

Responsible use of data is one of the biggest challenges in the context of digital innovations and artificial intelligence, including data security, the fear of surveillance, etc. How do you treat this topic?

SK: We perceive data security as a core responsibility and important aspect of sustainable products at Miele. We keep very high standards of data security, but we are aware that misuse, leakage, etc., always remain a risk, not only in our sector, but everywhere. Therefore, it is important to estimate whether these risks outweigh the benefits of new technologies in the innovation process. Next to the protection of data, the transparent use of it is equally important with clear information to the consumer. This also includes the right to choose whether, and which, data is collected. In 2019, Miele announced the new product, Generation 7000, with full data network capability, yet customers are able to choose whether they want to connect and share data or not. Data security, transparency, and the freedom of choice are key pillars of the Miele brand's essence and an important basis for customers to build trust in us. For a premium brand, in particular, this is more than mere corporate social responsibility, but part of its core business and competitiveness.

Integrated responsible solutions for homes cannot be achieved by a single company. How can businesses across sectors successfully collaborate to responsibly design the smart home of the future?

SK: Several platforms exist that allow collaboration on different levels, all of which highly depend on convening the right experts and stakeholders. One such platform that Miele uses and co-founded is Universal Homes, a network of premium manufacturers and service providers for homes. It started from the question how to design a livable future for all and improve the ways in which humans live and work at home. The initiative connects experts from design, innovation, research, marketing, ICT, product management and more, enabling knowledge sharing and cross-sectoral systemic solutions. A big topic regarding more integrated solutions for the future is the creation of common standards across sectors of the home industry and it is these platforms where the necessary exchanges take place.

Lastly, scientists would benefit largely from understanding the broader context of any policy problem. They should cultivate their political consciousness and improve their understanding of the different interests embedded in the problems they research. In doing so, they should foster their contacts to civil society and make use of "citizen knowledge" in their research. Scientific evidence that considers societal tensions policymakers have to face would be much more successful in attracting their attention.

What is your vision of the role that Miele will play in 2030?

SK: In 2030, we will still be the most desirable and trustworthy brand of the industry. Creating quality will still be on the top of our agenda, becoming "*Immer Besser*" for our customers, our employees, and the planet. We will still be an independent, family-owned business. We will be an important player in ecologicalization, as well as digitalization, and we will be a provider of services and ecosystems that make our customers' lives both easier and more enjoyable.

A8

Responsible Innovation and artificial intelligence

AN INTERVIEW WITH HARALD LEITENMÜLLER

Harald Leitenmüller is Chief Technology Officer at Microsoft Austria. He supports future-oriented IT initiatives in order to enable a fast, smooth, and useful adoption of new technologies. Before joining Microsoft Austria, he gained experience in various international innovation projects across industries. Topics, such as the ICT location Austria, a fair, open marketplace, social innovation, technology policies, and the competitiveness of the local IT ecosystem have always been a core concern of his.

How would you define artificial intelligence and what are common use cases?

Harald Leitenmüller: In contrast to common definitions, I would start from the notion of an intelligent technology designed to support humans in order to perform more complex tasks, do and achieve more, and to better participate in society. From a strategic perspective, it is, therefore, a means to an end. The term "intelligent" refers to the technology's ability to take over tasks that would have otherwise been done by humans, requiring human senses and/or intellect. On the technological side, AI is an umbrella term for concrete areas, such as machine learning, deep learning, etc. Although people are often unaware of it, it permeates many of the most common applications. Every state-of-the-art search engine, whether on Netflix, Amazon, etc., selects suggestions based on AI and machine learning algorithms. Likewise, X-ray diagnostics vastly applies image analysis and optimization through AI. Digital photography on mobiles, communication tools, encryption, virus detection, and many more technologies all apply AI to improve in one way or another.

DOI: 10.4324/9781003319481-10

The vast range of applications and seemingly unlimited possibilities offered by AI raise both questions and fears. These concern, among others, automated data collection and decision-making, misuse of data, and, more generally, the resulting control over people's lives paired with a lack of transparency. Responsible use of AI includes both the responsible design and application of concrete solutions. Applying clear, ethical frameworks and procedures helps companies to select use cases and design responsible solutions depending on local context and values. More generally, I would argue that innovation is moving toward the holistic design of solutions, including questions of societal and other impacts. Co-creation and interdisciplinary collaboration between AI, industries, etc., quickly open new possibilities in this regard, but they require the establishment of a common language.

What is needed for the responsible use of AI?

HL: In the simplest terms, responsible use of AI depends on actors' responsibility on two levels. The first concerns the innovator and her/his ability to design holistic solutions. This requires new competencies, such as systemic and abstract thinking, especially for combining social and technological innovation and the inclusion of ethical and sustainability aspects. Second comes the responsibility of the end-users. Although designers and engineers may define the purpose and use cases of a technology, every system can still be misappropriated in various ways. This requires the user's competencies analogously to a car driver that needs to know how to drive, regardless how safely designed the car is. In Europe, the GDPR provides a legal foundation in the right direction to address the misappropriation of data and define rules for responsible data management. However, there remain various gray areas that the regulation cannot cover – for example, an insurance company using data on mobile phone charging patterns of customers to predict their reliability of paying fees and liabilities – and which require involvement of ethics. Such ethical, value-based frameworks need to be applied both during the innovation of a technology and during its use. Guiding decisions through such a framework with the aim of better understanding their impact and minimizing the risk of data misuse are, therefore, a key topic at Microsoft.

In which areas are autonomous decisions by AI necessary and reasonable, in your view?

HL: At its core, machine learning is the generation of new data by means of existing data with a certain probability that this new data is either correct or not. From that perspective, additional input is made available to inform decisions, although this input may be biased due to insufficient training of the algorithm, etc. Whether decisions are to be taken autonomously by AI based on data, or only improve a human's knowledge base, is, therefore, a multifactorial question with ethical implications, especially in sensitive areas, such as medical diagnosis and treatments. In response, many organizations develop guidelines to discern when to prefer autonomous over human decision-making. At Microsoft, we defined three important areas as a first starting point on the topic of responsible AI use cases in our customer relations. The first is that of use cases, in which decisions are to be made extremely fast, for example, self-driving cars that have to decide within milliseconds which action to take in order to avoid an accident. Human mediation or intervention would be counterproductive and increase risk in this case. As a side note, human drivers also do not take decisions based on ethical reasons, but rather follow instincts and intuition to stay safe on the road. Second, situations in which communication is limited demand higher autonomy of AI decision-making. For example, a Mars robot cannot rely on human remote control, because communication is delayed by 30 minutes or even impossible. In this case, the robot needs to navigate and conduct tasks autonomously. The third area concerns dangerous tasks that would normally require human intervention in a high-risk environment. For example, in a nuclear accident, it can hardly be argued why not to send in an autonomous AI-controlled machine instead of humans to measure radiation, etc.

What do ethical guidelines for responsible AI look like at Microsoft?

HL: The above-mentioned three areas of autonomous AI are only simplified illustrations to start a discussion with partners and customers on the responsible use of AI. The actual decision process regarding potential and responsible use cases is based on a more nuanced ethics framework. The framework covers six main criteria and starts from a basic question catalog to discern a project's foundation in terms of topic, specified scope, existing capacities, sustainability, ethical concerns, etc. If these questions are answered insufficiently, a dedicated ethics committee will be responsible for further evaluation. The committee follows a more complex framework based on a specified value system and applies various quantitative and qualitative instruments, such as impact and risk assessments, cost-benefit analysis, etc., for a much more thorough and informed decision. This process may appear simple and straightforward, but, in practice, the concrete decisions require intricate and effortful considerations.

How do you apply this framework in a specific use case?

HL: Microsoft's framework operates on two levels that go hand in hand. It addresses both the issue of what we want to innovate and how best to do so. The latter translates into ethics design guidelines to be used during development and follows what we call value-sensitive design. Taking the simple case of a chatbot, how should a chatbot interact in a dialogue with a human interlocutor? The design guidelines then define rules for engineers, such as "humans are the heroes," which is aimed at respecting needs, values, etc., of humans. Another would be "know the context" in order for the bot to understand, for example, the important relation of humans' emotions and intelligence. A typical reaction of human speakers is to switch to the emotional level during technical discussions they do not understand. In these situations, a bot should be able to recognize that a statement is out of context. A major ethical rule in our design guidelines for chatbots is that it has to identify itself as such in order to avoid misuse, such as manipulation, etc. This includes that, upon request, the bot will explain what it is, as well as the purpose for which it is used in a given context. However, this example already reveals the ethical intricacies connected to AI technology, because there are exceptions to this rule. In the US, Microsoft is running the pilot, Project Intercept to develop AI-supported interventions against human trafficking for prostitution. AI-bots automatically intercept online conversations between forced prostitutes and illegal buyers in order to educate the latter about the nature and consequences of their criminal actions. Forced and often incarcerated prostitutes are provided with a hotline to receive immediate help. The pilot project has been very successful so far, but it depends on the bot not revealing its identity from the beginning. Only if the human interlocutor directly asks would the bot identify itself.

Where do you see the difference of systemic design of holistic solutions compared to other types of innovation?

HL: I would distinguish between three innovation concepts, namely invention, discovery, and design. Invention is the rational engineering of technology resulting from experimentation and mathematical optimization. Discovery starts more openly and adds the element of coincidence and surprise. Design is more open than an invention, yet more streamlined and directed toward expected outcomes than discovery. It includes multiple parameters on top of technological feasibility concerning the environment and society. This approach is based on the insight that more holistic solutions comprise more than one solution for more than one problem and/or purpose, and depend on a higher level of abstraction. Among the three, I believe that design has already become the dominant mode of innovation, commonly operationalized through well-known tools, such as Design Thinking. It is common standard that software developers are asked to design programs by means of engagement with multiple actors ranging from partners to customers, in order to understand a potential innovation better in terms of technology, business model, society, environment, etc. This makes innovation processes and management much more complex, yet also more exciting and responsible with a very different commitment by developers and other stakeholders.

What is the value proposition of Design Thinking?

HL: Some companies may be hesitant, because of the complexity of such design processes and the resulting time investments required in following them to the very end. It is honestly a shame that we take ever less time, also in the corporate world, to investigate problems from different perspectives and combine them for the development of innovative ideas and concepts. The potential to get different views on a single problem or combine several problems into an entirely new solution path is one of Design Thinking's real value propositions. This goes hand in hand with Design Thinking as a co-creative process that – if taken seriously – brings together different actors and disciplines, quickly opens new business opportunities in an inclusive and, thus, more responsible manner. This holds especially true in the context of AI. AI as a digital solution has vast potential across many sectors and, therefore, more and more are exploring its use cases, whether in agriculture, health, education, or elsewhere. Suddenly, actors from multiple fields are getting together to discuss AI in terms of its usability and impact, discovering new directions and creating many new ideas that result in the design of innovative products and services. A very interesting example is a project in Africa called Premonition. It develops a smart sensor system for detecting and monitoring the spread of animal diseases. Instead of spending significant technical effort and time collecting animals' blood samples, the project uses flytraps to collect mosquitos and analyze their blood, because they are biting many animals. This has proved to be a very smart and cheap solution as the result of a co-creative design process. An important prerequisite for the successful application of co-creative Design Thinking is a common language. Not too many years ago, for example, data protection was a small field mostly comprised of lawyers sharing a very specific technical language. Nowadays, it is normal that lawyers and online security experts discuss data protection in order to develop, implement, and improve legal and technical solutions, respectively.

How do you, as part of a multinational corporation, experience and handle regional differences regarding responsibility and innovation?

HL: I would say that all regions follow value-based ethic frameworks, the question is which value systems they are based on and with what priorities. These are often incompatible with each other and, therefore, challenge policymakers and businesses alike. In simple terms, one may say that Europe follows a people-first strategy, but this may not be the case in China or the US in the same way. On a geopolitical level, resulting frictions require dialogue in order to solve global challenges, as we are increasingly facing them in the vastly unregulated digital space. Much of our regulatory frameworks is still based on a territorial-national logic that does not apply to the borderless cyberspace and issues, such as online surveillance, misinformation, or even digital warfare. To address this issue on the international stage, Microsoft started the bold initiative to propose a Digital Geneva Convention. On the company level, corporations are tasked to take a clear stance. Microsoft commits globally to the mentioned people-first strategy in order to support individuals and organizations to achieve their goals. This constrains our ability to participate in all markets equally and not all our solutions are marketable to the same extent across the globe. Obviously, this approach makes Microsoft's commercial success more difficult in countries, such as China. However, this has been the deliberate decision by the company and I would argue that such decisions are essential for responsible business conduct.

How will digitalization advance in the next five to ten years?

HL: We can currently see a four-step integrated process evolving around digitalization. The first step was, and still is, the migration toward cloud-based systems, that is, basically an infrastructure innovation enabling data sharing. It forms an important foundation for the internet of things (IoT) as the second step, which uses sensor technology to automate data collection. The data can then be stored and processed via the cloud infrastructure and together this ecosystem exponentially boosts big data analytics. The third step is the upcoming topic of edge computing. Transferring vast amounts of data to central data nodes is not the most efficient approach and, therefore, edge computing focuses on the pre-processing of data through machine learning algorithms close to the site of collection. The last step is AI and machine learning as such to automatize and, therefore, substantially scale big data analysis to generate new data and support decision-making. The more an AI system has been trained and the better it performs, the less data it requires to make decisions. Vast amounts of data are only required for the training period. This four-step process is growing in parallel and many companies are developing strategies of how to manage and integrate the above-mentioned steps. Ideally, this will allow us to return to less overall, yet more high quality, data and information that we need for a sustainable future and the entailed massive transformation of our lives.

The future of artificial intelligence inspires fear and raises hope. How do you perceive these two sides?

HL: Humans are making mistakes that we often attribute to technology. However, it would be wrong to focus only on the downsides and dangers in view of the vast potential of AI also to solve problems. Most certainly, we need the right framework conditions and instruments to mitigate the risks involved. Just to mention one innovative approach in this regard, sandboxing is an upcoming idea to create secure spaces in which AI can be tested and to learn and improve from mistakes. Overall, a positive view on this technology under due consideration of its responsible management is important if we want to tap the technology's full potential and direct it toward sustainable outcomes.

A9

From science to fiction and back

AN INTERVIEW WITH MARC ELSBERG

Marc Elsberg is a best-selling Austrian author. Before becoming a renowned author, he worked as a strategy consultant and creative director in the advertising industry and as a columnist for an Austrian daily newspaper. His books have been translated into numerous languages, sold several million copies worldwide, and made into a series and a film. Since 2021, he has been teaching Storytelling at the University of Applied Arts Vienna as a university lecturer.

As a best-selling author of books, such as *Greed* and *Zero*, how do you choose the topics and plots for your books?

Marc Elsberg: In general, I select topics about social and technological innovations with strong risk potential for society that must fulfill three criteria. Obviously, I need to be interested in it. A topic also should not be too widely discussed in the broader public already. Lastly, it needs to have a thorough scientific basis or background. Usually, I spend significant time on researching a topic and once I decide to write a book, this research intensifies and continues for roughly another year while drafting starts in parallel. In the case of my book, *Helix*, I myself was surprised to discover manuscripts and research on genetics and biotechnology on one of my old laptops that went back ten years before the book's publication. Although I am writing fictional stories, I try to stay as close as possible o real-life situations and outcomes in the application of technology. The book, *Blackout*, for example, portrays different scenarios, such as collapsing infrastructure (e.g., blackouts), or the book *Zero*, social media manipulation. These have either already been reality or at least their scientific foundation has been established, and, as we have seen in the context of online manipulation, even became true with the

DOI: 10.4324/9781003319481-11

Cambridge Analytica data scandal. In short, I select a certain topic and form its scientific foundation, theories, and potential outcomes into a concrete plot with real-life situations, events, and actors.

Digitalization, smartification, and AI in everyday life are important topics featuring in your books that often include science fiction elements. What will our lives look like in 10 to 15 years, in your view?

ME: Most likely, the range of lifestyles will widen and the gap between them as well. Some will retain their current way of living while others will be fully "smartified." We may assume that smarter homes will increase convenience; the question remains about their Responsible Innovation and use in terms of data security and privacy, as well as, more generally, their sustainability. At the same time, societal pressure will probably increase on everyone to participate in these new developments or risk social exclusion. Most of us have relatives, friends, or colleagues, particularly among older generations or in poorer countries, that cannot, refuse, or struggle with the use of the internet and smartphones. This comes at the price of less access to information that is a key enabler of social inclusion in today's knowledge societies. As with most technologies, digitalization also has the strong potential to separate people, which requires them to decide on the extent to which they want, and/or need, to adopt the use of new technology.

It is expected that the amount of sensors and data will increase massively due to digitalization, big data, and AI. What impact will this have on our society?

ME: The accumulation, collection, and analysis of data will definitely be driven much further, and it will be a key challenge for us to find responsible ways how to do so. Although it may seem a bit abstract, one of the most important impacts will potentially be a much-altered approach to knowledge creation. Instead of investigating causal relationships in order to understand, predict, and reproduce or emulate real-world phenomena, we will work much more AI-based with correlations. There is the fundamental rule that correlation does not equal causality and there are many illustrative examples on the internet that demonstrate how two strongly correlated phenomena are not causally connected. AI and machine learning identify patterns and, therefore, correlations in order to make predictions, regardless of any causality. This changed mode of knowledge creation bears the challenge and responsibility for human society not to become blind to the processes that created knowledge and blindly trust its results. It is known, for example, that AI algorithms are much less neutral than expected in many instances. Pro Publica's publications in recent years revealed how racial bias was detected in the algorithms used for predictive analysis in US judiciaries. Even more so, due to lacking knowledge about causal relations in the use of these algorithms, it is extremely difficult to understand the reasons for the bias. It may be connected to both data collection and its processing.

When researching big data, AI, and surveillance for your book, *Zero*, published in 2014, what surprised you the most, and have the book's events been confirmed?

ME: On the one hand, I was, and still am, surprised, if not irritated, by the ongoing indifference most people have and their reluctance even to inform themselves about this topic and the potential consequences of data collection, use, and misuse. On the other hand, I was also shaken at that time by the hesitancy of responsible public authorities and private companies to act against the manic surveillance to which the public is increasingly exposed. The trend of big data, AI, etc., during the last years only confirmed this experience, as well as the ideas and concerns depicted in *Zero*. In particular, the manipulation through social media proved to be closer to reality than one may have thought. *Zero* describes a certain scenario in which a company similar to Facebook experimented with the potential of user manipulation. In the same week the book was published, Facebook announced that it had conducted precisely this type of experiment already two years ago. In contrast, the publication of the GDPR in response to the growing threat of data misuse is a very positive development that I would not have anticipated as such. It demonstrates that a united Europe can, indeed, sometimes function in tackling societal challenges.

In contrast to the mentioned general reluctance of people in this regard, innovations like Google Glass received significant criticism due to data privacy issues and did not succeed in becoming the anticipated revolution so far. Why and how did the public care in this case?

ME: The rejection of Google Glass was connected to people's intuition that it transgresses certain limits of data privacy. This intuition was likely triggered by the fact that the wearing of glasses much more directly brings to the surface issues of surveillance compared to other tremendously invasive technologies, such as mobile phones. A person watching you with a device that can collect data through pictures, videos, etc., conveys a very strong symbolism in this regard. Moreover, it is hard to estimate whether a different, much faster, and broader marketing approach would have suppressed the critique against it in the long run. It needs to be seen whether this technology will re-emerge within the next 10–15 years in the form of glasses again or perhaps even contact lenses that already exist. Smart glasses are still used in professional contexts, and this will further boost their development. Although this remains speculation at this point, increased use cases and functionality are certainly additional sales arguments that may enable broader adoption.

In *Zero*, one of your characters states, "Most people ultimately prefer security and convenience over freedom and independence." Do you believe that data privacy will soon not be a topic at all any more?

ME: As hinted above, data privacy is already highly marginalized in modern society and was only reinvigorated by the GDPR inside the European Union to a certain extent. I have to include myself here, because I also am constantly carrying a smartphone, which is a surveillance machine. The issue is that we increasingly contrast, especially security and freedom, as mutually exclusive opposing forces. There must be either security or freedom, but both cannot co-exist in such a worldview. However, security can only truly exist based on freedom and vice versa. This is something we have to relearn despite continuing interests of different stakeholders to construe these dichotomies. We need to build more cooperation and decrease polarization in order to understand the synergies between our security and freedom and openly discuss both risks and opportunities of digital technologies on an equal footing.

In the same vein, another protagonist in your book states that the existence of surveillance alone guarantees our subjugation. In times of digitalization, is our free will only an illusion?

ME: According to studies in the aftermath of Edward Snowden's revelations, roughly a third of journalists asked stated that they would be more careful what and how to write in their email communication and that they would not have done so before. Self-censorship and the drive toward conformity are a common result of surveillance, the other, less frequent one being aggression. One may say that our free will is not constrained, as such, because it is the very free will, by which I constrain myself. However, this does not change the fact that the available options to act and think are being restricted. This, I would argue, is not only problematic for the individual well-being, but also for society as a whole, due to the risk of destroying openness and diversity as prerequisites for creativity and innovation. I am, therefore, surprised that the economy is not strongly resisting the pressure of conformity, because innovation is a major economic driver. A society of surveillance will hardly bring forth the people needed in companies to think outside the box and compete on the market.

You also raise the interesting question whether to make use of instruments that are able to improve people's lives, yet for the price of manipulation. Is artificial intelligence a possible solution to make us better, even if it means humans are no longer making the decisions?

ME: As you may guess, there is no straightforward answer to this question. First comes the normative issue of defining "improve" and "better," including the question who is in charge of any such definition. Is it existing lifestyle apps telling me how to become healthier, smarter and even sexier? Nutritional trends are equally dictating to us what to eat for many decades, changing from no eggs to no sugar, no meat to meat instead of carbohydrates, etc. The important point is to have the ability for an open and transparent discourse based on which consensus can be formed that may change over time and hopefully improve. However, most of these apps and trends are less the result of such democratic processes than the singular efforts by individual actors with, or without, scientific foundation. Even less so in the context of AI, where self-learning algorithms are literally operating in a black box, lacking any transparency even for experts to comprehend decision-making processes ex-post. In addition, this also includes AI's manipulative potential, such as a navigation system suggesting a certain route not because it is the fastest alternative to a jammed road, but because there is a fuel station of the brand sponsoring the software. The lack of transparency is a major issue of AI that only intensifies with use cases, such as health, education, etc., regardless of its potential to solve problems and improve lives, because it denies the possibility of an informed discourse that is an intimate part of the improvement process.

In addition to open and informed decision-making processes, do we also lose skills and competencies with increased use of AI?

ME: Coming back to the example of navigation systems, I am the best example of lost skills, because without their help I completely lack orientation. However, I would neither see this as a major issue, in general, nor one that is specific to AI. The loss of competencies due to the use of technology was already criticized over 2000 years ago when Greek philosophers, for example, expressed their concerns about the use of scripture, because it would negatively affect our ability of memorization. New technology also opens tremendous possibilities to acquire new knowledge and skills. It is important to be conscious about certain basic abilities that should be maintained. Other than that, the use of technology, in general, is not problematic in this regard as long as we gain new knowledge and know how to apply it responsibly.

Turning to AI, it certainly requires close attention whether, when, and to which extent to allow knowledge and skill reduction of human actors and transfer competencies to an AI system. Taking the use case of medical diagnosis, it would certainly be too early to transfer final conclusions about patients' health to an automated system. Even if these systems become fully fit for purpose, it would be crucial to retain the mentioned transparency of the decision-making processes for a physician to understand, act, and also intervene accordingly. Transparency and replicability of knowledge and its creation processes are fundamental to human science. This is what sets science apart from other forms of knowledge, for example, religious, namely, the possibility of tracing a certain technology back in its entirety to its causal roots and reproduce it, based on the causal relations that establish its functionality. As long as AI can serve this purpose, it will also be able to refine and increase our knowledge base and, thus, improve our skillset.

A10

Innovation and virtual reality

AN INTERVIEW WITH ARMEN OVANESSOFF

Armen Ovanessoff is the Principal Director of Accenture Research. His work sits at the intersection of business, government, and society, collaborating with institutions like the G20, the G7, and the World Economic Forum. Formally based in London, he established Accenture's think tank in India, which he ran from New Delhi for three years, helped build the firm's think tank in China, and currently lives between the UK and Latin America, having set up and run the regional think tank in São Paulo, Brazil, for five years. A major emphasis of his work for 20 years has been to persuade businesses and governments to prioritize acting responsibly and ethically. He has published on the advent of intelligent and immersive technologies, the future of learning, public-private partnerships, and trends in globalization.

There co-exist multiple notions, such as extended, mixed virtual and augmented reality that are all associated with a variety of emerging technologies. How would you best characterize this field and how to distinguish it from others?

Armen Ovanessoff: Since there are so many terms that are used in this sphere, it is helpful to provide some context. I usually use the notion of "immersive technologies" to encompass all tools that use and enhance our natural senses. Virtual reality is when you are entirely immersed by wearing a headset that completely shuts out your view of the physical world around you. In contrast, augmented reality blends the physical and the digital worlds through, for example, smart glasses. Therefore, with augmented reality, you can see what is actually in front of you, as well as additional information overlaid on top, like videos, images, or text. Smartphones are increasingly being used to do this; by putting the phone in front of physical objects, you can see the overlaid information on the screen. The type and degree of immersion make a difference in terms of use cases. In training, for example, virtual reality

DOI: 10.4324/9781003319481-12

is especially effective in building social and behavioral skills, due to full immersion in an experience. Augmented reality can be more useful in building technical skills – you can imagine an engineering or plumbing trainee simultaneously working and viewing additional material through smart glasses that guide their actions and answer their real-time questions. Moreover, immersive experiences are not restricted to watching and listening. We are seeing great advances to incorporate other senses into the experience, like haptics for touch and feel, and even smell and taste. In fact, a number of companies are even experimenting with "mind control," translating brain signals into binary code in order to control objects through eye movements or thoughts. For example, years ago, we collaborated with a company to help paralyzed patients control the lighting and music in their surroundings through a headset that interprets brain waves. Therefore, the range of potential immersive applications is quite extraordinary and exciting. Recently, the term "metaverse" has increased in popularity – we can imagine that as a world where all these immersive tools can inhabit the same space as the physical world, and the distinctions between them become less important.

Immersive technologies are still mostly considered an emerging technology. What does the current market situation of XR (extended reality) look like and what are the projections of its future?

AO: When I ask audiences at events, gaming always emerges as the most dominant exposure to these technologies. Fewer people have experience using immersive technologies at work. Right now, the gaming industry still represents the main arena for XR, and this is also where much of the investment is located. However, we are currently experiencing a tipping point for change. We can see from 2021 data that non-gaming industry spending on XR is already growing at approximately twice the speed of the gaming sector. By 2024, we expect it to have reached 2.5 times the gaming sector. The technologies are maturing to a level where they have become real value propositions; products that people can use in offices, factories, and other environments. We can see how accelerated innovation is driving this: For example, from 2014 to 2016 (the latest data available), there was a five-fold increase in XR patent applications. Likewise, the funding of start-ups in the XR space grew by around 240% in that same period. At Accenture, we work on a wide range of XR-driven offerings with clients across industries, and the pandemic has only accelerated interest in these tools. We are in an entirely different position than only two years ago; the hype is finally turning into real investments and innovations.

What are concrete use cases for XR and what are its benefits?

AO: The range of XR's current and potential applications is vast, but I will point to four major areas. The first is about increasing work productivity; that could be through research and design or other contexts. For example, car manufacturers have virtual environments, where designers can create vivid 3D objects and experiences simply by moving their hands in the air. In warehouses, augmented reality is used through smart glasses to indicate the quickest routes and to advise on how to pack trolleys efficiently with goods of different shapes and sizes, all without the need for scraps of paper that often are lost or damaged. The second area is training, where different types of XR can be used in different contexts, as I briefly mentioned earlier. A concrete example would be how oil and gas companies train engineers to work in the complex environment of offshore drilling operations without having to be there physically or to train workers in preparation for hazardous and dangerous situations that cannot be safely simulated in real life. In a completely different field, retailers use virtual reality training to prepare store managers for stressful situations like hectic environments during sales, or dealing with frustrated customers waiting in queues. A third area that has become increasingly common and useful during the recent pandemic lockdowns is customer experience. When buying a sofa or a kitchen, for example, you can use your phone to see the sofa superimposed on your room. A popular usage has been to see how make-up might look on your face before buying it. Finally, an important usage of XR is in the social sphere, including mental health and therapies that use virtual reality, for example, to treat post-traumatic stress symptoms through triggering feelings of pain, relief, etc. Accenture has also developed an award-winning VR experience for child welfare caseworkers, helping them to interpret signs of safety and risk. A very interesting characteristic of XR in all these applications is that the real value is in augmenting and improving human performance and productivity, rather than replacing the tasks of humans like some other technologies.

What are the major risk areas to be considered in the development and use of this technology?

AO: As with all technologies, the benefits of XR come with their own risks closely connected to the specific use cases. Therefore, we first need to ask what makes immersive technologies special or different, and I would point to three main factors. The first is that we are dealing with data that is profoundly connected with personal identity, intimate behaviors, and even thoughts. The second factor is that immersive technologies entail direct connections to our mental faculties and our perceptions of reality, which are not yet fully understood. The truth is that we still do not understand much about the human brain despite tremendous recent progress in neuroscience. The third factor is that of irreversible consequences. The incredible power of technology, the speed of innovation, and the decentralized nature of today's digital tools mean that any problems and mistakes will proliferate incredibly quickly and are extremely hard to reverse. The cost of inaction and attempting to fix mistakes retrospectively is simply too high, so decisive action needs to be taken from the start, from the early design stages. Therefore, the power and intimacy of these immersive tools offer both unique potential, but also uniquely dangerous risks.

Based on the three areas mentioned above, what are concrete examples of new risks posed by XR?

AO: I tend to place XR's risks in two categories. One set is specific to immersive technologies. The other set are risks that already exist with other technologies, but which will be magnified and intensified due to the immersive nature of XR.

For example, think of the misuse of personal data that already exists. It is about protecting things like credit card numbers, purchase histories, likes and dislikes, etc. In the context of XR, personal data becomes much more intimate, including a person's behaviors, their choices, their movements, all kinds of biometric data, and potentially even their thoughts. This magnifies the existing issues connected to data privacy.

Another concrete example is that today we have "fake news," which spreads through articles and videos. However, in an XR world, where people receive information in immersive environments, it becomes much easier to influence people's perceptions and ultimately their behaviors and decisions. If this is based on false information, or through "fake experiences," we can imagine a magnification in what we already see in terms of stimulating social divisions, eroding civil institutions, and even inciting physical harm.

Another risk that may be amplified is cybercrime, including through ransomware attacks, where data flows are obstructed until the criminals are paid. Today, ransomware is escalating fast, for example, hospitals regularly pay criminals not to release private patient healthcare data. Imagine an XR world where surgeries are performed with surgeons and patients in different locations (which is already happening, by the way), or where hazardous engineering projects are accurately controlled from a distance, through XR. Now, imagine the risk of those data flows being blocked until ransom payments are made. As always, huge leaps of progress are accompanied by commensurate new risks.

Perhaps the best-known risk of extended reality is technology addiction, mainly in the context of entertainment. The World Health Organization already classifies gaming disorder as a formal mental health condition and neuroscientists are exploring other potential disorders connected to the extended use of immersive technologies. Likewise, lockdowns across the globe have revealed how the extensive use of social media negatively affects stress and anxiety due to the gap between the idealized online world and the realities of the physical world. This gap only widens with the use of extended reality and younger population groups seem to be particularly at risk – it is interesting to observe how these issues are being discussed in Japan, where the use of immersive technologies is much more advanced.

Immersive worlds can also exacerbate the effects of anti-social behavior, such as trolling or cyber bullying. The number of people, especially children, who fall victim to cyber bullying has been constantly increasing over the last few years. We can only imagine how virtual cyber bullying through avatars and negative experiences can intimidate and traumatize people. Again, XR simply magnifies the effects of risks that already exist.

With all these risks that relate to extended exposure to virtual worlds, it is useful to consider what scientists call the Proteus Effect. This refers to how behaviors in the virtual world translate into the physical world. I touched earlier on how this can be used positively in trauma therapy, but we can also imagine unintended negative behaviors and trends.

I will end with a final, slightly different risk, and that is the widening of the technological divide. In the context of XR, this can manifest in two ways. The more familiar issue is that of unequal access to this new technology, leading to deepening socio-economic divisions. This applies to all technological innovation as it rolls out first to those who can afford it before eventually reaching others. The remedies here require business and government to collaborate in ensuring affordable access through infrastructure, devices, content, and skills. The second aspect is more specific to XR. Virtual worlds are designed with very specific purposes, such as training or entertainment. Irrelevant and undesirable content is omitted, for example, a simulated experience through a city rarely includes the homeless, pollution, or rubbish in the streets. Therefore, the longer people spend in idealized and controlled virtual environments, the easier it is for them to disengage from the physical world, including its problems and societal challenges. This can bring up questions around social cohesion and, indeed, unspoken social contracts that we have built over millennia in the physical world.

In view of this entire range of risks, how prepared are we actually to mitigate them?

AO: Recent experiences of risk mitigation in the digital world do not bode particularly well for us. Data privacy and cyber security are areas in which Europe is advanced. Nonetheless, there remains substantial work to be done in the context of social media, fake news, mental health issues and others. We have known about many of these risks for several years, yet progress is too slow. Adding to this picture, we are still struggling to define the new set of risks brought by artificial intelligence, such as unintended biases in algorithms. These issues also hold true in the non-digital sphere, for example, the gig economy has existed for decades and legislation still has not caught up with what has essentially become a standard form of work in the twenty-first century. We have not been able to catch up with the risks and responsibilities related to current technologies and developments, so we should be even more concerned about understanding and addressing the risks of XR before these tools become more widespread. This view is not meant to be pessimistic, but rather a sincere call to action to address the Responsible Innovation agenda.

Who is called to action, generally, and what is the responsibility of businesses, in particular?

AO: The truth is that everyone is called to action. It is business, policymakers, and civil society alike, because it affects all of us and we each have responsibilities. To begin, it is crucial to convene actors and experts across sectors and industries to jointly research and address the different benefits and risks mentioned above. This is already taking place to some extent through different initiatives and committees, with academics and practitioners (e.g., neuroscientists, ethicists, etc.) exploring and discussing these issues. Companies have a particular responsibility to objectively assess and improve their day-to-day business practices that affect Responsible Innovation.

This goes beyond mere compliance exercises and ticking boxes, it demands governance rules and performance incentives that require individual workers (from the CEO to the coder) to understand the impact of their actions and decisions. Businesses also need to acknowledge the boundaries of their knowledge and expertise and be more open to collaborate with external experts to address these risks. We have seen the beginnings of this with the rise of "Responsible AI," and similar efforts need to be extended to XR. Then, of course, we need appropriate government policies and legislation, which would be informed by the experts and practitioners. These policies need to both stimulate innovation and enforce appropriate safeguards. Legislation should also be as harmonized as possible across regions. What would be your message on how to innovate XR technology more responsibly, given the urgent need?

AO: My overarching message is that these technologies are a booming reality, creating ever more data and inevitably becoming part of our everyday lives at a very fast pace. The benefits will be extraordinary. However, the cost of trying to retrospectively fix the issues connected to this technology is going to be horrendous compared to taking the time to proactively design responsibility and ethics into the innovation processes from the start. Compare it to the invention of the automobile: car crashes came as an inevitable risk, yet it took us decades to develop standardized seat belts, and decades more to develop the airbag. Imagine if the designers of the car had taken the effort of designing seat belts and airbags while designing the car, or soon after. With XR, we are not dealing with car crashes, but with the economic, social, and health risks I have outlined, and which are potentially devastating. The call for attention and action is urgent.

Part B
Projects and experiences

Part B describes the design, implementation, experiences, and business implications of eight EU-funded responsible research and innovation projects:

- The **RESPONSIBLE INDUSTRY** project explores which practices in commercial research and innovation environments can be transferred to the RRI debate and how public RRI research funding principles can be translated to privately funded environments.
- The **COMPASS** project applies co-creation approaches and pilot-tests of methods and tools to support small and medium-sized enterprises (SMEs) to create their own Responsible Innovation visions and roadmaps.
- The **PRISMA** project conducts eight pilot studies to create guidelines that help businesses to include societal values in the development strategy of innovative products.
- The **I AM RRI** project develops a complex network model to investigate webs of innovation value chains in additive manufacturing and identify openings for RRI.
- The **SISCODE** project conducts ten co-creation labs to investigate the operationalization of RRI in real-life ecosystems.
- The **SeeRRI** project implements a process for bringing RRI into regional planning by engaging stakeholders in the creation of a strategy for research and innovation. The chapter illustrates results from the plastics industry in Lower Austria.
- The **RRI2SCALE** project provides methodological guidance to embed RRI processes into research and innovation ecosystems.
- The **DigiTeRRI project** develops frameworks and roadmaps to enable traditional industrial regions to seize the opportunities of digitalization. The chapter presents the findings of the Styria region in Austria.

Responsible-Industry

Duration:	February 1, 2014–July 31, 2017
Total cost:	€1,881,663.65
EU contribution:	€1,496,992
Contract No.:	609817

Coordinator:

- DE MONTFORT UNIVERSITY (United Kingdom)

Participants:

- KARLSRUHER INSTITUT FÜR TECHNOLOGIE (Germany)
- UCLAN CYPRUS LIMITED (Cyprus)
- FUNDACIÓN TECNALIA RESEARCH & INNOVATION (Spain)
- UNIVERSITEIT TWENTE (The Netherlands)
- ASSOCIAZIONE ITALIANA PER LA RICERCA INDUSTRIALE – AIRI (Italy)
- EUCLID NETWORK (United Kingdom)
- TEKNOLOGIAN TUTKIMUSKESKUS VTT (Finland)
- SYDDANSK UNIVERSITET (Denmark)

https://cordis.europa.eu/project/id/609817

B1

Responsible-Industry

First steps toward the inclusion of Responsible Research and Innovation in industry

Bernd Stahl and Catherine Flick

1.1 INTRODUCTION

The concept of Responsible Research and Innovation (RRI) started to gain prominence in the early 2010s. It constituted a central part of the Science in Society program of the Seventh EU Framework Programme. It was further rooted in national research programs, for example, in the UK, the Netherlands, or Norway. Despite the prominent inclusion of the term "innovation," however, RRI engaged only to a limited extent with the way research insights can be turned into socially and commercially relevant innovations. If RRI has the aim to ensure that processes and products of research and innovation are desirable, acceptable, and sustainable (Von Schomberg, 2011), or, to paraphrase the European Council, if RRI is about aligning research and innovation to the values, needs, and expectations of society (Rome Declaration, 2014), then it is clear that this has to be done in collaboration with industry. The logic of research and innovation systems in most Western societies is that early-stage blue-sky research is carried out mostly by publicly funded research, typically in universities and research institutions. The closer ideas get to broader rollout, typically via market mechanisms, the more prominent the role of commercial organizations becomes. The situation is in practice, of course, more complicated, and universities can undertake applied research just as companies can do basic research. In any event, companies are not only active players in the research and innovation ecosystem. They contribute the majority of research and innovation funding, and their work is typically closest to citizens and consumers, which means that it has significant influence on the social consequences of the applications of science and research, often in the form of novel technologies.

Due to the importance of industry in research and innovation, it was recognized early on that RRI without the inclusion and support of industry would be lacking

DOI: 10.4324/9781003319481-14

an important part of the research and innovation ecosystem and, thus, be unlikely to fulfill its aim of aligning research, innovation, and society. This recognition was presumably the reason why the European Union (EU) launched a call in 2012 for research to understand the role of RRI in industrial processes better.

This chapter gives an account of the project that was funded by the resources associated with this call, the Responsible-Industry project. The chapter starts with some more detail on the background, scope, and challenges that the project sought to address. It then recounts the approach and methods, what was discovered and learned as a result of the project, and what implications for business could be distilled. The chapter concludes by contextualizing its findings in the current and ongoing discourse on the future of RRI and its relationship to industry.

1.2 BACKGROUND, SCOPE, AND CHALLENGES

The concept of RRI was novel in the early 2010s. However, many of the activities that it describes and the intentions that it embodies predate it by decades or even centuries. The idea that science and research should benefit society has long been established. However, during the twentieth century it became increasingly clear that society cannot simply rely on the intrinsically good nature of science, research, and innovation. Large-scale slaughter of civilians and soldiers in modern warfare, exploitation of the poor in industrial production or environmental degradation that threatens humanity's survival are key examples of unacceptable developments that are at least partially caused or facilitated by research and innovation. Various disciplines or streams of activities, such as philosophy of technology, science and technology studies or technology assessment, have spent significant efforts on better understanding and addressing the problems related to research and innovation.

The timing was, therefore, right when the European Union emphasized its focus on RRI at the start of its eighth research framework program called Horizon Europe. This coincided with similar developments in the UK, where the Engineering and Physical Science Research Council adopted a framework on Responsible Innovation (Owen, 2014) and similar developments could be observed at the Dutch and Norwegian research councils. Simultaneously, a thriving academic debate evolved on the topic of Responsible Innovation (Stilgoe *et al.*, 2013). Funding opportunities and academic interest combined to form the basis for the development of a thriving academic community.

Despite the convergence of these different aspects, it is clear that the term RRI had different meanings and connotations, leading to different requirements and implementation practices. The EU's flavor of RRI heavily emphasized a number of well-established policy aims, which carried over from the Seventh Framework Programme and, in many cases, even preceded this. These are expressed as the "pillars" or "keys" of RRI, notably engagement, gender equality, science education, open access, ethics, and governance (European Commission, 2012a). While all of these are plausible components of an agenda bringing science and society together, they are very different in scope and scale, and they leave out prominent issues or topics, such as integrity or sustainability. The academic discourse has picked up on these problems of the EU's concept of RRI and built on Stilgoe *et al.*'s (2013) position to focus on the processes of engaging with stakeholders and reflection on the processes and outcomes. There has been debate whether this means that there are two fundamentally different concepts, sometimes referred to as Responsible Innovation versus responsible research and innovation (Owen & Pansera, 2019), or whether they are different aspects of the same thing. This conceptual question is far from settled (Owen *et al.*, 2021), but it is important to revisit it here to understand the approach of the Responsible-Industry project and to be able to assess the degree to which its findings are still relevant.

The other reason for discussing the conceptual basis of RRI is that Horizon 2020 has been succeeded by the EU's Ninth Framework Programme called Horizon Europe and the EU's focus and rhetoric have moved away from RRI to other policy goals. Agendas on the RRI pillars still exist, but they are changing in content (e.g., from gender equality to broader equality and diversity covering other aspects beyond gender; European Commission, 2020) and are maturing (e.g., the EU's ethics review process or the open access/FAIR information agenda; Wilkinson *et al.*, 2016). Therefore, it is worth asking whether RRI is yesterday's fashion or whether it still has something to offer.

As neither the keys/pillars of RRI, nor the activities of engagement, reflection, anticipation, or responding are novel or unique to RRI, the concept will have to have further characteristics if it is to have a future and ongoing relevance. Therefore, we have suggested that the unique nature of RRI does not lie in its components, but rather in the way in which it brings these together. We have used the term meta-responsibility to denote this. Meta-responsibility points to a higher-level responsibility that "aims to shape, maintain, develop, coordinate and align existing and novel research and innovation-related processes, actors and responsibilities with a view to ensuring desirable and acceptable research outcomes." This quote is taken from the Description of Action of the Responsible-Industry project and it has also been published in (Stahl, 2013, p. 708). A more detailed account of this idea was developed in (Stahl *et al.*, 2019). The uniqueness of RRI then is not based on the individual topics, nor specific activities, but in the way these are orchestrated. This view of RRI has the advantage that it accommodates both the EU's position and the broader academic debate. It also means that the concept of RRI can remain relevant, even if the European funding streams no longer emphasize it to the degree they did previously during Horizon 2020.

A further advantage of RRI as meta-responsibility is that it is no longer tied to a particular policy agenda and clearly prescribed actions or targets (e.g., gender balance, open access to data or publications), but that it is context-dependent and open to exploration and discovery. Which responsibilities exist in a particular situation and how they can be aligned, shaped, and promoted is not given *a priori*, but is subject to research and discourse. This opens the way for the integration of RRI into industry, where different incentives prevail, a different terminology is used and different pre-existing responsibilities are assumed from what can be found in publicly funded research.

The Responsible-Industry project was a first attempt to understand better what RRI in the industry context would look like. It was developed in response to the call FP7-SCIENCE-IN-SOCIETY-2013-1, topic SiS.2013.1.1.1–2: "Demonstration of Responsible Research and Innovation practices in industrial processes."[1] The topic description made it clear that the expectation by the EU was to bring together different actors, including those from industry and civil society, and to define an implementation plan for RRI, covering both the development process and the final product. The following sections explain how the consortium interpreted this task and what our findings and insights were.

1.3 APPROACH AND METHODS

The Responsible-Industry project's consortium was comprised of universities, industry research centers, and multipliers reaching out to civil society. The key approach devised by the consortium was to enable and guide discussions between industry partners, RRI experts, policy advisors, and Civil Society Organizations (CSOs) to understand how RRI might be implemented in an industry setting throughout the research and innovation process. In order to provide a focus for this work and have a methodological position that would allow for the comparability of insights from the different data sources described below, the project focused on one specific technology application, namely the use of ICT for health, demographic change, and wellbeing. By focusing on ICT, the project retained a broad scope, but was limited to types of technologies of interest to digital technologies. This means that some widespread technology-related concerns were expected to be relevant, such as data protection and privacy, while not all concerns about technology played a role, such as toxicity of materials. The focus on health, demographic change, and wellbeing was chosen, because this topic was discussed as a "grand challenge" (Bhan *et al.*, 2007) and the funding logic of Horizon 2020 was heavily influenced by the aim to address such grand challenges (Cagnin *et al.*, 2012; European Commission, 2012b).

The first task of the Responsible-Industry project was, thus, to understand how research and innovation on ICT, with the aim of addressing challenges related to health, demographic change, and wellbeing, was undertaken and in what way RRI already formed part of such work or could be integrated into it. To meet this task, the project started with a synthesis of a literature review of the state of the art of RRI in industry, a series of 30 in-depth interviews with industry representatives, 5 bottom-up case studies and 2 reports on what the sector might look like in the future, based on the previous results.

Second, the project carried out a series of in-depth stakeholder dialogues with industry, CSOs, policymakers, and other stakeholders that explored the existing processes, barriers, and opportunities for responsible research and innovation in specific value chains of products and applications. An international Delphi Study was carried out on RRI in industry, with 130–150 stakeholders, culminating in an international multi-stakeholder workshop.

All of these studies were brought together to develop the key output of the project: a detailed implementation plan for RRI in industry in the domain of health, demographic change, and wellbeing. This plan was then tested in 4 pilot projects, 15 industry-driven focus groups on the viability of this implementation plan, and, finally, the development of models of RRI in industry and an Exemplar Implementation Plan of RRI in Industry.

1.4 RESULTS AND LESSONS LEARNED

The key findings in the initial stages of the project (Søraker & Brey, 2014) identified 18 domains that, at the time, required further research. At the time, RRI principles were still frequently quite vague, and many were seen as not appropriate for industry. Principles that were deemed appropriate for industry may not have been well articulated in that field; these specifically were highlighted as areas that the project could address. The 18 domains identified are listed in Table B1.1.

These domains formed the basis for the rest of the Responsible-Industry project's exploration of ways of better integrating Responsible Innovation in industry.

One key finding from this systematic review was the importance of evaluating responsible innovation frameworks against methods and practices that already existed within industry. The need to avoid a "one-size-fits-all" approach to RRI in industry was also highlighted – this requirement identified here has carried on beyond this project and throughout subsequent projects, such as COMPASS and Living Innovation. The

Table B1.1
Eighteen domains for further research in RRI

Democratization and inclusion	Learnings from Corporate Social Responsibility (CSR)	Standards and certification
Codes of conduct	Importance of distinguishing between sectors	Operationalization of the public good
Underrepresented academic disciplines and frameworks	Underrepresented societal needs	The workplace environment
Education in ethics	Support infrastructure	Market demographics
New and emerging forms of research and innovation	New forms of consumer power and online tools	Branding and public relations
Workplace equality	Science communication/open access	Power and politics

initial findings that "the long history of CSR and its explicit attention to Industry incentives needs to be better integrated with RRI research in order to not reinvent the wheel" (Søraker & Brey, 2014) are similarly reflected in the strategy and outputs of these other projects.

Industry incentives were a significant theme for Responsible-Industry – at the time, there were few business case outlines for integration of RRI principles within industry. The review identified certifications as a possible way to provide incentives and value to companies that adopt the principles, but recognized that motivations for adopting certifications were still unknown at that point. An option, identified here, which seems to have been resisted by policymakers so far in terms of incentivizing RRI adoption is the suggestion for integrating these into public procurement requirements. Instead, as more substantial business cases have been developed over the years, the onus has been placed on individual companies to take on Responsible Innovation practices independently.

The requirement, identified here, for there to be different approaches for different-sized companies and different sectors has largely been ratified by the COMPASS and Living Innovation projects, as well. While there are shared areas of interest, good practice, and potential for improvement, the operationalization of Responsible Innovation within companies depends significantly on the size of company, sector, research intensity, and other factors. Similarly, the lack of research into what causes actors to behave ethically, and how that affects their wellbeing, is identified as a key aspect of Responsible-Industry. As later projects showed (e.g., COMPASS), without CEO and upper management buy-in to the integration of ethics and Responsible Innovation practices, there is unlikely to be significant uptake and, at worst, CSR and RRI can become a part of "ethics washing" for the company (Wagner, 2018). This ties in with the public visibility of Responsible Innovation dimensions that the review mentions "may be a promising venue for increasing transparency and accountability" – the increase in ethical consumerism in recent years supports this finding.

Finally, efforts around increasing diversity and equality practices were recognized here as being important to the uptake and effectiveness of Responsible Innovation practices within industry, not only in the workplace, but also in terms of external company image and consumer uptake of products and services. Once again, the focus on equality and diversity within companies has increased in recent years, with the rise of more public scrutiny of discrimination and demand for representation, particularly within the technology industry.

While some of these issues identified were definitely not new at the time, many of them were under-developed within the Responsible Innovation field, and particularly for industry. In Responsible-Industry, and projects that have come through since, and with shifts in public opinion and politics, many of these have been subsequently much more developed.

Indeed, the review was somewhat prophetic in this case as well, contextualizing van Oudheusden (2014) in the very first issue of the *Responsible Innovation* journal to suggest that "we need to better understand how [Responsible Innovation] plays out in the market, how politics may be an obstacle to responsibility, and to what extent political and strategic considerations could support responsibility".

A two-round Delphi Study (Adler & Ziglio, 1996; Linstone & Turoff, 2002) was conducted that brought together experts from industry, academia, policy, and end-user organizations (Borsella *et al.*, 2015). The first round was a questionnaire that explored the following topics:

- awareness of RRI concepts;
- integration of RRI in the product value chain;
- responsible governance tools/procedures;
- how to include the EU RRI pillars (ethics, public engagement, gender equality, education, transparency, governance) in the field of ICT for an aging society.

The results from the first round were compiled and sent back out in a second round to discover convergences of opinion among the responses. These responses, along with a series of interviews with key industry personnel and the challenges presented above, formed a first set of results, including a justification and business case examples for innovating responsibly, which was one of the first attempts at doing this within European projects (see Section 1.5 "Implications for businesses," for this business case). Also included in these results were a set of key concerns about specific aspects of ICT for an aging society including:

- real-time monitoring of user lifestyles and health through sensors;
- brain-computer interfaces;
- privacy-sensitive data analysis;
- robotics;
- social networking;
- data protection issues, such as transmissions of data to third parties, data storage and management, and automated transmissions between devices.

A series of good practices followed for operationalizing RRI within organizations, including suggestions for allocation of responsibilities, guidance on how to perform ethical and social impact analysis, integration of RRI within the value chain, and a set of tools that could be used to help facilitate RRI, such as codes of conduct, CSR tools, risk management and quality certifications and technical standards. Finally, some policy options and suggestions for communication about RRI issues and principles were suggested.

After a series of stakeholder engagement dialogues and in-depth case studies to elicit feedback on these initial results, which were attempting to generalize across all levels of business and policy, the project recalibrated the results into a series of reports aimed at different levels: (1) an executive summary aimed at CEOs and senior executives on the benefits for RRI in ICT for an aging society; (2) a guidance document on implementation of RRI in the industrial context aimed at project managers and those responsible for implementation; and (3) a set of EU policy guidance for RRI in health and aging.

The key results aimed at CEOs and senior executives explained the sectors with the highest ethical concerns for ICT are an aging society (see the list above), provided a set of case studies showing the importance and implementation benefits, and listed the benefits of adoption of RRI and how these will be achieved, including a set of Key Performance Indicators that were tested in the in-depth case studies and found to be helpful.

Results aimed at helping project managers and senior executives implement RRI in ICT provided a list of the key principles and values that

> should be respected in developing ICT products for older persons in need of care (vulnerable consumers): individual rights and liberties; personal safety and health; autonomy, authenticity and identity; implications for quality of life; social isolation; integrity and dignity; bodily integrity and self-determination; social safety; justice (distributive) and access; equality; and avoidance of dual use.

The implementation framework itself largely revolved around the key questions of "Who is responsible for what?"; "How can RRI be integrated along the value chain?"; "What voluntary tools can be used for RRI?" and "How can ethical and social impact analysis be performed?". Alongside these questions was a list of RRI drivers: reflection on social and ethical impacts; alignment of research and innovation with users and societal needs; engagement of stakeholders in the research and innovation process; and equality and transparency in information and communication, education, and ethics. A list of RRI facilitators was also provided with communication and policy options for the key aspects: increasing awareness, education and training, fostering a RRI culture, setting incentives for good practice. Finally, an "RRI in a Nutshell" brief commentary summarized the key actions for implementation, which were:

- reflection on vision, culture, and capacity for RRI;
- integration of RRI into existing CSR, research and innovation, and other company functions;
- promotion of awareness and reflection on ethical/societal issues with analysis from an early stage of the value chain, with identification of preventative and precautionary measures;
- fostering stakeholder engagement, keeping communications open and transparent;
- performing ongoing risk and impact assessment of the technology;

- ensuring training and professional development opportunities, especially on ethical aspects;
- fostering multidisciplinarity and equality in the workplace and recruitment strategies.

Finally, a set of results aimed at EU policy-makers focused on a clear message aimed particularly at those in the EU's Directorate-General for Research and Innovation (DG RTD), calling for action to "step up [the DG RTD's] efforts to raise awareness of RRI inside the EU Commission"; to integrate RRI principles into future procurement directives; and to continue to fund research into RRI in future research agendas.

Overall, these results were well received, and we can see how the research conducted to develop it has gone on to form the basis of other RRI projects throughout the subsequent years, and how some of the questions that were raised back at the very beginning of the project continue to be difficult to answer today.

Toward the end of the project, a significant paper was published that came out of the framework and other research conducted within the project, which tied together all of the concepts, issues, and approaches into an RRI maturity model for businesses (Stahl *et al.*, 2017). This model was trialed on three of the case studies with companies that were part of the project, and was one of the more potentially transferable aspects of the project to other domains outside of health, demographic change, and wellbeing.

Finally, the case studies and other efforts made throughout the project formed part of the core repository of knowledge at the Orbit website, which then went on to establish the *Journal of Responsible Technology* and become a spin-off endeavor from this project and other, related projects (e.g., FRRIICT).

1.5 IMPLICATIONS FOR BUSINESSES

The implications for business from this project were evidenced on several levels: on the one hand, the specific domains of interest were particular to companies in the ICT for health and aging domain. On the other hand, there were largely similar, high-level concepts that continue to dominate Responsible Innovation in industry discourse: particularly there being no "one-size-fits-all" approach; conversations around who is responsible; evidence of good practice within other approaches, such as CSR, and how these relate to Responsible Innovation; how Responsible Innovation can be championed or advocated for in ways other than purely voluntary methods (e.g., certification, etc.); and, finally, the business case for Responsible Innovation.

The business case for Responsible Innovation is now more evidenced and distinct than it was in this early project. The original ideas that came out from the Responsible-Industry project were articulated as:

By doing innovation responsibly you will contribute to a better world and you will benefit!

How will this be achieved?

- By strengthening links with customers to get insights into their needs.
- By better matching societal expectations.
- By undertaking foresight activities as part of risk management.
- By stimulating and motivating the working environment.
- By mitigating environmental impacts.
- By ensuring compliance with qualified norms and standards.

Thereby:

- Enhancing your company reputation.
- Decreasing business risks and unintended consequences.
- Strengthening public trust in the safety of your products.
- Increasing acceptability of your products.
- Adopting an environmentally friendly profile.
- Optimizing your medium-term competitiveness/profitability.

The logic of these points was that organizations, in order to engage with Responsible Innovation, would need to understand what they can do and which results these actions will have. The starting point was an assumption that the companies wanted to do their research and innovation activities responsibly, that they welcome the possibility to contribute to a better world, but would benefit from guidance on practice and outcomes. Of key interest is the question how being responsible can benefit a company.

The first set of bullet points in the above text box, therefore, highlights how integration of Responsible Innovation will lead to societally beneficial and desirable outcomes. These points show the processes that will support and carry Responsible Innovation. They start with a strengthening of the links with customers as key stakeholders whose needs and preferences a company needs to understand. Customers are not the only stakeholder group, but they also make up part of the broader societal environment whose expectations determine whether a company's work is deemed legitimate. The engagement with Responsible Innovation topics contains an aspect of risk management and compliance with various regulations, e.g., in terms of environmental protection or labor relationships, two aspects with which companies are broadly familiar. The purpose of highlighting these points was to underline that Responsible

Innovation is not fundamentally alien to companies, but that it aligns with various activities and processes that they typically already have in place.

The second set of bullet points then aimed to show how the company's Responsible Innovation activities could lead to the desired outcomes of contributing to a better world and simultaneously benefit the company. We proposed that engaging in Responsible Innovation is likely to be beneficial to the company's reputation. This has to do with a better control of business processes, which can reduce risks and unintended consequences. Consequently, one can reasonably expect increased trust by customers and the public, which can lead to a higher acceptance of products and thereby in the medium to long term to increased competitiveness.

When we drew up these points, they were taken from our experience and related literatures, such as those on CSR. However, in the meantime, many of them have been demonstrated as being true. For example, engagement with diverse sets of stakeholders (including customers and those indirectly affected) was shown to improve the technology developed within Living Innovation, for example the smart mobility aspects with Siemens.[2] Two early-stage standards for Responsible Innovation now exist, one originating from the UK's innovation funder Innovate UK (BSI, 2020); one being derived from the EU project PRISMA,[3] one of the successor projects of Responsible-Industry (CEN, 2021). This implies that there is a demonstrable value in committing to RRI. The rise of ethical consumerism shows the value in committing to environmental sustainability and matching of societal expectations (Doane, 2001; Tomşa *et al.*, 2021).

On some of the questions posed by Responsible-Industry at the very beginning of the project, we have some better answers than were available at the time; on others, more research and analysis still need to be done. The most consistent finding across all of the projects that came out of Responsible-Industry is that there is much existing good practice already happening in companies, such that even if they do not know of the Responsible Innovation concept, they are still implementing many of its aspects. This once again points to the importance of Responsible Innovation, as not so much creating new knowledge of good practice, but as acting more as a way of tying these together in a coherent, consistent framework through meta-responsibility.

1.6 CONCLUSION AND RECOMMENDATIONS

The Responsible-Industry project was the first EU-funded project that focused specifically on RRI in industry. It was followed by a number of successor projects exploring similar areas and aimed at the role of RRI in private companies (COMPASS, SMART-map, PRISMA, LIV_IN). Some of the basic characteristics of research and innovation in industry remain unchanged and continue to raise barriers to the uptake of RRI. This starts with the terminology, which is not familiar to those in the private sector. There are also aspects of RRI, such as open access, which are problematic in a profit-oriented setting, for example, when they interfere with legitimate use of intellectual property. Another key issue is the difference in incentive structures between privately and publicly funded research and innovation. In publicly funded research, the funder, typically a public sector body, such as a funding council, can stipulate the rules of engagement, including a requirement to engage with RRI. Where the source of funding is private, the reasons for engaging with RRI are different. By definition, private companies need to keep their bottom line in mind to ensure the viability of the organization. RRI activities can be resource-intensive, for example, when they involve large-scale stakeholder engagement or by tying up resources for reflexivity exercises that could be used for the actual innovation process. The justification of such expenditure, therefore, needs to consider the business case in more detail than is typically the case for publicly funded work. This does not mean that companies cannot engage with RRI. A business case for RRI can be made and the Responsible-Industry project has identified arguments from reputation management to employee retention that demonstrate the value of RRI for an organization. A key difference between public and private RRI activities remains, however, that in the private sector it is not an end in itself, but must find its justification in the (often long-term) benefit that it bestows on the organization.

Another fundamental difference is the general ethical and social evaluation of research and innovation in public and private settings. Public research, typically undertaken in universities, is broadly understood as an ethical good that needs no further justification. This view can trace its roots to Greek antiquity and the conviction that the creation of knowledge is a good in itself. Research, as the way to create new knowledge, is, therefore, a tool in the pursuit of an intrinsic value. Furthermore, more knowledge is typically recognized to have further benefits, such as better goods and services, ranging from healthcare to consumer products. While this logic applies to some degree to industrial research and innovation, as well, the positive perception can clash with the profit motive of companies. Whereas research and innovation by universities is typically perceived to be altruistic, the profit motive of companies can lead to the perception of egotistical motives, thus, devaluing the moral value of their research and innovation.

As indicated earlier, this is no doubt a simplistic view of research and innovation systems. Universities are increasingly profit-oriented and companies may well work for altruistic reasons. However, one can find numerous examples of the sentiment that private companies' motivations render their actions unacceptable. A prominent example is provided by Zuboff (2019), who uses the term "surveillance capitalism" to denote the exploitative use of personal data by the large tech companies, which are simultaneously some of the most successful research and innovation organizations. Another current example refers to the vastly different evaluations of the contributions by universities and companies in combatting the COVID-9 pandemic. While there is much consensus that the quick development of COVID-19 vaccines was a unique success of research and innovation systems and that companies' role in this was crucial, there is now much more criticism of companies, because of the significant financial gains they have made in the wake of this success.

What these examples show is that we remain far away from a uniform application of RRI across various research and innovation settings. Terminologies remain different, incentives diverge, and logics can be incompatible. At the same time, however, the starting point of the Responsible-Industry project remains, namely the fact that private organizations play a key role in research and innovation and, thus, need to be incorporated for RRI to achieve its aim of aligning societal needs and preferences with the products and processes of research and innovation. The Responsible-Industry project has provided some initial insights and suggested ways of considering industrial activities, such as the RRI maturity model, which we hope will remain relevant. We also believe that the idea of framing RRI as a meta-responsibility retains the power to bridge different aspects of the RRI debate and facilitate the discourse across different types of research and innovation ecosystems.

Many challenges remain. This is probably not surprising. Questions of ethical acceptability, social desirability, and sustainability are rarely subject to simple resolution. They are more likely to remain ongoing discourses that should allow the formulation of questioning of positions. In some cases, consensus will be possible to achieve, but due to the dynamic nature of science, research and innovation, new challenges will appear. In addition, the complexity of research and innovation ecosystems pose fundamental challenges to our traditional ideas of ethics, as well as governance (Stahl, 2022). Therefore, we should not approach the topic of RRI in industry in the hope of being able to comprehensively answer all questions or resolve all issues. Rather, we would be well advised to ask how these questions could be addressed in an open, transparent, and inclusive manner that allows for the development of democratically legitimate and practical ways forward. We hope that the work that we have undertaken in the Responsible-Industry project has provide a good foundation to continue to engage in this discourse in an academically rigorous and practically relevant manner.

DISCLOSURE STATEMENT

No potential conflict of interest was reported by the authors.

FUNDING

The Responsible-Industry project has received funding from the European Union's Horizon 2020 research and innovation program under grant agreement No. 609817. The opinions expressed in this chapter reflect only the authors' view and in no way reflect the European Union's opinions.

NOTES

1. https://ec.europa.eu/research/participants/portal/desktop/sedia/opportunities/fp7/calls/fp7-science-in-society-2013-1.html (accessed January 25, 2022).
2. https://www.youtube.com/watch?v=8A3cKnPddGc (accessed February 19, 2022).
3. https://www.rri-prisma.eu/ (accessed February 19, 2022).

REFERENCES

Adler, M. & Ziglio, E. (1996). *Gazing into the oracle: The Delphi Method and its application to social policy and public health*. Jessica Kingsley.

Bhan, A., Singh, J.A., Upshur, R.E.G., Singer, P.A., & Daar, A.S. (2007). Grand challenges in global health: Engaging civil society organizations in biomedical research in developing countries. *PLoS Medicine*, *4*, e272–1459. https://doi.org/10.1371/journal.pmed.0040272

Borsella, E., Porcari, A., & Mantovani, E. (2015). Delphi Exercise Report and 1st Draft Implementation Plan. Responsible-Industry project.

BSI. (2020). *PAS 440:2020 Responsible Innovation – Guide*. British Standards Institution.

Cagnin, C., Amanatidou, E., & Keenan, M. (2012). Orienting European innovation systems towards grand challenges and the roles that FTA can play. *Science & Public Policy (SPP)*, *39*, 140–152.

CEN. (2021). Responsibility-by-design: Guidelines to develop long-term strategies (roadmaps) to innovate responsibly. (CEN Workshop Agreement No. CWA 17796). CEN, Brussels.

Doane, D. (2001). *Taking flight: The rapid growth of ethical consumerism*. New Economics Foundation.

European Commission. (2012a). *Responsible Research and Innovation: Europe's ability to respond to societal challenges*. European Commission, Publications Office, Brussels.

European Commission. (2012b). *Investing in Research and Innovation for grand challenges*. European Commission, DG Research, Brussels.

European Commission. (2020). A union of equality: Gender Equality Strategy 2020–2025. (Communication from the Commission to the European Parliament, the Council, the European Economic and Social Committee and the Committee of the Regions No. Com(2020) 152 final). European Commission, Brussels.

Linstone, H.A. & Turoff, M. (2002). *The Delphi Method: Techniques and applications*. Addison-Wesley Publishing Company, Reading, MA.

Owen, R. (2014). The UK Engineering and Physical Sciences Research Council's commitment to a framework for Responsible Innovation. *Journal of Responsible Innovation*, *1*, 113–117. https://doi.org/10.1080/23299460.2014.882065

Owen, R. & Pansera, M. (2019). Responsible Innovation and Responsible Research and Innovation. In D. Simon, S. Kuhlmann, J. Stamm, & W. Canzler (Eds.), *Handbook on science and public policy* (pp. 26–48). Edward Elgar.

Owen, R., von Schomberg, R., & Macnaghten, P. (2021). An unfinished journey? Reflections on a decade of responsible research and innovation. *Journal of Responsible Innovation*, *8*(2), 217–233. https://doi.org/10.1080/23299460.2021.1948789

Rome Declaration. (2014). Rome Declaration on Responsible Research and Innovation in Europe. European Commission.

Søraker, J.J. & Brey, P. (2014). Systematic review of industry relevant RRI discourses (Responsible-Industry deliverable No. D1.1).

Stahl, B.C. (2013). Responsible research and innovation: The role of privacy in an emerging framework. *Science and Public Policy*, *40*, 708–716. https://doi.org/10.1093/scipol/sct067

Stahl, B.C. (2022). Responsible innovation ecosystems: Ethical implications of the application of the ecosystem concept to artificial intelligence. *International Journal of Information Management*, *62*, 102441. https://doi.org/10.1016/j.ijinfomgt.2021.102441

Stahl, B.C., Obach, M., Yaghmaei, E., Ikonen, V., Chatfield, K., & Brem, A. (2017). The Responsible Research and Innovation (RRI) maturity model: Linking theory and practice. *Sustainability*, *9*, 1036. https://doi.org/10.3390/su9061036

Stahl, B.C., Timmermans, J., Rainey, S., & Shaw, M. (2019). Ethics in innovation management as meta-responsibility: The practice of responsible research and innovation in human brain simulation. In J. Chen, A. Brem, E. Viardot, & P.K. Wong (Eds.), *The Routledge companion to Innovation management* (pp. 435–454). Routledge.

Stilgoe, J., Owen, R., & Macnaghten, P. (2013). Developing a framework for responsible innovation. *Research Policy, 42*, 1568–1580. https://doi.org/10.1016/j.respol.2013.05.008

Tomşa, M.-M., Romonţi-Maniu, A.-I., & Scridon, M.-A. (2021). Is sustainable consumption translated into ethical consumer behavior? *Sustainability, 13*, 3466.

van Oudheusden, M. (2014). Where are the politics in responsible innovation? European governance, technology assessments, and beyond. *Journal of Responsible Innovation, 1*, 67–86. https://doi.org/10.1080/23299460.2014.882097

Von Schomberg, R. (2011). *Towards Responsible Research and Innovation in the information and communication technologies and security technologies fields*. Publication Office of the European Union.

Wagner, B. (2018). Ethics as an escape from regulation: From ethics-washing to ethics-shopping. In E. Bayamlioglu, I. Baraliuc, L.A.W. Janssens, & M. Hildebrandt (Eds.), *Being profiled: Cogitas ergo sum* (pp. 84–90). Amsterdam University Press,

Wilkinson, M.D., Dumontier, M., Aalbersberg, Ij.J., Appleton, G., Axton, M., Baak, A., Blomberg, N., Boiten, J.-W., da Silva Santos, L.B., Bourne, P.E., *et al.* (2016). The FAIR Guiding Principles for scientific data management and stewardship. *Scientific Data, 3*, 160018.

Zuboff, P.S. (2019). *The age of surveillance capitalism: The fight for a human future at the New frontier of power*, 1st edn. Profile Books.

RESPONSIBLE INNOVATION COMPASS

Duration: May 1, 2016–April 30, 2019
Total cost: €1,505,945.63
EU contribution: €1,499,945.63
Contract No.: 710543

Coordinator:

- WIRTSCHAFTSUNIVERSITÄT WIEN (Austria)

Participants:

- DE MONTFORT UNIVERSITY (United Kingdom)
- UCLAN CYPRUS LIMITED (Cyprus)
- FUNDACIÓN BANCARIA CAIXA D'ESTALVIS I PENSIONS DE BARCELONA LA CAIXA (Spain)
- EUROPEAN BUSINESS AND INNOVATION CENTRE NETWORK AISBL (Belgium)
- STICHTING B LAB EUROPE (The Netherlands)
- STRATEGIC DESIGN SCENARIOS SPRL (Belgium)

https://cordis.europa.eu/project/id/710543

B2

COMPASS

Small and medium-sized enterprises on course to Responsible innovation

Norma Schönherr and Florian Findler

2.1 INTRODUCING COMPASS

In the last two decades, European research and innovation policy has intensified its efforts to reconcile scientific excellence with the societal relevance of research and innovation. The concept of Responsible Research and Innovation (RRI) was established in 2010 and has since become a cross-cutting theme in European research and innovation policy (de Saille, 2015). In this context, the European Union's aim is to transfer the concept and practice of RRI to other contexts, in particular to industry and business (Scholten & Blok, 2015).

Private sector companies tend to focus much more on innovation and applied research and development (R7D) than other types of research institutions, which is why the abbreviated term Responsible Innovation (RI) is used in this field (Jarmai *et al.*, 2020). RI adds a new dimension to the ongoing discourse on the role and responsibility of companies in society, but has yet to penetrate far into the minds of entrepreneurs and corporate managers (Martinuzzi *et al.*, 2018). It stands to reason, however, that just as practices related to research integrity, open science, ethics, gender equality, and societal impact are important tenets of the work of researchers conducting basic research in public sector research institutions, RI practices play an equally significant role in achieving excellent applied research and innovation outcomes in research-intensive private sector companies. Within this space, small and medium-sized enterprises (SMEs) have even more specific needs and logics with which RI must connect if the concept and practice are to be successfully integrated into research and innovation activities, management, and outcomes (Flick *et al.*, 2020).

The aim of the COMPASS project was to make RI accessible, understandable, and actionable for SMEs. This was realized through the joint development and pilot testing of methods and tools that enable SMEs to create their own RI visions and roadmaps – taking into account the specificities of their respective sector and business

DOI: 10.4324/9781003319481-15

context (Iatridis & Schröder, 2016). In addition, SMEs and innovation support organizations were provided with tailored, easy-to-use tools and resources; including a self-check tool and teaching and training materials (Tharani *et al.*, 2020). The COMPASS project was built on the premise that recognition of the value of RI thinking, methods, and tools among entrepreneurs is a necessary prerequisite for mainstreaming RI (Iatridis & Schröder, 2016). The major conceptual challenge for the COMPASS project was that the resonance of RI in industry, in general, and among SMEs, in particular, is currently low. At the start of the COMPASS project, there were few, if any, proactive corporate users of the concept (Auer & Jarmai, 2017). To address this challenge, the multi-stakeholder COMPASS consortium worked specifically with highly innovative SMEs to develop methods and tools for RI implementation that are tailored to the needs of entrepreneurs and promote organizational learning (Auer & Jarmai, 2017; Tharani *et al.*, 2020).

The practical challenges faced by the project were:

1. developing an RI definition and narrative that is useful in a business context (Schönherr *et al.*, 2020);
2. describing RI practices and outcomes in a way that is consistent with business practices and the innovation process implemented in SMEs (Jarmai, 2020a; Jarmai *et al.*, 2020);
3. developing a methodology that is flexible enough to allow companies to develop their own roadmap for RI, while providing actionable guidance throughout the process (Yaghmaei & Poel, 2020);
4. identifying RI good practice examples and other resources suitable for helping entrepreneurs implement specific RI practices (Flick *et al.*, 2020).

This chapter provides an overview of how the COMPASS consortium addressed these challenges and presents the project results and their application in an SME environment. The following section outlines the conceptual framework used throughout the project and explains the scope of the project activities. Then the approach and specific methods used throughout the project are outlined, while an overview of the results is given. The COMPASS Self-Check Tool and COMPASS co-creation method kit that aim to support business practitioners in SMEs to implement RI in their innovation processes are introduced, and the chapter concludes with future recommendations.

2.2 TRANSLATING RESPONSIBLE INNOVATION FOR SMALL AND MEDIUM-SIZED ENTERPRISES

There is still conceptual ambiguity around RI (as a term distinct from RRI and mainly applicable to industrial environments) and a variety of definitions currently exist. These definitions of RI are often comprehensive, but vague. Notwithstanding the variety of definitions and approaches, there are several common features in the RI literature that have influenced the COMPASS project. First, it is safe to say that RI builds on, and extends, concepts and theoretical approaches previously used in academic studies of corporate responsibility, such as Corporate Sustainability (Martinuzzi & Schönherr, 2019), technology assessment (Grunwald, 2014), ethics and the philosophy of technology (Griffy-Brown *et al.*, 2018), as well as ethical, legal, and social aspects of research (ELSA/ELSI) (Zwart *et al.*, 2014). RI embeds accountability in very early stages of innovation by drawing attention to issues of research integrity, different institutional environments, and dynamics that have a strong influence on the societal impact of organizations (Martinuzzi *et al.*, 2018).

Second, RI takes a holistic view of the responsibilities associated with corporate innovation processes and outcomes, encompassing environmental, ethical, social, and political dimensions (Stilgoe *et al.*, 2013).

Third, the actors whose responsibility it is to manage research and innovation responsibly can vary widely, from individual researchers and innovators to funding agencies and venture capitalists, policymakers, or companies as a whole (Stahl, 2019). Consequently, the implementation of RI requires a joint effort of different stakeholders to find sustainable solutions based on the ethical acceptability, sustainability, and societal desirability of the innovation process (how it is carried out) and its marketable products (impact on society; Stahl *et al.*, 2017).

Companies need not start from scratch on the path to embedding RI. In fact, companies of all shapes and sizes are already successfully engaging in many practices that fall under the umbrella term RI. However, these practices are often disconnected, dispersed across business functions, or not connected to companies' core business (Auer & Jarmai, 2017). RI is an opportunity for companies to integrate these elements and practices into a coherent framework for a better management of innovation processes and improved outcomes for the mutual benefit of business, society, and the environment (Schönherr *et al.*, 2020).

In translating RI for SMEs, the COMPASS consortium faced several conceptual and practical challenges. Conceptually, it was necessary to align academic definitions and approaches to RI with business logics (Jarmai *et al.*, 2020). This is because the project aimed to target SMEs as well as innovation funding agencies as primary target groups. At the time, the organizations affected by the project were largely unaware of and/or unfamiliar with the discourse on RI. The consortium's experience during the project was that there was a general openness to engage with the concept of RI, but entrepreneurs needed to be given convincing answers to two pressing questions: "What do I and my company get out of it?" and "What exactly do I need to do?" (Jarmai, 2020a).

To answer the first question, the COMPASS project had to build a business case for RI, taking into account that different companies operate under different conditions (depending on e.g., business model, size, product offering, and contextual factors, such as legal framework or industry dynamics; Schönherr *et al.*, 2020). To answer the second question, it was necessary to break down RI thinking into specific business practices that SMEs with limited resources and manpower could understand and implement (Tharani *et al.*, 2020). Each project output, therefore, ideally needed to present low barriers to entry for time- and resource-starved entrepreneurs.

This conceptual challenge then presented a set of practical problems that the COMPASS project needed to address, namely:

1. how to develop an RI narrative that is useful in the business context;
2. how to describe RI practices and outcomes in a way that is aligned with business practices and the innovation process implemented in SMEs;
3. how to develop methodologies that are flexible enough for companies to develop their own roadmap for RI;
4. how to identify and present proven RI practice cases and other supporting resources to entrepreneurs in implementing specific RI practices.

The COMPASS consortium decided early on to focus on collaboration to address these challenges (Jarmai & Vogel-Pöschl, 2020). On the one hand, collaboration among different stakeholders is a key practice of RI and was, therefore, essential to demonstrate to SMEs and innovation support agencies that the COMPASS project was following the spirit of RI. On the other hand, collaboration allowed the COMPASS project to pool the expertise and resources available in its multi-stakeholder consortium, work directly with its target groups and their broader stakeholder environment, and test project results directly in the field before they were published, thereby ensuring that they were fit for purpose (Flick *et al.*, 2020). More detailed information on the COMPASS approach and methods follows below.

2.3 DESIGNING THE COMPASS APPROACH

The COMPASS project was based on a three-pronged approach to translate RI for SMEs. First, co-creation was the primary method for developing tools and resources for implementing RI in the SME sector. Second, targeted stakeholder engagement was a key principle throughout the project. Third, the COMPASS project integrated lessons learned from previous projects and connected with other existing initiatives and platforms to improve its outreach and impact.

2.3.1 Innovating with users through co-creation

COMPASS was guided by the belief that translating RI into business practice requires both ownership of RI practices by SMEs and their organizations to support innovation and a collaborative effort among the various stakeholders shaping their business environment (Blok *et al.*, 2015). Figure B2.1 illustrates the approach of the COMPASS project, giving insights into the way in which the key stakeholders were addressed. Co-creation[1] is an approach that allowed the consortium to place collaboration at the center of project activities and work with a set of proven, established methods while building a relationship with target audiences (Deserti *et al.*, 2022).

Figure B2.1
The COMPASS approach

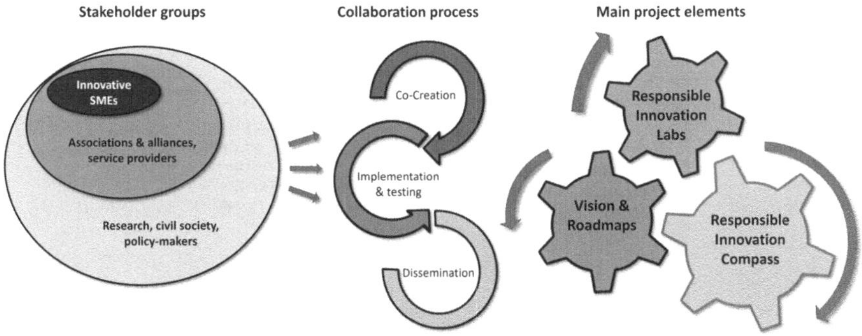

Co-creation approaches to R&D and innovation have gained increasing recognition in industry and academia for their unique ability to structure creative co-creation processes involving multiple stakeholders (Robinson *et al.*, 2021).

> Co-creation involves users of a product or service in exchanging their knowledge and resources with the aim to deliver a personalized experience. Co-creation relates... to the relationship between an organization and a defined group of users, who are engaged directly by involving them in the creation of a product or a service, i.e. in its design and in its development processes.
>
> (Mirri *et al.*, 2018)

The main venue for co-creation throughout the project was the so-called RI Labs, which were used to develop sectoral and SME-specific RI roadmaps (Jégou *et al.*, 2017). This methodology was co-developed by the multi-stakeholder consortium in winter 2016 and continuously adapted after each interaction with project stakeholders and target groups. The RI Lab methodology is divided into a so-called "choreography" as shown in Figure B2.2. It consists of a fact-finding phase with scoping interviews and a peer-to-peer webinar to determine the status quo, a forward-looking visioning phase to determine the desired impacts of RI implementation, and a back-casting phase to develop the timeline and actions needed to move from the status quo to the desired impacts, as well as a testing phase that served to assess the robustness and feasibility of the roadmap (Jégou *et al.*, 2017). A streamlined version of this methodology was also included as part of the methods toolkit published in the Responsible Innovation Compass (Jégou *et a*l., 2019).

2.3.2 Involving stakeholders in a targeted manner

Targeted stakeholder engagement was a key feature of COMPASS. The project strategically engaged industry, research, and civil society representatives in co-creation processes at a very early stage to ensure usefulness, feasibility, and ownership of outcomes among target groups (Flick *et al.*, 2020).

Figure B2.2
The RI lab methodology

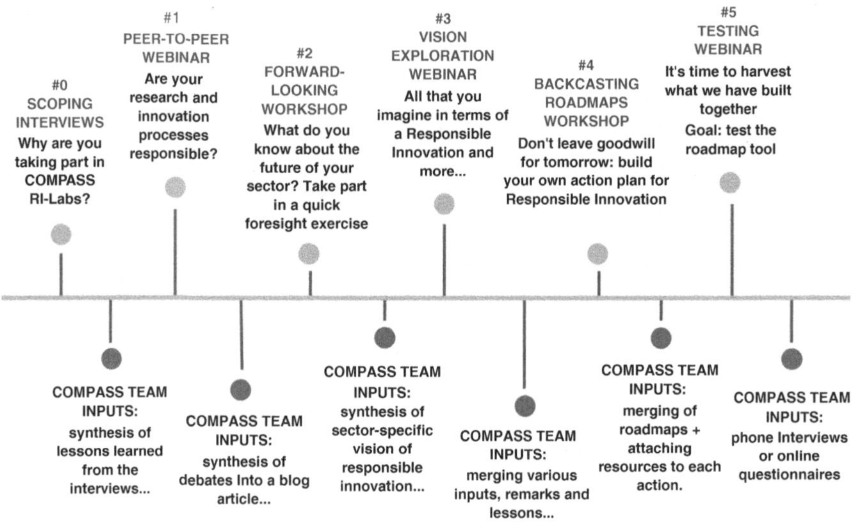

COMPASS ensured that the right actors were targeted for the right task by distinguishing between actors involved in co-creation, implementation, and dissemination activities. The primary target groups of the project were innovative SMEs and their innovation support organizations. The second level of stakeholders included actors from industry, research, and civil society who actively supported the co-creation of visions and roadmaps at the sectoral level. A third level of stakeholders was involved throughout the project as multipliers of results and "test groups" of the Compass for Responsible Innovation. This group of multipliers included business associations, SME support organizations, civil society organizations, and science and policy stakeholders. In addition, an Advisory Board of high-level experts provided regular feedback and input on issues in the areas of their expertise throughout the project duration.[2]

2.3.3 Building on relevant projects, initiatives, and networks

COMPASS built and established synergies with other relevant projects and initiatives whenever possible. The COMPASS project collected, applied, and leveraged lessons learned from previous projects in the areas of RRI, CSR, and business model innovation (Antoniou, 2020; Jarmai, 2020b; Nwafor *et al.*, 2017). In this context, it was beneficial that all members of the multi-stakeholder consortium brought their experience as coordinators or project partners in previous European projects in one or more of these three areas. In doing so, the project also addressed the significant fragmentation of expertise, resources, and knowledge on RI in the business community. Existing sources of information were limited to anecdotal best practice cases that might not be easily replicated, scaled, or transferred to other business contexts. Service offerings and advice for businesses tended to be fragmented and dispersed across different communities of practice (Iatridis & Schröder, 2016). It was also found that highly innovative SMEs, in particular, were underserved and had difficulty navigating a variety of information and service offerings, all with different focuses, and adapting them to their own context. The exorbitant information costs associated with engaging with RI were, therefore, a significant barrier to entry for SMEs (Auer & Jarmai, 2017).

The COMPASS project addressed this issue by building a comprehensive, customizable, user-friendly online portal, the Responsible Innovation Compass, which can serve as a one-stop shop for interested SMEs.[3]

2.4 PRESENTING THE OUTCOMES OF COMPASS

As a result of three years of collaborative work within the multi-stakeholder consortium and with a number of external stakeholders, the COMPASS project resulted in an online platform, the Responsible Innovation Compass,[4] which was geared at supporting SMEs from emerging technology industries with managing their R&D and innovation activities in a way consistent with RI. The Responsible Innovation Compass provides guidance to understand the large amount of evidence sources and resources in the communities, taking into account the specific needs of SMEs, and includes available tools, service offerings, inspiring case studies, and sector-specific RI roadmaps. By increasing transparency, structuring, and contextualizing available evidence, and linking it to practical implementation tools, the Responsible Innovation Compass is an attempt to reduce barriers to access for SMEs, make existing incentive structures visible, and facilitate partnerships between SMEs and stakeholders. Key components of the Responsible Innovation Compass are:

- A diagnostic **Self-Check Tool** enabling SMEs to assess where their company stands in implementing RI practices, how they compare to their peers, and what they can do to make their innovation practices more responsible.
- A forward-looking **co-creation method kit** that enables SMEs to develop their own RI roadmap and action plan by means of a tried and proven process.
- **RI sector roadmaps**, setting out key RI issues and operational measures for addressing them at the sectoral level. These roadmaps may serve as inspiration for SMEs wishing to use the COMPASS method kit to develop their own specific roadmap and point out sector-specific action points for companies from the nanotechnology, cybersecurity, and biomedicine sectors.
- A set of inspiring **case studies** showcasing RI best practices of SMEs as well as **thematic executive reports**. These serve as a door opener to becoming familiar with the meaning of the concept in a business context and highlight potential benefits of implementing RI practices in day-to-day operations.

- **Training materials and teaching cases** tailored to the needs of SMEs. These materials were designed to support organizational learning on RI within SMEs and the innovation support organizations that collaborate with them.
- An **RI project directory**, which allows for easy identification of, and access to, relevant projects and RI initiatives in Europe.

In the following, the two core elements of the Responsible Innovation Compass are presented in more detail, with a brief commentary on their characteristics, applicability, and potential benefits for business practitioners. First, the COMPASS Self-Check Tool will be introduced as a diagnostic resource to help SMEs assess their state of RI. Second, the COMPASS co-creation method kit will be described as a stand-alone resource that enables SMEs and their innovation support organizations to design forward-looking roadmaps for embedding RI in their innovation processes.

2.5 FACILITATING RESPONSIBLE INNOVATION PRACTICES WITH THE COMPASS SELF-CHECK TOOL

The COMPASS Self-Check Tool aims to facilitate self-diagnosis and monitoring of RI practices in SMEs without the need for expert advice or consultation. It helps practitioners to go beyond existing RI tools by systematically deconstructing Responsible Innovation into observable practices, thus contributing to a better alignment of Responsible Innovation with business realities and processes (Tharani *et al.*, 2020).

The primary target group of the COMPASS Self-Check Tool is business practitioners working in industries characterized by a high degree of innovation. Therefore, the tool was developed with the participation of nanotechnology, cybersecurity, and biomedical companies; however, it was designed to be applicable by other organizations and in other industry contexts without adaptation. The COMPASS Self-Check Tool can be implemented by anyone in the organization who has a good understanding of how the organization operates, as well as the policies and procedures that govern the organization's management and innovation process. The tool guides its users through a questionnaire on RI practices, explains why these practices are important, and illustrates how to implement them. It is designed to facilitate learning about what Responsible Innovation is, how the concept applies to business management and innovation processes, and how it is implemented. At the same time, the users receive an analysis of their strengths and opportunities for improvement to initiate change.

The COMPASS Self-Check Tool is structured according to key phases of the innovation process (idea generation and research, development and testing, and market and impact) in conjunction with a section on general governance that invites reflection on broader organizational structures and practices. The focus of the tool is on the company and its processes as a whole, rather than on a single innovation project (although the modular approach of the tool also allows parts of it to be used for a specific innovation project without evaluating the entire company). Each section includes a set of accountable innovation elements that apply to each phase of the innovation process or governance. The elements are broken down into questions and answer choices that indicate good Responsible Innovation practices. Recognizing that Responsible Innovation is still an evolving concept in business environments, most of the questions have an open comment option where users can enter their own approach to how they address that specific problem if that particular approach is not presented as a possible answer option in the multiple-choice answers.

The Self-Check Tool includes 43 questions and 249 response options that highlight best practices for Responsible Innovation. Each question relates to a specific and observable corporate practice or policy. Answers to each question are scored for verifiable corporate practices. The questions and scoring system do not assess the user's awareness, understanding, or opinion on specific topics related to Responsible Innovation in the company, but examine what the company does and does not do. For example, the COMPASS Self-Test Tool asks what policies the company has implemented to anticipate potential impacts of its innovations, rather than whether the company/user is aware of the impacts its innovations may have. This approach also guides the user to specific action items or practices that can help implement and ensure Responsible Innovations in company processes in the future. In this way, diagnosis and recommendation occur simultaneously.

There are three main outputs that the tool provides to its users:

1. percentages of total possible points scored in each of the four sections;
2. scores compared to all others who completed the tool;
3. a summary of questions that the user flagged for follow-up improvement.

The tool is based on a principle of equal weighting of elements of Responsible Innovation. This is implemented by giving equal weight to each sub-section (equal total points available per sub-section). In this way, the questionnaire does not prioritize any Responsible Innovation element over others. All questions within a sub-section can have the same score. Two different weighting systems of answer options per question are possible:

1. Each positive answer scores an equal fraction of the total points available for the question.
2. Each positive answer scores the total number of points available for the question. By providing an overview of a user's performance across functions and topics, the tool enables a structured and informed prioritization of which areas of business functions and Responsible Innovation should be addressed first. As the user goes through the questionnaire, they can mark specific questions as action items for their company. In the results phase, the user can download a list of bookmarks for further action.

2.6 DEVELOPING RESPONSIBLE INNOVATION ROADMAPS WITH THE COMPASS CO-CREATION METHOD KIT

The COMPASS co-creation method kit is a consistent set of materials that business practitioners in SMEs can use to develop their own RI roadmaps and action plans. In contrast to the COMPASS Self-Check Tool, the method kit is forward-looking in nature and builds on the principle of co-creation, involving stakeholders from inside and outside the business. The method kit guides users through a co-creation process, which was developed, piloted, and refined in collaboration with businesses over the course of the COMPASS project. Secondary target audiences for the toolkit include business and innovation support organizations, which may find the method kit useful in collaborating with their members, as well as consulting companies that wish to facilitate this kind of interaction. The toolkit was developed over three years, with an initial testing session conducted with the consortium at a project meeting. This "crash test" of the method allowed for refinement of aspects of the method, coupling knowledge of the sectors and suggestions for successful facilitation. The final "choreography" of the method was then set out for the Responsible Innovation Labs to use (Jégou *et al.*, 2019).

In order to help SMEs understand more about road-mapping for Responsible Innovation and the available tools offered by the Responsible Innovation Compass, a virtual crash course is also a part of the methods toolkit. The virtual crash course is presented in the form of a video featuring COMPASS experts. It allows interested audiences to get a quick and thorough understanding of Responsible Innovation, shows them how to run their own roadmap co-creation workshop and equips them with a basis for their own tailored roadmaps. It also includes pieces of practical advice on how to facilitate the process in different contexts.

2.7 CONCLUSION AND RECOMMENDATIONS

The COMPASS project showed that SMEs that engage with RI practices require a significant organizational commitment, but can also create synergies that enhance both innovation processes and outcomes. While the concept of RI may be unknown to many business practitioners in SMEs, the experiences from the COMPASS project show that it is easy to start thinking about the different elements that constitute it and introduce the potential advantages of implementing them. The COMPASS project has successfully uncovered applications of RI that have supported businesses in reconnecting with the communities they serve, while becoming more prosperous and successful. This entails immediate benefits for the business, but also sets the framework for a long-term strategy that can support both social and environmental change.

Indeed, many SMEs already implement a range of different practices that can be considered RI. This includes practices to anticipate the potential consequences of research and innovation activities on customers and end users (e.g., patients, physicians, and hospitals), the inclusion of many different stakeholders to compensate for the lack of internal resources, as well as the timely response to new or changing customer needs. The challenge is to integrate them into a consistent whole. This can be critical for SMEs that work on innovations which engender new concerns that are difficult to evaluate in their entirety, for example, in relation to data privacy, or the potential long-term toxicity of new materials. The tools developed by the COMPASS project can support business practitioners in coping with these concerns and ensure that innovations ultimately improve people's lives.

Innovative SMEs must decide for themselves what they consider as their responsibility toward society, and how much this decision is based on success measured in economic terms. As such, the trailblazers in the realm of RI, some of which have shared their experiences as collaborators in the COMPASS project, are united in that they acknowledge an intrinsic motivation to engage with RI, going beyond short-term profit generation. However, there are also external drivers for engaging with RI, for instance, external pressure exerted upon companies (e.g., legal pressure or funding and financing requirements), or stakeholder pressure. The lesson we learned from this is that the exact configuration of a business case will depend on determining the right fit between the drivers of RI within the company in question.

In order to enhance the uptake of RI, SMEs need external support (Schroeder & Ladikas, 2015). In this context, the collaboration with SMEs in the COMPASS project has resulted in recommendations that aim to incentivize SMEs when integrating RI into their innovation processes. First, EU research and innovation policy should explore measures to externally reward companies that adopt a Responsible Innovation approach. The most important incentive for companies to follow an RI approach is currently an intrinsic wish to produce a positive impact and reduce the negative potential impact on society and the environment. EU research and innovation policy could potentially do a lot to incentivize the uptake of RI practices by rewarding businesses implementing them (i.e., by including societal impact/RI in funding criteria) or by connecting public programs to extant corporate initiatives that aim to increase responsibility of businesses' research and innovation processes.

Second, research and innovation policy programs should provide additional support to SMEs that wish to develop Responsible Innovation capacities. Many companies likely to implement RI practices are found in sectors that directly cater to the wellbeing of end-customers (e.g., medical, care, lifestyle, food, and health companies) or sectors that are considered high-risk (e.g., nanotechnology, cybersecurity). External support to improve innovation and compliance processes, for example, in the form of free of charge coaching and consultancy, as well as training in relevant areas (ethics, impact assessment, innovation, and quality management) may well be essential to SMEs wishing to penetrate the market more easily and thus level the playing field.

Third, research and innovation policy should focus on facilitating collaboration and network formation. RI practices (like CSR and other so-called non-market strategies) tend to reach scale only if, and when, they are pursued at the sectoral level.

DISCLOSURE STATEMENT

No potential conflict of interest was reported by the authors.

FUNDING

The COMPASS project has received funding from the European Union's Horizon 2020 research and only the authors' view and in no way reflect the European Union's opinions.

NOTES

1. More information about co-creation can be found in Chapter C1 of this volume.
2. For further information on the Advisory Board, see Insights – Responsible Innovation Compass: https://www.innovation-compass.eu/
3. For further information, see Responsible Innovation Compass – Set your course to Responsible Innovation: https://www.innovation-compass.eu/
4. See Responsible Innovation Compass – Set your course to Responsible Innovation: www.innovation-compass.eu

REFERENCES

Antoniou, J. (2020). What responsible businesses can learn from social innovation. In K. Jarmai (Ed.), *Responsible Innovation* (pp. 37–50). Springer Netherlands. https://doi.org/10.1007/978-94-024-1720-3_4

Auer, A. & Jarmai, K. (2017). Implementing responsible research and innovation practices in SMEs: Insights into drivers and barriers from the Austrian medical device sector. *Sustainability, 10*(2), 17. https://doi.org/10.3390/su10010017

Blok, V., Hoffmans, L., & Wubben, E. F. M. (2015). Stakeholder engagement for responsible innovation in the private sector: Critical issues and management practices. *Journal on Chain and Network Science, 15*(2), 147–164. https://doi.org/10.3920/JCNS2015.x003

de Saille, S. (2015). Innovating innovation policy: The emergence of 'Responsible Research and Innovation.' *Journal of Responsible Innovation, 2*(2), 152–168. https://doi.org/10.1080/23299460.2015.1045280

Deserti, A., Real, M., & Schmittinger, F. (2022). *Co-creation for Responsible Research and Innovation: Experimenting with design methods and tools* (vol. 15). Springer International Publishing. https://doi.org/10.1007/978-3-030-78733-2

Flick, C., Fisk, M., & Ogoh, G. (2020). Engaging small and medium-sized enterprises in responsible innovation. In K. Jarmai (Ed.), *Responsible Innovation* (pp. 71–83). Springer Netherlands. https://doi.org/10.1007/978-94-024-1720-3_6

Griffy-Brown, C., Earp, B. D., & Rosas, O. (2018). Technology and the good society. *Technology in Society, 52*, 1–3. https://doi.org/10.1016/j.techsoc.2018.01.001

Grunwald, A. (2014). Technology assessment for Responsible Innovation. In J. van den Hoven, N. Doorn, T. Swierstra, B.-J. Koops, & H. Romijn (Eds.), *Responsible Innovation* (pp. 15–31). Springer Netherlands. https://doi.org/10.1007/978-94-017-8956-1_2

Iatridis, K., & Schröder, D. (2016). *Responsible Research and Innovation in industry: The case for corporate responsibility tools*. Springer.

Jarmai, K. (2020a). Introduction. In K. Jarmai (Ed.), *Responsible Innovation* (pp. 1–5). Springer Netherlands. https://doi.org/10.1007/978-94-024-1720-3_1

Jarmai, K. (2020b). Learning from sustainability-oriented innovation. In K. Jarmai (Ed.), *Responsible Innovation* (pp. 19–35). Springer Netherlands. https://doi.org/10.1007/978-94-024-1720-3_3

Jarmai, K., Tharani, A., & Nwafor, C. (2020). Responsible Innovation in business. In K. Jarmai (Ed.), *Responsible Innovation* (pp. 7–17). Springer Netherlands. https://doi.org/10.1007/978-94-024-1720-3_2

Jarmai, K., & Vogel-Pöschl, H. (2020). Meaningful collaboration for responsible innovation. *Journal of Responsible Innovation*, *7*(1), 138–143. https://doi.org/10.1080/23299460.2019.1633227

Jégou, F., Gouache, C., and Bonneau, M. (2017). Responsible Innovation Lab Methods Report (Deliverable 2.1). Available at: https://innovation-compass.eu/wp-content/uploads/2017/07/COMPASS_D2-1_RI-Lab-Methods-Report_v02.pdf

Jégou, F., Gouache, C., Bonneau, M., Mebrahtu Kidanemariam, S., Dujardin, B., Lerouge, E., & Flick, C. (2019). Responsible Innovation Co-Creation Method Kit (Deliverable 2.5). Available at: https://innovation-compass.eu/wp-content/uploads/2019/04/D2.5-Co-creation-Method-Toolkit-final.pdf

Martinuzzi, A., Blok, V., Brem, A., Stahl, B., & Schönherr, N. (2018). Responsible Research and Innovation in industry: Challenges, insights and perspectives. *Sustainability*, *10*(3), 702. https://doi.org/10.3390/su10030702

Martinuzzi, A., & Schönherr, N. (2019). Introduction. In N. Schönherr & A. Martinuzzi (Eds.), *Business and the Sustainable Development Goals* (pp. 1–17). Springer International Publishing, https://doi.org/10.1007/978-3-030-16810-0_1

Mirri, S., Roccetti, M., & Salomoni, P. (2018). Collaborative design of software applications: The role of users. *Human-Centric Computing and Information Sciences*, *8*(1), 6. https://doi.org/10.1186/s13673-018-0129-6

Nwafor, C., Jarmai, K., Stacherl, B., & Montevecchi, F. (2017). Benchmark report and policy paper: "Integration of the RRI approach into collaborative R&D&I and SME participation in European funded collaborative research in healthcare, nanotechnology and ICT" (Deliverable 1.4). Available at: https://innovation-compass.eu/wp-content/uploads/2017/09/D1.4-Benchmark-Report_Integration-of-the-RRI-approach-into-collaborative-Research-Development-Innovation-.pdf

Robinson, D.K.R., Simone, A., & Mazzonetto, M. (2021). RRI legacies: Co-creation for responsible, equitable and fair innovation in Horizon Europe. *Journal of Responsible Innovation*, *8*(2), 209–216. https://doi.org/10.1080/23299460.2020.1842633

Scholten, V.E. & Blok, V. (2015). Foreword: Responsible innovation in the private sector. *Journal on Chain and Network Science*, *15*(2), 101–105. https://doi.org/10.3920/JCNS2015.x006

Schönherr, N., Martinuzzi, A., & Jarmai, K. (2020). Towards a business case for Responsible Innovation. In K. Jarmai (Ed.), *Responsible Innovation* (pp. 85–97). Springer Netherlands. https://doi.org/10.1007/978-94-024-1720-3_7

Schroeder, D. & Ladikas, M. (2015). Towards principled Responsible Research and Innovation: Employing the difference principle in funding decisions. *Journal of Responsible Innovation*, *2*(2), 169–183. https://doi.org/10.1080/23299460.2015.1057798

Stahl, B.C. (2019). Who is responsible for Responsible Innovation? Lessons from an investigation into Responsible Innovation in Health Comment on "what health system challenges should Responsible Innovation in health address? Insights from an international scoping review." *International Journal of Health Policy and Management*, *8*(7), 447–449. https://doi.org/10.15171/ijhpm.2019.32

Stahl, B., Obach, M., Yaghmaei, E., Ikonen, V., Chatfield, K., & Brem, A. (2017). The Responsible Research and Innovation (RRI) maturity model: Linking theory and practice. *Sustainability*, *9*(6), 1036. https://doi.org/10.3390/su9061036

Stilgoe, J., Owen, R., & Macnaghten, P. (2013). Developing a framework for responsible innovation. *Research Policy*, *42*(9), 1568–1580. https://doi.org/10.1016/j.respol.2013.05.008

Tharani, A., Jarmai, K., Schönherr, N., & Urban, P. (2020). The COMPASS self-check tool. Enhancing organizational learning for responsible innovation through self-assessment. In E. Yaghmael & I. van de Poel (Eds.), *Assessment of Responsible Innovation: Methods and practices* (1st edn, pp. 198–217). Routledge.

Yaghmaei, E. & van de Poel (Eds.) (2020). *Assessment of Responsible Innovation: Methods and practices*. Routledge.

Zwart, H., Landeweerd, L., & van Rooij, A. (2014). Adapt or perish? Assessing the recent shift in the European research funding arena from 'ELSA' to 'RRI.' *Life Sciences, Society and Policy*, *10*(1), 11. https://doi.org/10.1186/s40504-014-0011-x

PRISMA

Duration: August 1, 2016–July 31, 2019
Total cost: €1,708,096.25
EU contribution: €1,708,095
Contract No.: 710059

Coordinator:

- TECHNISCHE UNIVERSITEIT DELFT (The Netherlands)

Participants:

- RIJKSINSTITUUT VOOR VOLKSGEZONDHEID EN MILIEU (The Netherlands)
- KARLSRUHER INSTITUT FÜR TECHNOLOGIE (Germany)
- ASSOCIAZIONE ITALIANA PER LA RICERCA INDUSTRIALE – AIRI (Italy)
- THE UNIVERSITY OF WARWICK (United Kingdom)

https://cordis.europa.eu/project/id/710059

B3

PRISMA

A standard to go beyond the status quo and roadmaps to innovate responsibly

Emad Yaghmaei, Steven Flipse, Pim Klaassen, Zenlin Kwee, Maria Maia, Elvio Mantovani, Elena Mocchio, Daniela Pimponi, and Andrea Porcari

3.1 INTRODUCTION

Responsible Research and Innovation (RRI) is a governance framework for research and innovation that seeks to support the development of products and processes that are safe, ethically acceptable, and responsive to the needs and expectations of society. It is considered one of the cornerstones that drives Europe's future growth (European Commission, 2014) when dealing with transformative and enabling technologies that have an increasing impact on our everyday life, society, and the environment. The ability to translate such technologies into innovations that generate societal benefits, as well as direct value for the developing organization and its affected stakeholders, is a core aspect of any corporate strategy taking into account responsibility and sustainability principles.

Where commercial research and innovation are concerned, RRI shows a close affinity to Corporate Social Responsibility (CSR). The essential difference between RRI and CSR is the explicit focus in RRI on the ethical and social impacts during the research and innovation process, starting from the earliest stages to prototyping and all the way to market launch (Kwee *et al.*, 2021). Additionally, while CSR has quite a long history of practical implementation, initiatives to put RRI in practice are still limited. The few explicit examples one can find (see e.g., Lubberink *et al.*, 2017; Yaghmaei & Van de Poel, 2020) tend to be limited to cooperative projects within the EU framework programs or national equivalents (such as the Dutch MVI program, the British EPSRC program).

For an effective RRI uptake, it is essential to identify strategies and practices that fit with the realities and constraints in which the specific company operates. At the industry level, one of the methods that has been widely used in strategy

DOI: 10.4324/9781003319481-16

planning is Technology Roadmapping (Phaal *et al.*, 2004; Van de Poel *et al.*, 2017).[1] A Technology Roadmap aligns technology with an organization's goals and encompasses the visualization of strategic aims (vision/development plans) of the organization and can be used to structure the research, development, and business activities (Gerdsri *et al.*, 2009; Phaal *et al.*, 2004). In recent years, the concept of the Innovation Policy Road-Mapping (IPRM) methodology has been developed to connect the development of technologies and innovations to a wider societal sphere. The main aspect of IPRM is to identify those societal needs, which create a potential demand for new solutions and possibly favor the emergence of new products and markets. IPRM can help articulate societal needs and link these with technological and industrial developments. IPRM integrates foresight exercises on enabling technologies, applications, products, and markets into analyses of socio-economic and sectoral drivers, as well as policy and regulatory tools and strategies.

To bring RRI uptake into an industry context, this chapter presents a guideline that has been developed in the PRISMA project, in close collaboration with representatives of PRISMA's collaborating industrial partners and is now published as a technical document by the European Committee for Standardization (CEN), under the name CWA 17796:2021-Responsibility-by-design (CWA, 2021). A total of eight industrial RRI pilots were run, each dealing with the application of a transformative technology, in a different sector. In the pilots, the RRI dimensions were integrated into these companies' strategies and actions, to develop specific "pilot RRI roadmaps," and to improve the societal value and overall performances of the outcomes of their research and development activities.[2]

The guideline adapts the basic architecture of a generic IPRM to the identification of long-term visions and action plans for the uptake of RRI within companies' innovation strategies. It provides a framework to develop long-term strategies (roadmaps) to innovate responsibly, integrating technical, ethical, social, environmental, and economic issues into research and innovation practices. In doing so, companies may improve the ethical and social impacts of marketable outcomes. The guideline described in this chapter is applicable to all organizations or actors involved in planning and performing research and technological development, with a focus on transformative and/or enabling technologies. The guideline has been designed to be optimally consistent with existing management system standards and with management or governance standards (such as the widely used ISO 9001 standard for quality management, and the standard on social responsibility, ISO 26000).

The chapter starts with a synthesis of the aim, and the definitions and principles used in the CWA 17796 guideline, followed by a description of the methodological steps proposed to design a roadmap to implement RRI in industrial practices. The concluding remarks provide insights and recommendations from our experience in using the guideline.

3.2 PRINCIPLES OF RESPONSIBLE INNOVATION

A wide set of publications provide different definitions and principles for RRI (for a review of the definitions and dimensions, see e.g., Burget *et al.*, 2017; Kwee *et al.*, 2021). We adopted von Schomberg's widely used definition for the guideline, which states that RRI is "a transparent, interactive process by which societal actors and innovators become mutually responsive to each other with a view to the (ethical) acceptability, sustainability and societal desirability of the innovation process and its marketable products" (2013, p. 19). This definition focuses on the societal value in product development, and, thus, is relevant from an industrial perspective, and has been created considering the EU normative framework, with explicit reference to the Charter of Fundamental Rights of the European Union.[3]

Building on, or responding to, this definition, a heterogeneous set of concepts and principles has been developed in the literature (Klaassen *et al.*, 2018; Lubberink *et al.*, 2017; Stilgoe *et al.*, 2013) to support the implementation of RRI in different kinds of decisional and operative structures and practices. Such "management" principles are connected to specific action lines for RRI implementation along the research and innovation (R&I) value chain and product life cycle, as reported in Table B3.1.

These principles are further described in the following (Stilgoe *et al.*, 2013):

- **Reflection:** scrutinize each activity, commitment, and assumption in order to connect them with a moral value system and the good practices of science, taking into account the limits of knowledge and that a particular framing of an issue may not be universally held. Reflexivity in RRI context is not only about the moral responsibility of the single researcher or developer nor a self-critique of the single professional, but it is also intended as an institutional practice. It can also be intended as a public matter, since people external to the organization

Table B3.1

Set of principles and actions for RRI implementation

Principles for RRI implementation	Action lines
Reflection and Anticipation	Integrate an Ethical, Legal and Social Impacts (ELSI) analysis from the early stages of product development
Inclusiveness	Promote stakeholder engagement and involve stakeholders from the quadruple helix to inform all phases of product development and ensure that research and innovation activities are societally relevant and desirable
Responsiveness	Integrate monitoring, learning, and adaptive mechanisms to address (changing) public and social values and normative principles in product development

can be part of reflexivity actions. Reflexivity is equally important with respect to the other phases of the product value chain or other functions inside the organization (besides R&D) that could be affected by an R&I action or result.

- **Anticipation:** systematically extrapolate all the plausible scenarios for the application of the R&I results; identify in these scenarios the possible risks, opportunities, uncertainties, critical issues, and draw possible ways to prevent, manage, or exploit them. Anticipation is not only intended to prevent undesirable events, but also to organize activities and resources toward shaping desirable futures. When describing desirable futures, anticipation should be realistic, for example, avoid overestimating the benefits of the innovation.
- **Inclusiveness:** introduce participatory approaches in the R&I processes from the very early stages by engaging people interested in the innovation process or results. Inclusion entails the engagement of both internal and external stakeholders. Inclusion is also connected to the other three dimensions of RRI, because reflexivity, anticipation, and responsiveness can be improved by the broad participation of different stakeholders.
- **Responsiveness:** change the direction of the innovation process to answer to stakeholders and public indications, needs, and values or to react to changing circumstances. It could also be necessary to adjust innovation actions when recognizing lack of knowledge and control, or in response to new knowledge, perspectives, or regulatory requirements. The entire R&I processes should be shaped to be as responsive as possible.

3.3 A ROADMAP FOR RRI

Based on the principles described above, the methodological steps of the process leading to the design of a roadmap for the implementation of RRI in industrial practice are concisely indicated in Table B3.2. Key elements of the RRI roadmap include:

- the Research and Innovation product(s) on which to focus the RRI roadmap;
- the vision for RRI implementation in the product development;
- the timescale for the implementation of the RRI roadmap;
- the drivers and challenges, risks, and barriers to achieve the vision, based on the assessment of the present status;
- the RRI actions to pursue, as possible path(s) between present and future to achieve the vision;
- the resources and process owners needed, their feasibility and consistency with the overall organization strategy and the innovation ecosystem.

The process proposed in this guideline is circular: top management commitment prompts and facilitates the process of roadmap design and is simultaneously informed by it.

Table B3.2

List of methodological steps for the roadmap design

	Step	Goal	Roadmap preparation
	Commitment and leadership	Ensure top management's endorsement of the organization toward RRI values and approach	Setting of the initial RRI vision, and selection of RRI product candidates
	Context analysis	Analyze the organization, the R&I product(s) to focus on, the technologies to use; identify ethical, social, and legal impacts of the product and stakeholders of the product innovation ecosystem	Compilation of the fourth line of the roadmap (R&I Tech and products)
	Materiality	Identify and prioritize drivers and challenges for RRI, risks and barriers to overcome, stakeholders to work with, and significant RRI actions to pursue	Compilation of first and second lines of the roadmap; refinement of the vision; first version of the RRI actions (third line)
	Experiment and engage	Perform exploratory/pilot RRI actions, engaging with stakeholders to inform the RRI roadmap	Review of the overall roadmap with stakeholders
	Validate	Evaluate impact of the roadmap on both the product development and the organization (Key Performance Indicators)	Review of RRI actions, in view of their technical, ethical, social, environmental, and economic impacts
	Roadmap design	Consolidate and visualize the long-term RRI strategy, covering all the R&I value chain and product life-cycle	Final roadmap

Source: adapted from Porcari *et al.* (2020).

3.4 DETAILED METHODOLOGICAL STEPS FOR THE RRI ROADMAP DESIGN

We will now take you through the steps in the design of an RRI roadmap, discussing each of the above-mentioned elements in some detail, following the process shown in Table B3.2 and in Figure B3.1.

Figure B3.1
Overall approach and steps leading to the definition of the RRI roadmap

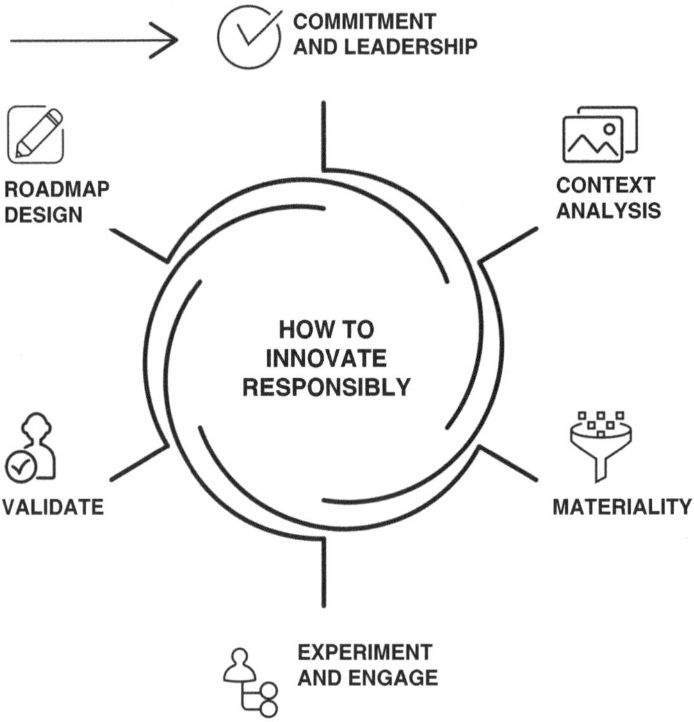

3.4.1 Top management commitment and leadership

A prerequisite for RRI implementation is top management commitment. This commitment is necessary, but not sufficient to achieve the intended RRI outcomes, as the top-down approach should be integrated with a bottom-up approach, involving other roles providing leadership. Ideally, top management demonstrates leadership and commitment with respect to the RRI by doing the following:

- ensuring that the RRI roadmap, related actions, objectives, and vision are established and are compatible with the values and identity and stakeholders the organization is referring to;
- providing that RRI principles are integrated into the organization's management systems and governance to ensure that the RRI achieves its intended outcome(s);
- ensuring the integration of the RRI principles into the organization's management systems and governance;
- ensuring that the resources needed for both the roadmap design and its future implementation are available (also in the long term);

- identifying and sustaining the motivation for the company to engage with RRI, and ensuring that the RRI roadmap achieves its intended outcome(s); communicating the importance of effective RRI, supporting the application of this guideline;
- supporting other relevant roles for RRI implementation, for example, supporting RRI promoters.

This process will lead to an initial formulation of the vision for the RRI roadmap and a selection of possible R&I projects or products to focus on in the design of the RRI roadmap ("RRI product").

3.4.2 Context analysis

RRI is connected to a broad spectrum of factors related to the type and management policies of a company, the technology, and products it works on, the sectors and markets, the pertinent regulatory frameworks, and stakeholders involved. For an effective and efficient RRI uptake, it is essential to identify strategies and practices that fit with the realities and constraints in which the organization operates. Consideration of the needs and expectations of interested parties can help the organization. As such, the following elements should be identified, at least in draft form:

- the ethical, legal, and societal impacts of the RRI product;
- the specific technologies and products, and related R&I projects, the RRI roadmap design will be focused on;
- the level of technology readiness of the RRI product;
- the stakeholders interested/involved in the development of the RRI product throughout the innovation ecosystem, and their needs and perspectives.

3.4.3 Materiality analysis

A key aspect of RRI is anticipation. Identifying materiality aspects of the RRI product and the organization early on in the R&I value chain is essential to anticipate impacts, and, thus, have time to change and adapt the process to ensure the creation of value (e.g., maximize positive impacts and minimize negative ones). The term materiality brings two concepts into play:

- understanding what (content) is relevant in terms of RRI with respect to the context in which the RRI product and the organization are found and operate;
- understanding how significant the relevant content is.

An example of questions involved in a materiality analysis are the safety and privacy issues related to operations of autonomous vehicles. What are the safety concerns (both actual and perceived by stakeholders) related to the different conditions of work of the device? How to manage the data that the device could or have to collect during its operations? Is the collection of these data critical from a social, ethical, and legal point of view? What could be the ethical issues related to autonomous decisions that these vehicles might have to take during their operations? All these aspects are relevant, but depending on the specific device (e.g., autonomous cars or drones), the technology (e.g., the type of data collected, the way these are managed by the device, etc.), the use scenarios (e.g., use of the device in buildings, cities, farms, etc.), and the stakeholders concerned, the definition of significant issues for the specific products (materiality) could completely change.

3.4.4 Experimentation and engagement

Stakeholder engagement is one of the pillars of RRI, and it is essential to validate the materiality analysis and the design of the roadmap. Based on the previous steps, it is possible to identify one or several RRI pilot actions that the organization should perform in order to ascertain the appropriateness and the feasibility of the RRI roadmap. Thus, in this phase, the following aspects are addressed:

- at least one inclusiveness action is performed, involving stakeholders in the innovation ecosystem in discussing and analyzing key ethical and social impacts of the project and in reviewing the draft roadmap;
- additional RRI actions are performed to practice and pilot activities planned in the roadmap.

3.4.5 Validation

The success of RRI uptake is strongly context-dependent and is affected by several factors, as underlined in the context analysis clause (e.g., company size, complexity of the organization, features of the technology, the level of innovation, and the associated risks). RRI actions could have both tangible and intangible impacts, ranging from long-term strategic factors at the company level (e.g., company reputation) to short-term factors in product development (e.g., alignment with user needs and stakeholder values). In this phase, the organization evaluates and validates the value of the roadmap in terms of its impact on the product development and the company, based on selected criteria. This process is needed both to evaluate the feasibility of the roadmap for the organization, and, if necessary, to refine it. The definition of the criteria is also helpful to provide documented information on the roadmap that could be controlled and maintained by the organization during the uptake of the roadmap actions. Thus, in this phase, the following aspects are addressed:

- Identify what needs to be monitored and measured, selecting criteria to perform evaluation of impacts of RRI actions.
- Select the methods for monitoring, measuring, and evaluating the impacts of the roadmap on the RRI product and the organization.

Table B3.3
RRI key performance indicators (KPIs)

Item	Principles for RRI implementation	RRI KPIs
1	Reflection and Anticipation	Awareness of public and social values
2		Awareness of ethical issues of innovations
3		Integration of public and social values into company innovations
4		Anticipation of social effects in the company innovations
5	Inclusion	Stakeholder engagement
6		Diversity and gender equality
7	Responsiveness	Transparency and accountability about RRI relevant choices
8		Learning mechanisms to address public and social values in product development
9		Capacity to align to societal goals
10		Active monitoring of RRI impacts
11	Purpose of innovation	Outcome-focused measures (backward- and forward-looking)
Source: adapted from CWA (2021).		

- Evaluate (at least qualitatively) the impacts of the RRI actions defined in the roadmap, focusing on the added values, both tangible and intangible, based on the selected criteria.
- Explore whether, and to what extent, the roadmap could be embedded in the usual innovation, risk, quality, or social responsibility policies of the organization.

A list of Responsible Innovation indicators to help monitor the implementation of Responsible Innovation principles and actions has been developed based on project activities (see Table B3.3).

3.4.6 Roadmap design

Based on the outcomes of the above-mentioned steps, the final RRI roadmap synthesizes the relevant aspects that emerge during the road-mapping process into a chart (Figure B3.2). The RRI actions are the core part of the roadmap and help to put into practice the principles for implementing RRI previously described. Three main actions are identified:

1. Integrate analysis of ethical, legal, and social impacts since the early stages of product development (reflection and anticipation).

Figure B3.2
Visualization of the PRISMA RRI roadmap

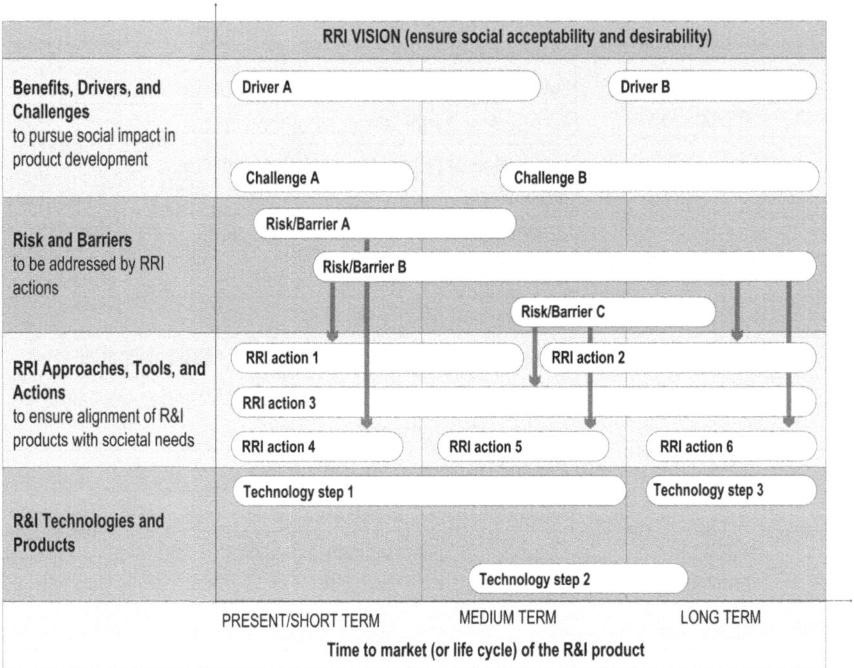

2. Perform stakeholder engagement to inform all phases of product development (inclusiveness).
3. Integrate monitoring, learning and adaptive mechanisms to address public and social values and normative principles in product development (responsiveness).

These actions are considered the minimum requirement for RRI implementation. In the course of the PRISMA project, a series of examples of more specific sub-actions referring to these three main areas has been identified (as briefly described in Section 3.5).

The chart template (Figure B3.2) includes:

- At the top of the chart: the RRI vision, setting the desired outcome of RRI implementation.
- On the y-axis: the benefits, drivers, and challenges to purse social impact in product development; the risks and barriers to be addressed by RRI actions; the RRI actions to put into practice along the product (or project) development (broadly indicated as approaches, tools, and actions); the R&I technologies and products, showing the technology steps foreseen for the specific product (or project) development.

- On the x-axis: the expected duration of the research and product development, until the entry into the market (time to market). This is the period in which the different RRI actions indicated on the y-axis need to be pursued. It might also include the use and end of life of the product, if a life cycle perspective is considered in the definition of the roadmap (in this case, time to market is replaced by life cycle).

This chart facilitates sharing and (deliberative) communication activities, both with internal and with external stakeholders.

3.5 RESULTS AND LESSONS LEARNED

The PRISMA project involved working with eight industrial case studies, piloting the application of this guideline. The pilot case studies were related to the development of innovative products using transformative technologies, such as nanotechnology, synthetic and industrial biotechnology, the Internet of Things, drones, and autonomous vehicles for different application sectors. The organizations involved included seven small and medium companies, and a public-private cooperative R&I project.

During the pilots, different PRISMA partners supported these organizations in developing an RRI roadmap to fit the specific organization, technologies, and products, as well as putting into practice some of the short-term RRI actions identified in the RRI roadmap. They did so by adopting either of two strategies: (1) providing external advice and consultancy to the company during the design of its specific RRI roadmap, or (2) providing an embedded ethicist within the company, co-operating with the different organization's functions. Irrespective of the strategy chosen, most significant RRI actions pursued included the following actions:

- performing an ELSI analysis of the R&I project;
- realizing awareness-raising and training initiatives for R&D personnel;
- helping to design for values and formulating value scenarios to inform R&I products design;
- advising on implementation of RRI and CSR methodologies and tools;
- organizing dialogues and co-creation initiatives with stakeholders;
- engaging with business partners to address RRI aspects.

The specific RRI pilot roadmaps developed for each of the pilot companies involved in the project were tailored to define a strategy that fits with the features of the organization and the specific sector in which it operates, with the aim of improving the societal value and the overall performances of their products. Some RRI actions have been experimented on during the two-year cooperation with the pilots; others will be implemented in the future.

The experience in designing the RRI roadmap and performing specific RRI actions helped the pilot case studies to evaluate the most significant ELSI expected by the development of their products and to identify operative actions to address them (see e.g., Kwee *et al.*, 2021). Across the eight pilots, the most significant normative issues emerged in relation to transformative technologies included privacy, data ownership, safety, efficacy and reliability, transparency, and open access, democratic participation, and consent (on technological decisions), distribution of benefits, risk and harm, and sustainability and social responsibility.

Early identification of societal needs and concerns helped the pilot organizations in designing products that will be better aligned with societal expectations and, thus, could gain more acceptability by the end-users. Engagement with R&I partners, supply chain actors, regulators, authorities, certification bodies, market operators, clients, and end-users (e.g., patients, local communities, consumers, etc.) has been essential to identify, in the early stages of the development, research opportunities, product design improvements and solutions, as well as ways to address potential regulatory barriers.

A summary of the eight case studies is reported in Table B3.4, including the technology and sector concerned, the RRI vision, and key ELSI addressed (as identified in the materiality analysis). A report, including the details of each case and the eight RRI roadmaps developed, is publicly available online for further details.[4]

The results of specific RRI pilot roadmaps from the eight pilots demonstrate that RRI can be helpful to anticipate social or market trends or requirements, technological scenarios, possible regulatory changes and, thus, inform the overall business strategy and help to save money and time. As RRI is considered crucial to building trust and legitimacy, the companies involved in PRISMA pilots specifically asked for instruments to make RRI implementation more recognizable by society. A list of key performance indicators (KPIs) both at the organizational and RRI level has been provided to companies and can be adapted during the course of their RRI implementation (see the full list of KPIs in Yaghmaei *et al.*, 2019).

Several actions addressing RRI principles and dimensions discussed during the project were already part of the usual business practices, at least for some of the pilot organizations, though they were not classified as such (*de facto* RRI). However, a structured and strategic approach to responsibility in research and innovation was, in most cases, lacking. There are significant barriers for RRI uptake, including the lack of expertise, limited resources, challenges to commit all functions within the company and the project partners and value chain actors, unclear added value of RRI approaches, lack of long-term vision.

The application of transformative technologies typically implies a certain degree of uncertainty, both from a technical and societal point of view, and, thus, is the initial driver for companies to look at RRI approaches. However, the reasons why a company could decide to apply a structural and long-term approach to RRI are much broader; there is a complexity of reasons and factors influencing a company's choice, often not related to the specific technology concerned.

Table B3.4

Overview of the RRI vision and key ELSI addressed by the pilot case studies

Pilot case study	Sector, technology	RRI vision	Significant ethical, legal, and social impacts addressed
Company 1	Nanotechnologies, healthcare	Realize a personalized point-of-care therapy, for highly effective, accessible, and affordable treatments of severe diseases	Product efficacy and safety, risk perception and user acceptability, patients' rights, precautions, safety, beneficence, dignity, informed consent, data ownership, transparency
Company 2	Nanotechnologies, cosmetics, and medical devices	Create nano-based dermo-cosmetics products, based on ethically acceptable and sustainable production methods and safe and more effective use of natural and organic ingredients	Product efficacy, safety and safe production, risk perception and user acceptability, improved quality, affordability, compliance with sustainability norms, information to consumers
Company 3	Synthetic biology for healthcare and nutrition	Create a mutual understanding of a desirable innovation pathway that can benefit both the synthetic biotechnology value chain as well as other stakeholders	Safety of genetically modified organisms, value chain/ benefit sharing, environmental sustainability, information to consumers
Company 4	Internet of Things for public health and hygiene applications	Develop new cleaning technologies that contribute to public health and hygiene (and respect other relevant values) and offers the possibility to increase market share	Public/patient health and hygiene, sustainability, privacy, security, transparency, autonomy, reliability, and trust
Company 5	Internet of Things for Unmanned Aerial Vehicles (UAVs)	Developing drones, combine data collection and AI, ensuring safety, and safeguarding users' rights, including privacy and fair use of data	Safety, security, and users' rights, including privacy, data protection, and data ownership
Company 6	Internet of Things and online applications for data sharing	Develop distributed data platform as a mechanism for increased personal control of data	Information privacy, data ownership, commercial use of private data, respect of users' rights, transparency, and security
Company 7	Autonomous vehicles for smart cities	Developing automated and personalized public transport to reduce traffic, pollution, and parking land use in urban areas	Information privacy, commercial use of private data, and urban planning, and safety
Industrial Project 8	Syn biotec for algae feedstocks production for consumer and industrial sectors	Developing bio-based (algae) feedstock to replace petrol-chemicals, based on RRI-aware Life-Cycle Assessment	Environmental and social and economic impact, open innovation, and transparency

The PRISMA experiences show that RRI implementation is context-sensitive, depending on the sector, technology, type of company, and business. RRI actions involve different company functions, and could have both tangible and intangible, short- and long-term impacts at different levels.

The added value of this road-mapping process is to equip companies with a practical and effective way to bring RRI into their innovation process, regardless of their sector or dimensions and their knowledge about RRI practices. The PRISMA roadmap could help companies introduce structural changes in their usual business practices, toward more anticipatory, inclusive, and responsible research and innovation practices.

3.6 CONCLUSION AND RECOMMENDATIONS

Until recently, there was only very limited experience with embedding RRI in real industry innovation processes and the added corporate value of opening up the innovation process to inclusion of social perspectives has been minimal. The methodological approach presented in this chapter helps companies to identify a vision and operative actions to put RRI in practice (the RRI roadmap), integrating considerations of technical, ethical, social, environmental, and economic aspects into ongoing innovation processes. It is aligned with existing management standards in the areas of social responsibility, risk management, and quality management standards (e.g., ISO 26000, ISO 31000, ISO 9001), and, thus, can be easily embedded into existing company procedures. The approach is now part of the CWA 17796 technical guidance, and, thus, available to all stakeholders and business operators.

It is essential for companies to identify strategies and practices that fit within the realities and constraints in which they operate. After running the pilots, we concluded that besides helping to identify a vision, a set of actions, and a timeline (roadmap) for implementing Responsible Innovation activities, the guideline also helps to analyze the potential barriers, opportunities, and benefits in pursuing Responsible Innovation (Porcari *et al.*, 2020). The guidelines include examples of methods for materiality and stakeholder analysis, stakeholder engagement, impact analysis, and KPIs. The proposed list of indicators upholds monitoring the implementation of Responsible Innovation principles and actions at the company level.

There are some further areas for future research that emerge from the PRISMA work. First, we have found that there is a limited understanding of the costs of RRI. There exist some studies that considered the associated benefits and costs of RRI (Porcari *et al.*, 2020; Yaghmaei & Van de Poel, 2020), but an expansion of evidence on benefits and costs of RRI will be useful to explain under which contingencies companies can realize RRI as a fruitful strategy. Second, while neither RRI nor CSR have come to a halt after PRISMA was finished, it would be interesting to hold up our work against other contemporary developments. A few scholars have looked at different research and innovation governance modes such as Safe-by-Design (see e.g., work by Bouchaut & Asveld, 2020 or Van Gelder *et al.*, 2021), or Sustainable finance and ESG risks (see European Commission, 2019). Thus, future research could elaborate further if (process) lessons come out of the other socio-technical notions that are also relevant to the further development of (industrial) RRI. Third, the PRISMA approach helps R&I-intensive companies do what they do responsibly, so they not only do things right, but are also supported in thinking through second-order questions about what it means to do the right thing. However, this does not, in itself, help deal with what might be the biggest challenge for RRI in industry, namely how to get companies interested in taking a look in the first place. Hence, further research would appear to be necessary to elaborate on further development of the conceptual and practical frames for RRI to call on businesses of all sizes to use the RRI principles to innovate responsibly.

ACKNOWLEDGMENTS

Parts of this chapter have been published as deliverable 5.2 from the PRISMA project. All authors have participated in the PRISMA project. Emad Yaghmaei wrote the first version of this contribution, which has been subsequently drafted by the other authors. All other authors have contributed with their ideas and have read and commented on earlier versions of this chapter.

DISCLOSURE STATEMENT

No potential conflict of interest was reported by the authors.

FUNDING

The PRISMA project has received funding from the European Union's Horizon 2020 research and innovation program under grant agreement No. 710059. The opinions expressed in this chapter reflect only the authors' view and in no way reflect the European Union's opinions.

NOTES

1. Other business and innovation management methods and practices and the relevance of such methods for RRI are provided in Dreyer *et al.* (2017).
2. The pilot reports and other supporting documentation can be found at: https://www.rri-prisma.eu/road-map-rri-for-companies/
3. See https://www.europarl.europa.eu/charter/pdf/text_en.pdf (accessed April 25, 2022).
4. The pilot report can be found at: https://www.rri-prisma.eu/road-map-rri-for-companies/

REFERENCES

Bouchaut, B., & Asveld, L. (2020). Safe-by-Design: Stakeholders' perceptions and expectations of how to deal with uncertain risks of emerging biotechnologies in the Netherlands. *Risk Analysis*, *40*, 1632–1644.

Burget, M., Bardone, E., & Pedaste, M. (2017). Definitions and conceptual dimensions of responsible research and innovation: A literature review. *Science and Engineering Ethics*, *23*(1), 1–19. https://doi.org/10.1007/s11948-016-9782-1

CWA (2021). 17796:2021 Responsibility-by-design: Guidelines to develop long-term strategies (roadmaps) to innovate responsibly. European Committee for Standardization (CEN). Available at: https://store.uni.com/catalogo/cwa-17796-2021-314554

Dreyer, M., Chefneux, L., Goldberg, A., von Heimburg, J., Patrignani, N., Schofield, M., & Shilling, C. (2017). Responsible Innovation: A Complementary view from industry with proposals for bridging different perspectives. *Sustainability*, *9*(1), 1719.

European Commission (2014). Responsible research and innovation: Europe's ability to respond to societal challenges. European Commissioner for Research, Innovation and Science Message delivered at the conference 'Science in Dialogue —Towards a European Model for Responsible Research and Innovation in Odense, April 23–25, 2012, Available at: https://ec.europa.eu/research/swafs/pdf/pub_rri/KI0214595ENC.pdf (accessed February 2, 2021).

European Commission (2019). EU sustainable finance taxonomy: Technical report. In EU Technical Expert Group on Sustainable Finance (Ed.), *Financing a sustainable European economy. taxonomy: Technical report*. European Commission.

Gerdsri, N., Vatananan, R. S., & Dansamasatid, S. (2009). Dealing with the dynamics of technology roadmapping implementation: A case study. *Technological Forecasting and Social Change*, *76*(1), 50–60. https://doi.org/10.1016/j.techfore.2008.03.013

Klaassen, P., Rijnen, M., Vermeulen, S., Kupper, F., & Broerse, J.E.W. (2018) Technocracy versus experimental learning in RRI: On making the most of RRI's interpretative flexibility. In R. Gianni (Ed.), *Responsible Research and Innovation: From concept to practices*, Routledge.

Kwee, Z., Yaghmaei, E., & Flipse, S. (2021). Responsible research and innovation in practice: An exploratory assessment of Key Performance Indicators (KPIs) in a nanomedicine project. *Journal of Responsible Technology*, *5*, 100008. https://doi.org/10.1016/j.jrt.2021.100008

Lubberink, R., Blok, V., van Ophem, J., & Omta, O. (2017). Lessons for Responsible Innovation in the business context: A systematic literature review of responsible, social and sustainable innovation practices. *Sustainability*, *9*(5), 721. https://doi.org/10.3390/su9050721

Phaal, R., Farrukh, C. J., & Probert, D. R. (2004). Technology roadmapping: A planning framework for evolution and revolution. *Technological Forecasting and Social Change*, *71*(1–2), 5–26. https://doi.org/10.1016/S0040-1625(03)00072-6

Porcari, A., Pimponi, D., Borsella, E., Klaassen, P., Maia, M. J., & Mantovani E. (2020). Supporting RRI uptake in industry: A qualitative and multi-criteria approach to analysing the costs and benefits of implementation. In E. Yaghmaei & I. van de Poel (Eds.), *Assessment of Responsible Innovation: Methods and practices*. Routledge.

Stilgoe, J., Owen, R., & Macnaghten, P. (2013). Developing a framework for responsible innovation. *Research Policy*, *42*(9), 1568–1580. https://doi.org/10.1016/j.respol.2013.05.008

van de Poel, I., Asveld, L., Flipse, S., Klaassen, P., Scholten, V., & Yaghmaei, E. (2017). Company strategies for Responsible Research and Innovation (RRI): A conceptual model. *Sustainability*, *9*(11), 2045.

van Gelder, P., Klaassen, P., Taebi, B., Walhout, B., van Ommen, R., van de Poel, I, …, & Jung, D. (2021). Safe-by-Design in engineering: An overview and comparative analysis of engineering disciplines. *International Journal of Environmental Research and Public Health*, *18*(12), 6329. https://doi.org/10.3390/ijerph18126329

von Schomberg, R. (2013). A vision of responsible research and innovation. In R. Owen, J. Bessant, & M. Heintz (Eds.), *Responsible Innovation: Managing the responsible emergence of science and innovation in society* (pp. 51–74). Wiley. https://doi.org/10.1002/9781118551424.ch3

Yaghmaei, E., Porcari, A., Mantovani, E., & Flipse, S. M. (2019). Monitoring the value of Responsible Research and innovation in industrial nanotechnology innovation projects. In I. Eisenberger, A. Kallhoff, & C. Schwarz-Plaschg (Eds.), *Nanotechnology: Regulation and public discourse* (pp. 147–175). Rowman & Littlefield.
Yaghmaei, E. & Van de Poel, I. (2020). *Assessment of Responsible Innovation: methods and practices* (1st ed.). Routledge.

I AM RRI

Duration: May 1, 2018–October 31, 2021
Total cost: €2,995,565
EU contribution: €2,995,565
Contract No.: 788361

Coordinator:

- MONTANUNIVERSITAET LEOBEN (Austria)

Participants:

- AIT AUSTRIAN INSTITUTE OF TECHNOLOGY GMBH (Austria)
- TECHNISCHE UNIVERSITEIT DELFT (The Netherlands)
- TAMPEREEN KORKEAKOULUSAATIO SR (Finland)
- LITHOZ GMBH (Austria)
- DESKARTES OY (Finland)
- UNIVERSITY OF LANCASTER (United Kingdom)
- MATERALIA (France)
- FUNDACIÓN TECNALIA RESEARCH & INNOVATION (Spain)
- GRADO ZERO ESPACE SRL (Italy)
- NORDLANDSFORSKNING AS (Lithuania)
- INTERESANSA – INSTITUT ZA RAZVOJ INIZDELOVALNE TEHNOLOGIJE ZAVOD (Slovenia)
- CENTRO RICERCHE FIAT SCPA (Italy)
- VOESTALPINE ADDITIVE MANUFACTURING CENTER GMBH (Germany)

https://cordis.europa.eu/project/id/788361

B4

I AM RRI

Roles of Responsible Research and Innovation keys in the additive manufacturing webs of innovation value chains and business

Brigitte Kriszt, Marianne Hörlesberger and Izaskun Jimenez Iturriza

4.1 INTRODUCTION

The European approach of Responsible Research and Innovation (RRI) was introduced to steer research and innovation activities toward solutions to European societal challenges. RRI as a paradigm for orientation to responsibility in innovation aims at being anticipative to future developments, reflect their impact, and develop concepts to be reactive and respond to the challenges in Europe. Its six keys include "reaching gender equality" to prevent discrimination and female poverty in the future. The outreach for "science education of young people" (Barroso, 2010)[1] should help to increase European knowledge capacity in solving upcoming challenges, such as climate change and carbon neutrality and help create a resilient society. Since the impact of research and innovation solutions are always difficult to access, a stronger ethical orientation in any science and innovation action is up for debate. The engagement of civil society (the public), also an RRI key in research and innovation, should promote more democratic decision-making in innovation. Therefore, foresights become a new instrument for engaging stakeholders. Giving open access – another RRI key – to research outcomes should raise transparency and improve knowledge transfer in research and innovation. This approach goes remarkably beyond the current business strategy of sustainability. Owen *et al.* (2021) summarized the development of the RRI approach and anticipated the future paths of RRI. Often referred to as the sixth key is the implementation of processes and actions (governance) in research, business, or public organizations and comes under the umbrella of institution change (Niamh Delaney, 2020).

The concepts of the six RRI keys give the innovation manager guidelines as to which future challenges should be addressed. This approach was developed and tested for innovation systems, in general, but put specific emphasis on innovation in business.

DOI: 10.4324/9781003319481-17

The locations in the web of innovation value chains (WIVC) where RRI can be successfully implemented are referred to as RRI openings.

The aim of this chapter is to build knowledge about the influence of RRI on the innovation process in companies and to explain the interrelationships and effects of RRI keys, using the example of innovations in additive manufacturing (AM). Strategic guidelines for corporate decision-makers in innovation management are derived from the analysis of the innovation system of AM. The chapter discusses the following questions: "What are the optimal openings for current RRI keys for companies being active in an innovation system and can their impact can be maximized by combining openings or RRI keys?" Today, the keys are treated as independent objectives, but the question is raised whether the interrelationship of the RRI keys leads to other strategic actions by companies in implementing RRI. This perspective becomes crucial in a complex, knowledge-driven innovation environment, such as that offered by the interacting web of innovation value chains.

The case of AM was selected for the investigation of that complex innovation system. This chapter will highlight the good practices to implement RRI in an upcoming new innovation segment. Business decision-makers should focus on introducing RRI into their innovation activities in order to achieve society-oriented research and innovation. In detail, the principal assumptions and conceptualizations are explained first, and then the applied methodology is introduced. The outcomes of an assessment of RRI keys, with respect to their interrelations and openings to the innovation process and organization types, will be discussed.

4.2 BACKGROUND

4.2.1 RRI key approach

RRI was established as a European policy approach in the H2020 framework program (von Schomberg, 2013). Today, RRI is understood as follows:

> Responsible Research and Innovation[2] is a multi-actor and stakeholder approach that anticipates and assesses potential implications and societal expectations with regard to research and innovation, with the aim to foster the design of inclusive and sustainable research and innovation.
>
> (European Commission, 2021)

In addition to the explained understanding of RRI, the approach is also often defined as a process-oriented action, the process steps are called anticipative, inclusive, reflective, and responsive. Sometimes that approach is found under the abbreviation AIRR – the RRI process dimension in research and innovation. They are defined as RRI keys, namely, gender equality, public engagement, open access, science education, and ethical orientation in research and innovation. The RRI keys stand for the orientation toward current societal challenges in innovation. Implementing actions for fostering RRI key orientation in the organization is understood as institutional change toward RRI (Niamh Delaney, 2020).

4.2.2 Additive manufacturing

AM is the name for a large number of production technologies. These are characterized by building new, designed products layer by layer. These production technologies offer new ways of designing products, such as bionic, lightweight structures or individual, small quantity products. The trend of digitalization additionally supports the application of these new, upcoming technologies. Small batch sizes of products characterized by new functionality, produced on demand by the customers are typical of AM (Wohlers Associates, Inc., 2021). In additive manufacturing, innovations are seen in new production technologies, machines, materials, software, and even more in new products. Innovations do not happen independently; in most cases, AM technologies, the machine, the material, and the AM product are combined. They build a web of innovation value chains. Software innovations are linked to design, technology, and machine innovations. In the AM system, several innovation value chains run in parallel and form a network of innovation value chains that create non-linear innovation paths.

4.2.3 Web of innovation added value chain and innovation processes

The characteristic of innovation systems consisting of the web of innovation value chains (WIVC) is that many types of innovations are running parallel and interconnected at specific locations of the chains (Spring *et al.*, 2019). Each innovation follows a specific innovation value chain, including the phase of idea generation, of product development, and of market diffusion (Hansen, 2007). The transitions from one innovation phase to another need decision-making on whether to go on or to stop, or to go back to the previous phase for improvement. Such decision-making points are called gates (Cooper, 1986; 1990). In the case of an RRI-oriented innovation system, gate criteria can come directly from RRI keys or from the socio-economic environment. Typically, regulation, norms, and standards, external financing (e.g., funding) or societal goals and values can offer such gate criteria. Partners can be involved in many innovation value chains; they can join or leave the innovation value chain in any phase or gate. Typical partners are research and educational institutions, companies, clients, intermediaries, or other AM special stakeholder groups. They bring their knowledge and resources to the innovation value chain; they create knowledge and value, but take learning and knowledge with them when they leave the innovation process. Any time they change the innovation value chain, a knowledge transfer happens, and the innovation value chains become interlinked by the transfer. That process is called criss-crossing and builds the complexity of webs of innovation value chains. Typical actors in AM are research organizations, technology companies, machine producers, material developers and suppliers, producers of B2B or B2C[3] products, and customers. The WIVC is embedded in a socio-economic environment. Actors, such as politicians (for regulations) and public administration, funding, and standardization, and insurance companies or the societal representatives, are a part of the "organization of the innovation environment" and also influence innovation. The concept of the web of innovation value chains is described in detail in the deliverables of the I AM RRI project (Spring *et al.*, 2019).

4.2.4 Openings of Responsible Research and Innovation in the webs of innovation value chains

Openings are seen as the location in the WIVC where RRI can be implemented. These places can be at any stage of the innovation process, but also at the gates or with the actors themselves. However, in principle, they are defined as the criteria for fulfilling measures or any organization in the WIVC that implements RRI measures in their organizational structure. Openings can be seen on the level of the overall webs of innovation value chain, on the innovation value chains itself, and the individual organization participating in the innovation system.

4.3 APPROACH AND METHODS

The methodology concentrates on the following steps:

1. **Observations and analysis** of use cases and interviews with actors in innovation cases of additive manufactured products delivered insight into the opening of RRI on the organizational basis. Case studies of WIVC for the production of parts for the automotive industry and for medical implants are used for the investigation and interpretation of the openings of RRI keys and for the guidelines for business decision-makers. Interviews and workshops with the actors involved in these AM case studies gave an understanding of the role of RRI in the innovation value chain and built the basis for the established analysis and assessments. Literature on the individual RRI keys supported the analysis.
2. **Impact assessments and cross-impact analyses** of the RRI keys in the different stages of the innovation process and associated organization types were carried out. These assessments were done in cooperation workshops with various actors from the AM innovation system. The assessment outcomes were visualized. These tables build the database for the interpretation on the location of RRI openings in the innovation and system and show how to maximize the impact in gaining RRI orientation.

   The impact analysis is used for many different purposes, e.g., social impact analysis, or environmental impact analysis. An impact assessment asks about the effects of one element of a system on other elements. It asks how strongly a set of factors will affect a different system. In the case of our analysis, we asked how strongly the RRI keys will impact the innovation system and the individual innovation processes in AM. Impact assessment is used to develop the results shown in Figure B4.2 and Figure B4.3 on p. 000 and p. 000. Graphical representations show how they affect each other – the arrowheads point in the direction of those keys that are affected by the others (Figure B4.2), or they show the importance of the keys in the innovation phase or gates (Figure B4.3) by values from zero to one.

Cross-impact analysis studies the relationship (the cross-impact) between various factors. It estimates how certain factors are likely to interact with each other. Cross-impact analysis has the advantage of processing both quantitative and qualitative information. Gordon and Hayward (Gordon, 1968) introduced the concept of asking how certain emerging technologies interact with each other. A cross-impact analysis is conducted by assessing the influence of the factors on each other. The interaction was assessed with factors from three categories. In our use case, we asked stakeholders of the AM system if there is:

a) no influence (zero points)

b) a weak or indirect influence (two points) or

c) strong influence between two factors (three points).

The assessment is established in an interaction matrix first. Then the cross-sums for passive and active behavior are built and normalized, so that the maximum cross-sums are set to one. Then the normalized passive and active are drawn into a grid with four quadrants. The factors with the highest active and passive sums are located on the top right quadrant and show the strongest interlinkage. In this work, the cross-impact analysis was performed by interdisciplinary AM teams.

3. **Deriving the guideline by deductive analysis**. All lessons from the study on impact of RRI built the basis for the guidelines for stakeholders in the AM innovation system. The relevant guidelines for business decision-makers are outlined in Section 4.4.

4.4 RESULTS AND LESSONS LEARNED

Governance turned out to be the RRI key that has to be classified as an important key for the web of innovation value chains. Under the RRI key governance, all aspects of regulation, standardization or setting of rules or implementation of innovation management processes in the companies or in the innovation environment are summarized. Governance also includes the role of politics, financing, and standardization. All influencing mechanisms that affect the innovation environment are included in this key.

4.4.1 Open access

The RRI key "open access" follows the idea that sharing science or research outcomes and co-creating approaches derive knowledge that leads to a higher probability of successful innovations. Barriers to gaining access to knowledge are reduced and technology transfer, inter-institutional and inter-disciplinary collaboration will be stimulated. The European Union provides, in a background note, the information on open access to science publication and research data at the EU level (EC-Directorate General for Research and Innovation (TD), 2016). The impact of open access on academics, the economy, and society are discussed (Tennant, 2016). As learned in the workshops with AM stakeholders, open access influences the three phases of the AM innovation process in the following way (see Table B4.1) and different impacts of open access were found in the innovation phase.

The open access publications offer the actors in the AM WIVC different options; they broaden the knowledge base and provide a higher level of specific knowledge to the actors involved in the process and the innovation system, as well. New trends and technologies become visible and can be easier assessed for standardization. Open access publications contribute to the formation of the web of innovation value chain because competence partners become visible. The dissemination of new ideas and products is supported by the implementation of the RRI key open access.

Table B4.1

Open access key in the phases of the AM innovation value chain

Idea generation	Idea development	Idea diffusion
Accessible knowledge base in AM – material, technology, knowledge from open repositories and publications	Accessible existing knowledge, data, or research results from open repositories	Publish research methodology, results, and data in open access repositories (multiple use), non-scientific publications attract interest of societal actors
Open access supports finding and selecting experienced partners and experts based on their publications and makes them attractive for cooperation	Deliver low barrier publication for starting standardization processes, which leads to general standards, which address societal needs, often they become part of legal regulation	Reach a wider reader community and show AM competences via open publication
Open access or low barrier access to the company's intellectual properties will reduce the competitive advantages of companies in the innovation value chain.	Open access or low barrier access to the company's status on product development will reduce their competitive advantages and their leading position	High diffusion rate on innovation will increase business success, many successors will help to improve the products and foster the position of technologies on the market
New evolving innovation topics might be faced with a low number of open access journals		Low number of options of open access publication and type of journals might reduce diffusion of knowledge

A bibliometric analysis of AM literature with Web of Science showed that, in AM, the share of open access publication is approximately 30% globally, but slightly higher in the European countries, at 38%. In the classical disciplines, in engineering and material science, the share of open access publications is only 10%.[4] From that, it is indicated that the open access publications have a supportive role in the development of new innovative technologies.

Even if the use cases revealed that the companies are rather reluctant to publish their own results in idea generation and product development phase, the benefit for companies in the innovation process becomes apparent from Table B4.1. The cooperation with research organizations and universities opens the way to the key "open access." Open access gives deep information about the innovation to the customers and helps to increase business success and increase the market reach.

4.4.2 Ethics

The AM use cases have shown that ethical considerations are an integral part of the research from start to finish. Compliance with ethical principles was shown to be crucial to attain innovation. With AM medical products, ethical considerations, such as privacy and handling of individual patients' data, were emphasized by the companies. In the automotive case, general rules for passenger safety are mentioned as ethical issues. The discussion with the AM manager revealed the ethical topics are very important in exchange with societal stakeholders. The detailed analysis of the relation of RRI ethics and AM innovation value chain is shown in Table B4.2.

The consideration of ethics differs in the different stages of the innovation process, especially in the idea generation and development phases, as well as in the diffusion phase. In the development and diffusion phases, considerations need to be made to ensure products comply with AM standards or regulations related to safety, health, or environmental aspects in production and use phase.

4.4.3 Science education

Scientific education is a crucial factor in the knowledge-based economy, where innovation is driven by the transfer of scientific findings to innovative products and services. Science education is also important to ensure a high human capital for innovation and has a strong link to gender equality in AM. Gender equality action and science education of females in STEM are seen as a key for RRI orientation. This enables a general increase of knowledge in society, and science education leads to a better knowledge base for new and rapidly developing technologies. Science education is, therefore, an essential element for the innovation process in a rapidly evolving sector, such as AM. Table B4.3 shows the influence of science education in the phase of the innovation value chain in AM.

Workshops with the AM actors from companies and from higher education organizations showed that science education can be addressed in any phase of the innovation

Table B4.2

Ethics key in the phases of the AM innovation value chain

Idea generation	Idea development	Idea diffusion
Alignment of the practices with the Code of Conduct for Research Integrity	Alignment of the practices with the Code of Conduct for Research Integrity	Ensure that the outcomes of the innovation process are used responsibly
Consult external research ethics expert or ethics committee	Consult external research ethics expert or ethics committee	Ensure that the production process is according to social and engineering state-of-the-art standards, seek improvement with your products
Engage different research and innovation actors and beneficiaries in the ethics-related reflection	Engage different research and innovation actors and beneficiaries in the ethics-related reflection	Apply environmentally friendly AM technologies and materials, ensure the technology standards in recycling of your AM products
Check internal standards, rules, and regulations related to health, safety, environmental aspects	Use future studies (such as participatory foresight) to anticipate the benefits and risks of the project	Set up socially oriented business models for AM products
Follow ethical consideration in your field, such as passenger safety or ethical standards in medical application of implants	Adjust your design, material product process of your product to the ethical requirement in your field. Follow the standardization of the product category or materials.	Do not discriminate or harm any party of society (female/male, young/old), do not exploit children by low-cost production in developing countries

Table B4.3

Science education key in the phases of the AM innovation value chain

Idea generation	Idea development	Idea diffusion
Include youngsters and students in ideation processes through co-creation methods; train them in new technologies and scientific findings, highlight their contribution	Include youth and students in the development process (through teaching/learning factories methodology, for instance), try to achieve gender equality in your teams	Adapt texts/formats according to target groups, communicate scientific outcomes
Organize science shops to generate research ideas	Motivate your scientists to establish start-ups	Use different outreach channels, including innovative science communication formats
Become engaged in science education, motivate your co-workers to join science education programs	Apply attractive teaching methodology from science education like modeling and simulation in your product development	Get involved in science education and training with new products and services, show benefits, be open to new teaching methods

process, because students can be involved in any innovation phase. Since AM is a rather new production technology, education in AM is not implemented widely in the curricula or training programs yet, not even in practical industry-oriented training (Simpson *et al.*, 2017). The continuous implementation of science results in all education programs was seen as the most important task. The teaching program should be adapted to the level of education. The idea diffusion phase was seen as the most important phase for higher education. AM companies did not participate in the creation of new educational programs, but were open to engaging in teaching. This was seen as their way of contributing to science education. In general, it was agreed that teaching should also include innovative methods to show the attractiveness of STEM careers for female and male students. The AM companies expressed their general need for a high number of excellently qualified co-workers to have the potential to bring new ideas to innovation. However, the AM partners also stated that they cannot take on the responsibility for offering study programs for young people. Public and private education institutions are in charge of adapting study programs or establishing new ones to react to the need of the AM industry. For the AM community, educational organizations are not perceived as direct partners in the innovation value chain, but they play an important role in shaping the RRI environment. Companies can support the establishment of new education programs by formulating their needs from the economy, joining panels for development of studies, or offering internships for students. One option that was raised was the appointment of researchers from AM companies as lecturers for science education.

4.4.4 Public engagement

Co-creating the future with citizens, civil organizations, and other stakeholders is at the heart of public engagement, bringing on board the widest possible diversity of people to interact on matters of science and technology. The engagement of the public is shown in Table B4.4. The necessary openness of science and innovation to the public can be clearly seen in the first stages of the innovation process, namely, in the idea generation and idea development phases. The discussions with the AM partners had shown that they see the commitment to dialogue with the public as the role of universities and research centers. They expect that these bodies will give information on the benefits of AM technologies to increase the acceptance of new technologies in general, but do not ask for the input of civil society in the innovation actions. When it comes to the idea generation for new AM products, companies see, in general, their customers as more important than civil society.

A broader range of actors of the AM WIVC is affected by the "public engagement" key, when it comes toB2C relations, such as in consumer products. When opening the innovation process to society, different actors are relevant in terms of providing different visions to the firms and knowledge providers.

External partners, such as policy-makers, clusters, NGOs, or industrial associations and civil society organizations, play an important role in the AM innovation process. From a strategic point of view, the AM firms and knowledge providers could include

Table B4.4
Public engagement key in the phases of the AM innovation value chain

Idea generation	Idea development	Idea diffusion
Include other actors in the value chain in the idea generation (including end-users, policy-makers, and investors), open innovation	Establish spaces for deliberation for projects that are in collaboration	Involvement of the public in new products and considering new perspectives of application scenarios
Include citizens and civil society organizations in the idea generation through co-creation methods, include citizens and civil society organizations in future study processes (i.e., participatory foresight)	Engage stakeholders in the product definition, establish spaces for deliberation with NGOs and citizens, request feedback from affected actors (through surveys and other means)	Include public feedback in your product improvement
Research organizations and intermediary organizations should give more general information on new technology to the public, companies can support that process, foresights should help to create future scenarios and give help in finding new products and services		Join platforms to get into discussion and dialog with the public

the stakeholders in the definition of their research agendas. Public discussion sessions on different research and innovation topics offer a more operational perspective. This would help increase the scientific literacy and the empowerment in society. An interesting methodology, which should enable a dialog with society, or any other stakeholder, are foresight studies. These should help to address the future needs and will give a wider perspective in innovation prior to the product development process.

4.4.5 Gender equality

Gender equality is relevant in the AM sector for several reasons, particularly because of the lack of female students in engineering for STEM degrees, resulting in a lack of females in engineering jobs and AM companies. Adapting the product to the individual helps overcome gendered design. However, it is important to ensure gender equality in the innovation process of the product. Table B4.5 shows the influence of gender equality in the phase of the innovation value chain in AM.

The gender dimension can be seen in all stages of the innovation value chain, especially in the idea generation and idea development phases. The different needs,

Table B4.5

Gender equality key in the phases of the AM innovation value chain

Idea generation	Idea development	Idea diffusion
Identify gender stereotypes during the ideation process	Create a gender-balanced development team	Gender considered in dissemination activities
Create a gender-balanced ideation team	Consider different needs, behaviors, and attitudes of men and women for product development	Gender dimension in production
Analyze the different needs, behaviors, and attitudes of men and women		Gender dimension in accessibility of products and services
Consider gender relevance of research topics		

behaviors, and attitudes of men and women should be assessed, and gender stereotypes must be identified. The creation of a gender-balanced innovation team could contribute to achieving these objectives.

All AM stakeholders engaged in the WIVC stressed that they took actions to achieve gender equality in their own organizations. From a research and innovation process perspective, fostering gender balance in AM research teams and integrating the gender dimension in the content of research and innovation might be some of the measures to be taken by those actors. The low number of women with STEM qualifications is seen as critical for achieving gender balance in teams. This situation will be solved within a short period of time.

4.4.6 Results of the cross-impact of RRI keys in the AM innovation system

The results of the workshops with AM actors provided the understanding and the knowledge basis for establishing cross-impact analysis of the RRI keys. As already seen in the analysis of Tables B4.1 –B4.5, some keys might be interrelated, but a quantitative analysis for AM was done by the cross-impact analysis. The result of the cross-impact analysis is shown in Figure B4.1.

The RRI keys that are more likely to be classified as active are located in the upper left quadrant of Figure B4.1; they are referred to as the drivers of the system. They are not influenced that much by the other keys. In the case of AM, innovation system open access is classified as the only rather independent key in the AM system. Open access is, therefore, seen as the only RRI key that can drive the AM web of innovations value chain RRI keys. Located in the upper right corner, other active keys can act as a driver, but also have the potential to moderate the system. These keys are closely interrelated (see Figure B4.1).

Figure B4.1
Cross-impact analysis of RRI keys in AM WIVC

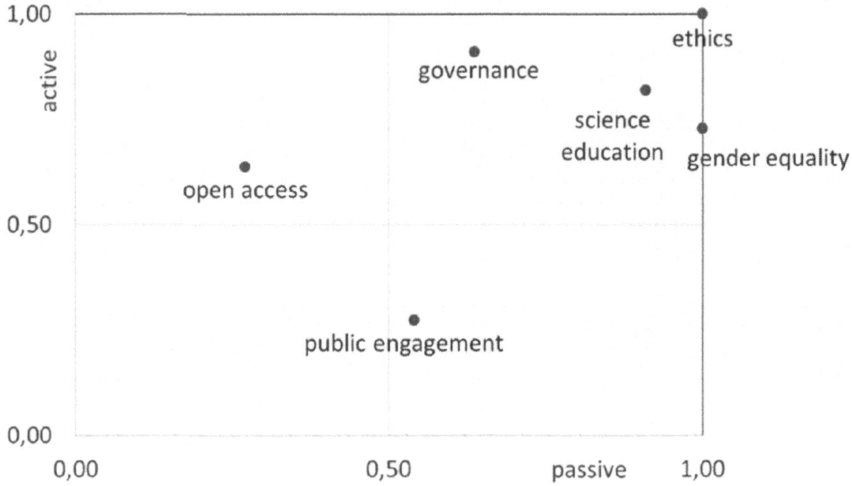

The only driver of the AM innovation system is the RRI key "open access." Any actions in open access will push the AM innovation system forward. Engagement of companies in open access actions will strengthen RRI innovation. As already explained, companies can benefit from open access by having low barriers to knowledge base, by supporting publication of the cooperation partners or preparation of their own publications to inform customers about their innovation activities.

Governance, science education, ethics, or gender equality RRI keys are strongly interrelated and they are not independent. Thus, all strategic measures to strengthen one key in the WIVC also have an impact on the others and strengthen all RRI-oriented innovation measures equally. The RRI key ethics has the highest active impact on the current AM innovation system; it is also understood as the most important key to obtaining socially accepted innovation. However, the RRI key ethics also has the highest passive impact position. It is, thus, assumed that a lack of ethical orientation will lead to a system that does not meet the RRI objectives, even when other RRI keys are implemented. The conclusion was drawn that the societal acceptance of innovation will be low.

Science education can bring tremendous benefits to RRI-oriented AM innovations. Highly qualified employees have the knowledge to develop new ideas, solutions, and innovations, but the lack of scientifically trained employees is an obstacle to growth. However, the introduction of new education programs is not the responsibility of AM innovation actors, so this RRI key is not as powerful for the AM innovation system. The environmental influence on the innovation system is rather high. Furthermore, it must be taken into account that the development of new educational programs takes time and so does the training of students. For the case of higher education, the passive role as a barrier and the active role as a driver of RRI in the innovation value chain are very evident.

Gender equality is in a similar place in Figure B4.1 as science education, but the passive part is slightly higher. Gender equality is closely related to science education to activate the innovation system, even if the additional obstacle of motivating women to choose a STEM career has a slightly lower active impact on the innovation system. In discussion with the AM companies, it was seen as an advantage that RRI-oriented higher education, including ethical aspects or gender equality, will appeal more to young people. Increasing the number of AM students will help the companies meet their demand for highly qualified employees.

Governance is understood as a very active key in the current WIVC. Governance comes into AM by regulations like standards, laws, or funding. Currently, the AM innovation system is more influenced by supportive governance mechanisms than by regulative actions, such as standardization or legal limitation. The AM innovation has been developed rather without any external restrictions. During the last few years, the ISO standards on AM were agreed and set in force. They concentrate more on the classification of the type of AM technologies. Already established standards in automotive and medical application help the AM companies to reduce the risks in product development and were seen as positive by the AM company partner. For companies, the establishment of RRI principles helps them to reduce risks until standardization is available, which gives them a competitive advantage in the early stage of innovative technologies.

Public engagement was characterized as a buffer in the AM innovation system. This means that public engagement has a more passive character. The influence on the other RRI keys is rather low. Public engagement is not assessed as an activating driver for RRI in the current AM innovation system.

The cross-impact analysis also provides information on how the RRI keys are directly related to each other and how they influence each other (see Figure B4.2). Open access is the key that is hardly influenced by other RRI keys. Its strongest impact points directly to the RRI key of science education. The positive relationship between open access and science education is interpreted by the AM partners as the possibility for students and teachers to have barrier-free access to current AM research literature. Gender equality affects both ethics and science education and supports herewith the most active RRI keys. A disadvantage could be that the establishment of science education programs is a rather time-consuming measure. An attractive opening for increasing the RRI key orientation in AM innovation system will be to increase open access publications. This offers students of scientific training programs tailored to the needs of the AM innovation system the opportunity to build their knowledge in a short time. Companies have the potential to formulate their needs to higher education. Cooperation with universities and higher education institutions opens up the possibility of participating in new educational programs. In addition to that, a gender

Figure B4.2
Interrelation and interaction of RRI keys

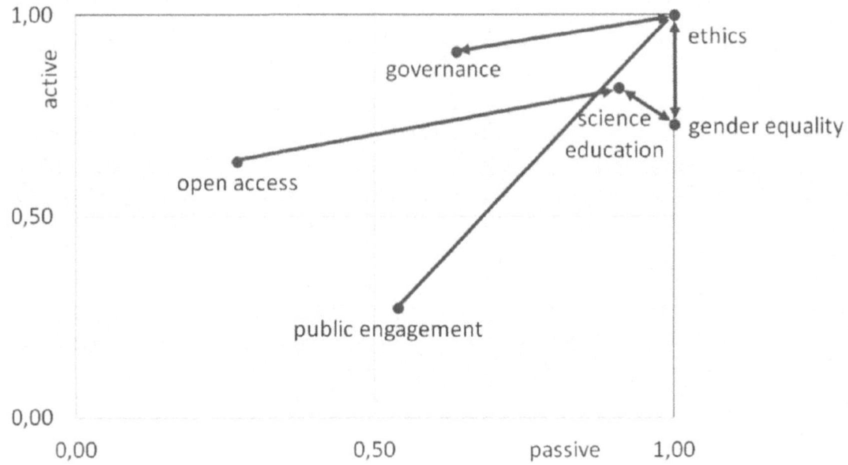

equality-oriented science education and ethical courses in science education will be the strongest opening for RRI in the WIVC. This will also attract more female students to engineering topics like AM.

Another strong opening is the interrelation of ethics and governance. They influence each other and become a strong pair in promoting the RRI orientation in the AM innovation system. As described above, implementing ethical principles in innovation management processes will help reduce risks in the early stages of innovation, but also attract highly skilled employees and send positive signals to society and customers. In the workshops, it was stressed that self-regulating mechanisms through standardization will have a more positive effect on the development of the innovation system than legal regulation, even if both mechanisms build on societal ethical norms. Standardization and regulation have the power to change the behavior of the actors in AM very quickly when put into force. The AM actors classified standardization as an open, bottom-up process of the innovation community itself. Legal regulation was seen as a top-down process, mirrored by societal needs.

The legislator can require that harm to society be averted at a very early stage of innovation; in most cases, the regulation stops the innovation actions. The power of legal regulation to create new, individual innovative solutions to the grand challenges of European society was considered to be rather low, because the innovative creativity comes from the actors in the AM innovation network. Governance through legal regulation can define the framework and set societal standards when new solutions are needed. A very astonishing outcome of the analysis was that the RRI key ethics influences public engagement and not the other way around. Explanation might be found in the fact that additive manufacturing is a rather new type of production technology and the awareness in civil society is not very high.

4.4.7 RRI in the innovation and gates phases

The second analysis attempts to answer how strong RRI keys influence each of the three innovation phases. Figure B4.3 shows the results of the direct impact of the RRI keys in the three different phases and gates of the innovation value chain. RRI keys can offer openings in any phase and in any of the gates of the AM innovation value chains. The impact assessment helps to make it transparent at which phase or gate which type of RRI opening will have the highest impact. The evaluation gives insight into the advantage of RRI keys as openings, in general, but it also shows the potential for openings of the individual keys.

The potential for RRI keys being included in innovation is at its highest in the phase of idea generation. This phase is seen as the design phase and has the most freedom in decision-making. At the beginning of innovation, when RRI considerations require changes, the risk and resources for this are rather low. Funding organizations can support the RRI orientation by asking for open access, gender equality, including education aspects or assessments on societal impact.

When the innovation enters the second phase, the option for introducing RRI becomes remarkably lower. Nevertheless, science education has a direct impact, even if, as described above, it is not a very flexible and quickly adaptable key. When it comes to idea diffusion, governance by regulation is classified as a strong key to influence the innovation, occurring, however, too late in many cases. This dilemma was already described by von Schomberg (2013).

Another strong position for an RRI opening is the gate between the phase idea generation and idea development. RRI criteria that need to be implemented in innovation can act as a strong gatekeeper in AM, ethical considerations play an important role, in general, in the gates. It can be concluded that in the current state of AM webs of innovation value chains that the introduction of RRI will be most effective in Phase 1, which is research and idea generation, or in gate 2 between idea generation and idea development (transformation of idea to product).

Figure B4.3

Impact potential of RRI keys in the innovation process: (a) process steps, and (b) gates

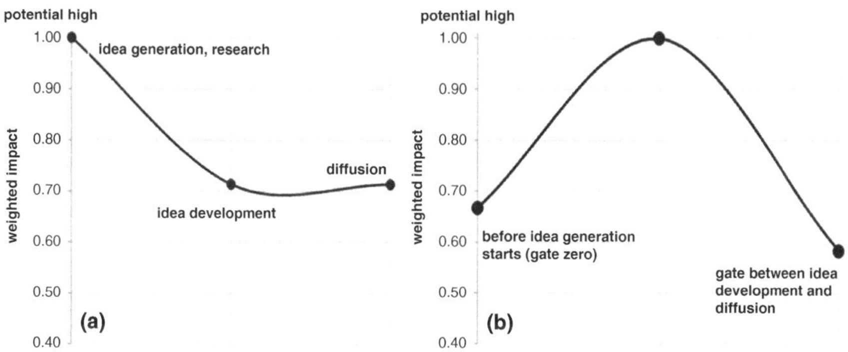

4.4.8 AM actors as openers for RRI

Many different actors with different competences are involved in the AM WIVC system. Some of them, such as research institutions, AM technology companies, material suppliers, and customers, have a direct influence on the innovation process and are responsible for implementing RRI keys in their actions. Others, such as policy-makers, funding agencies, standardization organizations, and educational institutions, create the environment for AM WIVC. They set the framework for development, they can be supportive, for example, through funding, science education programs, or standardization, or they can be restrictive, for example, through legislation, taxes, or limiting resources.

Customers, who are often seen by the AM community as representatives of the public or society also have a major influence on the RRI orientation in the innovation value chain network in AM. Customers have a greater influence than the public. In AM, customers are very often involved in all steps of the innovation value chain and are a strong opinion leader. RRI-oriented customers can play a strong role in incorporating RRI orientation into innovation processes.

Even though they are often seen as part of the environment in the web of innovation value chains, the RRI influence potential of universities and research organizations is quite high. They are the promoters of open access publications; they provide the foreground knowledge for new technologies and are responsible for the introduction of higher education and science education programs.

4.5 GUIDELINES FOR RRI IN INNOVATION MANAGEMENT

The guidelines for business decision-makers were derived from the case of AM companies. They proposed the main measures for the introduction of RRI in innovation management. In general, strategic decision-making for the implementation of RRI in the innovation action of a company is needed. This will initiate the institution's change process. In the implementation phase of RRI, clear management responsibility and transparent RRI criteria in innovation actions or decision-making in the innovation should be communicated. RRI needs a strong commitment to contribute to the solution of the European grand challenges. From the analysis, it is suggested that companies should focus their prime engagement in the RRI keys on open access, ethics, gender equality, and governance.

An option for a new perspective is to include the dialogue with society in the innovation process. Platforms for AM technologies might offer access to the public. This needs a strong commitment to cooperation with universities and other partners in the innovation value chains, and a willingness to be open, share knowledge, or for the implementation of diversity in any aspect of the cooperation. When forming project teams and collaborative alliances in the field of innovation, a gender balance should be sought. In general, more diverse teams, in terms of competence or age, help to find novel and innovative solutions. The different perspectives are more responsive to the needs of society.

A company that is RRI-oriented can take the role of an ambassador of RRI in webs of innovation value chains. Therefore, it is recommended to start implementing RRI orientation in corporate strategies, processes, and communication with employees, suppliers, customers, and society. Today, Corporate Social Responsibility (CSR) standards are already in force. To improve RRI orientation, implement CSR standard practices in your innovations. In particular, the participation of companies in the development of standards is seen as a valuable contribution of RRI. This is important for all those who develop new and innovative technologies; AM is one of them. The employees should be trained in RRI thinking, so that RRI is included in innovation work. The employees of companies should also get the opportunity to bring the knowledge from innovation actions to science education. The cooperation with higher education institutions and the involvement in the creation of new study programs need to be intensified. When it comes to open access publications, companies can take the lead in publishing or support the other actors in the innovation value chains. Co-authorships attract the attention of companies, which are then very often invited to participate in the value chains of innovation for new products. Open access is, thus, not only a barrier-free source of knowledge, but also builds high potential for new alliances in innovation processes.

4.6 CONCLUSION AND RECOMMENDATIONS

The concept of innovation value chains, consisting of phases and gates, helps to introduce specific RRI decision criteria into the innovation process and to establish the RRI orientation of other AM IVC. The cooperation of actors, such as companies and research institutions, in an innovation environment shaped by regulation or standardization helps to integrate RRI into the overall innovation network of innovation value chains. The work showed that RRI keys are interconnected, as well as how they influence each other to maximize RRI innovation orientation for companies. The cross-impact analysis highlighted open access publications as a driving force in an emerging innovation system. Open access has a direct impact on the important key of science education, ethics, governance, and gender equality.

Two groups of RRI keys were analyzed. One was the interrelation between ethics, science education, and gender equality. The other group of RRI openings was governance and ethics. While ethical orientation, governance, and gender equality can be directly addressed through companies in the AM innovation value chains, science education is seen more as an environment characteristic of companies in a RRI-oriented innovation system. Standardization, legal regulation, or financing are mainly seen as a regulating RRI key. The impact of science education on innovation value chains is twofold. Directly in the innovation process, scientific staff are needed to enable the realization of innovative ideas. As an environmental aspect, the development of higher education studies is seen to strengthen the RRI key science education. In the company's view, the RRI key gender equality has a similar position to science education.

The analysis of the impact of RRI keys in innovation value chains delivers guidance for implementation of RRI in businesses and innovation management.

DISCLOSURE STATEMENT

No potential conflict of interest was reported by the authors.

FUNDING

The research work delivering the results for this chapter was funded by the European Union's Horizon 2020 Research and Innovation Program under GA Number 788361. The opinions expressed in this chapter reflect only the authors' view and in no way reflect the European Union's opinions.

NOTES

1. European Strategy 2020 aimed to involve 40% of academic educated people. That threshold was already passed in 2015 (Vincent Bourgeais, 2015) for the population aged between 30 and 34 years.
2. Responsible Research and Innovation is abbreviated as RRI.
3. B2B = Business to business; B2C = Business to customer.
4. This analysis was done on the data of November 2020.

REFERENCES

Barroso, J. M. (2010). EUROPEA 2020 Strategy: A European strategy for smart, sustainable and inclusive growth. Available at: https://ec.europa.eu/eu2020/pdf/COMPLET%20EN%20BARROSO%20%20%20007%20-%20Europe%202020%20-%20EN%20version.pdf.

Cooper, R. (1986). An investigation into the new product process: Steps, deficiencies, and impact. *Journal of Product Innovation Management*, *3*, 71–85. https://doi.org/10.1016/0737-6782(86)90030-5

Cooper, R. (1990). Stage-gate system: A new tool for managing new products. *Business Horizons*, *33*(3), 44–54.

EC Directorate General for Research and InnovatioN (2016). Background note on open access to science publication open research data. Available at: https://ec.europa.eu/info/sites/default/files/research_and_innovation/strategy_on_research_and_innovation/documents/ec_rtd_background-note-open-access.pdf;

Europea Commission

European Commission (2021). Responsible research & innovation. 27 May. Available at:. https://ec.europa.eu/programmes/horizon2020/en/h2020-section/responsible-research-innovation

Gordon, T. T. (1968). Initial experiments with the cross-impact matrix method of forecasting. *Futures*, *1*(2), 100–116.

Hansen, M. B. (2007). The innovation value chain. *Harvard Business Review*, *85*(6), 121–130, 142.

Niamh Delaney, R. I. (2020). *Institutional changes towards Responsible Research and Innovation*. Publications Office of the European Union.

Owen, R., von Schomberg, R., & Mcnaghten, P. (2021). An unfinished journey? Reflections on a decade of responsible research and innovation. *Journal of Responsible Innovation*, 217–233.

Simpson T.W, Williams, C. B., & Hripko, M. (2017). Preparing industry for additive manufacturing and its applications: Summary & recommendations from a National Science Foundation workshop. *Additive Manufacturing, 13*, 166–178.

Spring, M. *et al.* (2019). Draft on web of innovation value chains. Leoben: Montanuniversitaet, https://doi.org/10.34901/mul.pub.2021.2

Tennant, J., Waldner, F., Jacques, D., Masuzzo, P., Collister, L., & Hartgerink, C. (2016). The academic, economic and societal impacts of Open Access: An evidence-based review. F1000, Research. https://doi.org/10.12688/f1000research.8460.3

Vincent Bourgeais, S. G. (2015). *Europe 2020 education indicators in 2014: The EU is moving closer to its Europe 2020.* Eurostat.

von Schomberg, R. (2013). A vision of Responsible Research and Innovation. In J. Bessant, R. Owen, & M. Heintxz (Eds.), *Responsible Innovation* (pp. 51–71). Wiley. Online.

Wohlers Associates, Inc. (2021). Annual Wohlers Report. Available at: wohlersassociates.com

SISCODE

Duration: May 1. 2018–April 30. 2021
Total cost: €3,999,268.75
EU contribution: €3,999,268.75
Contract No.: 788217

Coordinator:

- POLITECNICO DI MILANO (Italy)

Participants:

- AGENZIA PER LA PROMOZIONE DELLA RICERCA EUROPEA (Italy)
- TECHNISCHE UNIVERSITÄT DORTMUND (Germany)
- ASSOCIATION EUROPEENNE DES EXPOSITIONS SCIENTIFIQUES TECHNIQUES ET INDUSTRIELLES (Belgium)
- STICHTING MUSEUM VOOR INDUSTRIE EN SAMENLEVING (The Netherlands)
- SOCIEDADE PORTUGUESA DE INOVAÇÃO CONSULTADORIA EMPRESARIAL E FOMENTO DA INOVAÇÃO SA (Portugal)
- INSTITUT D'ARQUITECTURA AVANCADA DE CATALUNYA (Spain)
- CIENCIA VIVA-AGENCIA NACIONAL PARA A CULTURA CIENTÍFICA E TECNOLOGÍCA (Portugal)
- ASSOCIATION TRACES THEORIES ET REFLEXIONS SUR APPRENDRE LA COMMUNICATION ET L'EDUCATION SCIENTIFIQUES (France)
- ARISTOTELIO PANEPISTIMIO THESSALONIKIS (Greece)
- UNIVERSITY COLLEGE LONDON (United Kingdom)
- BIOSENSE INSTITUTE – RESEARCH AND DEVELOPMENT INSTITUTE FOR INFORMATION TECHNOLOGIES IN BIOSYSTEMS (Serbia)
- COLLEGE OF THE HOLY & UNDIVIDED TRINITY OF QUEEN ELIZABETH NEAR DUBLIN (Ireland)
- KRAKOWSKI PARK TECHNOLOGICZNY SP ZOO (Poland)
- DESIGN SOCIETY FOND (Denmark)
- MAKER (Denmark)
- EUROPEAN NETWORK OF LIVING LABS IVZW (Belgium)

https://cordis.europa.eu/project/id/788217

B5

SISCODE

Responsible Research and Innovation operationalization in ecosystems through co-creation

Alessandro Deserti, Jennifer Eckhardt, Christoph Kaletka, Daniel Krüger, Francesca Rizzo, and Felicitas Schmittinger

5.1 INTRODUCTION

It has been recognized, both in theory and practice, that the active involvement of stakeholders and final users (here the authors refer to the notion of co-creation) can support the development of solutions like products, services or innovations and make them more effective, appropriate, and implementable (Benington & Moore, 2010; Jones, 2018; Stilgoe *et al.*, 2020; Voorberg *et al.*, 2015).

With respect to the development of new products and services for the market, co-creation has been largely recognized as an approach to innovation that can lead to better solutions that can create new business opportunities (Prahalad, 2004; Ramaswamy *et al.*, 2014). What is less known is evidence in favor of the fact that turning stakeholders and customers from passive to active participants in the process of innovation development can automatically bring in higher levels of responsibility, for example, intrinsically by sharing problems and co-creating solutions, the results will become more sustainable for all (Schmittinger *et al.*, 2020).

RRI entails direct interaction with and among different actors taking cultural and behavioral diversity and various points of view into account, leading to an iterative and collaborative process of solution development. Through the elements of collaboration and exchange, a peer-to-peer learning process can be enabled that build new capacities and capabilities. RRI, on the other hand, aims to open innovation processes to a broader range of societal actors, including citizens, communities, and stakeholders, starting from the early phases of research to develop innovation responding to the real needs of society.

DOI: 10.4324/9781003319481-18

The similarities and links in their goals and approaches suggest the potential of connecting co-creation to RRI in order to identify the benefits and the possible application of co-creation as a means to operationalize RRI. Co-creation, being recognized as a way to deal with ill-defined problems, complexity. and multiple stakeholders with diverse interests (Grönroos, 2012), paves the way for including citizens, industry, and public sector organizations in a common process going beyond a single market. However, a major issue identified in the field of RRI is its lack of practice-orientation and missing implications on how to translate the concept – widely discussed in theory – into actions and operational processes (Emery *et al.*, 2014; Zwart *et al.*, 2014).

The perspective of co-creation can allow the concept of RRI to move forward from a set of recommendations to an applied practice embedded in research and innovation processes in innovation sectors, as well as in policy-making. Hence, co-creation can help to overcome some of the current limits and weakness of RRI by doing the following:

- filling the gap on how to introduce RRI into the implementation of real innovations;
- helping to deal with wicked problems like societal challenges that require non-linear models of innovation (iterative approach);
- introducing mechanisms for granting the participation of diverse stakeholders (including citizens) in the process of innovation and the management of their complex interactions.

Following this perspective, the SISCODE project[1] (Society in Innovation and Science through CO-DEsign, H2020, 2018–2020) has focused on the practice of co-creation as an approach to operationalize Responsible Research and Innovation (RRI). Aiming to bridge this gap, co-creation was developed as an approach deeply rooted in applied practices to foster the development of a set of innovations as answers to real and unmet challenges.

Given this framework, the approach embraced by the SISCODE project has been to consider co-creation as inherently bound to the notion of RRI and to develop it concretely as a bottom-up approach to the development of innovations that are meant to tackle societal challenges in 10 different co-creation labs across Europe. In doing so, SISCODE adopted various co-design methodologies (Deserti *et al.*, 2022). Furthermore, design and co-creation capacities were investigated as a new approach to be taken in and internalized for long-term change and impact on organizations and ecosystems.

Experiments were conducted through the implementation of co-creation journeys for around 18 months. In these experiments, each lab aimed to tackle a specific societal challenge, (meaningful for the context in which the lab is located, but, at the same time, transversal and relevant on a wider scale) and engaged with it a set of stakeholders in a co-creation process from the stage of co-design (e.g., analysis of the context, reframing of the problem, and envisioning alternatives) to that of co-production of prototypes in an iterative process. This process opens up many relevant issues related to how co-creation for RRI should be integrated within a specific organizational and institutional context, promoting more inclusive innovation to achieve better societal outcomes (Komatsu Cipriani *et al.*, 2021).

This chapter illustrates the findings on how co-creation can be embedded in processes of innovation development, which, in turn, results in producing solutions that are more responsible, and details how co-creation ecosystems, as contexts of/for RRI, can be implemented, how they work, and how they might develop over time. Insights on co-creation ecosystems reported in this chapter and the recommendations extracted for business contexts represent the synthesis of a comprehensive research activity in SISCODE based on the triangulation of data coming from: the analysis of the literature on RRI and its interactions with the notion of co-creation; the 10 long-term SISCODE experiments; and longitudinal studies of co-creation ecosystems across Europe using a database of 100 cases. The triangulation, as a systemic methodology to the data analysis, allowed the understanding of the changes and transformations needed in organizations, administration, techniques, procedures, and resources to embed co-creation into RRI ecosystems fully.

5.2 BACKGROUND, SCOPE, AND CHALLENGES

The notion of participatory approaches, such as co-creation, has grown significantly over the past years (Nazarko & Melnikas, 2019), calling for new processes in development and decision-making across sectors and fields. Co-creation has developed as a paradigm of innovation, involving stakeholders and end-users as co-creators, co-designers, and co-producers that recognize them as a precious source of knowledge and capacity for innovation (Vargo & Lusch, 2004; Von Hippel, 2007).

The SISCODE approach is based on the assumption that RRI and co-creation are interlinked, as co-creation is responsible in itself, because of its core principles of transparency, sharing and collaboration. In fact, to reach the project objectives, SISCODE has adopted the co-design approach, methodologies, and tools that have already been shown to be the most suitable knowledge domains to practice co-creation, starting from situated problems and developing solutions through a process of co-design and co-production that engages all the affected actors (Deserti *et al.*, 2022).

Since the early 2000s, in particular, the attention to include different stakeholder typologies in the process of developing innovation and value affected the notion of co-creation (Windrum *et al.*, 2016). Consequently, the idea of the ecosystem can be framed as a wider landscape, in which co-creation takes place, moving from a top-down to a bottom-up and user-driven innovation process (or combining top-down and bottom-up practices). Hence, citizen-driven innovation develops in co-creation ecosystems (Deserti *et al.*, 2021). The well-known triple helix innovation model, focusing on the relationship between university, industry, and government, first embeds a fourth helix, that of civil society and the culture-based public, and then includes the fifth helix of the environment and societal context (Carayannis & Campbell, 2010), and thereby gains a more comprehensive and ecologically sensitive perspective. Co-creation is situated in a framework that values and encourages the knowledge society and knowledge democracy as pillars for production and innovation. Different stakeholders enter the co-creation process with specific interests, motivations, and expectations, which need to be considered, managed, and included as promising sources of knowledge, thus, preventing differences in values, beliefs and needs from becoming potential barriers to innovation. Consequently, to set up novel models of interactions able to flow in new network configurations, the situated needs, specific competencies, expertise, and experiences of each actor have to be carefully taken into account.

The increasing complexity of systems, contexts, and stakeholder landscapes, as well as the prospects of co-creation, have evolved, leading to the development of the idea of a dynamic co-creation ecosystem. This ecosystem can be seen as an environment characterized by a dynamic bottom-up approach or a blended process of bottom-up and top-down initiatives. All co-creation processes involve a multitude of stakeholders and experience the influence of dynamics on a macro level, even when the co-creation initiative itself is conducted at a micro level (Geels, 2005; Moore *et al.*, 2015). Simultaneously, this connection implies the ability to scale initially small experiments on a niche level to large-scale ones that are able to impact policies, regulations, and established structures.

The SISCODE scope was to explore this potential by introducing an intermediate level defined as an interactive playground meant to function as a connection between the operative playground on the micro scale and the strategic playground at the macro scale (see Figure B5.1).

By investigating the findings and the insights from the small-scale experiments and observing the dynamic of these specific contexts, the project aimed at re-connecting the micro level with broader scales. To serve this scope, SISCODE implemented an intermediate-level playground based on reflective and collective learning and the activation of new processes and actors to be active as connectors. This connection level allowed a further definition of how co-creation ecosystems can be designed and evolve over time in relation to specific contexts and factors, and thereby provide concrete evidence on how co-creation and its ecosystems may support the operationalization of RRI.

The main challenges SISCODE has faced in the project's mission to operationalize RRI through co-creation have been related to the missing links between theory and practice in the RRI applications. The involvement of actors and stakeholders throughout the entire process until the implementation of the innovations in each of the experimental contexts, the lack of a co-creation culture in the actors involved, the lack of tools and practices to support the activation of the intermediate

Figure B5.1

SISCODE's Interaction Model between micro and macro dimensions of co-creation ecosystems

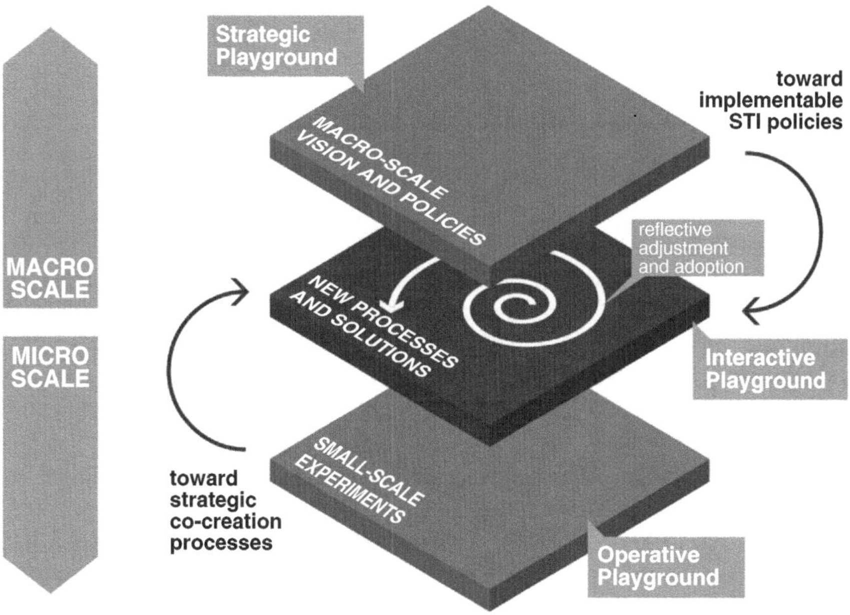

playground, as well as the need for evidence on the effectiveness of the process to influence policy-making and the missing proof of impact, are all indicators of the lack of understanding of co-creation as a complex phenomenon.

The highly complex nature of co-creation ecosystems was also revealed to be a challenge for the analysis and the development of recommendations. The multiple factors, levels, and extensions hampered the extraction of clear and unambiguous recommendations to be taken up by other practitioners of co-creation.

By following the earlier research within the project, the results from the ten SISCODE experiments, and by analyzing existing co-creation landscapes and cases, many signals for elaborating a dynamic model of co-creation emerged. This allowed the distinction of different instances, levels of maturity, and contexts of application. These categories needed to be further developed to do justice to the plurality of factors and their interrelation.

The direct dependency and interconnection of co-creation ecosystems with their surrounding context raised the issue of how even slight differences or shifts in the context can function both as opportunities or barriers for the ecosystem to evolve in relation to a specific instance. As a result, SISCODE investigated co-creation ecosystems, their building blocks, and dynamics as favorable environments for RRI operationalization.

5.3 APPROACH AND METHODS

On the basis of the theoretical groundwork regarding co-creation and underlying an open heuristic toward ecosystems of co-creation, SISCODE lined up to produce a profound comprehension of co-creation in practice and of the mechanisms affecting its implementation. Therefore, SISCODE aimed to generate an understanding of the configurations integral to co-creation practices, as well as of the transformative forces and dynamics within ecosystems of co-creation. Assuming a close relation between co-creation and social innovation, in which co-creation can be understood as an integral partial practice within phenomena of social innovation (cf. Eckhardt *et al.*, 2021), the concept of social innovation ecosystems (cf. Bason, 2010; Eckhardt *et al.*, 2017; Kaletka & Schröder, 2017; Pel *et al.*, 2020; Terstriep *et al.*, 2020). was applied to the research process in SISCODE. Alongside a multi-layered approach, functioning as a searchlight for the empirical data, four interrelated, non-selective, observation units were distinguished. On a (macro) normative level, the political and regulatory framework conditions were of interest, as well as societal attitudes and the specific "cultures of collaboration and innovation," which were assumed to be of impact regarding the success of co-creation initiatives. The context of structures then illustrates the meso level, as it asks for "constraints and path dependencies because of existing institutions, economic, political, and technological imperatives" (Eckhardt *et al.*, 2017, p. 85). Here, socio-economic and demographic parameters could be of relevance, but also infrastructural parameters and the structural alignment of, for example, a local-political landscape. With the level of roles, the heuristic moves toward the micro-perspective of actors, stakeholders, and beneficiaries of the co-creation routines, whereby their "political and social attitudes, motivations, socialization, self-concepts, image, capabilities, and skills" (Eckhardt *et al.*, 2017) are included. Within the fourth level, the context of functions, it asked for managerial aspects of the co-creation initiative, for how stakeholders get involved, how they are interlinked, how they collaborate and for the role design takes in the process. In addition, its modes of scaling, diffusion, and impact were examined. The interdependence of these layers was highlighted and iteratively carved out during the research process, leading to an impression of ecosystems of co-creation and the inherent drivers and barriers.

To gather the data necessary to understand ecosystem dynamics alongside the described approach, a mixed-methods research design for field research was developed. Figure B5.2 summarizes the design and shows the assets and workflow of the initiative, including information on the respective deliverables, which can be found online.[2]

In the three pillars of field research, both quantitative and qualitative data were gathered: (1) in a database; (2) in in-depth case-study research; and (3) in lab experiments conducted as action research.

1. **In the database**, 135 cases of co-creation were collected via desk research to generate a first, broad understanding and descriptive meta-analysis of practices

Figure B5.2
Workflow and elements of the analysis

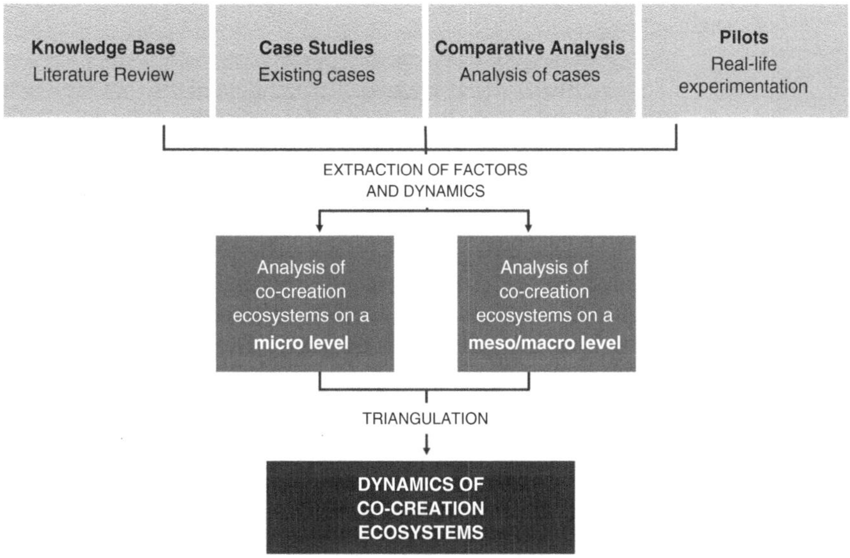

of co-creation in various contexts on a macro level. These cases, located mainly within EU countries, address several societal challenges, such as health, demographic change, wellbeing issues, Europe in a changing world, climate action, and questions of food security, energy efficiency, and sustainable mobility. They were not limited to the fields of RRI and policy-making, as the private sector was a part of the co-creation routines in the majority of cases.

2. **In the case studies**, the research focus shifted from the question of "what is actually going on in the field of co-creation?" to the examination of context-dynamics. The embeddedness of the practices, as well as their specific design and mode of operation, were now the focus. Furthermore, the interacting entities and the gradual description of contexts became important. To do so, 40 cases from the database were identified in a first step and examined following a specifically developed case study template. Some 15 cases were then identified as ones that could deliver profound information regarding the "biographical development" of the co-creation initiative to get closer to an understanding of ecosystems, relevant turning points in co-creation in practice, and the beneficial factors and obstacles.
3. **In ten co-creation labs**, planned co-creation processes alongside the SISCODE approach took place as action research across Europe. They all were members of the Fab City Foundation (managed in part by Fab Lab Barcelona), the European Network of Living Labs (ENoLL), or the European Network of Science Centres and Museums (Ecsite). The experiments were conducted through the implementation of SISCODE's co-creation journeys for around

18 months. On the one hand, knowledge of co-creation should be increased and the effectiveness of co-design methodologies to better integrate the phases of ideation and implementation was tested, whereby each lab aimed at a specific societal challenge.

The results were then triangulated via a systemic interpretation of the three research pillars tied back to the theoretical assumptions and to the ecosystems heuristic, allowing statements regarding the dynamics (in terms of drivers and barriers) and institutionalization (in terms of levels of implementation) of co-creation and its ability to cross-fertilize the fields of RRI and policy-making. Based on these categories, it was possible to derive further presuppositions to describe the maturity-levels of "ecosystems of co-creation" on a range from non-existent to far mature. Section 5.4 illustrates the results and lessons SISCODE was able to produce in a condensed form, highlighting implications for RRI and the transitions for industries and innovation management.

5.4 RESULTS AND LESSONS LEARNED

As a first result of the analysis, the dynamics of co-creation and the conditions of co-creation ecosystems were determined on the different heuristic levels from the micro to the macro perspective to build up a first set of influential factors regarding co-creation in practice. To do so, three analytical domains were identified from the theoretical groundwork and the data material conducted:

1. **Engaging**: As stakeholder engagement proved to be a critical phase during the co-creation processes, special attention was given to all activities leading to a reasonable and purposeful involvement of the relevant actors.
2. **Organizing**: Within this domain, internal processes, as well as cultural and organizational questions were raised, which could describe the "co-creative mindset" coming to light in the context of co-creation practices.
3. **Scaling**: While the first two domains are rather directed toward dynamics, meaning also the beneficial factors and obstacles, the scaling domain turns attention to the topic of institutionalization in terms of the outcomes and values of co-creation processes and their scalability and replicability beyond the project's lifetime.

From the knowledge gained in these research steps, a maturity scale of co-creation ecosystems was developed. It defines four different levels of maturity as ideal types (Weber, 1980) and, therefore, theoretical states which are unlikely to be found in practice, ranging from non-existent and somewhat existent to medium mature and far mature. Figure B5.3 illustrates the ideal types including a short description of their main features.

5.4.1 Far mature co-creation ecosystems

Far mature co-creation ecosystems were found mainly in cities and urban contexts with an established culture and tendency toward collaborative practices. Even

Figure B5.3
Maturity levels and their main characteristics

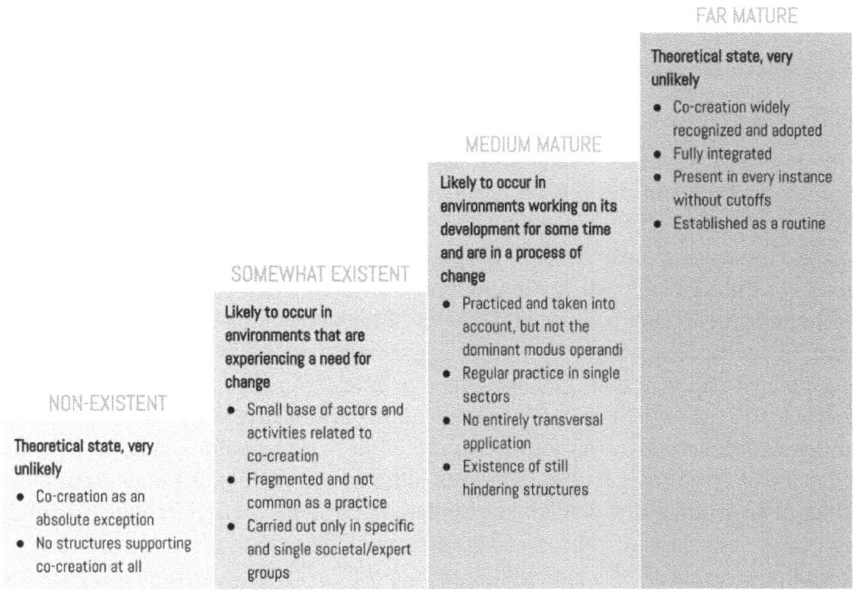

though some nearly corresponding situations were found during the elaboration, the far mature state remains a theoretical concept that is rather unlikely to occur in real-life settings, since there were always some remaining barriers identified that prevent the ecosystem from being entirely classified as far mature. On the other hand, the environments with co-creation embedded as a norm and remaining few obstacles allowed the extraction of some particular traits and characteristics of far mature ecosystems.

Co-creation may only be fully embedded when the current culture is sufficiently similar to allow this incorporation to be accepted and integrated. Often, these environments are already experienced in social innovation and are providing a policy context that favors democratic processes and citizen empowerment. The legislative frameworks in these contexts already implement shared decision-making in several fields and the sharing of knowledge is considered a normal practice, while knowledge asymmetries are continuously reflected. The values of participation and collaboration are established and determine practice. The full engagement of relevant actors in the processes of problem solving is a normalized societal process technology and the general will to uptake new co-creation practices is high.

Thereby, the full integration of co-creation also bears a number of risks when is becomes daily practice. The motivation of participants may decrease over time. Routines can also be established, where the same actors are always present, while others are being left out, risking that voices of smaller groups of interest are not considered.

Another risk related to the establishment of routines is that co-creation processes proven successful are continuously applied without being monitored or assessed further, and thereby become outdated and unresponsive to ongoing challenges and needs.

5.4.2 Medium mature co-creation ecosystems

Medium mature ecosystems are closer to reality than the highest level of far maturity, and were identified among the cases analyzed. In medium mature ecosystems, decision-making entities rely on participation to inform the public and to consult them in some parts of the decisions to be made, but the participation does not get beyond the stage of consultation of the public and relevant actors. At times, the public seems to experience "participation fatigue," because of past participation processes without purposeful outcomes. Some parts of the application context are generally open to questioning norms (e.g., of social (inter-)action, social practices of innovating, policy-making or living, etc.) and to overcome entrenched routines to take innovative pathways, and, therefore, progressive and participative policy agendas emerge and provide links and leeway for co-creation, while design methods and principles are known and sometimes applied. However, although co-creation is practiced in these kinds of environment, it is still being hindered by a series of barriers and structures, especially at the level of policies and governance. Often, these advances should come from upper levels of decision-making to support the already active practices at the citizens' level. Actors and groups of interest, like civil associations or communities, may be encouraged, supported in taking their actions further, develop, and implement solutions for real impact.

5.4.3 Somewhat existent co-creation ecosystems

The ecosystems classified as somewhat existent collaborative are similar to medium mature ones in terms of dynamics and structures, but the latter are less established and more fragmented across the ecosystem, lacking connection. Here, co-creation is not the usual practice (yet) and the single initiatives have little independence and range of action themselves. There are innovation policies already implemented, but not in the area in which the co-creation initiative is settled. For example, socio-political issues or communal development/spatial planning questions are already being solved collaboratively, but technical/ecological questions are treated "the old way," which means the possibilities of co-creation or participative policies are not recognized yet in large parts of the reference context.

There is a need to identify and engage additional actors and figures, who can help strengthen the fragile ecosystem and build it up further. These kinds of ecosystems are often beginning the process of integrating co-creation, which is often triggered by high, external pressure to change caused by pressing problems and challenges. This ongoing transformation process is positively showing the movement toward more collaborative practices, but their embedding will eventually take time.

5.4.4 Non-existent co-creation ecosystems

Non-existent collaborative ecosystems are characterized by the complete absence of co-creation practices and the environment is hostile to their introduction. At best, single initiatives or actor groups practice the active involvement of citizens and stakeholders and there is no broad vision on how co-creation could be permanently embedded across levels and disciplines. Often, in these cases, an initial reform of the policies and structures is necessary to enable the introduction of co-creation, as there are no official strategy papers implemented in the policy system. Furthermore, actors have to be identified (e.g., policymakers), who have to be informed about the benefits of participation and convinced to drive co-creation forward.

This also applies to the general population. As the traditional practices of solving things are top-down-oriented, there are no experiences in shared decision-making and participative approaches are generally perceived in a skeptical way, as large parts of society are interested in the preservation of traditional, established norms and values, and especially decision-makers tend to reject such approaches. If co-creation is to play a role in these contexts, the general public needs, first and foremost, to be informed about the topic, while also addressing existing values and norms to trigger a process of self-reflection and a progressive and collaborative culture.

5.4.5 Instances of the model of co-creation ecosystems

Acknowledging the complexity of co-creation ecosystems and recognizing that a single ecosystem may be more or less mature in relation to specific factors, the qualitative data of drivers and barriers was mapped to define seven descriptors of co-creation ecosystems. Each descriptor contains a set of specific factors and dynamics that influence co-creation. The seven dimensions identified are:

1. Infrastructure and context of co-creation
2. Knowledge exchange, learning, and organizational transformation
3. Culture of co-creation
4. Monitoring, assessment, and adaptation
5. Formalization of practices
6. Governance, interaction among actors, and mediation
7. Tangibility, the role of single initiatives and prototypes.

Each descriptor refers to different characteristics of the co-creation ecosystem, ensuring that the an empirical variety of ecosystems can be covered appropriately. While all instances are distinct, connecting the dimensions allows for the generation of the broader heuristics, showing different states of overall maturity (Figure B5.4). A more detailed and precise evaluation is enabled by considering the descriptors separately instead of forcing an overall judgment on the maturity of the ecosystem paired with general recommendations for improvement.

Figure B5.4
Dynamic model for the single instances of co-creation ecosystems

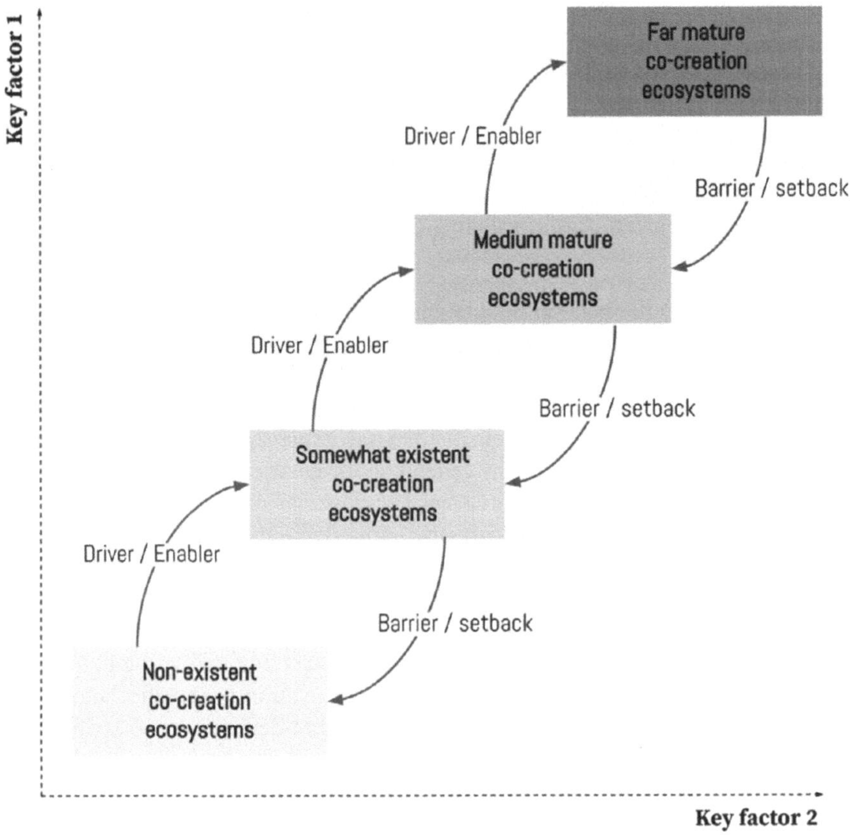

Each of these descriptors consists of a set of two key factors that, when combined, describe the maturity level of the system, as well as a set of specific drivers and barriers for each of the transition processes from one maturity level to the following one. By analyzing not only the levels of maturity, as a whole, but also for every instance, more detail is added to the drivers and barriers, which produces specific recommendations on how businesses can move forward in addressing the weaknesses identified in relation to a certain instance of co-creation. Figure B5.4 shows the model that was used for each of the instances to describe the specific enablers and setbacks characterizing the passage from one maturity level to another.

All instances listed are directly interconnected by dynamics (see Figure B5.5). This illustrates how the various instances, even though they may function as self-standing dimensions of analysis, are interdependent when shaping the overall ecosystem of co-creation.

Figure B5.5
Interrelation of the seven descriptors

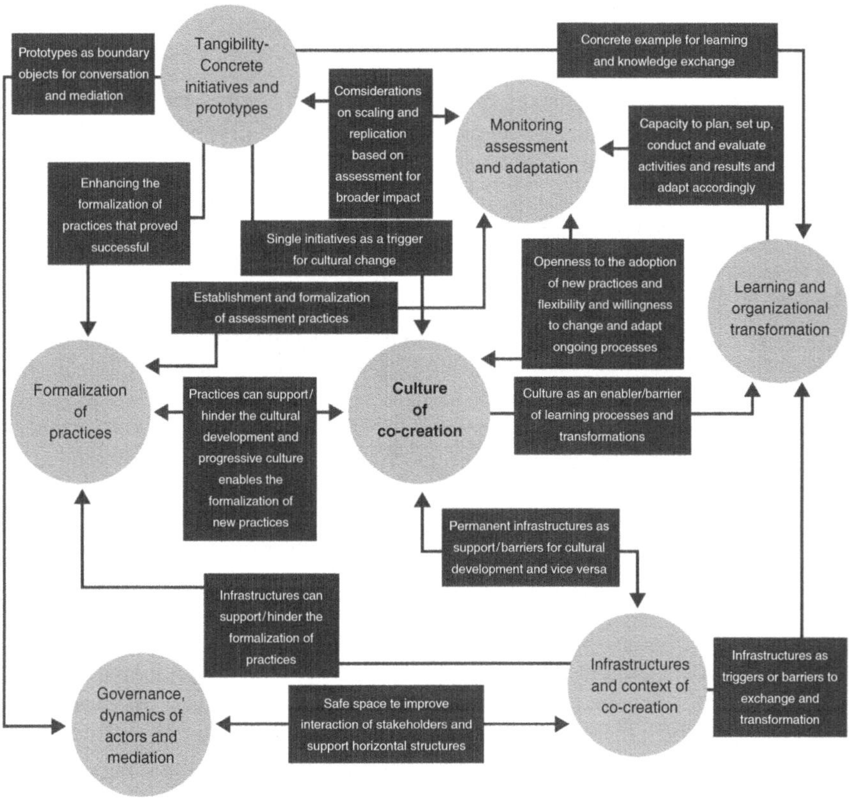

5.5 IMPLICATIONS FOR BUSINESSES

With RRI opening up innovation processes through co-creation to a broad spectrum of actors and all societal sectors, specifically including citizens and communities, businesses are in the midst of the game. With regard to the empirical results presented before, the implications for businesses can be summarized as follows:

- In mature co-creation ecosystems, businesses are initiators of RRI processes. They lead co-design solutions toward societal needs.
- In mature co-creation ecosystems, businesses actively participate in RRI processes from an early phase on, and they stay on board for the implementation and possible adaptation phases. This implies a number of challenges, for example, the need to prepare for and anticipate time-consuming phases for problem identification, which may be in conflict with the prevalent business culture.

- Businesses can enhance their performance in RRI operationalization by developing a culture of co-creation as part of their organizational culture. This culture can be developed and strengthened, i.e., through learning by projects and co-creation practices that can eventually be introduced, formalized, and standardized as daily practices in the company.
- Value creation actually means value co-creation: The different aspects of value, which define the organization's purpose and strategy beyond financial performance, can be co-defined and co-created with customers, investors, and other societal stakeholders. Such a strategy can increase the company's visibility and credibility and make them an important societal player.

The SISCODE project has put a strong focus on creating societal impacts through innovation. A number of service-based business models have been detailed and conceptualized in a way that puts co-creation processes and open innovation with, and for, society in the center (Glumac & Aibu, 2021). Through the lens of businesses, co-creation-based business models help to understand and make use of the value of stakeholders' involvement and provide opportunities for their self-empowerment, as well as fertilization of cross-sector and transdisciplinary collaboration.

In the course of the SISCODE project, primary emphasis has been placed on the service and the processes of innovation, with product innovation playing a subordinate role. Adopting co-creation for service and process innovations in businesses is a demanding process and requires a number of resources to be allocated: besides the usual suspects, competences are needed to introduce co-creation systematically and moderate the process as well as the conflicts. In the following, an example will be introduced which helps better understand and actively guide the implications of co-creation for businesses: First, a service design tool is detailed as one of the very concrete services developed within the SISCODE project. Second, the relevance of co-creation in the industrial digitalization processes will be explained.

In SISCODE, partners tailored Business Model Canvases and Customer Journey tools to their specific experimentation and applied them in a prototyping phase. The results were refined, reflecting on their application within the project to be then shared with the public as service-based business models. One of these examples is a service brief for knowledge-transfer and capacity building (cf. Glumac & Aibu, 2021, p. 35ff.), which addresses private and public businesses as a key target group. The tool was designed to make use of the experiences and knowledge acquired throughout the practice phase of the pilots and to make innovation communities, labs and their representatives, and private and public businesses familiar with co-creation methodologies:

> The labs have a relevant role in multiplying practice-based knowledge to other labs, practitioners and their communities. The labs have gained a substantial amount of knowledge and know-how on the application and adaptability of the SISCODE co-creation journey methodology and its tools … This service aims to ensure that the labs and networks jointly implement capacity-building activities

> for target audiences interested in adapting the journey for their own co-creation processes or simply acquiring knowledge on the subject.
>
> (Glumac & Aibu, 2021)

Therefore, using the tool also helps businesses to reflect on what happened during their co-creation journey, learn from these experiences, and develop competences for co-creation in different stakeholder constellations. What services can businesses expect from local labs? What is it that they themselves are expected to deliver? In addition, where can co-creation processes fail? This does not imply that businesses have to learn co-creation from scratch. Many have long-standing experiences in open innovation, one specific approach to co-creation. However, while open innovation is often about customer-oriented resourcing and usually a restricted collaboration with one stakeholder group, co-creation can also be about participating in more complex actor constellations with more potential for conflict. Here, learning systematically from experience is crucial for businesses and their co-creation partners.

Of course, it is important to note that co-creation with its different participatory approaches is not new to businesses and SISCODE did not work on a blank sheet. However, there are some notable tendencies and trends in the business world, including large industrial players, which currently lead to a more widespread use of co-creation and a more conscious conceptualization of R&I processes in this direction. Industries, such as the steel industry, increasingly have discovered the relevance of co-creation. They not only experiment and improve such approaches internally, for example, in industrial digitalization processes and innovative learning arrangements, for the development of new digital solutions, but also for a better understanding of, and integration into, local and regional communities:

> Co-creation practices based on social innovation processes show how new alliances and ecosystems are created (regional and local authorities, economic clusters and sector stakeholders, training providers and departments, companies and social partners), but also how new internal processes are implemented within companies and their employees in a collaborative way.
>
> (Kohlgrüber *et al.*, 2021, p. 10)

Without co-creative processes encompassing both the development and implementation of new solutions for internal and external challenges, the authors argue, the acceptance of innovations by suppliers and customers can suffer as much as the internal acceptance by employees (Kohlgrüber *et al.*, 2021, p. 1).

5.6 CONCLUSION AND RECOMMENDATIONS

A series of findings that can be translated into recommendations to be further considered from the innovation and responsible market perspectives have been identified in the following, in relation to the different scales, but also considering co-creation ecosystems as a whole and its relevance to more sustainable and responsible innovation.

The *importance of connecting and adapting co-creation to the specific context* became evident when designing specific journeys and roadmaps conscious of the surrounding environment. At the same time, tools and processes are to be selected and modified, paying attention to the involved stakeholders and the cultural, organizational, and structural characteristics of the context. The conscious planning, development, execution, and assessment of the process may result in the acquisition of both new competencies related to the application of tools, and soft skills to facilitate knowledge exchange and knowledge creation among actors.

Rather than employing a steady and pre-defined set of tools, it is necessary to provide guidelines on how to *select and adapt single methodologies and tools* from a toolbox and adapt them for the specific environment and situation of application. In doing so, the active engagement with co-creation tools and processes has been shown to be a facilitating factor for the longer-term adoption and integration of co-creation in organizational settings.

The intermediate playground developed and tested within SISCODE proved to be an effective way of *connecting bottom-up and top-down approaches* directed toward sustainable and responsible innovation. Moreover, the analysis highlights the problems deriving from the application of only one of the approaches: While top-down initiatives may be disentangled from actual needs and societal challenges to be solved, purely bottom-up experimentation often lacks a connection to existing policies and structures, and, therefore, support mechanisms for implementation. The results of the experimentation suggest a successful connection of both directions through co-creation.

A general need to *align the outputs and results of co-creation within policy-making procedures* emerged. The complexity of policies and policy development needs to be recognized and taken seriously, acknowledging the need to include the combination of top-down and bottom-up approaches to enable the development of effective solutions (Rizzo *et al.*, 2018). On the other hand, the connection of two such contrasting conceptions leads to conflicts and barriers when applied in practice (Kurath & Gisler, 2009; Smallman, 2020).

Tools and methodologies of co-creation can take a mediating and bridging role by facilitating dialogue, finding a common language, and working collaboratively toward a common goal. This function as a mediator is particularly relevant in environments dealing with complex and ill-defined problems, such as the one of policies and policy-making. Here, policies themselves can turn into objects of co-creation to transform abstract and challenging environments into a melting pot of diverse competences that work toward a structured, common goal (Rizzo *et al.*, 2018).

DISCLOSURE STATEMENT

No potential conflict of interest was reported by the authors.

FUNDING

The SISCODE project has received funding from the European Union's Horizon 2020 research and innovation program under grant agreement No 788217. The opinions expressed in this chapter reflect only the authors' view and in no way reflect the European Union's opinions.

NOTES

1. This work was supported by the European Union's Horizon 2020 Research and Innovation program under grant agreement No. 788217.
2. All deliverables of the SISCODE project are to be found on the project's homepage at https://siscodeproject.eu/resources/ (accessed March 2, 2022),

REFERENCES

Bason, C. (2010). *Leading public sector innovation: Co-creating for a better society.* The Policy Press.

Benington, J., & Moore, M. H. (Eds.) (2010). *Public value: Theory and practice.* Macmillan International Higher Education.

Carayannis, E. G., & Campbell, D. F. (2010). Triple Helix, Quadruple Helix and Quintuple Helix and how do knowledge, innovation and the environment relate to each other?: A proposed framework for a trans-disciplinary analysis of sustainable development and social ecology. *International Journal of Social Ecology and Sustainable Development (IJSESD), 1*(1), 41–69.

Deserti, A., Real, M., & Schmittinger, F. (2022). *Co-creation for Responsible Research and Innovation: Experimenting with design methods and tools.* Springer Nature.

Deserti, A., Rizzo, F., Kaletka, C., Eckhardt, J., Krüger, D., Schulz, A. C.; Crabu, S., & Schmittinger, F. (2021). Models of co-creation ecosystems, Deliverable 5.1. of the SISCODE project. Available at: www.siscodeproject.eu

Eckhardt, J., Kaletka, C., & Pelka, B. (2017). Inclusion through digital social innovations. Modelling an ecosystem of drivers and barriers. In *Universal access in human-computer interaction* (Part I, pp. 67–84). Springer.

Eckhardt, J. *et al.* (2021). Ecosystems of co-creation. *Frontiers in Sociology*, 6. Article 642289. doi:10.3389/fsoc.2021.642289.

Emery, S., Kendall, H., & Frewer, L. J. (2014). Independent evaluation of the public engagement with research and research engagement with society (PERARES) project. Available at: link.springer.com/chapter/10.1007/978-3-030.

Geels, F. W. (2005). *Technological transitions and system innovations: A co-evolutionary and socio-technical analysis.* Edward Elgar.

Glumac, T., & Aibu, O. (2021). SISCODE project. Available at: https://siscodeproject.eu/wp-content/uploads/2021/05/D6.4_SISCODE_Business_Model.pdf

Grönroos, C. (2012). Conceptualising value co-creation: A journey to the 1970s and back to the future. *Journal of Marketing Management, 28*(13–14), 1520–1534.

Jones, P. (2018). Contexts of co-creation: Designing with system stakeholders. In P. Jones & K. Kijima (Eds.), *Systemic design* (pp. 3–52). Springer.

Kaletka, C., & Schröder, A. (2017). A global mapping of social innovations: Challenges of a theory driven methodology. *European Public & Social Innovation Review*, *2*(1), 78–92.

Kohlgrüber, M., Maldonado-Mariscal, K., & Schröder, A. (2021). Mutual learning in innovation and co-creation processes: Integrating technological and social innovation. *Frontiers in Education*, *6*. https://www.frontiersin.org/articles/10.3389/feduc.2021.498661/

Kohlgrüber, M., & Schröder, A. (2019). Innovation reloaded. The social character of digitalisation in industry. In *Atlas of social innovation*, vol. 2: *A world of new practices* (pp. 47–49). Oekom.

Komatsu Cipriani, T., Deserti, A., & Rizzo, F. (2021). The role of design research in and for social innovation. In J. Howaldt, C, Kaletka, & A, Schröder (Eds.), *A research agenda for social innovation*. Edward Elgar Publishing.

Kurath, M., & Gisler, P. (2009). Informing, involving or engaging? Science communication, in the ages of atom-, bio- and nanotechnology. *Public Understanding of Science*, *18*(5), 559–573.

Moore, M. L., Riddell, D., & Vocisano, D. (2015). Scaling out, scaling up, scaling deep: Strategies of non-profits in advancing systemic social innovation. *Journal of Corporate Citizenship*, *58*, 67–84.

Nazarko, L., & Melnikas, B. (2019). Operationalising Responsible Research and Innovation–tools for enterprises. *Engineering Management in Production and Services*, *11*(3), 21–28.

Pel, B., Wittmayer, J., Dorland, J., & Søgaard Jørgensen, M. (2020). Unpacking the social innovation ecosystem: An empirically grounded typology of empowering network constellations. *Innovation: The European Journal of Social Science Research, 33*(3), 311–336.

Prahalad, C. K. (2004). The cocreation of value in 'invited commentaries' on 'evolving to a new dominant logic for marketing'. *Journal of Marketing*, *68*(1), 18–27.

Ramaswamy, V., & Ozcan, K. (2014). *The co-creation paradigm*. Stanford University Press.

Rizzo, F., Deserti, A., Crabu, S., Smallman, M., Hjort, J., Hansen, S., & Menichinelli, M. (2018). Co-creation in RRI practices and STI policies (D1.2) SISCODE project, EU Commission. Available at :www.siscodeproject.eu.

Schmittinger F., Rizzo F., & Deserti A. (2020). Experimenting design thinking in RRI as model of knowledge exchange between bottom-up initiatives and policy making. In *Proceedings of IFKAD, 15th International Forum on Knowledge Asset Dynamics*, September 9–11, Matera.

Smallman, M. (2020). 'Nothing to do with the science': How an elite sociotechnical imaginary cements policy resistance to public perspectives on science and technology through the machinery of government. *Social Studies of Science*, *50*(4), 589–608.

Stilgoe, J., Owen, R., & Macnaghten, P. (2020). Developing a framework for responsible innovation. In A. Maynard & J. Stilgoe (Eds.), *The ethics of nanotechnology, geoengineering and clean energy* (pp. 347–359). Routledge.

Terstriep, J., Rehfeld, D., & Kleverbeck, M. (2020). Favourable social innovation ecosystem(s)?: An explorative approach. *European Planning Studies*, *28*(5), 881–905.

Vargo, S. L., & Lusch, R. F. (2014). *Evolving to a new dominant logic for marketing* (pp. 21–46). Routledge.

Von Hippel, E. (2007). Horizontal innovation networks—by and for users. *Industrial and Corporate Change*, *16*(2), 293–315.

Voorberg, W. H., Bekkers, V. J., & Tummers, L. G. (2015). A systematic review of co-creation and co-production: Embarking on the social innovation journey. *Public Management Review*, *17*(9), 1333–1357.

Weber, M. (1980). *Wirtschaft und Gesellschaft: Grundriss der verstehenden Soziologie*. Mohr Siebeck.

Windrum, P., Schartinger, D., Rubalcaba, L., Gallouj, F., & Toivonen, M. (2016). The co-creation of multi-agent social innovations: A bridge between service and social innovation research. *European Journal of Innovation Management*, *19*(2), 150–166.
Zwart, H., Landeweerd, L., & Van Rooij, A. (2014). Adapt or perish? Assessing the recent shift in the European research funding arena from 'ELSA'to 'RRI'. *Life Sciences, Society and Policy*, *10*(1), 1–19.

SeeRRI

Duration:	January 1, 2019–October 31, 2021
Total cost:	€2,031,612.50
EU contribution:	€2,031,612.50
Contract No.:	824588

Coordinator:

- NORDLANDSFORSKNING AS (Norway)

Participants:

- AIT AUSTRIAN INSTITUTE OF TECHNOLOGY GMBH (Austria)
- FUNDACIÓN INSTITUTO DE INVESTIGACIÓN INNAXIS (Spain)
- WEDO PROJECT INTELLIGENCE MADE EASYSL (Spain)
- RESEARCH AND INNOVATION MANAGEMENT GMBH (Austria)
- UNIVERSITY OF HAIFA (Israel)
- ALMA MATER STUDIORUM – UNIVERSITA DI BOLOGNA (Italy)
- UNIVERSIDAD AUTONOMA DE BARCELONA (Spain)
- DEPARTAMENT D'ECONOMIA I HISENDA (Spain)
- ECOPLUS.NIEDERÖSTERREICHS WIRTSCHAFTSAGENTUR GMBH (Austria)
- NORDLAND FYLKESKOMMUNE (Norway)
- NAERINGSLIVETS HOVEDORGANISASJON (Norway)

https://cordis.europa.eu/project/id/824588

B6

SeeRRI

Bridging the gap between Responsible Innovation and environmental economics

Jens Ørding Hansen and Nhien Nguyen

6.1 INTRODUCTION

The concept of Responsible Research and Innovation (RRI) has been gaining traction in recent years, in policy-making circles, as well as in the academic literature (Hansen *et al.*, 2020). The overriding goal of RRI is to align research and innovation (R&I) with the values and needs of society (Burget *et al.*, 2017). With this goal in mind, the literature on RRI emphasizes the need for participative R&I processes that give stakeholders from different sectors of society a voice on where research and innovation is headed (Lubberink *et al.*, 2017; Owen *et al.*, 2012) This chapter explores the business implications of such stakeholder engagement activities.

In an influential conceptual framework by Stilgoe *et al.* (2013), the inclusion of a diverse range of stakeholders in decision-making is presented as one of four key dimensions of RRI. While inclusiveness is a cherished value in most democratic societies in and of itself, the justification for emphasizing the role of stakeholder participation in RRI lies in the realization that R&I activities are difficult to govern through top-down government regulation alone for two reasons (Stilgoe *et al.*, 2013). First, the future trajectory and consequences of R&I are exceptionally hard to foresee. Policy-makers, if left to their own devices, are liable to make non-optimal R&I policy decisions based on biased or incorrect views of the future. Second, R&I activities have complex social, ethical, and political implications. As mentioned, the ultimate purpose of RRI is to align R&I activities with the values and needs of society. Since it is not always obvious what the values of society are, let alone how those values may manifest themselves in the context of specific technological dilemmas, an element of bottom-up democratic participation is desirable in the governance and monitoring of science and innovation.

DOI: 10.4324/9781003319481-19

Viewed from a business-sector perspective, RRI joins other concepts, such as corporate social responsibility (CSR) and environmental, social, and corporate governance (ESG), in focusing attention on the ethical and environmental obligations of decision-makers in business and industry. RRI distinguishes itself by focusing explicitly on research and innovation activities, whereas the other related concepts have a broader scope. In the business context, one question worth pondering is whether RRI is simply a chore for firms, something they may practice out of a sense of duty, but which does not bring them any benefits, or whether there is, in fact, a business case to be made for RRI. The fledgling academic literature on RRI provides little in the way of answers to this question.

We may look to the literature on CSR for clues, as CSR has been studied and practiced for much longer than RRI. The CSR literature presents mixed evidence on whether companies' "socially responsible" conduct is associated with economic benefits (Bhardwaj *et al.*, 2018). It appears that CSR and economic performance may be connected, but it is difficult to disentangle the causal mechanisms involved (Ferrell *et al.*, 2016) and, therefore, hard to conclude that CSR brings economic benefits that outweigh its costs. We expect that the question of whether RRI is good for business will prove equally resistant to simple answers. Companies that engage in RRI in the hope of increasing their profits are likely to be disappointed in the short term. RRI activities are costly, and any economic benefits they may bring are likely to be of a long-term nature.

Nevertheless, we are intrigued by the idea that RRI might be good for business in addition to bringing benefits to society and the environment. The literature on RRI claims that we need RRI in order to solve societal challenges, but has largely neglected to propose incentive mechanisms for industrial actors to get involved in RRI beyond appealing to their conscience. If there is a legitimate economic argument to be made for practicing RRI, this could make it easier to persuade actors from the business sector to get on board the RRI train. In this chapter, we will develop an argument for why stakeholder engagement can be good for business, drawing on theory from environmental economics, as well as empirical observations from the Horizon 2020 project "Building Self-Sustaining Research and Innovation Ecosystems in Europe through Responsible Research and Innovation," or SeeRRI for short.[1]

The aim of the SeeRRI project, which took place from January 2019 to October 2021, was to develop and implement a process for bringing RRI into regional planning by engaging regional stakeholders in the creation of a regional strategy for R&I. SeeRRI experimented with initiatives in several European regions. One of these regions was Lower Austria, where actors, representing the plastics industry, were interested in exploring how RRI could help improve the image of their industry. We will use the experience of these actors in the SeeRRI project to support our theoretical argument that RRI can be good for business and create economic value for the benefit of all stakeholders, especially in industries with a controversial environmental track record.

While the RRI and environmental economics literatures are thematically overlapping, they contrast sharply in that the former tends to ignore the role of individual economic incentives whereas the latter focuses almost exclusively on self-interest as the driver of agents' behavior. We aim to help bridge the gap between the two research streams by exploring how the tools of RRI can be used to tackle obstacles to achieving efficient outcomes under the assumption that actors respond rationally to economic incentives. (Of course, we do not claim that responsible innovators ought to be motivated *only* by self-interest.) Our findings are of particular relevance to practitioners from industries burdened with a public image problem who are looking for ways to gain or regain the trust of the public.

The remainder of the chapter proceeds as follows. Next, we outline our theoretical argument, explaining why it may be in the self-interest of business actors to engage actively in RRI. Section 6.3 addresses several potential counter-arguments to our argument drawn from the existing RRI literature. The RRI methodology developed in SeeRRI is then introduced and Section 6.4 argues for the relevance of this methodology to the business case for RRI. SeeRRI's attempt at promoting RRI in the plastics sector in Lower Austria is presented and uses the takeaways from this experience to illustrate how RRI can be good for business. The chapter concludes with recommendations for future practice.

6.2 PROPOSING A BUSINESS CASE FOR RRI

A key concept in our analysis in this chapter is *asymmetric information.* Asymmetric information refers to a situation where some parties possess more or better information of relevance to the situation than other parties (Tietenberg & Lewis, 2018). Intuitively, having an information advantage might seem like a blessing. It is obvious that proprietary information can be a source of competitive advantage for firms. Sometimes, however, economic actors with an information advantage would be better off if they could eliminate the asymmetry, as doing so would make it easier for them to obtain full recognition of the value of their offerings and increase their scope for engaging in mutually beneficial transactions with other actors (Samuelson, 1984). Eliminating information asymmetries is not as easy as it sounds. In this chapter, we will look at the potential role of RRI in doing so.

As technological advances continue to erode barriers to the free flow of information, it is conceivable that a narrowing of information asymmetries is taking place in specific sectors of the economy, for example, among traders in financial markets (Marszk & Lechman, 2021). Nevertheless, asymmetric information phenomena remain pervasive and sometimes appear to be immune to the disruptive effects of enhanced information access. For example, the public has better access to information about science and technology than ever before, yet distrust in science appears to be on the rise, reflecting the public's difficulties in untangling the complex implications of R&I and their sense of being at the mercy of actors with information superior to their own (Aupers, 2012). One prominent example from recent times is the skepticism seen in many societies toward vaccines developed to combat the COVID-19 pandemic. Even intensive government-sponsored information campaigns and near-unanimous endorsement of COVID-19 vaccination by the medical community failed to convince millions of skeptics around the world that being vaccinated against COVID-19 was a good idea (Sallam, 2021).

The COVID-19 example illustrates an important point: as the accessibility and complexity of information continue to increase, asymmetric information issues no longer derive merely from differences in *access* to information; increasingly, they stem from discrepancies in stakeholders' ability to interpret information and assess its accuracy. Eliminating information asymmetries involves more than simply dispensing raw data to all interested parties. It requires a patient effort on the part of information providers to establish credibility, as well as a collaborative, open-minded effort of all stakeholders to develop a shared appreciation of the different lenses through which the information may be viewed. As we shall see, this is something RRI is designed to deliver.

Our business case for RRI goes like this. If an industry produces a product that is in high demand, but also has actual or potential negative impacts on the environment, the industry will rightfully be viewed with suspicion by regulators and consumers. Regulators, aware that profit motives may lead some industry actors to engage in unethical conduct, will seek to constrain such behavior by means of rules and regulations. Meanwhile, environmentally conscious consumers will try to use the power of their purchasing decisions to reward ethical behavior and disincentivize unethical conduct in the industry.

Unfortunately, regulators and consumers possess only imperfect knowledge. Worse, the stakeholder group with the most knowledge of the current and potential future environmental harm caused by the industry is the industry itself, owing to their direct involvement in the harmful activities (Field & Field, 2016). In other words, the group with the greatest information advantage is also the group with the greatest incentive to exploit this information for their own gain.

The information asymmetry between the industry, on the one hand, and consumers and regulators, on the other, presents an example of what is known in economics as the "lemon problem" (Akerlof, 1978). Even if an environmentally conscious industry actor were to invest resources in developing and marketing a product with genuinely superior sustainability features, a subset of environmentally conscious consumers might lack the ability to distinguish between genuine and false sustainability claims in the market and would unwittingly opt for a less environmentally friendly product instead. The environmentally conscious industry actor would predict this outcome *ex ante*. In the worst case, he or she might decide to forego the investment entirely, even though the product would have been financially viable if consumers were better informed. Asymmetric information has led to market failure of the environmentally friendly product.

A similar argument applies to the relationship between industry and regulators. Suppose environmental regulators wield the tools at their disposal – such as taxation – in a way that fails to reward innovation aimed at reducing negative externalities in an industry. Well-meaning industry actors may try to convince the regulators that the regulations should be changed, but the regulators, who are at an information disadvantage and imbued with sound skepticism, may struggle to distinguish between valid and spurious arguments coming from the industry. As a result, the regulations might not get changed.

Environmental economics suggests several avenues to resolving such problems. For example, in the case of emissions regulations, regulators may adopt a flexible scheme that obviates the need for them to try to obtain detailed information about industry actors and their production processes. Consider an emissions tax scheme that allows businesses to emit any amount of pollutants they want, but charges them a tax based on the quantity they emit. Such a scheme incentivizes businesses to use their private information to find the economically optimal balance between paying emissions taxes and incurring innovation costs to try to reduce emissions (Field & Field, 2016).

However, even such approaches have limitations rooted in asymmetric information. For example, in the case just discussed, regulators cannot predict how businesses will respond to the scheme or how much pollution they will choose to emit. We propose adding RRI methods to the toolbox. By this, we mean creating structures and activities that engage all relevant actors in the ecosystem around an industry – government, academia, and civil society, in addition to the industry itself – in direct dialogue to enhance mutual understanding, lower asymmetric information, and increase trust across the ecosystem. It is not simply a case of the business sector representatives "sacrificing" their private information for the benefit of other participants. All attending stakeholders possess unique information, which they contribute as part of the information exchange. The process of collective enlightenment helps good companies identify new business opportunities while simultaneously enhancing their legitimacy. One example of such an RRI process is the one designed by the SeeRRI project, which, as we shall see later, encourages constructive stakeholder collaboration in several ways that are amenable to analysis through the lens of asymmetric information.

6.3 COUNTER-ARGUMENTS TO OUR BUSINESS CASE

The topic of asymmetric information is familiar in the RRI literature. We are not the first to suggest that asymmetric information plays a significant role in RRI and stakeholder engagement processes, yet the view of that role commonly encountered in the literature is quite different from the perspective we present in this chapter. While we focus on the potential for RRI activities to reduce asymmetric information, the more popular notion is that asymmetric information presents a barrier to realizing the ideals of RRI (Blok & Lemmens, 2015; Borch & Throne-Holst, 2021; da Silva *et al.*, 2019; Salvini *et al.*, 2019). It is argued that knowledge disparities between different stakeholder groups may hinder effective dialogue and cause a significant imbalance of power, which conflicts with the ideal of inclusiveness that lies at the heart of RRI (Borch & Throne-Holst, 2021). Power imbalances also engender mistrust and are a threat to effective collaboration (Bryson *et al.*, 2006).

Another important point mentioned in the literature is that stakeholders who enjoy an information advantage may be protective of the advantage it gives them. This is especially true of stakeholders from the business sector. Blok and Lemmens (2015) point out that information asymmetries are a critical source of competitive advantage for innovative companies and argue that it would be "highly naïve" to think that such companies would be willing to forgo valuable private information for the sake of transparency toward other stakeholders. On the contrary, such companies often face a temptation to exploit their information advantage in unethical ways (Millar *et al.*, 2012). This observation is ironic, because it suggests that participating in RRI processes can, indeed, be good for business – if only because the informationally privileged company may seek to exploit the process to further their own agenda at the expense of other stakeholders' interests. Of course, this cannot be considered true RRI. For this and other reasons, Blok and Lemmens (2015) conclude that the idealized vision of RRI that has taken shape in the literature will never materialize in the real world.

We do not dispute the validity of any of these points. Neither of them directly refutes the business case for RRI that we outlined above, but they undeniably coexist with it. There are two sides to the asymmetric information coin. There may be benefits to keeping information private and there may be benefits to sharing it; sometimes the former outweighs the latter, sometimes not. A stakeholder engagement process that maximizes stakeholders' incentive to share information openly, while minimizing their incentive to keep information private, has the greatest chance of succeeding.

The practical question is: under which circumstances does the incentive for sharing information eclipse the incentive for not doing so? This question is important, because we cannot assume that the business sector will be willing to share information with other stakeholders if they perceive that doing so would jeopardize their competitive position in the market. The answer to the question may help policy-makers – such as the European Union, which has been championing RRI – create framework conditions that incentivize the business sector to share information. It might also help the business sector see the value in doing so. In our search for an answer, we will make use of empirical data from the SeeRRI project. Section 6.4 describes SeeRRI's approach to RRI and the role of the Lower Austrian plastics sector in the project. Then, we will draw on the SeeRRI experience in Lower Austria to attempt an answer to our question.

6.4 RESPONSIBLE RESEARCH AND INNOVATION IN PRACTICE: THE SEERRI WAY

6.4.1 The SeeRRI project

The Horizon 2020 project "Building Self-Sustaining Research and Innovation Ecosystems in Europe through Responsible Research and Innovation," or SeeRRI for short, took place from January 2019 to October 2021 and involved 12 partner organizations from 5 European countries. The aim of the project was to develop and implement a process for bringing RRI into regional planning by engaging regional stakeholders in the creation of a regional strategy for R&I. The resulting "SeeRRI process" comprises three stages (Nguyen *et al.*, 2021; Nguyen *et al.*, 2022).

In the first stage, regional policy-makers define a "core challenge" that the strategy will address. This focus on a specific challenge serves to reduce the complexity of the process and make it more manageable for the stakeholders who will be involved in the subsequent stages.

In the second stage, foresight workshops are organized, at which a diverse group of stakeholders from the region are invited to participate. In accordance with the RRI principle of inclusion, and to ensure a balanced representation of societal interests, the entire "quadruple helix" of government, academia, industry, and civil society must be represented. At the workshops, the invited stakeholders work together to envision possible future scenarios for the region and suggest measures the region can take today to put itself on a trajectory toward a desirable future. A shared vision and agenda are created. The regional government synthesizes the outputs from the workshops to produce a coherent regional strategy.

In the third stage, the regional strategy is jointly implemented by all relevant stakeholders. The experiences and lessons learned from the co-creation and implementation processes are shared and exchanged with other regions interested in the approach. When a new core challenge is ssidentified, the process starts over again. Figure B6.1 illustrates the SeeRRI process.

Figure B6.1
The SeeRRI process

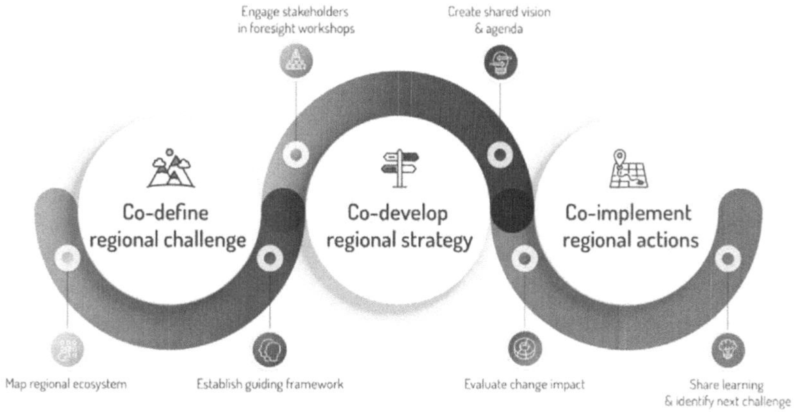

Source: Nhien Nguyen with graphic design by Mario Magaña.

The SeeRRI process is designed to maximize the chance that participants will feel encouraged to provide relevant and accurate information and share it with each other in a spirit of collaboration. In group work at the workshops, groups are mixed, so that stakeholders from different branches of the quadruple helix are forced to work together. This procedure lowers the risk of collusion among participants with a similar background and rewards participants' efforts to understand the perspectives of stakeholders with a different background to their own. If all stakeholder groups trust that the process is not biased against them, they will be more likely to engage in the process in a collaborative manner.

Most of the foresight process is deliberately *not* aimed at reaching agreement on one particular future scenario as the "best" one. Rather, the overriding objective is to delineate a wide variety of scenarios, some of which might (indeed, should) favor the fortunes of particular stakeholder groups over others. By allowing participants to explore a range of alternative future scenarios, the foresight process avoids a turf war between stakeholders with opposing interests. The process is designed to expose conflicts of interest among stakeholders without being distorted by some stakeholders' efforts to prevail over competing stakeholders in those conflicts. The scenarios draw attention to the existence of trade-offs between different societal objectives and the need to balance the interests of different groups of stakeholders. Stakeholders with divergent interests can only agree on a "middle way" if they have some shared understanding of where the middle is located. Mapping out the extreme scenarios of the possibility space helps to achieve this.

The SeeRRI approach is not designed to be applied exclusively in ecosystems centered on a polluting product or technology; it is envisioned as a more general tool for regional planning. However, we will argue that the approach and, indeed, the practice of RRI, in general, have a particular economic justification in such ecosystems. The method was tested in three European regions: Nordland (Norway), Lower Austria, and the B30 economic area in Catalonia, Spain. One of these regions – Lower Austria – provided a context and regional challenge that makes it particularly relevant for our purposes in this chapter.

6.4.2 The Lower Austria case in SeeRRI

The key actors involved in implementing the SeeRRI process in Lower Austria were the Austrian Institute of Technology (AIT), the Business Agency of Lower Austria (ecoplus), which has close ties to the plastics industry, and the Office of the Federal Government of Lower Austria (Hörlesberger *et al.*, 2021). Thus, three of the four branches of the quadruple helix were represented already from the start: academia, industry, and government. As prescribed by the SeeRRI model, the Lower Austrian actors defined a core challenge that would be the focus of the stakeholder engagement process: "The plastics industry in Lower Austria will contribute significantly to a climate-compatible, environmentally friendly, resource-conserving economy through research and development of products, taking into account the entire value chain" (Nguyen *et al.*, 2021).

The background for this choice was the actors' perception that the plastics industry in Lower Austria had a very one-sided negative public image, and that society was lacking awareness of the importance and responsible use of polymers. The team saw SeeRRI as an opportunity for the plastics industry in Lower Austria to renew itself and demonstrate its commitment to innovation for sustainability by reaching out to stakeholders and inviting them to take part in the work to develop a shared vision for the industry.

From an RRI perspective, this sort of stakeholder outreach requires no justification: involving stakeholders in drafting a strategy for innovation in a controversial industry like plastics is simply RRI in action. At the same time, the initiative in Lower Austria also makes sense from the perspective of managing the negative consequences of asymmetric information. The plastics industry wanted to improve its image. It could have tried to do so through a unilateral information campaign, but the effects would have been diminished by the public's mistrust. Sometimes it is hard to get rid of one's information advantage even if one actively tries to share information with others. A more effective way to convince stakeholders of the sincerity of one's commitment to an approach is to invite them to join in and co-create the approach, which is what the Lower Austrian SeeRRI team did.

This is the starting point for us to address the question of how, and under which conditions, an RRI approach can provide incentives for the business sector to share information with other stakeholders. Our findings, presented in the next section, embody our reflections on the processes and outcomes we observed in the SeeRRI project, especially in Lower Austria.

6.5 ADDRESSING THE COUNTER-ARGUMENTS: FINDINGS FROM THE SEERRI PROJECT

Above, we described how several studies have argued that asymmetric information can be a barrier to RRI, because innovation actors are protective of their private information. We do not object to this argument, but suggest that it may be possible to design a co-creation process that provides benefits to sharing information that outweigh the incentives to keeping it private. In what follows, we will propose five factors that we believe can increase the chances that actors from industry will see a potential benefit from getting involved in genuine RRI-style stakeholder engagement activities. The first factor is given by external circumstances outside of the control of the organizers of the RRI process. The remaining four factors can be brought about by design.

1. *It helps if the industry suffers from a negative public image that actors from the industry perceive to be unfair.* We have noted previously that polluters know pollution best. If an industrial actor feels that they have been lucky to escape attention for practices that would attract controversy if they became widely known, they have little to gain from open information exchange and may prefer to keep a low profile. On the other hand, if they feel that their industry

has been targeted to an unfair degree by regulators and the public, they have little to lose from sharing their views on the matter with other stakeholders. This was the case with the Lower Austrian plastics industry in the SeeRRI project.

2. *It is important that the entire "quadruple helix" of innovation actors, i.e., actors from industry, academia, government, and civil society, be involved in the process.* For industrial actors in polluting industries to engage in dialogue with regulators and other government representatives is nothing new. Indeed, regulators often rely to some extent on information from industry to do their job. It is also common for industrial actors to voluntarily provide information to regulators in an attempt to influence them, e.g., to induce them to lower taxes or relax standards. Unsurprisingly, the information thus provided is often incorrect or misleading; businesses frequently understate the environmental impact of their activities and overstate the costs imposed on them by regulatory measures, in order to make a case for less stringent regulation (Field & Field, 2016). The checks and balances provided by the presence of a broad range of stakeholders, each possessing unique information and expertise, lowers the benefits from opportunistic behavior and helps the industrial actors focus their energies on RRI, i.e., on joint initiatives that will benefit the entire ecosystem, including themselves.
3. *The topics for debate at the stakeholder events should take a long and broad view.* The stakeholder dialogue should not be focused on the nitty-gritty details of current regulations or production processes, but on the long-term future of the ecosystem. In such a future-oriented dialogue, industrial actors have less incentive to misrepresent information, because the discussion focuses less on current practices or technologies, in which they are heavily invested and which they have an incentive to defend, and more on potential future possibilities to which they are as yet uncommitted. The idea is to focus on topics that are very important to the participants, but not yet urgent enough to lure them into short-sighted opportunistic positions. All things being equal, the relatively weak incentive to present biased information enhances the credibility of the information provided by all stakeholder groups, including the industrial actors, and helps to reduce asymmetric information between them.
4. *The stakeholder dialogue should concern the future of the ecosystem as a whole and its impact on society and the environment.* The ultimate objective should be to strengthen the ecosystem while making *all* the involved actors more responsible and accountable in the process. An ecosystem with fair and just governance that rewards good behavior and penalizes misdeeds, and whose "green" innovations are recognized as such by consumers and regulators alike, is in the long-term interest of all stakeholders. Since the future of the ecosystem is not a zero-sum game, industrial actors are less likely to be bogged down in a stubborn defense of narrow self-interest when discussing it. Again, this characteristic of the participatory process enhances the credibility of the information provided by the industrial actors, which, in turn, helps to reduce asymmetric information between them and other stakeholders.

5. *A variety of representatives from industry should take part in the RRI process together.* If only one industrial actor participates, this actor will have an incentive to magnify their own experience and misrepresent their unique perspective as reflective of the interests of a larger universe of companies. If more businesses are represented in the process, the incentive of each participant shifts toward working for the interests of the ecosystem. If the process involves group work, it is important that the stakeholders are shuffled so that industry actors are forced to work with stakeholders of a different background. Again, the idea is to create conditions where the incentive for providing low quality, misleading information for short-term private benefit is as weak as possible while the incentive for exchanging high-quality, accurate information that fosters genuine mutual understanding and helps develop the community along a healthy path is as strong as possible.

Let us take a closer look at how some of these factors manifested themselves in practical terms in the case of the Lower Austrian plastics industry in the SeeRRI project. First, the plastics industry plays a complex role in modern society, because plastics are indispensable in many products, yet are also a major source of pollution and a contributor to climate change. The industry is justifiably viewed with suspicion, but the skepticism gives rise to a risk that the valuable contributions of the industry to the economy and society are overlooked. In SeeRRI, the representatives of the Lower Austrian plastics industry felt that the industry was unfairly maligned, and this was an important motivator for them to engage in dialogue with stakeholders (cf. factor 1 above).

Four stakeholder workshops were held in Lower Austria, with up to 30 participants in each. Participants represented the entire quadruple helix (factor 2 above) and included a variety of representatives from the plastics industry (factor 5 above). The details of all the activities at the workshops are beyond the scope of this chapter, but the foresight exercises eventually resulted in the creation of four hypothetical scenarios for Lower Austria in 2045, with the following titles:

- "Everything will be okay"
- "No rules, just profit" (fat industry)
- "Happy World and Greta smiles"[2]
- "World without plastics"

As can be seen at a glance, these scenarios cover a lot of ground. Interestingly, the most pro-plastic scenario and the most anti-plastic scenario both come across as thoroughly unattractive worlds to inhabit. "No rules, just profit" is a bleak vision of capitalism run amok. "World without plastics" is an even more dystopian scenario in which the prohibition of plastics leads to a catastrophic decline in living standards. The stakeholders at the workshops seem to have reached consensus that the best place to be is somewhere in between these two extremes. Such a consensus was possible because the debate took a long and broad view (factor 3 above) and because the dialogue concerned the future of the ecosystem as a whole (factor 4 above).

Workshop participants reported that co-creating such concrete future scenarios was a valuable exercise that helped open their minds. However, lest we forget the topic of this chapter: was it good for business? As always, it would be unwise to expect too much of a direct economic benefit for the industrial actors, but the SeeRRI process in Lower Austria seems to have generated a substantial impact after the workshops in the form of new collaborations and initiatives inspired by the project, including cross-sector initiatives (Kasztler *et al.*, 2021). In later interviews, participants highlighted the strength and value of the connections formed during the workshops. The plastics industry has reported improved working relationships with other stakeholders, as well as enhanced cooperation within the industry itself after the SeeRRI process.

Most importantly, the process inspired the industry to establish the Austrian Carbon Cycle Circle,[3] an organization devoted to exploring and spreading awareness of the positive role the plastics sector can play in building a sustainable society. The Austrian Carbon Cycle Circle will continue to seek dialogue at the quadruple helix level in the future. Overall, it appears that the plastics industry and other stakeholder groups achieved their objectives with the SeeRRI process in Lower Austria. As far as the industry is concerned, we think it is fair to say that they managed to reduce an information asymmetry that had been preventing them from improving their public image, and that this was favorable for their business.

In Lower Austria, SeeRRI observed a high willingness of industrial actors to participate in the project. Surprisingly, NGOs were the least keen to join. The reasons for this are unclear, but the limited success in involving NGOs warrants attention. To realize the potential benefits of RRI, it is essential that representatives from all stakeholder groups participate in the RRI process and lend it legitimacy. It is particularly important that stakeholder groups with sharply opposed interests or points of view, as in the case of the plastics industry and environmental NGOs, take part. One potential barrier to achieving this may be that NGOs are worried about unintentionally imparting legitimacy to the controversial industry itself (rather than to the RRI process) by participating in the initiatives, or even that the initiatives are nothing but a ploy by the industry to gain such legitimacy. This creates yet another asymmetric information problem for the industry and underscores the fact that if the industry is a major driver behind the RRI initiatives, a careful communication effort is required to make sure that the purpose and objectives of the initiatives are correctly perceived by other actors.

6.6 CONCLUSION AND RECOMMENDATIONS

We find it plausible, based on theory and empirical data, that practicing RRI can be good for business. The explanation that we have put forth focuses on reducing information asymmetries in order to promote mutual understanding and avoid market failure and other coordination problems that may exist between an industry and its surrounding stakeholders. We have used the SeeRRI process to show how industries can implement RRI in practical terms. However, it is not essential to adopt all of the specifics of the SeeRRI model to derive the economic benefits we have discussed in this chapter. The core recommendation is that industries should open themselves up to information exchange with a broad range of external stakeholders, including representatives from government, academia, and civil society. The stakeholders should be given a say in formulating a long-term vision for the evolution of the industry, which considers social and environmental impacts. The dialogue with the stakeholders should focus on the industry as an integrated ecosystem rather than on particular firms within the industry.

Admittedly, our case study from Lower Austria is tailored to our theoretical argument in the sense that it revolves around industrial actors who more or less stated from the outset of the study that they were victims of their own information advantage (without using those words). Outside of "tainted" industries that wish to redeem themselves in the eyes of the public, the relevance of our RRI case for business is less clear. More research needs to be done to explore the benefits of RRI in other settings. Nevertheless, any business involved in research and development would be well advised to keep in mind that there may be economic benefits from practicing RRI and that these benefits are most likely to be realized when RRI is practiced at the ecosystem level, with the full involvement of the local quadruple helix.

DISCLOSURE STATEMENT

No potential conflict of interest was reported by the authors.

FUNDING

The SeeRRI project was funded by the European Union's Horizon 2020 research and innovation program under grant agreement no. 824588.

ACKNOWLEDGMENTS

The authors wish to thank all SeeRRI partners and workshop participants, whose insights and contributions to SeeRRI have made this chapter possible. Our special thanks go to Harald Bleier, Simone Hagenauer, Marianne Hörlesberger, and Andrea Kasztler for driving the SeeRRI process in Lower Austria.

NOTES

1. https://seerri.eu. Retrieved July 28, 2022.
2. "Greta" refers to Greta Thunberg, a prominent environmental activist.
3. https://carboncyclecircle.at/. Retrieved July 28, 2022.

REFERENCES

Akerlof, G. A. (1978). The market for "lemons": Quality uncertainty and the market mechanism. In *Uncertainty in economics* (pp. 235–251). Academic Press.

Aupers, S. (2012). 'Trust no one': Modernization, paranoia and conspiracy culture. *European Journal of Communication, 27*(1), 22–34.

Bhardwaj, P., Chatterjee, P., Demir, K. D., & Turut, O. (2018). When and how is corporate social responsibility profitable? *Journal of Business Research, 84*, 206–219.

Blok, V., & Lemmens, P. (2015). The emerging concept of responsible innovation. Three reasons why it is questionable and calls for a radical transformation of the concept of innovation. In B. J. Koops, *et al.* (Eds.), *Responsible innovation* (vol. 2, pp. 19–35). Springer.

Borch, A., & Throne-Holst, H. (2021). Does proof of concept trump all? RRI dilemmas in research practices. *Science and Engineering Ethics, 27*(1), 1–21.

Bryson, J. M., Crosby, B. C., & Stone, M. M. (2006). The design and implementation of cross-sector collaborations: Propositions from the literature. *Public Administration Review, 66*, 44–55.

Burget, M., Bardone, E., & Pedaste, M. (2017). Definitions and conceptual dimensions of responsible research and innovation: A literature review. *Science and Engineering Ethics, 23*(1), 1–19.

da Silva, L. M., Bitencourt, C. C., Faccin, K., & Iakovleva, T. (2019). The role of stakeholders in the context of responsible innovation: A meta-synthesis. *Sustainability, 11*(6), 1766.

Ferrell, A., Liang, H., & Renneboog, L. (2016). Socially responsible firms. *Journal of Financial Economics, 122*(3), 585–606.

Field, B., & Field, M. K. (2016). *Environmental economics*. McGraw-Hill Education.

Hansen, J. Ø., Jensen, A., & Nguyen, N. (2020). The responsible learning organization: Can Senge (1990) teach organizations how to become responsible innovators? The Learning Organization.

Hörlesberger, P. *et al.* (2021). Future scenarios for RRI implementation in R&I ecosystems of the three territories. Deliverable 3.2 of the Horizon 2020 project SeeRRI.

Kasztler, A. *et al.* (2021). Report on Integrated Framework for Building Self-sustaining R&I Ecosystems. Deliverable 4.3 of the Horizon 2020 project SeeRRI.

Lubberink, R., Blok, V., Van Ophem, J., & Omta, O. (2017). Lessons for responsible innovation in the business context: A systematic literature review of responsible, social and sustainable innovation practices. *Sustainability, 9*(5), 721.

Marszk, A., & Lechman, E. (2021). *Digitalization of financial markets*. Routledge.

Millar, C., Udalov, Y., & Millar, H. (2012). The ethical dilemma of information asymmetry in innovation: Reputation, investors and noise in the innovation channel. *Creativity and Innovation Management, 21*(2), 224–237.

Nguyen, N., Hansen, J. Ø., Jensen, A., & Pereira, C. Á. (2022). Integrating responsible research and innovation into smart specialization: A question-machine approach. In B. Callegari, B. A. Misganaw, & S. Sardo (Eds.), *Rethinking the social in innovation and entrepreneurship*. Edward Elgar Publishing.

Nguyen, N., Hansen, J. Ø., Kasztler, A., Honrado, Á., Santangelo, A., Magaña, M., Gil, M., Prat, J., Snick, A., & Manent, M. (2021). *The SeeRRI booklet: Bringing responsibility and RRI into regional planning – from theory to practice*. Zenodo. Available at: https://zenodo.org/records/5567217

Owen, R., Macnaghten, P., & Stilgoe, J. (2012). Responsible research and innovation: From science in society to science for society, with society. *Science and Public Policy, 39*(6), 751–760.

Sallam, M. (2021). COVID-19 vaccine hesitancy worldwide: A concise systematic review of vaccine acceptance rates. *Vaccines, 9*(2), 160.

Salvini, P., Palmerini, E., & Koops, B. J. (2019). Robotics and responsible research and innovation. In R, von Schomberg & J. Hankins (Eds.), *International handbook on responsible innovation*. Edward Elgar Publishing.
Samuelson, W. (1984). Bargaining under asymmetric information. *Econometrica: Journal of the Econometric Society*, *52*(4), 995–1005.
Stilgoe, J., Owen, R., & Macnaghten, P. (2013). Developing a framework for responsible innovation. *Research Policy*, *42*(9), 1568–1580.
Tietenberg, T., & Lewis, L. (2018). *Environmental and natural resource economics*. Routledge.

RRI2SCALE

RESPONSIBLE RESEARCH & INNOVATION ECOSYSTEMS AT REGIONAL SCALE

Duration:	January 1, 2020–December 31, 2022
Total cost:	€2,009,981
EU contribution:	€1,999,775
Contract No.:	872526

Coordinator:

- AGENZIA PER LA PROMOZIONE DELLA RICERCA EUROPEA (Italy)

Participants:

- HOGSKULEN PA VESTLANDET (Norway)
- UNIVERSITEIT MAASTRICHT (The Netherlands)
- UNIVERSITEIT TWENTE (The Netherlands)
- Q-PLAN INTERNATIONAL ADVISORS PC (Greece)
- RESEARCH AND INNOVATION MANAGEMENT GMBH (Austria)
- WHITE RESEARCH SPRL (Belgium)
- VESTLAND FYLKESKOMMUNE (Norway)
- PROVINCIE OVERIJSSEL (The Netherlands)
- KRITI (Greece)
- AXENCIA GALEGA DE INNOVACIÓN (Spain)

https://cordis.europa.eu/project/id/872526

B7

RRI2SCALE

Responsible Research and Innovation ecosystems at the regional scale

Margot Bezzi, Chiara Buongiovanni, and Anne M. Dijkstra

7.1 INTRODUCTION

One of the most pressing issues that European regions face is how to introduce and develop, under a framework of democratic governance, Regional Research and Innovation (R&I) policies and strategies that promote sustainable development and achieve, at the same time, societal inclusion and participation of all stakeholders. The issue is not easy to deal with, considering the existing fragmentation among societal agents, each one with its own values and perceptions regarding the implications of regional R&I choices. How can every stakeholder who is impacted by these changes be empowered and encouraged to contribute actively to co-shaping regional R&I policies? How to achieve regional innovation that is governed by the principles of Responsible Research and Innovation (RRI)? The aim of the RRI2SCALE project, running from January 2020 until December 2022, is to address these questions in four pilot regional ecosystems: Galicia (Spain), Kriti (Greece), Overijssel (The Netherlands), and Vestland (Norway).

The project supports and provides methodological guidance to the four regional authorities in shaping regional development and innovation agendas and roadmaps that are growth-oriented, sustainable, and democratic. This means that the policy creation process should integrate the principles and methods of innovative and participatory governance, facilitating a sustainable and inclusive evolution of institutional structures, boosting democratic processes and being beneficial for the majority of territorial stakeholders (RRI2SCALE, 2020).

This is ensured through experimenting within regional R&I ecosystems, applying stakeholder engagement and co-design methodologies and tools that allow a timely and coherent inclusion of citizens' voices. The objective is to capture, as

DOI: 10.4324/9781003319481-20

early as possible in regional strategy processes, the so-called societal weak signals, meaning perceptions of a challenge, or indicators of a potentially emerging issue, which may become significant in the future. The approach used is systemic and based on

> [the] consciousness that there is no one single actor in any system who can arrive at a good understanding of the future, the innovator, the firm, the citizen nor the city, and so there is a need to make sense of and shape the future together in these systems.
>
> (Benneworth, 2020)

The aim is to provide specific options to support the increasing attempts of institutions to open up to cooperation and co-design, in order to harmonize political priorities, technological trends, financial opportunities, and sustainability issues with emerging societal needs, detecting and processing societal aspirations and concerns coming from the diverse stakeholders at any stage of the innovation process.

RRI2SCALE approach is nestled within the existing Research and Innovation Smart Specialization Strategies (RIS3) (see Foray *et al.*, 2012) and introduces a methodology to scan the regional RIS3 ecosystem while making citizens and diverse groups' contributions to the innovation policy-making meaningful and relevant. The S3 is an approach conceived within the so-called Cohesion policy of the European Union, aimed at identifying strategic areas for knowledge-based investments in each EU region, focusing on place-based strengths and comparative advantages. The distinguishing characteristic of this approach is the Entrepreneurial Discovery Process (EDP), a bottom-up mobilization of relevant local innovation actors consisting in an interactive and inclusive process, drawing on the collective intelligence of businesses, universities, government bodies, and other key territorial actors (Perianez-Forte & Wilson, 2021) to assess their proposals for future development and investment. The aim is to capitalize on the entrepreneurial knowledge existing in a region or country, also drawing from the cooperation of actors from the so-called quadruple helix: government, academia, industry, and civil society (organizations).

Based on this background, the project set and followed four steps: (1) identifying those situations where the pursuit of technical progress can generate dilemmas linked to human wellbeing and welfare dimension; (2) designing techno-moral scenarios; (3) using those scenarios in multistakeholder and cross-regional dialogues for collective future thinking; and, finally, (4) including stakeholder voices in regional innovation agenda and roadmap co-creation. The entire process is being implemented through a deep and extensive stakeholder engagement process and foresight methods, such as the Scenario Exploration System (SES, 2022).

In this chapter, we will discuss the results related to the two parallel series of multistakeholder dialogues and cross-regional dialogues completed between December 2021 and March 2022, putting their meaning for businesses in the spotlight.

Indeed, businesses are increasingly called upon – both from consumers' trends and by policy-makers – to adopt corporate responsibility practices: on the one hand, market trends show a progressive consumer "eco-wakening" attitude (Economist Intelligence Unit, 2021). On the other hand, policy-making at the international level calls for companies across all sectors to implement "comprehensive mitigation processes for adverse human rights and environmental impacts in their value chains, integrating sustainability into corporate governance and management systems …" (European Commission, 2022; UNESCO, 2015). Therefore, we will pay attention to the benefits deriving from the capacity of businesses to fit into these processes, notably embracing and managing a change of paradigm, where societal and environmental concerns become part of companies' value proposition and corporate identity, and where exchanges with society are managed with openness and transparency, contributing to shaping such an identity.

7.2 BACKGROUND, SCOPE, AND CHALLENGES

In this section, we provide the background and scope of the RRI2SCALE project, discussing the relevance and place of RRI in the context of regional development and innovation systems.

The traditional paradigm of growth, mostly driven by innovation and technology feasibility, is seeking new operative ways of proceeding that are able to incorporate social, ethical, and ecological considerations as early as possible in the process. The RRI approach provides an experimental basis for doing so. As a concept, RRI has been thoroughly described at the scientific and theoretical level. However, experiences and studies are still limited concerning the translation and operationalization of RRI principles into approaches and methods tailored around specific needs and characteristics (see Schuijff & Dijkstra, 2019). Within this transformational process of the concept of RRI, the local and regional levels have been shown to be a strategic and functional testing context for RRI experimentation for two main reasons. First, because any societal challenge must be addressed by analyzing the specific context and formulating case-by-case solutions, which makes implementation at the local level necessary. Second, the regional contexts make it easier, compared to wider contexts, to more tangibly appreciate and measure the direct connections between development policy orientations, techno-economic achievements, and positive social repercussions, such as wellbeing or inclusivity (Moghadam-Saman *et al.*, 2020).

The RRI2SCALE project, while taking into consideration in its preliminary analytic work all six intervention areas of the RRI European Union framework (public engagement, open access, science education, gender equality, ethics, and governance) (European Commission, 2020), has primarily focused, during its practical work, on the aspect of public engagement. Indeed, properly designed stakeholder engagement is considered a cross-cutting enabler and trigger of all RRI dimensions. This is because through involving citizens from the beginning in the development of solutions and allowing dialogue among different stakeholders can trigger a continuous and mutually responsive process that ensures societal needs and concerns are properly taken into account and integrated into research and innovation activities. Through stakeholder engagement, social, environmental, and moral issues and concerns, which may otherwise arise only in later phases of the research and innovation process, can be integrated and anticipated within the process, which mitigate or eliminate unintended harms before the implementation stage (van de Poel *et al.*, 2017). Based on the above, the RRI2SCALE project bases its approach on three main interconnected background assumptions:

1. *It is still difficult to represent stakeholders' voices within territorial R&I ecosystems and discourse, because we lack proper processes and methodologies for their involvement.* In the traditional technocratic innovation and development model, the different societal visions and positions about what is moral, acceptable, sustainable, or desirable in the matter of innovation and economic development are not usually reflected systematically in the process, with only certain interests or values prevailing. In the last decade, EU regional research and innovation ecosystems have started to promote multi-actor, transversal dialogic processes, which brought together a wide and differentiated range of regional knowledge actors, including business actors, with a view to stimulating innovative combinations of competences and capacities, and thereby create unique, cross-sectoral value propositions at the regional levels via S3 and EDP (Foray *et al.*, 2012).We still fail, however, to systematically and meaningfully reflect the wide and diverse scope of values and positions ascribable to the participation of the many voices that compose society, mostly due to a lack of effective and proper methodological approaches to support stakeholder engagement.
2. *It is difficult to capture and reflect stakeholders' voices in due time and in the earlier stages of the innovation cycle.* Incorporating citizens' needs or points of view in a meaningful way and as early as possible in the process reduces the risk of making research and development choices that are mostly led by economic or technology-related considerations, and disregarding actual or fundamental societal and human needs. An obstacle to the engagement of citizens on a wide scale is often represented by tight time constraints. Another difficulty in capturing and processing citizens' inputs relates to the so-called Collingridge dilemma. This concept states that it is difficult for stakeholders to form a well-considered opinion about a certain technology until its implications on society are clear and explicit. However, by the time the societal implications of the technology are finally explicit and recognized by society, and would allow conscious steering choices, the technological parameters are set in a quasi-irreversible way, making it impossible for users to contribute to shaping that technology to meet societal needs better (Benneworth, 2020; Collingridge, 1980).
3. *The RRI approach supports a conscious steering of technological development.* At the level of regional development, the quandary described above translates into the challenge of ensuring a fair balance between the tension toward techno-economic development and growth and the necessity of including societal and environmental aspects, such as inclusiveness, wellbeing, and

sustainability (Benneworth, 2020). The RRI approach supports the aim of mitigating such a dilemma by acting as a "societal attuning mechanism" able to incorporate such "weak societal signals" as early as possible into the innovation processes (Benneworth, 2020), ensuring a reflective, aware, and responsive technological and development steering model.

Combining these three assumptions, the RRI2SCALE project intends to experiment with methods that integrate RRI elements into regional R&I policy and strategic planning, as well as in regional R&I ecosystems (RRI2SCALE, 2020). The four different regions taking part in the experiment were chosen to ensure a wide coverage at the European level in terms of socio-cultural, economic, and political characteristics, in order to maximize the potential of the actions. Analysis and experiments were focused on three interconnected thematic areas highly relevant for future technological development, sustainable growth, and citizens' daily life: intelligent transport, intelligent energy, and intelligent cities. The methodology chosen supports the exploration of both the current situation and possible future trajectories, bringing the visionary, anticipatory and longer-term nature of RRI into the schemes of regional development policies (see Fitjar *et al.*, 2019).

7.3 APPROACH AND METHODS

This section describes in more detail the four steps anticipated in the introduction (Figure B7.1).

1. *Regional dilemmas identification*: As a first step, a review of the current regional research and innovation landscapes for each of the four partner regions was performed. This allowed the identification of regional dilemmas within the regional S3 innovation strategies and to catch the weak societal signals. This highlighted specific societal views on innovation policies in terms of both opportunities and threats, needs, aspirations, and concerns. As part of this step, a review of academic publications, gray literature, regional

Figure B7.1

The RRI2Scale pathway to Responsible Innovation Agendas

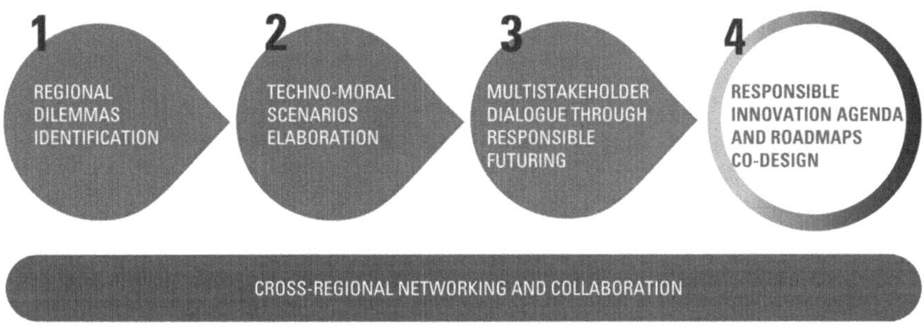

initiatives evaluations and relevant policy papers, and market reports was conducted, including the collection and analysis of 12 good practices on the matter of intelligent transport, energy, and cities. In parallel, information was collected through interviews and surveys. A total of 16 interviews with experts, 4 per region, were performed, gathering comments and views on the overall regional innovation landscape. In addition, a large-scale survey with citizens was conducted involving around 8,000 respondents – about 2,000 per region. Finally, to contextualize the dilemmas, a two-round Delphi survey was conducted to identify megatrends, trends, and drivers that are expected to impact on the socioeconomic and environmental landscape by 2030. A total of 120 experts on RRI, as well as domains experts, were asked to reflect on the potential implications of these trends and drivers and the probability of their appearance (Angelidou *et al.*, 2020).

2. *Techno-moral scenarios elaboration*: As a following step, six techno-moral scenarios were developed. Techno-moral scenarios foster anticipatory and reflexive thinking and support the exploration of future possibilities giving prominence – in an engaging and narrative form – to the moral values, concerns, and wider impacts that are at stake for an innovation (Boenink *et al.*, 2010). The scenarios were based on input from the above-mentioned sources and analyses, as well as a series of meetings with the regional stakeholders and experts and were created as preparatory steps to the Scenario Exploration System (SES) tool and its implementation during the multistakeholder dialogues. They incorporated into the narrative trends and drivers that were identified in the three thematic areas, including also general trends and megatrends. Each scenario's narrative was based on two axes, showing two orders of contrasting elements. The first axis contrasted the level of intervention in regional innovation policy – from adaptive versus rigid – and the second contrasted the level of citizen participation, ranging from high versus low (Dijkstra *et al.*, 2021). The six techno-moral scenarios were validated to assess whether they were "probable, desirable, different from one another, complete and internally consistent" (Angelidou *et al.*, 2021). Citizens in the four regions and project partners were asked to comment on aspects of the scenarios via social media and online. The scenarios were then refined and fed into the SES tool.

3. *Multistakeholder dialogue through responsible futuring*: As a third step, an extensive multistakeholder engagement process was prepared, providing dedicated and tailored training to project partners in the four regions. One training focused on the SES, aimed at increasing collective perspective and stimulating divergent thinking (Bontoux & Bengtsson, 2015; Bontoux *et al.*, 2020; Bontoux *et al.*, 2016). Another focused on the so-called "Responsible Futuring" approach, "a form of collaborative moral reflection-in-action that enables academics, industry, government, students, and citizens to become aware of their role, reflect on the short-term and long-term impact of ideas and technologies, and ideate potential solutions with moral imagination" (Van den Berg *et al.*, 2022).

After the training sessions, the SES methodology (Bontoux *et al.*, 2020) was applied in the multistakeholder dialogues. The SES tool, originally developed by the European Commission Joint Research Centre (JRC; Bontoux *et al.*, 2016), is an instrument to explore possible futures while engaging with relevant stakeholders in a safe environment. The SES tool pushes participants to step out from their daily role or responsibility and play the role of somebody else. In this way, it facilitates mutual understanding of the different voices in the arena (Bontoux *et al.*, 2020). The tool promotes both a temporal perspective (foresight approach) and a multistakeholder perspective, allowing one to expand one's own insight and gain a more holistic and non-divisive view on possible futures in given challenges, which provides better equipment to navigate collectively toward preferred futures (see Systasi Consulting *et al.*, 2017). RRI2SCALE realized a customized, digitalized version of the tool. The RRI2SCALE SES tool (see also Design Lab University of Twente, 2022) was tailored to local realities, to accommodate the different geographic, cultural, and socio-economic realities of the four regions (Bontoux *et al.*, 2020; Dijkstra *et al.*, 2021). Next to the multistakeholder dialogues, a series of three cross-regional dialogues were organized as an occasion for the four regional partners to exchange experiences, reflect on their institutional processes, and explore future collaborations.

4. *Responsible Innovation Agenda and Roadmap co-design*: As a fourth step, the project is preparing a co-design process, in which the regional teams work on how to best support the evolution and change in the institutional way of operating within each region, as well as on how to foster future cooperation and learning exchange among regions. The outcomes create a regional Responsible Innovation Agenda and Roadmaps for each of the pilot regions in co-creation with the different stakeholders. The process includes a two-step, co-creation program. In the first workshop, the constituting elements of the regional innovation agenda are developed, while the second transforms these elements into a more concrete roadmap. A final validation step with experts, businesses, and citizens ensures the acceptability of such responsible innovation principles (Schuijff & Dijkstra, 2019; Stilgoe *et al.*, 2013).

7.4 RESULTS AND LESSONS LEARNED

This section will summarize the findings and the evidence resulting from the multistakeholder and cross-regional dialogues, aimed at supporting governance change and the transition from triple to quadruple helix (institutions, academia, industry, and civil society). Our analysis highlights aspects where expectations and reality may collide, as well as the impact and perceptions of participants in terms of added value or difficulties. We will address the two questions stated in the introduction and will highlight points of interest for the business sector: how to achieve regional innovation that is governed by the principles of RRI?; and How can every stakeholder who is impacted by these changes be empowered and encouraged to contribute actively to co-shaping regional R&I policies?

7.4.1 How to achieve regional innovation that is governed by the principles of RRI?

In an attempt to change theory into practice, the partner regions tried to define what RRI is, or would be, within their region-specific realities and practices. We believe that the feedback received, although subjective, contributes to making this concept more concrete, understandable, and applicable. The concept of RRI was referred to as "ethical and societal norms embedded in innovation," where "participation is a means to achieve compatibility with ethical and societal aspects." Addtionally, "RRI is about the impact that innovation investments have in society in relation to the type of future we want," or "RRI is about what kind of relationship we want to achieve between society (stakeholders, citizens) and technology/innovation," or "RRI is about achieving consensus, sustainability, inclusivity, participatory decision-making." We found this definition particularly effective: "RRI is when the world is future proof."

This shows that the primary challenge when creating responsible and sustainable research and innovation strategies is about managing complexity, future impact, and integrating different societal voices and cultural drivers within innovation trajectories, while ensuring, at the same time, a fair balance and co-existence between techno-economic development and growth, on the one hand, and environmental sustainability and societal wellbeing, on the other hand. Such a process does not come without conflicts and dilemmas, the identification of which is therefore important, representing the room for building a meaningful dialogue through multistakeholder engagement and processes. Here are some extracts from the accounts of regions, which listed potentially conflicting priorities and interests in the context of their research and innovation strategies:

- One region recognized the need for a more sustainable use of energy and natural resources to ensure environmental benefits. Like other partner regions, energy management (e.g., energy storage and distribution provisions) represents a sensitive and controversial topic, showing conflicting interests between public administrations, business, and citizens. Points of attention related to creating a smarter relationship between urban and rural areas, preserving the traditional rural/non-urban way of living; also, transport and digital policies represented very sensitive areas, connected to potential divides in mountainous areas. Other reported controversies were in regards to the decision to invest in drones for emergency and services purposes, since this called for a revision of the existing legal framework in terms of environmental and ethical aspects.
- Another region put forward dilemmas connected to the digital divide, concerning the likely exclusion of elderly and less educated people from innovative and digitized public services.
- For the third region, energy transition represented the most pressing priority at the national level. At the regional level, this was the lack of consensus related to landscape management, with the need to ensure the creation and availability of future-proof infrastructures for sustainability (cables, grids, storage). Debated

problems related to acceptability issues connected to the landscape impact of wind turbines and solar panels, as well as to the low storage capacity of the current grid system, which was not properly anticipated and communicated to citizens.

- For the final region, the 2030 zero emission targets are the foremost priority and policy driver. Such objectives entail the full phasing out of fossil fuel in favor of a complete shift to renewable energies and a green and circular economy through regulations and incentives. At the sectoral level, a full electrification of the transport sector is expected, combined with the digitalization of the related information system and the revision of the energy management and exportation policy. Although the system has achieved a certain maturity in involving the business and research sector, time pressure still makes it difficult to involve people in the right way. The inclusion of citizens in the dialogue process remains a big challenge that still needs to be addressed along with representations of the problems on the media, which often complicates the understanding and exchange with citizens.

It is also interesting to report two different accounts on the role the business sector took in these processes. In the first account, one region compared two similar city shared-mobility services; one was created through a lengthy public deliberation process that led to the adoption of city bikes; the other was a commercially led initiative for shared electric scooters, which immediately took root. This showed how well working and widely accepted solutions might derive from different and mixed decisional approaches, where political, business, and practical interests are combined in different ways.

In the second account, another region told how drone experimentation was chosen as an innovation trajectory based on the needs of different sectors' industrial representatives, such as technology developers. Eventually, sectors were explored that could benefit from drone-based public services. This case, strongly influenced by the political level and by the point of view of only one dominant stakeholder, represents an old, technology-driven model to innovation, which needs to be surpassed in favor of strategies that take into account a wider plurality of voices and motivations, and a more complex preliminary assessment of the future implications of our technological choices.

The two accounts confirm the business sector as a main reference point in these processes. Therefore, we consider it vital for the business sector to become acquainted with the ongoing transition and debate on more open and inclusive processes to define innovation trajectories. This could eventually be reflected in corporate strategic and operational approaches or expectations, and pave the way for a more active and positive role of the industrial sector within the communities and societal contexts in which they operate.

7.4.2 How can every stakeholder be empowered and encouraged to contribute actively to co-shaping regional R&I policies?

The dialogue among different stakeholders is a subtle balance exercise depending on the blend of stakeholders, the right type of process, initiated at the right time, and with the right level of involvement. The correct combination of these elements proved essential to maintain high motivation and engagement among participants and generate impact. The lessons collected in the project about these aspects are summarized here.

7.4.3 The challenges of having the right blend of actors

The presence of all stakeholders is necessary to properly assess the opportunity and feasibility in discussions oriented toward priority-setting and problem-solving. However, even more critical in a stakeholder engagement process is having the *right* stakeholders at the table. Governance aspects, related to power level, decision-making power, and contact with politicians, or operational capacity, translate into different possibilities of leading and steering a process and affect its future directions, and, therefore, should be attentively considered. The same is true for specialist and technical knowledge. In some of our multistakeholder dialogues, the absence of participants who could bring the right perspective and insight led to the conversation making little headway.

Businesses normally have an important role in this by helping to shape scenarios and solutions that are realistic and feasible, and by facilitating the passage from ideas to action. Indeed, in the experiences explored, industrial stakeholders are involved more often and easily through well-structured and consolidated processes, such as in the Research and Innovation Smart Specialization Strategies (RIS3), representing a primary interlocutor for policy-makers when considering the orientations for future investment in technological development.

Put differently, the involvement of citizens still represents a vivid challenge for all regions, which highlighted the following:

- *Managing unexpected outcomes and reactions from citizens represents a challenge*: Contact and communication with citizens remain problematic in different stages. First, institutions lack orientation on how establishing ex ante contact with citizens; then it is difficult to predict to which extent and on what topic or policy areas citizens will complain; finally, it is difficult to deal with and manage such discontent.
- *The type of topic has an influence on the capacity to involve citizens*: Not all topics have the same engagement potential. Some are more understandable or more attractive than others are for certain groups of stakeholders.
- *People's goodwill to contribute should be cultivated and preserved*: This avoids counter-productive practices. A region reported the risks linked to citizens' over-involvement, mentioning the experience of a cross-topic lengthy participation process that, eventually, became associated with a sense of tension and fatigue, negatively affecting people's goodwill to contribute.

In summary, although all participants agreed that the presence of citizen voices should be strengthened in the dialogue with policy-makers to ensure a higher variety of points of view, for all regions, this represented a real challenge, requiring suitable and effective tools to appropriately manage the complexity of citizens' engagement processes and taking into account citizens' views. This is in line with findings from other engagement processes (Cormick, 2012).

7.4.4 Insights into the SES tool experimentation

Discerning the specificities of engagement tools and the type of process they can best support is increasingly important. The SES tool tested in RRI2SCALE (Bontoux *et al.*, 2016; Bontoux *et al.*, 2020) combined foresight and multistakeholder dialogue capacity. Here is the feedback received from the participants:

- *The specificities of the SES methodology allow all voices to be heard at the same time* in the process, compared to other processes, in which contributions are sought in silos or sequence.
- *The tool enables players to think and act out of the box,* widening their perspectives and giving the possibility to play roles and experience dynamics out of their usual social and professional role. This translates into an increased capacity to understand the motivations and interests of others. In fact, the more diversified the participating stakeholders are, the more useful and insightful the experience becomes.
- *The SES context helps to break and overcome real-life consolidated power structures and their inevitable influences on discussions and decision-making.* The way the process and the discussion are structured allows a more even distribution of power among participants, and a more balanced relationship. Such a balance makes it possible to represent different perspectives effectively and evenly, and to avoid cases, as a region reported, where "policy-makers complain that they have to do what only a few of the top businesses want."
- *In techno-moral scenarios, positive and negative elements can best be balanced in a realistic way.* Techno-moral scenarios represent a building block of the SES methodology, acting as food for thought and enabler of collective future thinking. Following the suggestion of previous developers of the SES tool, two contrasting scenarios – positive and negative – were developed for each region, keeping them general and open enough to adapt to different emerging situations flexibly, as in a real innovation system. However, our experience highlighted that high polarization and contrast could be detrimental to real-life complexity, making it too easy to choose one (positive) reality against the other. Therefore, it is important to represent the complexity and nuances of each context more realistically, as well as to guarantee a more complex blend of positive and negative elements in each scenario.

The business sector can be part of these experiences as a direct player, and as a role to be played by other participants in the SES session representing the point of view and interests of stakeholders from the business or industrial sector.

7.4.5 Other process-related considerations

Managing the communication among institutions, academia, large industry, SMEs, and citizens constitutes a complex task, since different stakeholders understand and see different aspects of problems based on their sectoral affiliations, cultural and specialist backgrounds, languages, priorities, and individualities. In this regard, the following steps have been considered important:

- *Define a common ground of understanding and a common set of rules beforehand*, stating what is to be discussed, for which reason, and what are the challenges.
- *Translate specialistic content information by academia or business stakeholders* into real-life, common language, allowing citizens or policy-makers to be on the same page as the specialists.
- *Choose the scope of debate attentively.* The narrower the agenda, the easier it is to involve stakeholders; the broader the agenda, the more difficult it becomes to take into account what stakeholders bring.
- *Consider the role of science literacy as a key enabling factor*, meant as the capacity to understand the scientific process, especially if the objective is to increase the variety of involved stakeholders.
- *Consider co-design and co-creation processes carefully.* When referring to structural and consolidated ways to relate to citizens, regions often referred to "consultations," which, as an approach, ranks quite low in the participation ladder, being a process taking place downhill in the innovation process, when strategic choices are made, and only non-structural contributions and marginal adjustments can be provided.
- *Harmonize the time of politics with that of engagement processes.* The pace and priorities linked to the election agenda often clash with the longer time a proper stakeholder engagement process requires to enable substantial contributions from citizens and build sustainable relationships.

7.5 IMPLICATIONS FOR BUSINESSES

The progress of institutions in outlining regional R&I strategies based on RRI values and multistakeholder processes directly impacts on the entire ecosystem, including the business sector. The aspects of the project's experience deemed most relevant to the business sector will be highlighted in this section.

- *Story of a consolidated cooperation and its expected evolution*: It was found that triple helix cooperation models (business, academia, and government), although implemented differently and not without challenges, represent a consolidated relationship throughout the different regional contexts. The experiences explored highlighted that the business and industrial sector is a primary reference point and interlocutor for policy-makers when dealing with future investments in regional research and innovation-oriented strategies and processes. Often, cooperation happened through well-structured and consolidated processes, which was strengthened by the introduction of the Entrepreneurial Discovery Process (EDP) as a key element of the S3 2014–2020. The value of businesses is, indeed, linked to their capacity to show the potential of technological innovation and indicate orientations and solutions that are realistic, feasible, grafted onto reality, and which facilitate the passage from ideas to action. In a paradigm strongly centered on technological feasibility, businesses often play a guiding role in orienting regional ecosystems to research and innovation. In doing so, businesses lead the way toward future pathways and reality options, which shape the social and technological environment in which we will live, by creating or meeting society's needs through innovative solutions. However, this model is now being surpassed in favor of open and inclusive processes that enhance evenly distributed power across all societal actors. It is important to embrace this challenge.

- *The quest for quadruple helix models is a commitment that cannot be postponed*: The challenge we are facing now is to head toward continuous and strategic quadruple helix dialogue, initiating and managing meaningful and transparent exchanges with citizens and a wider variety of actors. In a world characterized by complex societal and environmental challenges and an increasingly fragile democratic sphere, this is a commitment that cannot be postponed. Businesses, as well as governments, are increasingly being called upon and expected to commit to and contribute to building more open and sustainable relationships with society.
- *Responsibility and creation of shared value as new paradigms*: The traditional paradigm of growth, where innovation pathways were drawn predominantly by technological feasibility or economic interests, have been surpassed, and the same goes with the traditional concept of Corporate Social Responsibility (CSR). The reality of emerging experiences, such as B-corps or social businesses, goes in that direction by directly integrating values, such as sustainability, circularity, inclusivity, or wellbeing, at the level of organizational and business models, making them essential constituents of brands' identities and strategies that are able to foster their market positioning and competitiveness (see Porter & Kramer, 2006). Considering that consumers are increasingly expecting a direct and sincere commitment of the whole private sector on urgent environmental and societal issues, as well as a more conscious and active role within the societal context they inhabit (Porter & Kramer, 2011), it is time for all businesses to reflect on the extent to which societal and environmental concerns have been integrated substantially into their value proposition, corporate identity, and value chain organization.
- *Building a deeper connection with society*: Embracing such a change requires the capacity to listen to society in a different way (Godin, 2018) that goes beyond traditional business-consumer logics, which is mostly oriented to ensure proper

societal uptake and market share. This new role entails the attempt by businesses to capture and assess, in advance, the potential impacts of solutions and services at the societal and environmental level, which shows a strong connection with the communities and societal contexts in which they operate. In this view, the approaches to multistakeholder dialogue that enable increasing capability of anticipation and reflexivity might be relevant and valuable for the business sector in supporting them to understand future societal impacts and develop better market intelligence.

- *The challenge is open, and support is welcomed*: There is an urgency for businesses to actively take part in the above-described process. Such a transition toward more open and inclusive processes in the definition of regional development models opens the way for businesses to adopt a proactive and advocacy approach within their sectoral and territorial ecosystems, acting as forefront actors at any stage, with strong, consolidated cooperation relationships and specific know-how. The cultivation of continuous and long-lasting relationships with the scientific and research community at the territory level is highly recommended, not only to elaborate common visions and perspectives, but also to join forces toward a common challenge regarding effectively exchanging and communicating in initiatives involving citizens.

7.6 CONCLUSION AND RECOMMENDATIONS

The inclusion of RRI elements in governance processes raises challenges and difficulties. Committing to designing processes or taking decisions based on open approaches and multistakeholder dialogues is a process in and of itself and takes time. It entails, and requires, a whole set of governance evolutions and changes at several levels: cultural, organizational, procedural, and financial. It also requires the inclusion and mastering of professional facilitation skills, and what is true for institutions remains valid for the business world. Indeed, businesses are expected to be not only participants in this transition, but also initiators of dialogues and exchanges among stakeholders; the hope is that they can find in this account, if not solutions, at least inspirations or curiosity on the existing possibilities to tackle the challenges ahead. Here is a list of takeaways that we consider useful to set and address such challenges properly:

- *RRI: let's call it by its name*: In our discussions, the need to better understand and *name* the way RRI relates to the regions' specific playground – for example, using wording and terms that are more familiar in each specific context – has proved to be useful and critical to facilitate its integration into existing or emerging policies and practices
- *Involving public voices meaningfully is (hard) work*: The difference between stakeholder engagement and *meaningful* stakeholder engagement became evident in our experience. Genuine commitment and readiness in who initiates the process are a prerequisite to realize "meaningful" public engagement, taking equal care in all phases constituting the process.

- *Organizational adaptation and change as a prerequisite*: A model like the one extensively described above considers regional innovation agencies as the most suitable ecosystem orchestrator, yet a change in the organizational mindset was recognized as a prerequisite for all the involved stakeholders.
- *In-person interactions are only partially negotiable*: The global COVID-19 pandemic forced these processes into virtual situations, allowing experimentation and pushing the potential offered by online instruments forward. However, online processes can only partially address the complexity of multistakeholder dialogues. Power structures, conflicts, diversity of language and knowledge frameworks, mutual understanding, diversity of value systems and of interests at stake are still much better addressed through physical interactions.
- *Time for methods and tools*: RRI2SCALE considers public engagement methodologies as crucial to detect and capture those *weak citizen signals* from society, which, if properly conveyed and reflected in the process at the right time, could profoundly influence the directions taken by technological innovation (Moghadam-Saman *et al.*, 2020). The "practical" and instrumental dimension, therefore, stands out as an urgent need, in order to make RRI integration a reality. The choice of the most suitable tool does certainly represent the main challenge and learning path of all societal actors in the years to come, with a view to managing diversity and complexity and making sense out of them. Stakeholders who are eager to test and put into practice RRI approaches and principles need sound, implementable, and trustworthy methodologies and customizable tools, paired with specific training.
- *A tool to support systemic and future thinking*: The RRI2SCALE Scenario Exploration System (SES) tool was proved to stimulate reflections about future systemic implications, and to adopt an anticipatory approach, becoming more conscious about long-term or wider societal implications of our choices (including technological ones). In addition, it helped in shifting perspectives, breaking consolidated power structures, and understanding the points of view of others, in order to envision different pathways and possibilities.
- *Multistakeholder cooperation as a competitive asset*: The RRI2SCALE approach is based on regional multistakeholder fora, connecting relevant actors from different research and innovation ecosystems and enabling them to consequently co-shape the directions of their regional knowledge-driven economy. In such fora, a huge opportunity is in place for businesses as an active part of the ecosystem. On the one hand, as preeminent innovation actors, they are equipped to influence the regional trajectories by bringing their knowledge to the ecosystem, their assets, and investment capacities, as well as their needs to be complemented through other stakeholders' assets and capabilities. On the other hand, by embracing the ongoing change, they can learn about and exchange societal concerns, needs, and aspirations through a dialogical interaction. This could lead to an increased capability for anticipation and reflexivity from the businesses side, meant both as the capacity to anticipate and understand future societal influences, as well as offering better market intelligence.

DISCLOSURE STATEMENT

No potential conflict of interest was reported by the authors.

FUNDING

The RRI2SCALE project has received funding from the European Union's Horizon 2020 research and innovation program under grant agreement No 872526. The opinions expressed in this chapter reflect only the authors' view and in no way reflect the European Union's opinions.

REFERENCES

Angelidou, M., Politis, C., Psarra, F., Trendafili, K., Fellnhofer, K., Bakratsas, T., . . . Buongiovanni, C. (2020). Deliverable 2.1: Report on the identification of emerging territorial trends, drivers & potential impacts. RRI2SCALE project (Grant Agreement No 872526). Retrieved from https://rri2scale.eu/index.php/resources/reports/ (accessed June 2, 2022).

Angelidou, M., Politis, C., & Trendafili, K. (2021). Validation report on technomoral scenarios. Deliverable 2.3 RRI2SCALE project.

Benneworth, P. (Ed.). (2020). A common reference framework for RRI2SCALE. An internal report. Western Norway University of Applied Sciences.

Boenink, M., Swierstra, T., & Stemerding, D. (2010). Anticipating the interaction between technology and morality: A scenario study of experimenting with humans in bionanotechnology. *Studies in Ethics, Law, and Technology*, *4*(2). doi:10.2202/1941–6008.1098.

Bontoux, L., & Bengtsson, D. (2015). 2035 Paths towards a sustainable EU economy Sustainable transitions and the potential of eco-innovation for jobs and economic development in EU eco-industries 2035 (EUR 27376 EN; doi: 10.2760/80294). Retrieved from https://publications.jrc.ec.europa.eu/repository/handle/JRC96826.(accessed June 7, 2022).

Bontoux, L., Bengtsson, D., Rosa, A. B., & Sweeney, J. A. (2016). The JCR Scenario Exploration System: From study to serious game. Report 93. *Journal of Future Studies*, *20*(3), 93–108. doi:10.6531/JFS.2016.20(3).R93.

Bontoux, L., Sweeney, J. A., Rosa, A. B., Bauer, A., Bengtsson, D., Bock, A.-K., . . . Watson, R. (2020). A game for all seasons: Lessons and learnings from the JRC's Scenario Exploration System. *World Futures Review*, *12*(1), 81–103. doi:10.1177/1946756719890524.

Collingridge, D. (1980). *The social control of technology*. Frances Pinter.

Cormick, C. (2012). The complexity of public engagement. *Nature Nanotechnology*, *7*(2), 77–78.

Design Lab University of Twente (2022). Scenario Exploration System. Quick guide to responsible futuring for the RR2SCALE project. Available at: https://www.academia.edu/100728037/Scenario_Exploration_System_SES_for_RRI2SCALEs_Quick_Guide

Dijkstra, A. M., van den Berg, M., Angelidou, M., Politis, C., Psarra, F., Trendafili, K., . . . Turkeli, S. (2021). Techno-moral scenarios for territorial R&I futures in the domains of intelligent cities, energy and transport. Deliverable 2.2 for the RRI2SCALE project. Retrieved from https://rri2scale.eu/wp-content/uploads/2022/01/D2.2-Techno-moral-scenarios-for-territorial-RI-futures-in-the-domain-of-intelligent-cities-energy-and-transport.pdf (accessed April 25, 2022).

Economist Intelligence Unit. (2021). An eco-awakening: Measuring global awareness, engagement and action for nature. Retrieved from https://www.worldwildlife.org/publications/an-eco-wakening-measuring-awareness-engagement-and-action-for-nature.(accessed April 25, 2022).

European Commission. (2020). Communication from the Commission to the European Parliament, the Council, the European Economic and Social Committee and the Committee of the Regions A new ERA for Research and Innovation, COM/2020/628 final, https://eur-lex.europa.eu/legal-content/EN/TXT/?uri=COM%3A2020%3A628%3AFIN (accessed April 25, 2022).

European Commission. (2022). Proposal for a Directive of the European Parliament and of the Council on Corporate Sustainability Due Diligence and amending Directive (EU) 2019/1937, 2022/0051/COD, COM(2022) 71 final, https://eur-lex.europa.eu/legal-content/EN/ALL/?uri=COM:2022:71:FIN (accessed April 25, 2022).

Fitjar, R. D., Benneworth, P., & Asheim, B. T. (2019). Towards regional responsible research and innovation? Integrating RRI and RIS3 in European innovation policy. *Science and Public Policy*, *46*(5), 772–783. doi:10.1093/scipol/scz029.

Foray, D., Goddard, J., Goenaga Beldarrain, X., Landabaso, M., McCann, P., Morgan, K., . . . Ortega-Argilés, R. (2012). Guide to Research and Innovation Strategies for Smart Specialisation (RIS3). Retrieved from Luxembourg: https://ec.europa.eu/regional_policy/sources/docgener/presenta/smart_specialisation/smart_ris3_2012.pdf (accessed April 25, 2022).

Godin, S. (2018). *This is marketing: You can't be seen until you learn to see*. Penguin.

Moghadam-Saman, S., Coenen, L. M. A., Benneworth, P., Dijkstra, A., Wintjes, R., & Panori, A. (2020). D1.1: The Regional Dilemma: report on how EU regions integrate RRI in Territorial R&I Landscape. RRI2SCALE (Grant Agreement No 872526). Retrieved from https://rri2scale.eu/wp-content/uploads/2022/01/D1.1-The-Regional-Dilemma.-report-on-how-EU-regions-integrate-RRI-in-territorial-RI-Landscape.pdf (accessed April 25, 2022).

Perianez-Forte, I. & Wilson, J. (2021). *Assessing smart specialisation: The Entrepreneurial Discovery Process*. EUR 30709 EN, Publications Office of the European Union.

Porter, M. E., & Kramer, M. R. (2006). Strategy and society: The link between competitive advantage and corporate social responsibility. *Harvard Business Review*, *84*(12), 78–92.

Porter, M. E., & Kramer, M. R. (2011). Creating shared value. How to reinvent capitalism—and unleash a wave of innovation and growth. *Harvard Business Review*, *89*(1–2), 62–77.

RRI2SCALE (2020). Grant Agreement (Number 872526). Retrieved from https://rri2scale.eu/ (accessed April 25, 2022).

Schuijff, M., & Dijkstra, A. M. (2019). Practices of Responsible Research and Innovation: A review. *Science and Engineering Ethics*, *26*(2), 533–574. doi:10.1007/s11948-019-00167-3.

Stilgoe, J., Owen, R., & Macnaghten, P. (2013). Developing a framework for responsible innovation. *Research Policy*, *42*(9), 1568–1580. doi:10.1016/j.respol.2013.05.008.

Systasi Consulting, JRC Brussels, & VU Amsterdam (2017). Future nano-RRI application and techno-moral scenarios. D3.2 NANO2ALL. Retrieved from http://www.nano2all.eu/wp-content/uploads/files/NANO2ALL%20-%20685931%20-%20D3.2.Future%20nano-RRI%20application%20and%20techno-moral%20sc....pdf (accessed April 25, 2022).

The Scenario Exploration System (SES) (2022). Retrieved from https://knowledge4policy.ec.europa.eu/foresight/tool/scenario-exploration-system-ses_en (accessed April 25, 2022).

Van den Berg, M., Kousi, N., Markova, B., Swaak, J., & Wildevuur, S. (2022). On the process and outcomes of the regional multistakeholder dialogues. Deliverable 3.2 RRI2SCALE project.

Van de Poel, I., Asveld, L., Flipse, S., Klaassen, P., Scholten, V., & Yaghmaei, E. (2017). Company strategies for Responsible Research and Innovation (RRI): A conceptual model. *Sustainability*, *9*(11), 2045.

UNESCO. (2015). Sustainable Development Goals. Retrieved from https://sdgs.un.org/goals (accessed April 25, 2022).

DigiTeRRI

Duration: January 1, 2020–December 31, 2022
Total cost: €2,004,037.50
EU contribution: €2,004,037.50
Contract No.: 873010

Coordinator:

- AIT AUSTRIAN INSTITUTE OF TECHNOLOGY GMBH (Austria)

Participants:

- MONTANUNIVERSITÄT LEOBEN (Austria)
- NORDLANDSFORSKNING AS (Norway)
- WEDO PROJECT INTELLIGENCE MADE EASYSL (Spain)
- MATERALIA (France)
- ZENTRUM FÜR ANGEWANDTE TECHNOLOGIE LEOBEN GMBH (Austria)
- THE PAPER PROVINCE EKONOMISK FOERENING (Sweden)
- VÄRMLANDS LÄNS LANDSTING (Sweden)
- STANDORT UND MARKETING BRÜCK AN DER MUR GESMBH (Austria)
- KARLSTADS UNIVERSITET (Sweden)
- GRAND E-NOV (France)
- UNIVERSITE DE LORRAINE (France)

https://cordis.europa.eu/project/id/873010

B8

DigiTeRRI
Responsible Innovation in industry territories

Marianne Hörlesberger and Brigitte Kriszt

8.1 INTRODUCTION

This contribution deals with the European Responsible Research and Innovation (RRI) approach to transitioning traditional industry regions to digitalized industrial regions. DigiTeRRI, with the full title "Responsible Research and Innovation Approach for Transitioning the Traditional Industry Regions into Digitalized Industry Territories," contributes to the establishment of sustainable digitalized innovation ecosystems in three European territories, in Värmland in Sweden, Grand Est in France, and Styria in Austria. These three regions, besides others, are in the transition to digitalized industry territories, but with a long tradition in industry in the field of steel, non-ferro metals, and paper. This contribution's emphasis is on the Styrian case in Austria. Such territories already work on a high level of digitalization in their industrial sectors, e.g., a high level of digital development and use of ICT innovations, considering technical, business, as well as social elements (Grundke *et al.*, 2018). Industries and businesses must face the digital transformation and actively promote it. This transformation causes a change in the (regional) innovation system. This process can be viewed as a modification of wealth. The digital transformation can lead to different forms of innovation and path development activities in regional economies (Isaksen *et al.*, 2021). The digital transformation of a regional innovation system is a challenge for the actors in the region. This transformation requires dealing with the culture and skills, with digital education of the inhabitants of a region, and, thus, also with talents and digital culture, of course with infrastructure and technologies, with the quality of life in the region, with partnerships and networks in the region and beyond the region all over the world (Brunetti *et al.*, 2020). The literature on innovation systems and the business models of high-tech companies

DOI: 10.4324/9781003319481-21

underlines that cooperation and networks within the regional innovation and economic system, cooperation with research institutions and universities, with large companies and SMEs, and supra-regional cooperation are important factors for a successful region. The actors of the innovation ecosystem, the firms, the research organizations and universities, the policy-makers, and the education organizations need each other and benefit greatly from a well-organized collaboration. Thinking and understanding the innovation ecosystem as a whole, with implication for the environment and on society, are becoming increasingly important, especially in Europe, but also at the global level. A firm would like to understand the context and the implication of their products better regarding citizens and the environment. Ethical aspects play an increasing role, especially when it comes to digitalization. Therefore, a transformation into a digitalized industry region via the RRI approach is highly relevant.

Implementing RRI into an economic system and into industry is still a challenge. For instance, gender equality is not possible in industry, because there are not enough engineers in the first place. Open access and transparency conflict with IPRs and can be considered at the very beginning of the innovation. However, RRI can be designed in a specific way so that it covers the core idea, namely by seeking to align technological innovation with broader social values and anticipate the implications on the environment and society. The implementation of RRI in firms increases competitive opportunities, because RRI anticipates negative effects in the economy, society, and ecology. RRI is beneficial for companies, because social and environmental innovations can create economic benefits and business opportunities. This leads to better coordination between the actors. By adopting RRI, companies can achieve better alignment with society, government, and academia. By implementing RRI, companies are more profitable, because they can invest in business tools, equipment, and processes that directly affect productivity, but also invest in employee engagement and training, which have a positive impact on productivity. Implementing RRI strategies can create a sense of "meaningful work" for the employees. By aligning ethical values with their customers, companies will experience more engaged customers. Engaged customers do not need marketing directed at them and will recommend the company to others. Finally, RRI can also attract investors who intend to invest in environmentally and socially responsible manufacturing operations (Stahl, 2018).

The discussion about the responsibility of industry and business and their impact on society and the environment has taken place for approximately seven decades. The study "Responsible Research and Innovation in Industry – Challenges, Insights and Perspectives" provides an overview of the literature on Responsible Industry (Martinuzzi *et al.*, 2018). The concepts for this are approaches, such as Corporate Social Responsibility (CSR) (Carroll, 2015), Corporate Sustainability (Montiel & Delgado-Ceballos, 2014), or Business Ethics (Ferrero *et al.*, 2014). These approaches deal with ethical-normative requirements for companies (Kolk, 2016; Starik & Kanashiro, 2013). These approaches discuss the relevance of the influence of social and political aspects on companies and, thus, go beyond maximizing shareholder value (Bouglet *et al.*, 2012; Whiteman *et al.*, 2013).

The field of tension between corporate demands for profit, growth, competitive advantage, and market share, on the one hand, and social goals, such as prosperity, well-being, and sustainability, locally and globally, on the other, is discussed (Van der Byl & Slawinski, 2015). Operating in the global market and the pressure of the shareholders to succeed bring companies into a conflict, which seems insoluble. Individual interests prosper at the expense of citizens, future generations, or climate change, pollution (e.g., plastic in the oceans), or biodiversity (Starik *et al.*, 2013; Whiteman *et al.*, 2013). Corporate strategies to mitigate or avoid such conflicts have so far only been partially successful (Gautier & Pache, 2015). The EU has drawn up regulations so that the car industry, for example, has to deal with it in terms of environmental compatibility and ethics.[1]

RRI needs to be translated into business-language and relevant key performance indicators (van de Poel *et al.*, 2017). The implementation of RRI into business and industry might lead to better understanding of consumer and user needs. A well-implemented RRI approach supports building the trust of the stakeholders, consumer loyalty, a license to operate, employee engagement, and alignment with regulatory expectations. However, business and industry have to deal with the conflicts between the adoption of RRI and commercial interests (Chatfield *et al.*, 2017).

The RRI approach is closely linked to the context of the challenge of digitalization in the corresponding territories. The implementation of the RRI approach into an innovation ecosystem, where the actors coming from industry and business, science and research, policy-making, and also education and civil society create the knowledge and product flow, and collaborations between all these actors are the goal in the DigiTeRRI project.

DigiTeRRI uses the RRI approach by applying anticipative and participative processes with stakeholder engagement by the afore-mentioned actors, and by creating strategies with these stakeholders to address the RRI keys, such as science education, gender equality, open access, and public engagement, and those for supporting the transition into digitalization of the region, the innovation ecosystem in the region, in this case, Styria in Austria, and more specifically, Upper Styria. In this chapter, the case of Styria in Austria (inside the DigiTeRRI project) is discussed for its part in the territorial RRI-oriented transition process.

8.2 BACKGROUND, SCOPE, AND CHALLENGES

8.2.1 Innovation ecosystem

An innovation ecosystem consists of actors who are undertaking innovation activities and the interaction of these actors. The entirety of private and public organizations and individuals, who contribute by their activities and interactions to the creation and diffusion of new technologies, new products, or new knowledge, builds an innovation system. Freeman (1987) describes an innovation system as "the network of institutions in the public and private sectors whose activities and interactions initiate, import, modify, and diffuse new technologies." The study of innovation systems started more than 30 years ago. Innovation systems approaches can focus on the national level as Nelson (1993) or Lundvall (2007) or Edquist (2012) worked out. The innovation system on the regional level was described, for instance, by Braczyk *et al.* (2004). The sectoral innovation system was characterized by Malerba (2004; 2005), by Dolata (2009), by Carlsson and Stankiewicz (1991), by Johnson and Jacobsson (2001), or Hekkert *et al.* (2007), and, thus, considered the technological innovation systems. A smooth interplay between the actors is fundamental to a successful industry and business in a region. The composition of the following aspects and forces are the basis for flourishing innovation ecosystems: the conditions set by the policy-makers, the knowledge and technology creation in a region in universities or research organizations, the collaboration between research and industry, a cohort of highly educated employees, either from the region or also attracted from the best education providers in the world, and the infrastructure in the region. The success of a region (which is the summary of the economy and the wellbeing of the people there) depends on the constructive interplay and collaboration between these elements. Therefore, industry and business are greatly interested in co-creating the future together with all other actors in a region.

8.2.2 Transition multilevel approach

The transition to digitalization combines multiple perspectives in different ways and encompasses multiple levels. The multilevel approach can be seen as inspired by theories of structuration. Structuration theory by Giddens (1984) tries to balance the role of actors. It combines a view of how economic structures and institutionalized systems, and orders of inter-locking rules maintain path continuity. The relation between structure and action consists of rules and institutional complementarities, which selects actions that support the trajectory and tend to exclude others. At the same time, structures may open up for and allow a dynamic, which starts with micro level actors, such as entrepreneurs, niches, and innovators, who decide to move outside the limitations of the structural path of development. In this way, the structural and institutional macro level context is likely to work as a selection mechanism, a filter, which accepts certain new niches and opportunities of growth, and rejects others. This process of structuration involves: (1) the micro level, for example, transformative innovations, seen as entrepreneurial discoveries or emerging niches; (2) the meso level, for example, a dynamic where successful niches or discoveries start to grow and multiply into a patchwork of orders; and (3) the macro-level, for example, transforming the economic structure of the region, as well as the institutions in the socio-technical order (the landscape). This process of transformation takes place within the context of a territory or region, which includes material infrastructures, public sector institutions, institutions of research and learning, as well as labor markets. That is where DigiTeRRI comes in.

8.2.3 Responsible Research and Innovation (RRI)

The RRI approach aims to bridge the gap between the scientific community and society, as well as tackle the grand societal challenges (Stilgoe *et al.*, 2013). Applied RRI foresees those researchers and innovators actively design and align their work with responsibility for society and environment. This requires reflecting the need for researchers to communicate and discuss their results to build social support for and permit social guidance of their research efforts (Owen *et al.*, 2012; Stilgoe *et al.*, 2013). Social scientists and RRI approach designers stress that society has lost control over science and innovation, although the public funding has increased to stimulate and support research and innovation. Research policy has become increasingly oriented to scientific excellence, and innovation policy increasingly oriented to competitiveness. This orientation entails that social values are lost in research and innovation. RRI proponents contend that these policy arrangements create governance frameworks that are insufficient to control the development of research and new technology in potentially ethically problematic areas, such as genetics, biosciences, and information technology. Research, innovation, new technology development, manufacturing of products, the use of products, all applied processes, including business, should serve the wellbeing of society and the environment. The interplay between all the actors concerned may create the best way to achieve this wellbeing of society and the environment. The Responsible Innovation approach anticipates and assesses potential implications and societal expectations, in order to make innovation inclusive and sustainable. DigiTeRRI worked out an interlinked approach between this RRI approach, forward-looking methodologies, and stakeholder engagement.

This approach was applied to Upper Styria. Styria has a long tradition in the steel and paper production, the automotive industry, and as aerospace suppliers. These industries are familiar with global business, and they are aware of their impact in the region (Braczyk *et al.*, 2004). Such traditional industry regions have been through tough times, especially in the steel crisis in the 1980s. This crisis was caused by baleful competition and global overcapacities of steel production. Previously, the steel industry was largely a national affair, although the basis for the internationalization of the steel industry was laid as early as 1952 with the establishment of the European Coal and Steel Community. Companies in these regions are subject to constant development if they want to survive. Many of them are embedded into a network on the globe.

A paradigm shift within industries requires a new socio-technical system to be created with a different supporting infrastructure. A sociotechnical system is an organized set of people and associated technologies that are structured in a specific way to produce a specific outcome. It is a special case of a complex adaptive system. The behavior of such systems differs from the behavior of socio-ecological systems. In this context, the literature talks about regimes. A socio-technical regime describes the dominance of certain social and institutional routines and associated technical solutions that are connected to a functioning part (see Figure B8.1):

> The socio-technical regime forms the 'deep structure' that accounts for the stability of an existing socio-technical system. It refers to the semi-coherent set of rules

Figure B8.1
Meta-coordination through socio-technical regimes

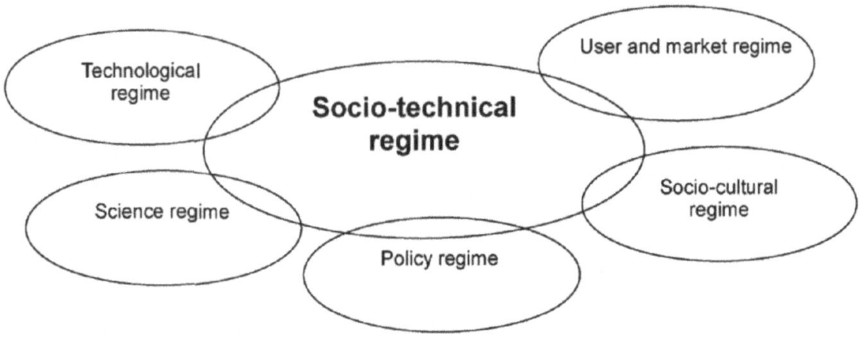

Source: Geels (2004).

> that orient and coordinate the activities of the social groups that reproduce the various elements of socio-technical systems.
>
> (Geels, 2011)

Rip and Kemp (1998) conclude that technological development is not a continuous process following along the dimensions of increasing performance and functionality. It is more like the way yeast cells grow. Developments branch in different directions, cross-connections and interactions between technological regimes, companies, and other actors occur. New technologies are always introduced against the background of existing regimes and socio-technical landscapes. They are not well defined at the starting point. Their opportunities and their success are also linked to structural problems or even crises in existing systems. Co-evolution of the technology by multi-actors in the regime can overcome challenges. Such co-evolution processes can lead to a relatively stable situation (Schot & Kanger, 2018). The ability of the actors in a region (the innovation ecosystem there) to adapt to the latest developments in technology and product development is a basic requirement for success of the economy in the region. Today, paradigm shifting into the digitalized territory is the challenge.

Digital tools, digital processes, data flood society, flood the industry, business, public administration, education system, science, and research. Digitalization is already a foundation for doing business and earning money. The core question is how to deal with these developments and how to shape the future with digitalization. However, within the low-tech industry, the gap between those who stick to their traditional business and others who are adopting digitally transformed business is becoming greater every day. Therefore, this transition process should be well defined and reflected to make sure the change process will be successful for the distinct companies and the entire region. Digital transformation causes a complete paradigm shift of production and innovation options. When talking about "digitalization," we distinguish different types:

- *Digitization*: Digitization is the technical process of converting analog signals into a digital form, and into binary digits (Hess, 2019; Tilson *et al.*, 2010).
- *Digitalization:* The term digitalization describes the manifold sociotechnical phenomena and processes of adopting and using digital technologies in broader individual context, in a broader organizational, and a broader societal context (Legner *et al.*, 2017). Digitalization is the use of digital technologies to change a business model and provide new revenue and value-producing opportunities; it is the process of moving to a digital business.[2]
- *Digital transformation*: Digital transformation is a strategy to adapt/transform business activities, processes, competencies, and models profoundly, so that the opportunities of digital technologies are leveraged and can exert their impact across society. It affects the dimensions of strategy, leadership, products, operations, culture, people, governance, and technology. Within an organization, digitalization can be characterized as proceeding along increasing maturity levels from being either "unaware," "conceptual," "defined," and "integrated" to finally "transformed" (Azhari *et al.*, 2014). Digital transformation is also understood as the seamless or end-to-end connectivity of all areas of the economy digitally and as the way in which the various players adapt to the new conditions that prevail in the digital economy (Bloching *et al.*, 2015).

The RRI approach supports and guides the digital transformation in an adequate way, in order to make sure that the outcomes of the process meet the needs of society in the region. The transition to a digitalized innovation ecosystem should provide value for the economy, address social and ecological challenges strongly and early, as well as consider certain ethical principles and normative aims. RRI processes provide suitable procedures to deal with the transformation challenge within traditional industries, in particular because of the reflexive nature of the implemented innovation process. Early involvement of stakeholder groups in the transition process, users, and citizens, as well as the development of additional or alternative knowledge sources provide a broader, more plural, and, thus, more legitimate basis for decision-making and change.

Therefore, DigiTeRRI has worked out a framework, elaborated a roadmap, and implemented actions in a participatory process to manage the challenges set by the interplay between the actors of the innovation ecosystem, which are the organization types, such as science and research, education, industry and business, policy, and the civil society organization of the region. The establishment of a self-sustaining innovation ecosystem is supported by anticipative and participative concepts by considering inclusiveness and openness.[3]

For a better understanding of the context of Styria,here is a brief summary. Styria is a federal province located in the south of Austria with a population of approximately 1.2 million inhabitants. Styria is traditionally both a resource-based and industry-oriented region. It hosts automotive industry and electronics industry, such as semiconductors or electronic components around Graz (284,000 inhabitants). In the northern part of Styria, referred to as "*Obersteiermark*" (Upper Styria), metallurgy of iron and steel, as well as material production, traditionally dominate the industry of this mountainous region, especially in the Mürz valley. Today, many suppliers or customers in the steel industry are settled in this area. The emphasis is on material production and other material-producing sectors, such as polymer engineering, industrial logistics, or environmental engineering. Today, many companies in steel production or in the automotive sector belong to large global players. The various crises in the steel industry initiated a heavy loss of jobs in the region during the last 30 years. This loss of jobs was correlated with a decrease in the population, especially young people moving to urban centers. The reason for participating in the DigiTeRRI project is based on the necessity of the further development of Styria into a region with a focus on technology and creativity, innovation, and quality of life, going digital, attractiveness as a business location, bridging the gap between strategic planning and realization of the future. Styria is recognized as a province in a European-level high-technology innovative region. Styria and especially Upper Styria are considered a robust economic and future-oriented region, having sufficient potential to innovate and to react in advance to new trends, such as digitalization, and implement its benefits, even if the qualifications and requirements on the labor market will be different.

The rate of employees with general qualification for university admittance is lower in Styria than the Austrian average today. The share of female employees is lower than that of male employees. In 2017, the general employment rate of females was about 40%. When considering, especially the industrial segments, the rate of female employees is lower than 35%. The universities and colleges in Styria offer well-recognized education and research. Generally, there is close collaboration between universities of applied sciences and the industry in Styria. Furthermore, there are strong network activities between research, the public, and industrial organizations. With the start-up Centre of Applied Technology and its collaboration with the Montanuniversität Leoben and the local industry, a lively culture of entrepreneurship and a new orientation in technology has emerged.

8.3 APPROACH AND METHODS

Collaboration in innovation systems is crucial. The conditions for cooperation between industry and research, between big, leading companies and SMEs are an important foundation for an appropriate innovation climate. In addition, the legal framework and support from policy-makers accelerate the innovation success. DigiTeRRI goes one step further and examines how innovation impacts society and especially digitalization and how that works in specific territories.

DigiTeRRI has combined the concepts discussed in Chapter B7 with the RRI by design approach and combined these with a roadmapping process. Therefore, civil society is also engaged in the DigiTeRRI innovation system. The actors in such an innovation ecosystem can be structured into five categories: industry and business, education, science and research, citizens and civil society, and government and policy. The

Figure B8.2
The DigiTeRRI approach

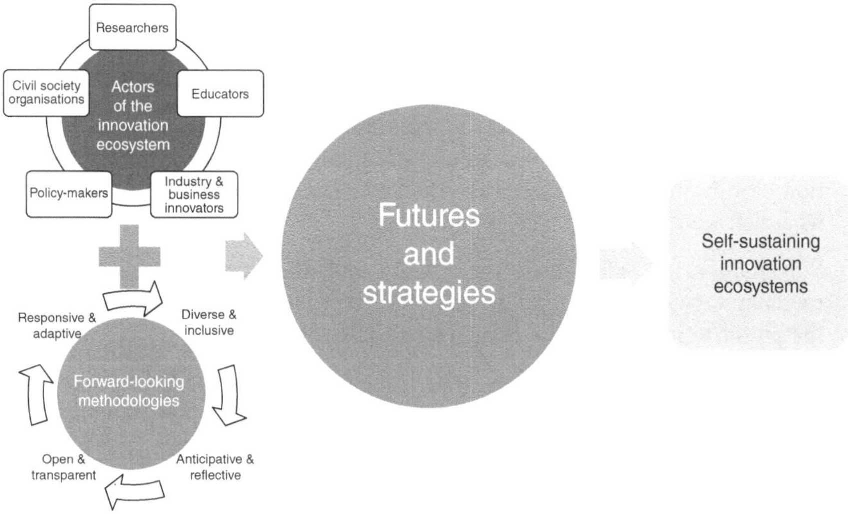

interlinkages and collaborations between these actors of the innovation ecosystem generate and create innovation, products, economic success, governmental conditions for living and doing business. Figure B8.2 presents the scheme of the DigiTeRRI RRI approach.

8.3.1 Roadmapping and stakeholder engagement

Forward-looking methodologies, combined with stakeholder engagement, align very well with the RRI approach, because it interlinks the co-creation of the stakeholders coming from science and research, education, industry and business, policy-makers, and civil society organizations with the RRI process dimensions, which are diverse and inclusive, anticipative and reflective, open and transparent, and responsive and adaptive to change. There are various forward-looking methodologies, such as Delphi study, trend analysis, foresight, and also roadmapping. In DigiTeRRI, roadmapping is applied, because it considers a time span of approximately five years into the future and DigiTeRRI wants to implement and monitor thefirst actions during the project duration of two years.

The creation of roadmaps has its roots in technology-intensive companies. Due to the increasing complexity of products and processes, these companies faced the problem of how to keep track of important technologies. There was a shortage of explicit, framework-structured representations of future developments in products and production processes for many organizations. Roadmapping offers an approach to address this challenge (Machate, 2006). The following terms play an important role in a roadmap process (International Energy Agency, 2014; Machate, 2006):

- *Roadmap* is a specific type of strategic plan. It outlines activities of an organization, which have to be undertaken over specified time frames to achieve stated goals and outcomes.
- *Roadmapping* is the evolving process. This process creates a roadmap, implements, and, monitors actions, and updates the roadmap if necessary.
- *Setting a vision* is necessary for developing a roadmap. The vision gives the direction for the roadmap. It is a motivating, positively formulated representation of a desired future state. The vision expresses where you want to be and what you want to stand for in the future.
- *Stakeholders* are affected by the actions, and, therefore, they co-create the roadmap together. They have an interest in the roadmap, support it, and have the power to implement the developed goals and measures.
- *Implementation* of the measures is the process of putting a roadmap into action, by carrying out projects and initiatives that address roadmap tasks and priorities, and by monitoring progress using a tracking system.

The DigiTeRRI roadmapping is based on a classical roadmap process. It is a four-phase process, composed of (1) stocktaking and mapping, (2) visioning, (3) working out the roadmap with the goals and objectives and with the gaps and action plans, and (4) implementation and improvement. The stocktaking and mapping of the innovation ecosystem creates a common understanding of the current situation and serve as the starting point. Visioning develops, together with all stakeholders affected, a vision statement, so that the region gets an idea where to go. The development of the goals and objectives works out concrete achievable targets and action plans on how to reach them. The implementation phase realizes the action plans. Figure B8.3 provides an overview of the road mapping process in DigiTeRRI.

The development of the roadmap considers the logic illustrated in Table B8.1.

Figure B8.3

The four phases of the roadmap process in DigiTeRRI project

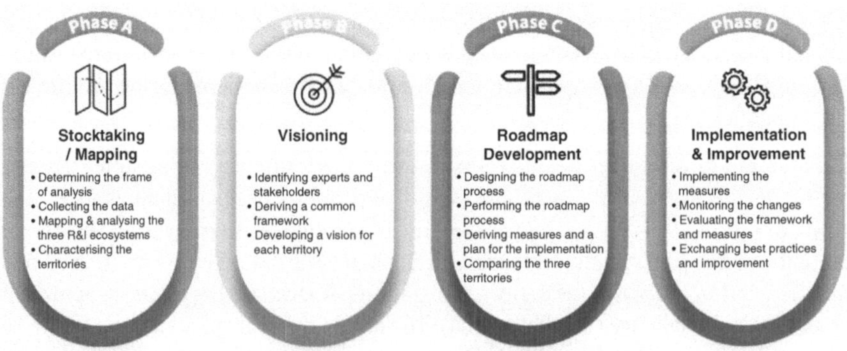

Source: Authors, AIT with graphical support by WeDo Project Intelligence Made Easy.

Table B8.1

Logic of the development of the roadmap

Logic item	Description
Goals	The goals are a clear and concise set of targets that, if achieved, will result in the desired outcome. In management literature, sometimes, there is a distinction between a "goal" and an "objective." A goal can be somewhat abstract and provides a big picture. A goal defines the general intentions and ambitions, however, can be difficult to measure.
Objectives	Once a core goal is set, defining objectives is the next step toward fostering a clear understanding of how to reach the desired outcome. The main difference between objectives and goals is that objectives cover precise actions including measurable steps individuals and groups take to move closer to the goal. They are specific targets that typically have a time-bound schedule or timeline for completion. *(For example, a company may have a goal of becoming the most profitable advertising agency in the country. Objectives related to this goal might include increasing their new business sales by 5% each quarter, growing their market share by a set timeframe, improving client retention rates by 10% each month, or adding two new products to their product line by the end of the fiscal year.)**
Milestones	Milestones are interim performance targets for achieving the goals with specific dates (e.g., "50% of the municipalities will have built the hardware for high-speed internet by October 2023")
Gaps and barriers	The roadmapping process will detect a list of potential gaps in knowledge, technology limitations, market, structural barriers, regulatory limitations, public acceptance, or other barriers to achieving the goals and milestones
Action items	The actions are developed to overcome any gaps or barriers. Actions are measures to overcome obstacles, to pave the way to achieve the goals. Typical solution actions include technology development, development of regulations and standards, policy agendas, creation of financing mechanisms, and public engagement.
Priorities and timelines	The actions will be prioritized with timelines. The most important actions that need to be taken in order to achieve the goals and the timeframes will be specified. There will be interconnections among those actions. These interconnections have to be carefully considered with regard to the affected stakeholder roles and relationships.

* Note: https://www.samewave.com/posts/the-difference-between-goals-and-objectives-create-an-actionable-business-planning-process

The goals and actions were developed in the following roadmap domains, a structure for the goals and objectives of a roadmap: knowledge and skills, technology, networks and collaboration, infrastructure, culture and values, leadership, business and market, as well as communication. These roadmap domains have been developed in the DigiTeRRI project based on Bumann and Peter (2019), however, they have been adapted to the innovation ecosystem. Bumann and Peter developed domains for the digital transformation in companies.

8.4 RESULTS AND LESSONS LEARNED

The applied process in DigiTeRRI provides results in the steps: stocktaking and mapping, visioning, roadmap development, and implementation. The implementation is not discussed in this contribution. For the first three steps, highlights of the results in Styria are presented.

8.4.1 Stocktaking and mapping

The scientific literature assigned to digitalization, EU projects, and patents data were analyzed to create a stocktaking picture. Presenting the details would go beyond the frame of this contribution. The extensive report is available in the deliverable, which is publicly available (Paier *et al.*, 2020).

Figure B8.4 shows the relative technological specialization in ICT patents from 2014–2018 in the three DigiTeRRI regions and compares this with the EU28 plus Switzerland and Norway together (value 1). It reveals that Styria has a higher level of patent activities in semiconductors and measurements than all other countries. Styria is also more active in patenting in consumer electronics.

Figure B8.4

ICT patents of the regions Grand Est in France, Styria in Austria, and Värmland in Sweden

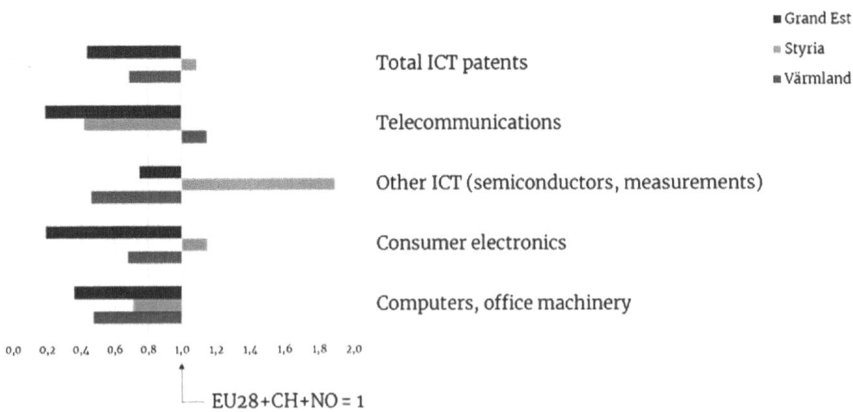

8.4.2 Vision statements

After the stocktaking and mapping, which was an important starting point for the discussion with the stakeholders, a vision statement for Upper Styria was developed. The vision statement provides the common orientation, where to go. It is the basis for developing the goals and objectives in the next step (see also Figure B8.3).

An important aspect is that the stakeholders will insist that all people in the territory can have trust and confidence in the future of Upper Styria and its innovation ecosystem. Trust should lead to close cooperation between big, leading companies, SMEs, and universities. Nonetheless, venture capital for digitalization is needed. The change should manage to create diversity and decentralization in the territory.

The condensed vision statement is formulated in the following way:

> Upper Styria is an attractive and open living space for all generations. Digitalization accelerates learning in the region and opens new perspectives in traditional and new fields. It is knowledge- and business-oriented. The pillars for international competitiveness and high quality of life are excellent research and innovation, implemented with modern infrastructure and cooperation.

8.4.3 Main goals

The main goals are as follows:

1. *Digital Transformation in the Field of Education*: The purpose of education and training is to be clearly defined and communicated to all those involved. Digital competencies are to be built upon, starting in nursery and continuing through to the university level. Some projects have already been initiated, using labs designed for pupils and to support teaching staff. Interdisciplinary work among the various subject areas is to be intensified. Professional training is to be designed to meet the needs of new job profiles. Networking among the training facilities and an exchange of knowledge with all those affected are essential objectives here. A transnational exchange in online training is to be boosted throughout the region. The educational opportunities and initiatives are to be communicated widely and made known throughout the region as well.
2. *Digital Solutions for Cities, Municipalities, the Public Sector*: Cooperation among cities, municipalities, and rural regions regarding digitalized solutions is to be intensified. A regular exchange on the current state of the art, best practices, and project ideas is to take place. Realizing standardized, user-friendly leading projects in the region is the aim. Comprehensive consulting services with respect to financial assistance and access to what is needed are to be offered to members of the public, start-ups, and companies in the region. Financial assistance for digitalization projects must be made available.
3. *Technology and Knowledge Transfer for Digitalization*: Private individuals, companies, and the public sector should have access to e-services and be able

to use them accordingly. New business models will be generated with the help of new technology, such as artificial intelligence. Research-oriented lighthouse projects will be implemented in the region and will contribute to progress being made.

4. *Creating Work-Environments and Countering the Lack of Skilled Labor*: The needs of those in the workforce, and the state of the art, as well, have been subject to constant change. Employers and the public sector need to react to this accordingly and place a well-functioning digital infrastructure at everyone's disposal. The parameters for all of this need to be set in order to encourage much-needed, highly-qualified experts in the field of digitalization to settle and stay in the region. New digital job profiles have to take gender needs and society's urgency for work-life balance into consideration. Thus, girls and women will be empowered into gaining a foothold in technical professions.
5. *A Universal Platform for Networking*: A new multi-functional platform for exchange is to be established for all the stakeholders involved. The platform is to serve as a visualization of the present situation in various fields and is to counteract any bottlenecks in the job market or in the training sector by providing the information needed. Deriving from that, the individual stakeholders will be able to gain access to various initiatives. Some of the activities might be the presentation of events or projects relevant to citizens. Data already available should be linked with real-time information. It might be conceivable for those living and working in the region to be given the latest information on avalanche, storm, or flood warnings. Any e-services the region might need have to be developed and be made available to those living and working in the region.

8.4.4 The objectives and actions defined

The main objectives and actions to be defined are as follows:

- *Digital Transformation in the Field of Education*: Building up the knowledge and skills to offer highly-qualified human resources to the regional labor market is essential for the economy, for SMEs and for large companies, as well. Highly-qualified experts in digitalization are also needed for higher education organizations, as well as for science and research organizations in the territory. Training for the elderly generations will give them access to e-governmental applications and to the labor market. Training in digitalization will not be an action for selected target groups of society; it will be an action for all societal members. Interaction and cooperation, as well as joint education programs, will be bridges, and the primary, secondary, tertiary, and academic education segments will also offer new training opportunities for lifelong learning. Table B8.2 lists the actions for achieving the developed goals.
- *Digital Solutions for Cities, Municipalities, the Public Sector*: The cooperation of the cities and the territorial government will offer new digital services for society and the economy. New digital solutions should be developed and

Table B8.2

The specific actions for the main goal "Digital Transformation in the Field of Education"

Specific action	Gap	Time frame
Digital competences in digital segment	Not sufficient general knowledge available, special knowledge has to be built up	Continuous action
Increase of competences for apprentices and pupils in digital labs (e.g., MUL, FH)	Access to excellent hardware for supporting learning process not always available	Starting in short-term, continuous action
Digital training for teachers, implementation of digital experts at schools	Teachers have to be trained; topics were included in curricula recently	Starting program development short-term, periodic activity
Digi@school: comprehensive program for digital skills addressing pupils and other target groups of society	No flagship project on digital learning in the territory	Starting program development short-term, continuous action
Knowledge exchange with transnational lectures for online courses	Option has hardly been used yet.	Starting first initiatives short-term, periodic activity (pilots exchanges from DigiTeRRI-project team)
Exchange platform of professors, lectures, and students, that is transregional for idea sharing and learning	Exchange of knowledge and co-creation between lectures are not established on a formal base (platform)	Design a demonstrator platform short-term, first pilot actions short-/medium-term
Open database on education and training programs in the territory	Barrier-free data access to information on training programs not established yet	Mid-term, continuous updates

implemented in cooperation, so they can benefit from synergies in software solution, programming, and data interfaces. Citizens should also be involved in generating user-friendly services. The defined specific actions for achieving the set goals in "Digital Solutions for Cities, Municipalities, the Public Sector" are described in Table B8.3.

- *Technology and Knowledge Transfer for Digitalization*: Digitalization leads, in general, to increased innovation velocity. Every action or institution, which provides knowledge and technology transfer, supports the ecosystem of a territory and gives added value to companies. Typical organization types are prototype lab, fab lab, or innovation lab. Cooperative interdisciplinary research initiatives have to be intensified. Digital solutions cannot be "stand-alone" knowledge, but should be offered as interdisciplinary knowledge (e.g., circular economy, tunneling, metallurgy, materials). Knowledge and technology transfer should be targeted to SMEs. An example is a digital hub. To implement all this, action networks between the stakeholders, companies, science education, and public

Table B8.3

The specific actions for the main goal "Digital Solutions for Cities, Municipalities, the Public Sector"

Specific action	Gap	Time frame
Exchange panels for digital solutions in the territory (citizen, cities, public authorities)	Cooperation on development of commonly used digital tools not established yet	Short-term, continuous activities
E-parking, e-charging stations	Analog solution (devices) is still in place and working properly	Mid-/long-term
Access to all public services with electronic signature	Electronic signature not commonly used. Software for public services is still under development	Mid-/long-term
Define and perform cooperation projects between municipalities	Municipalities are faced with different challenges and have focus on implementation of different solutions	Continuous, ongoing action
24-hour e-governance, providing physical document interfaces, connecting digital and physical administration	Interfaces between online services and physical services also have to be improved	Mid-term
Getting financial resources (funds)	Critical financial situation of municipalities because of COVID-19 expenditures	Short-term and ongoing action

authorities should be built. Table B8.4 presents the developed action for achieving the goals in "Technology and Knowledge Transfer for Digitalization."

- *Creating work-environments and countering the lack of skilled labor.* The territorial labor market is suffering from a lack of highly-qualified human resources. Measures to improve this situation in the Styrian territory are seen in the creation of attractive working environments and the attraction of external co-workers (e.g., highly-qualified immigrants). A core issue in this measurement cluster is the improvement of the family situation (e.g., childcare opportunities, new career path, and flexible working conditions for females). Table B8.5 lists the actions for reaching the goals in "Creating Work Environments and Countering the Lack of Skilled Labor."
- *A Universal Platform for Networking*: The digital platform reflecting the profile of the territory and giving access to digital services should be developed and implemented. The roadmap process asks for the following functionality:
  - Home base for networks: The networking and cooperation between all stakeholder groups will need a digital home base.

Table B8.4
The specific actions for the main goal "Technology and Knowledge Transfer for Digitalization"

Specific action	Gap	Time frame
Demonstrator cloud for data sharing	Common hardware and software not established	Short-term
Lab	Investment for equipment and operation has to be provided	Mid-term
Interdisciplinary initiatives and solutions	No room for experimental approach defined, change of culture needed	Short-term
Consulting for SMEs and craft business for digital business solutions	Offer special programs to SMEs and address them in a proper manner	Short-/mid-term
Digi network 4 Styria: providers, economy, science education, public administration	Many individual activities and networks on various objectives, general framework missing	Mid-term
Research initiatives	Definition of research topics is needed, financing has to be ensured (cooperative funding)	Short-term and ongoing
Development and implementation of Artificial Intelligence-solutions, high performance computing initiatives	Capacities on Artificial Intelligence and High-Performance Computing (HPC), etc., have to be built up. Experts should be attracted by the territory.	Mid-term

- One-stop-shop for third parties interested in the territory.
- Portal to digital e-government solutions.
- Career portal.
- Gender equality initiatives and career opportunities for females.
- Specific information services for citizens (e.g., storm and avalanche warning in alpine areas).
- Information on regional fairs.
- Description of companies, science, and education organizations.
- Training opportunities and education programs.

Table B8.6 presents the action, the gap, and the timeframe for the development of this multifunctional platform.

Table B8.5

The specific actions for the main goal "Creating Work Environments and Countering the Lack of Skilled Labor"

Specific action	Gap	Time frame
Co-working space – family	New models are not appreciated in the existing work environment (industrial production)	Mid-term, ongoing action
Childcare	Financial resources have to be provided and attractive locations for children have to be found	Short-term, ongoing action
Attract highly qualified immigrants	Region has to put more effort into becoming attractive	Mid-term, ongoing action
Strengthening entrepreneurship	Citizens of the region have to be motivated to become entrepreneurs and see the advantage of being the owner of a company	Mid-term, ongoing action
Open career paths between training and professional activity	Strict barriers between higher education organizations and companies prevent application of employees for higher qualifications	Mid-term, settle the programs

Table B8.6

The specific actions for the main goal "A Universal Platform for Networking"

Specific action	Gap	Time frame
Multifunctional digital platform	Current webpages do not offer these services, concept for platform and services software, hardware and operation model are missing	Short-term concept and specification and financial plan Mid-term start implementation

8.5 CONCLUSION AND RECOMMENDATIONS

In Styria, several high-tech companies act worldwide as specialists for specific technologies. They work globally but grow locally. All industry and business organization depend on the resources, competences, infrastructure, regulations, and laws of the innovation ecosystem to which they belong. The values of society shape the orientation of education and create competences. The digital transformation of industry and research requires the transition of the whole innovation ecosystem in a region, because of the needed competences through well-educated engineers. There is also a need for the latest technologies and well-implemented infrastructure for all people living in a region, so that the foundation of this culture in a territory supports the companies in further development and success. The success of industry and business is linked to the specific culture and the established values, trust, leadership, and networks in a region.

The co-creation of strategies and a roadmap, together with the actors of the innovation ecosystem, provides a common orientation and develops common goals and actions. It strengthens the network in the territory between companies and research, between education and science, as well as education and industry, between policy-makers and companies as well as research, and uncovers the needed competences in the whole society, so that the knowledge creation for top engineers finds fruitful ground. This process creates awareness for the competences, a common understanding and supported communication. Furthermore, it builds a common understanding for the implications of innovation on society and the environment. In this way, the interfaces between these organization types and the gaps become obvious and, thus, can be solved and closed. Such a common approach strengthens the innovation ecosystem because the opportunities for all actors become visible and networks and collaboration start. Schools and students learn about interesting jobs in industry and business. Digitalization allows work to take place anywhere in the world, for example, a high-tech firm in Styria. However, the tie and commitment to the employer are much stronger if the employees live in the surroundings, which was discussed in several workshops.

The DigiTeRRI project applied a comprehensive approach, which started with a stocktaking and mapping of the innovation ecosystem in Styria. This work revealed a lot of competences, knowledge, products, networks, technologies, etc., available in the region. The result of this stocktaking was an excellent starting point for the stakeholder workshops, because a common understanding about the current situation regarding digitalization had been reached. Next, the stakeholders, representatives from companies, SMEs, from universities and colleges, from high schools, from municipalities, from other public organization, as well as students, co-created together (in highly structured workshops) their vision statement, and, based on this, the goals and defined the actions to be implemented.

The five main goals are:

- Digital Transformation in the Field of Education
- Digital Solutions for Cities, Municipalities, the Public Sector
- Technology and Knowledge Transfer for Digitalization
- Creating Work Environments and Countering the Lack of Skilled Labor
- A Universal Platform for Networking

In these five main goals, specific objectives and actions have been developed for bridging gaps. The concrete action plans and their implementation created the first success within the affected group of people in the region (outlined in Tables B8.1–B8.6).

Companies have brough their needs regarding skilled employees, the necessity for transferring the processes of small companies into digital ones. The stakeholders have learned that the collaboration between big, global companies in the region with universities and research organization there, and also with SMEs, can: (1) create high potential for successful innovation to the big company, (2) also create technology and knowledge for the university, and (3) give SMEs the possibility to deliver high tech products or services and, thus, also create knowledge and technologies. Such collaboration offers interesting jobs for highly-educated people. DigiTeRRI workshops have managed to create awareness in high schools and especially in specific action for girls for such jobs. Supporting girls and making scientific fields more attractive, such as ICT, physics, or mathematics, could open the path for more engineers. The DigiTeRRI approach has supported the trust building of stakeholders and consumer loyalty.

Industry and business are well acquainted with roadmapping processes and, therefore, this procedure was well received in the stakeholder group.

The DigiTeRRI approach is RRI by design. This means that the affected actors in the innovation ecosystem of Styria have co-created their future in a diverse, anticipative, and reflective, open, transparent, responsive, and adaptive-to-change process. This process reinforces the networks for companies and support their needs. The process also uncovered that girls need support and specific training so that it will be easier for them to become an engineer for the high-tech companies in Styria.

The DigiTeRRI work in Styria underlines that implementation of RRI in firms increases competitive opportunities, because RRI anticipates negative effects in the economy, society, and ecology. The workshops in Styria, with participants from industry and business, science and research, education, public administration organization, have become aware of this context. The RRI by design approach created common orientation and implemented actions, such as supporting education for information technologies for girls, digital fairs and exhibitions for SMEs, according to the RRI criteria. By implementing RRI, companies are more profitable, because they not only can invest in business tools, equipment, and processes that directly impact productivity, but also invest in employee engagement and training, which has a positive impact on productivity. Implementing RRI strategies can create a sense of "meaningful work" in employees. By aligning ethical values with their customers, companies will experience more engaged customers.

The work in DigiTeRRI revealed further necessary development. The major development relates to evaluation, as it seems necessary to have further investigation of the way to assess digital initiatives relevant to RRI on a different scale: impact on the territory, impact for beneficiaries of the proposed actions, and impact on the members of the territorial ecosystem. The RRI approach for industry and business still has some limits regarding operating globally, or IPRs. RRI needs to be adjusted or further developed for business. However, digitalization, which is a strong driver for many businesses and many industries, is strongly linked to ethics (e.g., the ethical guidelines for trustworthy AI in the EU). Therefore, at least several aspects of the RRI approach can be found in Horizon Europe technical calls. The practice of RRI in technically driven projects provides a fantastic context for further proving the RRI concept.

DISCLOSURE STATEMENT

No potential conflict of interest was reported by the authors.

FUNDING

The DIGITERRI project has received funding from the European Union's Horizon 2020 research and innovation program under grant agreement No 873010. The opinions expressed in this article reflect only the authors' view and in no way reflect the European Union's opinions.

NOTES

1. https://ec.europa.eu/commission/presscorner/detail/en/ip_20_1530
2. Gartner Glossary, https://www.gartner.com/en/information-technology/glossary/digitalization.
3. For more information on the DigiTeRRI framework, see Nyguen *et al.* (2021).

REFERENCES

Azhari, P., Faraby, N., Rossmann, A., Steimel, B., & Wichmann, K. S. (2014) *Digital transformation report. Eine empirische Studie.* neuland digital vision & transformation / Wirtschaftswoche.

Bloching, B., Leutiger, P., Oltmanns, T., Rossbach, C., Schlick, T., Remane, G., Quick, P., & Shafranyuk, O. (2015). The digital transformation of industry - How important is it? Who are the winners? What must be done? Available at: www. rolandberger. com/publications/publication_pdf/roland_berger_ digital_transformation_of _industry_20150315. pdf

Bouglet, J., Joffre, O., & Simon, E. (2012). How to reconcile business with sustainable development: an innovation approach. *Society and Business Review*, *7*(2), 212–222.

Braczyk, H.-J., Cooke, P., & Heidenreich, M. (2004). *Regional Innovation systems: The role of governances in a globalized world.* CRC Press.

Brunetti, F., Matt, D. T., Bonfanti, A., De Longhi, A., Pedrini, G., & Orzes, G. (2020). Digital transformation challenges: Strategies emerging from a multi-stakeholder approach. *The TQM Journal*, *32*(4), 697–724.

Bumann, J., & Peter, M. (2019). Action fields of digital transformation: a review and comparative analysis of digital transformation maturity models and frameworks. In *Digitalisierung und andere Innovationsformen im Management* (pp. 13–40). Editiosn Gesowip.

Carlsson, B., & Stankiewicz, R. (1991). On the nature, function and composition of technological systems. *Journal of Evolutionary Economics*, *1*(2), 93–118. https://doi.org/10.1007/BF01224915.

Carroll, A. B. (2015). Corporate social responsibility. *Organizational Dynamics*, *44*(2), 87–96.

Chatfield, K., Borsella, E., Mantovani, E., Porcari, A., & Stahl, B. (2017). An investigation into risk perception in the ICT industry as a core component of Responsible Research and Innovation. *Sustainability*, *9*, 1424. 10.3390/su9081424.

Dolata, U. (2009). Technological innovations and sectoral change: Transformative capacity, adaptability, patterns of change: An analytical framework. *Research Policy*, *38*(6), 1066–1076. https://doi.org/10.1016/j.respol.2009.03.006.

Edquist, C. (Ed.). (2012). *Systems of innovation: Technologies, institutions and organizations* (1st edition). Routledge.

Ferrero, I., & Sison, A. J. G. (2014). A quantitative analysis of authors, schools and themes in virtue ethics articles in business ethics and management journals (1980–2011). *Business Ethics*, *23* (4), 375-–400. https://doi.org/10.1111/beer.12057.

Freeman, C. (1987). *Technology policy and economic performance: Lessons from Japan.* Pinter.

Gautier, A., & Pache, A. C. (2015). Research on corporate philanthropy: A review and assessment. *Journal of Business Ethics*, *126*(3), 343–369.

Geels, F. W. (2004). From sectoral systems of innovation to socio-technical systems: Insights about dynamics and change from sociology and institutional theory. *Research Policy*, *33*(6–7), 897–920. https://doi.org/10.1016/j.respol.2004.01.015.

Geels, F. W. (2011). The multi-level perspective on sustainability transitions: Responses to seven criticisms. *Environmental Innovation and Societal Transitions*, *1*(1), 24–40. https://doi.org/10.1016/j.eist.2011.02.002.

Giddens, A. (1984). *The constitution of society*. Polity Press.

Grundke, R., Marcolin, L., Nguyen, T. L. B., & Squicciarini, M. (2018). Which skills for the digital era?: Returns to skills analysis (OECD Science, Technology and Industry Working Papers No. 2018/09). OECD Publishing. https://doi.org/10.1787/9a9479b5-en

Hekkert, M. P., Suurs, R. A. A., Negro, S. O., Kuhlmann, S., & Smits, R. E. H. M. (2007). Functions of innovation systems: A new approach for analysing technological change. *Technological Forecasting and Social Change*, *74*(4), 413–432. https://doi.org/10.1016/j.techfore.2006.03.002.

Hess, T. (2019). Digitale Transformation strategisch steuern. Vom Zufallstreffer zum systematischen Vorgehen. In *Die Enzyklopädie der Wirtschaftsinformatik erscheint im GITO* Springer Verlag. https://doi.org/10.1016/S1048-9843(02)00096-6.

International Energy Agency (2014). Energy technology roadmaps: a guide to development and implementation. https://doi.org/10.1787/9789264086340-en.

Isaksen, A., Trippl, M., Kyllingstad, N., & Rypestøl, J.O. (2021). Digital transformation of regional industries through asset modification, *Competitiveness Review*, *31*(1), 130–144. https://doi.org/10.1108/CR-12-2019-0140

Johnson, A., & Jacobsson, S. (2001). Inducement and blocking mechanisms in the development of a new industry: The case of renewable energy technology in Sweden. In *Technology and the Market*. Edward Elgar Publishing.

Kolk, A. (2016). The social responsibility of international business: From ethics and the environment to CSR and sustainable development. *Journal of World Business*, *51*(1), 23–34.

Legner, C., Eymann, T., Hess, T., Matt, C., Böhmann, T., Drews, P., Maedche, A., Urbach, N., & Ahlemann, F. (2017). Digitalization: Opportunity and challenge for the business and information systems engineering community. *Business & Information Systems Engineering*. *59*, 301–308. https://doi.org/10.1007/s12599-017-0484-2.

Lundvall, B. Å. (2007). National innovation systems—analytical concept and development tool. *Industry and Innovation*, *14*(1), 95–119.

Lundvall, B.-Å. (Ed.). (2010). *National systems of innovation: Toward a theory of innovation and interactive learning*. Anthem Press.

Machate, A. (2006). Zukunftsgestaltung durch Roadmapping: Vorgehensweise und Methodeneinsatz für eine zielorientierte Erstellung und Visualisierung von Roadmaps. (Doctoral dissertation, Technische Universität München.

Malerba, F. (Ed.). (2004). *Sectoral systems of innovation: Concepts, issues and analyses of six major sectors in Europe*. Cambridge University Press. https://doi.org/10.1017/CBO9780511493270.

Malerba, F. (2005). Sectoral systems of innovation: A framework for linking innovation to the knowledge base, structure and dynamics of sectors. *Economics of Innovation and New Technology*, *14*(1–2), 63–82. https://doi.org/10.1080/1043859042000228688.

Martinuzzi, A., Blok, V., Brem, A., Stahl, B., & Schönherr, N. (2018). Responsible research and innovation in industry; Challenges, insights and perspectives. *Sustainability*, *10*(3), 702.

Montiel, I., & Delgado-Ceballos, J. (2014). Defining and measuring corporate sustainability: Are we there yet?. *Organization & Environment*, *27*(2), 113–139.

Nelson, R. R. (Ed.). (1993). *National innovation systems: A comparative analysis* (1st edition). Oxford University Press.

Nguyen, N., Ørding Hansen, J., & Jensen, A. (2021). Framework for RRI implementation in R&I ecosystems of the three territories. Deliverable for DigiTeRRI project. DOI: 10.5281/zenodo.5969119.

Owen, R., Stilgoe, J., Macnaghten, P., Gorman, M., Fisher, E., & Guston, D. (2012). A framework for Responsible Innovation. In *Responsible Innovation* (pp. 27–50). John Wiley & Sons, Ltd. https://doi.org/10.1002/9781118551424.ch2.

Paier, M., Kasztler, A., Toussaint, S., Heller-Schuh, B., Schiebel, E., Zahradnik, G., & Stegmann McCallion, M. (2020). Description of the R&I ecosystem landscapes of Grand-Est, Styria and Värmland. DigiTeRRI Deliverable 2.3. (V1.1). Zenodo. https://doi.org/10.5281/zenodo.4467757

Rip, A., & Kemp, R. (1998). Technological change. In S. Rayner, & E. L. Malone (Eds.), *Human choice and climate change* (vol. 2, pp. 327–399). Battelle Press.

Schot, J., & L. Kanger (2018). Deep transitions: Emergence, acceleration, stabilization and directionality. *Research Policy*, *47*(6), 1045–1059.

Stahl, B. (2018). RRI in industry: On the translation of the RRI discourse into the private domain. *The ORBIT Journal*, *1*(3), 1–11. https://doi.org/10.29297/orbit.v1i3.64.

Starik, M., & Kanashiro, P. (2013). Toward a theory of sustainability management: Uncovering and integrating the nearly obvious. *Organization & Environment*, *26*(1), 7–30.

Stilgoe, J., Owen, R., & Macnaghten, P. (2013). Developing a framework for responsible innovation. *Research Policy*, *42*(9), 1568–1580. https://doi.org/10.1016/j.respol.2013.05.008.

Tilson, D., Lyytinen, K., & Sørensen, C. (2010). Digital infrastructures: The missing IS research agenda. *Information Systems Research*, *21*, 748–759. https://doi.org/10.1287/isre.1100.0318.

van de Poel, I., Asveld, L., Flipse, S., Klaassen, P., Scholten, V., & Yaghmaei, E. (2017). Company strategies for Responsible Research and Innovation (RRI): A conceptual model. *Sustainability*, *9*, 2045. 10.3390/su9112045.

Van der Byl, C. A., & Slawinski, N. (2015). Embracing tensions in corporate sustainability: A review of research from win-wins and trade-offs to paradoxes and beyond. *Organization & Environment*, *28*(1), 54–79.

Whiteman, G., Walker, B., & Perego, P. (2013). Planetary boundaries: Ecological foundations for corporate sustainability. *Journal of Management Studies*, *50*(2), 307336.

Part C
Tools and methods

Part C provides detailed insights into the methods and tools that were developed and applied in another EU-funded project, called “LIVING INNOVATION.” The project was coordinated by André Martinuzzi and aimed at changing the view of industry from perceiving RRI as an additional burden to understanding RRI as a business opportunity.

- Chapter C1 shows how the LIVING INNOVATION project explored the business case for Responsible Innovation and aimed at changing the view from risk to opportunity.
- Chapter C2 on “Co-Creating Innovations” provides ideas on how to engage with users and citizens in Responsible Innovation.
- Chapter C3 on “Responsible Design Thinking” explains how responsibility and sustainability can best be integrated into Design Thinking processes.
- Chapter C4 on “Real-Life Inclusion” provides comprehensive insights and learning from a case study on how to innovate with low socio-economic status families.
- Chapter C5 on “Inclusive Workshops” presents a toolbox on how to facilitate workshops with blind and visually impaired people.

C1

Exploring the business case for Responsible Innovation

How to change the perception of Responsible Innovation from risk to opportunity

André Martinuzzi and Svetlana Ivanova

1.1 BACKGROUND AND CHALLENGES

Responsible Innovation in general and RRI in particular are often regarded as European, policy-driven approaches. This perspective has been reinforced by the European Union's substantial funding of approximately 180 RRI-related projects over the past decade, with a total contribution of €365 million. Most of these projects targeted the public sector, including government entities, science funds, administrative bodies, universities, and individual researchers. In contrast, the private sector has played a minor role in these EU-funded projects (Ivanova *et al.*, 2023). In parallel to their implementation, the scientific discourse started to explore the particularities of RRI within the business sector and competitive environments. For instance, Iatridis and Schroeder (2016) demonstrated the usability of CSR tools (i.e., standards, global initiatives, and principles) for RRI, whereas Dreyer *et al.* (2017) argued that RRI-related concepts, tools, and methodologies are not aligned with current industrial practices. Ceicyte and Petraite (2018), meanwhile, provided a network-based view on RRI to better understand the driving forces behind RRI activities, revealing how firms' multi-stakeholder networks shape Responsible Innovation practices throughout the different stages of an innovation process (Ceicyte *et al.*, 2021). Brand and Blok (2019) analyzed the deliberative engagement of companies with stakeholders and the wider public and identified several forms of tension in the ways that competitive markets operate, on the one hand, and the social and ethical requirements of innovation processes, on the other. Schönherr, Martinuzzi, and Jarmai (2020) outlined a business case for RRI, showing that responsibility and innovation can mutually strengthen each other, and suggested that additional research is required to provide insights into how Responsible Innovation may support companies in generating a competitive

DOI: 10.4324/9781003319481-23

advantage. Owen *et al.* (2021) identified the factors influencing the dynamics of the institutionalization of RRI in a major national public research-funding organization, while Steen, Nauta, and Gaasterland (2018) provided insights into institutionalizing RRI in a major research-performing organization. Both studies emphasized the need for similar investigations into the institutionalization of RRI in the business sector but acknowledged that their findings might not be directly transferable due to different logics and interests.

In 2017, a topic within the European Framework Programme Horizon 2020 called for a project in which large corporations would join forces and experiment with new ways of developing their research and innovation activities in line with the principles of RRI. The funded project should establish a neutral and open space in which companies, citizens, scientists, and other stakeholders could participate, network, and learn from each other. The project should develop, test, and disseminate new approaches to innovation in industrial contexts, building on and improving existing tools and disseminating good RRI practices within industrial communities.

The LIVING INNOVATION project was designed to address these challenges while operating on the fundamental premise that promoting the recognition of RRI's value within the industry was crucial for advancing its adoption in industrial contexts. The project's core objective was to establish a flagship initiative for RRI in the business sector, going beyond the isolated, firm-level cases available at that time and showcasing effective integration of RRI in industry that is transferable across sectors. This vision was to be realized through the implementation of four key strategies:

1. *Activating industry leaders, experts, and citizens*: Encouraging these stakeholders to actively engage in experimenting with responsible methods of co-creating innovations.
2. *Building capacity for RRI implementation*: Enhancing the skills and readiness of industry participants to effectively incorporate RRI principles into their activities.
3. *Developing tools applicable across industry sectors*: Creating versatile tools and resources that could be employed in diverse industrial contexts.
4. *Transforming attitudes toward RRI from risk to opportunity*: Changing the perception of RRI from a potential liability to an opportunity for growth and innovation.

To achieve this ambitious vision, the project required a coordinated and simultaneous focus on three distinct dimensions (Figure C1.1):

- *Outcomes*: The project sought to motivate industry leaders, experts, and citizens to experiment with responsible ways of co-creating innovations. The outcomes dimension of the project pertained to the effectiveness of RRI integration in the industrial sector. To achieve this, physical and virtual spaces were established,

Figure C1.1
The target dimensions of the LIVING INNOVATION project

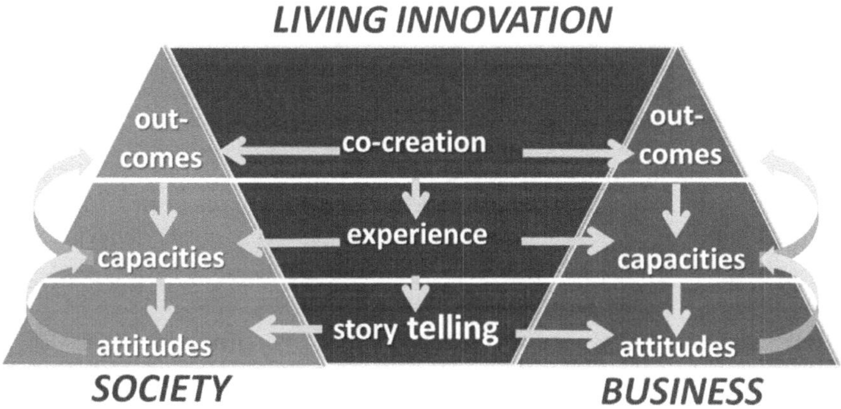

bringing together industry professionals and citizens to co-create new approaches to innovation and showcase the value of integrating RRI into industry practices. Within these collaborative spaces, the project aimed to produce innovation blueprints that were sufficiently detailed to enable rapid prototyping and roll-out at the industry level after the conclusion of the project.

- *Capacities*: The project set out to increase the capacity for RRI implementation and to showcase tools that could be used across industry sectors. This second dimension referred to the knowledge, skills, and tools necessary to achieve desired RRI outcomes. Previous attempts to integrate RRI have often relied on checklist approaches or external professional facilitation. This has presented challenges, particularly when industries lacked the internal capacity to understand, design, and execute such RRI processes independently, leading to risks of failure and disillusionment. To address this, the project aimed to build the necessary capacities for RRI implementation and to allow both industry leaders and citizens to experience first-hand how co-creation leads to mutually beneficial solutions.
- *Attitudes*: The project's third primary goal was to change the perceptions of RRI from being perceived as a risk to being viewed as a business opportunity. The attitudes dimension referred to the values, motivations, and cultures that determine resistance to engage with RRI. As these attitudes might differ significantly, the project planned to demonstrate the effectiveness of RRI throughout the innovation process through carefully designed outreach and dissemination activities based on audio-visual storytelling. Moreover, active engagement in dialogues with CSR- and RRI-related initiatives should contribute to a wider shift in perception and the development of positive attitudes toward RRI.

1.2 SCOPE AND METHODS

The LIVING INNOVATION project set out to become a flagship initiative for Responsible Innovation in the industry sector, with a key focus on demonstrating the benefits of co-creating innovations in a truly inclusive manner. The selection of the sector and the specific field of innovation was therefore done with great care and with certain criteria in mind.

First and foremost, the chosen sector needed to exhibit significant innovation potential, both from a technical perspective, with the development and application of numerous new technologies, and from an economic standpoint, with substantial growth and profit prospects. Consequently, the Information and Communication Technology (ICT) sector and the theme of digitalization were carefully selected.

Furthermore, the field of application had to be one that would profoundly impact people's lives and where questions of responsibility and sustainability held paramount importance. This led to the selection of housing as a central area of focus, specifically exploring how people would live in the year 2030. This emphasis allowed the project to place societal needs and acceptance at the heart of the innovation process, a task that a single company might not have been able to accomplish on its own.

It quickly became evident that the project should encompass not only smart homes but also smart health, as these two topics are intricately intertwined in practice. While smart homes are often associated with technology enthusiasts, the health aspect holds significance for a broader spectrum of individuals, including health enthusiasts, those seeking self-optimization, as well as those focused on childcare and providing assistance for the sick, elderly, and disabled. Both smart homes and smart health are integral components of the vision for smart future living and provide excellent opportunities for developing responsible future solutions.

All these considerations were reflected in the consortium composition, which brought together major multinational ICT companies, such as Siemens, ATOS, Ottobock, Telefonica, Infineon, and Ericsson, alongside universities and research institutions possessing expertise in citizens' involvement, co-creation, and multistakeholder dialogues.

The LIVING INNOVATION project comprised two primary streams:

1. *Community building*: This stream aimed to foster a community of practice by empowering and motivating experts from companies, academia, and non-governmental organizations (NGOs) to engage in the exchange of information and knowledge concerning various aspects of Responsible Innovation.
2. *Co-creation experiments*: In this stream, companies collaborated closely with citizens to address specific challenges and develop innovative solutions through concrete problem-solving efforts.

These streams were strategically designed to yield outcomes across three distinct dimensions:

1. *Process-oriented results*: This dimension encompasses experiences and instructions on how Responsible Innovation can be implemented in concrete terms. It addresses which aspects need to be taken into account and how a high level of process quality can be ensured. The target group for these outcomes consisted of innovation managers, designers, and facilitators.
2. *Tangible results in the areas of smart health and smart homes*: These outcomes represent developments that would either not be available at all or would be of lower quality without the application of Responsible Innovation. The intended recipients of these results were innovators, engineers, and venture capitalists.
3. *Business cases and stories*: This dimension includes cases and narratives that illustrate the benefits of Responsible Innovation and aim to persuade top-level managers to follow the example set by the partner companies of the LIVING INNOVATION project.

1.2.1 Community building

The LIVING INNOVATION project established a "community of practice" for RRI within the industrial sector. This community would bring together corporate managers, consultants, researchers, and other stakeholders by providing a platform where they could collaborate, learn from each other, exchange knowledge, and enhance their expertise in RRI-related matters. The envisioned community was intended to have an informal character, with participation being entirely voluntary and driven by members' genuine interest. Given that the term RRI was not widely recognized in the target industry, determining a specific subject or domain of focus presented a challenge. As a result, the project adopted an approach that encompassed a diverse range of topics. These topics spanned from specific technologies in smart homes and smart health to broader themes, including surveillance, competitiveness, and the responsibility of the ICT sector. This approach allowed for a more inclusive and adaptable framework that accommodated a variety of interests and knowledge levels within the community.

To create, cultivate, and sustain the LIVING INNOVATION community, the project established an online platform, organized a broad range of community events, and made use of audio-visual storytelling. All these activities were designed to raise awareness of the potential business opportunities associated with RRI; empower the community members in this area; initiate collaboration; encourage the exchange of experiences, insights, and even resources; and foster a sense of belonging and identity among its members. In establishing and further developing the LIVING INNOVATION community, we distinguished between the following types of members:

- *Consortium members*, who led the first interactions with new community members, participated in discussions, and initiated and delivered online events.

- *Citizens*, who voiced their specific needs and expectations, and provided insights into their daily living conditions. They were perceived as prospective users of future technologies and, simultaneously, advocates of socially responsible development and use.
- *Experts* from business, civil society, policy, and science, who exchanged knowledge and experiences, networked, and participated in joint activities, events, and discussions. As the project covered a broad spectrum of topics, the experts could have diverse thematic and institutional backgrounds:
  - Corporate research and innovation managers with thematic links to smart homes and smart health, working in medium-sized or large companies.
  - CSR managers in such companies (e.g., ICT sector, health sector, smart homes) and independent experts (e.g., consultants, researchers) on smart homes and smart health.
  - Founders or partners of startups and SMEs with thematic links to smart homes and smart health.
  - Experts with a specific background in societal trends and user need with thematic links to smart homes and smart health.
  - Experts in RRI, design thinking, co-creation, stakeholder dialogues, and other facilitation methods.

1.2.2 Community platform

As the LIVING INNOVATION project sought to raise awareness of the benefits of Responsible Innovation in industry, the above-mentioned experts were the primary target group of the community platform, while citizens were the focus of the co-creation experiments (as discussed in Chapter C2). The community platform was designed to serve as a primary access point for information on the corporate benefits of Responsible Innovation, as an entry point for collaboration between the consortium and other community members, and as a source of information about the project's activities. As the primary focus was on facilitating exchanges related to innovation processes rather than on specific technologies, we encouraged discussions on management challenges, strategies for designing and implementing Responsible Innovation processes, and the resulting business benefits. The information provided was practical and actionable, following a "lead-by-example" approach. To achieve this, the community platform concentrated on a few key thematic areas:

- General information about Responsible Innovation in the business sector, sharing best practices, and disseminating knowledge on the realm of Responsible Innovation.
- Specific information on smart homes and smart health, showcasing how Responsible Innovation can be successfully implemented.

- Process-related experiences and tools, covering specific aspects of co-creation, inclusive innovation, and other key concepts of Responsible Innovation.
- New thematic areas in response to COVID-19, such as challenges related to remote working, teaching, and learning.

The online community platform was designed, implemented, and moderated over a three-year period. It allowed experts to register, actively participate as community members, and receive a weekly newsletter. To achieve this, the platform was structured with specific sections accessible to all users without requiring them to register, such as general information about the project and a news section. In contrast, other sections, including an event calendar, knowledge units, and the ability to connect with other members, were exclusively available to registered users. The platform adopted a tiered approach to content, offering a preview of the project's core information to all users while reserving additional, exclusive content for registered members. This strategy proved effective in motivating new users to register and become active participants in the community. Over the course of three years, approximately 2,000 experts registered on the platform and opted to receive the weekly newsletter. The community platform incorporated the following key features:

- *General project information*: This section provided an overview of the project, offering insights into its objectives and key activities.
- *News*: This section provided up-to-date and reliable information, highlighting global trends and recent events related to technologies, policies, and successful implementation of Responsible Innovation. It established the project as a source of valuable and actionable information and provided a reason to regularly visit the platform.
- *Network*: Personalized user profiles encouraged networking among the community members based on their areas of interest. A sophisticated user credit system was implemented to incentivize active participation, enabling highly active members to unlock additional functionalities and assume specific roles.
- *Events*: This feature promoted events organized by the LIVING INNOVATION project but also allowed community members to showcase their own events. Over a period of three years, the project successfully organized 36 online events, including dialogues, workshops, and webinars.
- *Knowledge units*: This section offered comprehensive information developed by the project and provided an editorial system that allowed community members to share their own publications.
- *Joint actions*: This dedicated feature facilitated collaboration among community members and supported them in co-developing new technologies, tools,

roadmaps, or visions. Consortium members acted as facilitators and organized several online meetings and webinars for each joint action. In total, 12 joint actions were implemented, covering topics such as "Co-creating the smart kitchen," "Benchmarking your Responsible Innovation maturity," "Exploring affordable smart home solutions," and "Co-developing a framework for inclusive ICT solutions."

1.2.3 Online conferences

To promote the project and the community platform, the project organized an opening virtual conference approximately a year after its launch. The choice of an online format was a strategic one, enabling the project to reach a global audience while minimizing the need for travel and thus reducing associated carbon emissions. It is worth noting too that this decision was made before the onset of the COVID-19 pandemic, underscoring the project's forward-thinking and innovative approach to leveraging digital technology to stage a large-scale online conference.

The opening conference was a dynamic and inclusive event that seamlessly blended pre-recorded speeches with interviews with prominent experts. These segments were complemented by live online discussions conducted through chat forums. The conference spanned a total of 60 sessions, shining a spotlight on the myriad advantages of RRI. In doing so, it gave industry leaders and experts insights into pertinent questions, issues, and themes in the context of smart future living, covering topics such as smart homes, smart health, digitalization, and sustainability, and showcasing roughly 50 RRI stories. The opening conference was made accessible to the public and offered free of charge. The entirety of its content was available for on-demand viewing for a week, thereby accommodating participants who were unable to attend the live session. In total, the conference attracted 376 participants from 51 different countries. Most registered participants were affiliated with the business and academic sectors, with a smaller percentage coming from other sectors and policy backgrounds. This international and multi-sectoral engagement underscored the conference's success in reaching a diverse and global audience.

The final conference was held in collaboration with the 5th edition of the Responsible Innovation Summit. Over a span of four days, distinguished leaders, innovation and CSR managers, policy specialists, and academics came together for a series of online events. The aim was to collectively explore how the force of innovation could be harnessed to redefine conventional business practices and foster the creation of a more sustainable economy. Due to the constraints imposed by COVID-19, the summit was implemented as a virtual conference in which the LIVING INNOVATION project curated and conducted four sessions:

1. A high-level discussion on Responsible Innovation with the Austrian Federal Minister for Digital and Economic Affairs, the CEO of Infineon Technologies Austria AG, and the CEO of Microsoft Austria.
2. A session tailored to guide innovation managers, facilitators, and practitioners in designing responsible innovation processes.

3. A reflective session exploring various perspectives on inclusive innovation, featuring insights from academics, laypeople, and technologists.
4. A session offering a glimpse into an exciting future characterized by smart homes, health, technology, and responsibility, including a discussion with the Youth Panel.

This strategic and comprehensive approach ensured a dynamic and influential final conference, facilitating meaningful conversations and setting the stage for a more responsible and innovative future. Each session attracted substantial interest, with more than 200 participants in attendance and over 500 registrations secured for the Responsible Innovation Summit.

1.2.4 Webinars

In addition to the two major conferences focused on public outreach, a series of monthly webinars were organized to foster extensive engagement among community members, focusing on timely and attention-grabbing subjects. A total of 32 webinars were conducted, featuring distinguished professionals from various sectors, including industries, start-ups, policy advocacy, and academic research. To encourage networking and facilitate in-depth discussions, the presentations during these webinars were kept succinct, limited to just ten minutes. Subsequently, participants were divided into smaller breakout sessions where they could engage in more detailed conversations. The webinars covered a broad range of areas related to Responsible Innovation, often presenting challenging perspectives on the topic:

- Too old for tech? Co-creating with older people
- Will robots care for you?
- Preventive healthcare and fitness
- Smart health use cases and champions
- Vertical and indoor framing
- Responsible innovation for smart public transport
- Distance teaching and learning during lockdowns
- Video games and virtual reality in distance teaching
- Challenges of remote working – leadership and technology
- Trust, surveillance, and AI in remote working
- Holograms and virtual reality in remote working
- Balancing work, life, and health in remote working

Staging regular events has proven to be an effective method for increasing the number of experts within the community, as depicted in Figure C1.2.

Figure C1.2

How webinars boosted the number of registered users

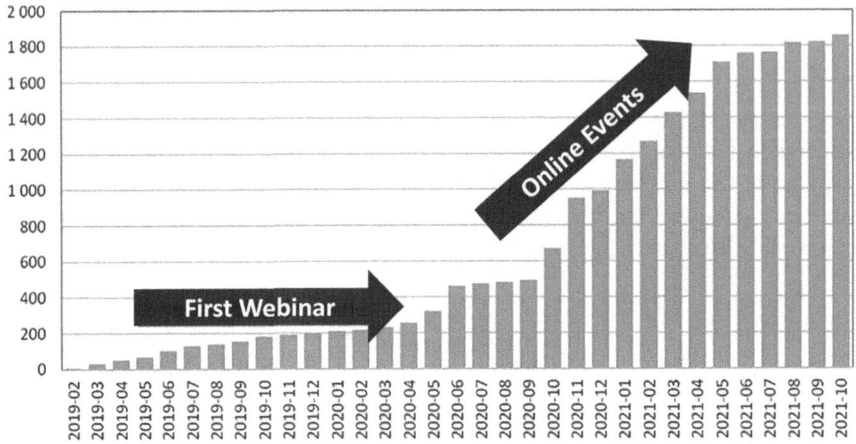

1.2.5 Responsible innovation stories

The project employed audio-visual storytelling as a central strategy for presenting project findings and success stories. Recognizing that this mode of dissemination resonated more effectively with businesses than traditional reports or academic publications, the project successfully created a series of approximately 100 videos featuring experts, business leaders, and policy-makers. These responsible innovation stories received substantial attention, amassing over 20,000 video views on YouTube and more than 110,000 impressions, indicating the frequency with which thumbnails of the videos were displayed on YouTube. Notably, stories featuring CEOs and top-level experts generated the highest number of views. The most relevant outcomes, innovations, and tools developed in the LIVING INNOVATION projects were presented in ten high-end videos that made use of 3D animation and rendering.

1.2.6 Co-creation experiments

The second stream of activities of the LIVING INNOVATION project allowed industry leaders to explore and experience co-creation as a key concept of Responsible Innovation. Over the course of three years, around 30 co-creation workshops were conducted across six countries, involving several hundred participants, and covering the following themes:

- *"Future homes and lifestyles"* focused on the effects of new technologies on homes and daily lives, explored new application areas for technologies making homes smarter, explored citizens' needs, and elicited citizens' concerns around these smart technologies. It consisted of six workshops, covering topics such as "Measuring and influencing sleep," "Robotics in the care sector," and "Indoor climate and energy management."

- *"Lifelong health and care"* focused on specific needs and challenges regarding the implementation of new technologies for blind and visually impaired persons, older persons, and persons with learning disabilities. It consisted of five workshops and several sessions at a major conference in collaboration with organizations representing people with reduced mobility.
- *"Internet of Things in daily life"* employed a developmental approach, which involved the same group of people consecutively over a period of half a year in six workshops. This format allowed for substantial progress in one specific thematic area and provided the most intensive and in-depth exploration of how to co-create real solutions.
- *"Communities and collaboration"* sought to collaboratively establish an online community for amputees, emphasizing active participation and integration. Across a series of four workshops, a small but diverse group of amputees explored the need for personal interaction and information exchange, culminating in the co-development of a solution that was subsequently implemented and expanded on a global scale.
- *"Preventive health and fitness"* focused on the generation of ideas for Responsible Innovation around smart health, with a specific emphasis on prevention and well-being, geared toward meeting the needs of young individuals with the assistance of technology. It consisted of a series of four on-site and online workshops following the design thinking method. The results were further processed by health experts from a corporate partner.
- *"High tech at home"* explored visions of socio-technical change among lower socio-economic status families, with a particular focus on children. Twelve families participated in a series of workshops and related activities.

All co-creation experiments were not singular events but, rather, comprised a sequence of three to six workshops, each lasting several hours. At the beginning of the project, the workshops were conducted on-site at the premises of the corporate consortium partners. However, due to the COVID-19 pandemic, face-to-face participation became unfeasible. Consequently, the experiments shifted to digital collaboration formats, which presented new challenges but also provided an opportunity to accumulate insights from online workshop experiences.

1.2.7 Workshop formats

As the co-creation experiments consisted of several workshops, three different formats were implemented and explored:

- In a *sequence and developmental approach*, the same group of participants met over the course of several different workshops. This allowed for intensive and in-depth work over a longer period of time, encompassing the development of tangible solutions and work phases between the workshops. This approach was applied in the co-creation experiments on the "Internet of Things in daily lives," "Communities and collaboration," and "High tech at home."

- In a *cross-country and comparative approach*, the same workshop formats on the same topics were implemented at different locations, which allowed for the consideration of different cultural backgrounds and contexts. This approach was implemented in the co-creation experiment on "Preventive health and fitness" involving young people from Spain and Austria.
- In a *sub-themes and exploratory approach*, the workshops dealt with the same general topic but focused on different specific sub-themes, enabling the involvement of an increasing number of diverse actors and allowing for rapid ideation and testing. The co-creation experiment "Future homes and lifestyles" applied this format.

1.2.8 Innovation blueprints

The diverse outcomes of the co-creation experiments were enriched by several activities that took place on the project's virtual community platform, such as webinars, online meetings, and joint actions. The results were summarized in eight so-called "innovation blueprints," each of which comprehensively described a specific idea from the workshops and consisted of the following:

- a short *description of the product or service* including a detailed description of user advantages, accompanied by images or illustrations and design specifications;
- a *business case* including required investments, expected profits, financial feasibility, customers' willingness to pay, and a best-case and a worst-case scenario;
- a *customer journey* comprising actions, motivations, questions, and barriers to the uptake of the new product or service.

As most of the innovation blueprints were endorsed by one of the corporate consortium partners for post-project development, they were not made publicly available so as to protect intellectual property rights. However, some of them were featured in the high-end showcase videos at the end of the project.

1.2.9 Outcomes and dissemination

To change the perception of the ICT sector and demonstrate that RRI represents a business opportunity across various sectors, we generated a wide range of deliverables and executed an array of dissemination activities.

- *Nine high-end showcase videos*[1] presented the key findings of the projects, covering tangible results in the areas of smart homes and smart health (e.g., a smart office chair, a smart mobility app for blind and visually impaired people, a holobox sharing system that could replace business travel) as well as process-oriented results (e.g., tools for inclusive workshop design and a framework for how to integrate responsibility and sustainability into design thinking). The visual design was based on the visual identity of the project and essentially consisted of a watercolor design commonly found in interior design concepts and drawings. This design choice symbolized the novelty of the products, solutions, or ideas presented, emphasizing that they were new and not yet available. The showcases were narrated by real individuals, as this tends to generate greater interest and trust than using drawn or animated characters or unknown off-screen voices. The length of the videos was 8–10 minutes, which corresponds to the viewing habits of conventional explanatory videos on YouTube.

- *Two toolboxes* targeted innovation managers in companies and provided them with comprehensive advice on how to ensure high-quality co-creation processes[2] (see Chapter C2 of this book) and how to run innovation workshops for blind and visually impaired participants[3] (see Chapter C4 of this book). These new tools were promoted through several virtual events and disseminated via the well-established platform: www.RRI-TOOLS.eu
- *Three policy briefs* were created to engage with national and EU-level policy-makers and to share the project's outcomes. The first brief[4] presents a new narrative on responsible innovation for the business sector, focusing on business opportunities and providing a compelling business case. It recommends the establishment of Responsible Innovation dialogues across different sectors in an effort to empower citizens, foster capacity building for co-creation, and emphasize the systemic character of missions in the EU Framework Programmes. The second policy brief[5] draws on the results of a comprehensive analysis of CSR- and RRI-related initiatives and recommends the establishment of a multi-stakeholder initiative on Responsible Innovation in the digital sector based on a set of principles and viable mechanisms for voluntary monitoring and enforcement. The third policy brief[6] focuses on the importance of maintaining high-quality co-creation processes and calls for resources to raise awareness of this approach and disseminate best practices.
- *Academic publications* were not the main type of outcome of the project. However, several journal articles,[7] conference papers,[8] as well as this book resulted from the LIVING INNOVATION project.

The project's extensive outreach to the business sector and the wider public is evident in several KPIs: The videos on the project's YouTube channel were viewed more than 20,000 times, more than 12,000 citizens were reached, the toolkits were downloaded more than 2,500 times, and nearly 2,000 experts registered on the project's community platform.

1.3 LESSONS LEARNED AND RECOMMENDATIONS

The LIVING INNOVATION project delivered a wide range of tools and deliverables that support the implementation of responsible innovation in companies and showcased that Responsible Innovation provides attractive business opportunities (see Chapters C2–C5). Based on three years of exploration and experience, we can derive learnings and recommendations on community building, co-creation, and business perspectives on Responsible Innovation.

1.3.1 On community building

- *Establishing a community is not an end in itself but rather a means to an end.* As such, it is crucial to establish a clear purpose that guides all subsequent activities and is transparent to potential community members. We recommend communicating the purpose openly and clearly, otherwise the target group will assume hidden agendas and refuse to participate.
- *Facilitating and nurturing a community of practice* requires a clear identification of the target audiences, their contexts, and needs. For example, we found substantial differences between top-level managers, CSR and sustainability managers, and innovation managers in their understanding, perceived benefits, and challenges of Responsible Innovation. We therefore recommend conducting in-depth interviews with potential community members and deriving key messages that attract their needs.
- *Activating community members is difficult.* Approximately two-thirds of our community members participated in only one interaction or event, and many of them attended but without contributing to the knowledge or exchange among the members. Therefore, we suggest ensuring that a new community involves a relatively large number of members from the very beginning to guarantee that interactions take place.
- *Linking activities to cutting-edge topics attracts attention and increases outreach.* When COVID-19 hit, the LIVING INNOVATION project suddenly received far more attention than it had previously because living at home suddenly became the only form of living. We reacted quickly to this change and focused on topics strongly related to these recent developments, such as new forms of distance working, distance learning, and remote care for elderly and sick people. We therefore suggest high thematic flexibility and contextualizing the key theme of a community with cutting-edge topics.
- *Building trust follows a stepwise strategy.* In the beginning, when a community is not well known, trust can be built up by involving high-profile figures, such as CEOs, leading researchers, or policy-makers. In the next phase, high-quality content supports trust and establishes a community as a valuable source of information. Subsequently, open, transparent, and participatory processes contribute to trust and facilitate active involvement. As a last step, a community can establish a brand that stands for all its activities. We recommend following these steps and keeping the perspective of (potential) community members in mind.

- *Using well-established social media platforms* and existing content management systems is easier than developing a new platform from scratch. In addition, we have found it challenging to establish a platform on which participants exchange information in an asynchronous and written form. We therefore made use of LinkedIn (for promoting and administrating events) and YouTube (for disseminating audio-visual content) and used our platform primarily as a central access point for accessing various activities and managing community members. Therefore, we advise establishing a community platform as a main access point and directory but suggest organizing interactive elements through other platforms.

1.3.2 On co-creation

- *Co-creation requires time* to ensure an in-depth understanding of needs, benefits, challenges, and potential barriers to acceptance. Emphasizing and understanding user needs are relatively easy, while finding innovative solutions is more challenging, but the selection of the best solution is the biggest challenge. We suggest a minimum duration of four hours, although we are aware that this might not be in line with the motivation and availability of some participants.
- *Selection of participants is key*, as they should represent the majority of future users, provide a broad diversity of contexts and perspectives, and be able to articulate their needs and concerns. Addressing potential participants beyond the "usual suspects" of young, urban, male, highly educated, and techno-savvy users is highly innovative but also challenging. We therefore suggest a recruitment strategy that allows for a targeted selection based on well-defined criteria.
- *Collaboration is based on mutual trust*, which is difficult to build and easy to lose. Interactions with the future participants before co-creation workshops (e.g., through interviews or visits to their homes) can be beneficial. The processing of results needs to be organized well in advance and openly communicated to the participants so as to manage expectations and avoid the feeling of being exploited. In addition, co-creation requires professionally trained facilitators who are perceived as neutral by the participants.
- *Inclusion should be carefully planned and supported* by tools, locations, and communication. In order to better understand special needs, we suggest collaborating with aid organizations, associations, and NGOs, while also involving representatives of target groups with special needs in the preparation of the co-creation activities.

1.3.3 On business perspectives on Responsible Innovation

- *The most commonly used RRI frameworks*[9] *do not sufficiently consider business practices,* do not speak the language of businesses, and do not address their main logics of profits, competitiveness, and growth. Responsible Innovation is therefore perceived to be a policy-driven issue that leads to additional burden and potentially undermines competitiveness, especially in markets where competitors from outside Europe do not need to consider aspects of Responsible Innovation. Institutionalizing Responsible Innovation in the business sector therefore requires a new narrative (as outlined in the concluding chapter of this book, A strategic approach to Responsible Innovation in the business sector).

- *Responsibility and sustainability require institutionalization and organizational change.* CSR and sustainability management are well-established areas, but they are only rarely linked to innovation. Responsibility for technologies and ethical concerns are often perceived to be an issue of sectors or of policy, but not of an individual company. We therefore suggest fostering the organizational links between CSR and sustainability management, on the one hand, and innovation management, on the other.
- *Open innovation is well established but limited to a relatively narrow group of potential users.* Although many companies use design thinking, hackathons, or innovation challenges, they complain about a lack of innovative ideas. This may be attributable to the fact that it is primarily employees and their families who participate in such events. We suggest interpreting responsible innovation as a "real opening" of innovation processes to a broader diversity of stakeholders and citizens and utilizing the vast knowledge of CSR and sustainability managers on stakeholder engagement for co-creating experiments.
- *The business benefits of Responsible Innovation are not sufficiently operationalized.* The narratives promoting Responsible Innovation are frequently unclear and may revolve around concepts like customer loyalty or gaining a competitive edge in attracting top talent. When these narratives do address Responsible Innovation, they tend to emphasize the increased creativity and innovation resulting from co-creation but often neglect to mention the potential adverse consequences. Therefore, we recommend evaluating and quantifying the costs of inaction to mitigate risks and prevent unwarranted expenditures.
- *Build on what you already have.* Inventing and establishing new tools are far more challenging than extending existing tools through Responsible Innovation. We therefore suggest including Responsible Innovation in CSR and sustainability reports and extending well-established innovation management methods by incorporating aspects of responsibility and sustainability (e.g., into design thinking, as shown in Chapter C3).

NOTES

1. https://www.youtube.com/@livinginnovation-euproject9587/videos
2. https://www.sustainability.eu/liv_in/LIV_IN_Co-Creation_Toolkit.pdf
3. https://www.sustainability.eu/liv_in/LIV_IN_Inclusive_Workshops.pdf

4. https://www.sustainability.eu/liv_in/LIV_IN_PolicyBrief1.pdf
5. https://www.sustainability.eu/liv_in/LIV_IN_PolicyBrief2.
6. https://www.sustainability.eu/liv_in/LIV_IN_PolicyBrief3.pdf
7. For example, Applin & Flick (2021); Ivanova *et al.* (2023).
8. For example, Firth & Flick (2020); Flick *et al.* (2021).
9. The so-called EU RRI keys (see Owen *et al.*, 2021) and the so-called ARRI framework (see Stilgoe *et al.*, 2013).

REFERENCES

Applin, S. A., & Flick, C. (2021). Facebook's Project Aria indicates problems for responsible innovation when broadly deploying AR and other pervasive technology in the Commons. *Journal of Responsible Technology*, *5*, 100010.

Brand, T., & Blok, V. (2019). Responsible Innovation in business: a critical reflection on deliberative engagement as a central governance mechanism. *Journal of Responsible Innovation*, *6*(1), 4–24. doi:10.1080/23299460.2019.1575681.

Ceicyte, J., & Petraite, M. (2018). Networked responsibility approach for responsible innovation: Perspective of the firm. *Sustainability*, *10*(6), 1720.

Ceicyte, J., Petraite, M., Blok, V., & Yaghmaei, E. (2021). Responsible Innovation in industry: The role of firm's multi-stakeholder network. In E. Koukios & A. Sacio-Szymańska (Eds.), *Bio#Futures: Foreseeing and Exploring the Bioeconomy* (pp. 581–603). Springer International.

Dreyer, M., Chefneux, L., Goldberg, A., von Heimburg, J., Patrignani, N., Schofield M., & Shilling, C. (2017). Responsible Innovation: A complementary view from industry with proposals for bridging different perspectives. *Sustainability*, *9*(10). DOI:10.3390/su9101719.

Firth, R. M., & Flick, C. (2020). Digital capital and sociotechnical imaginaries: Envisaging future home tech with low-income communities. Proceedings of the ETHICOMP 2020.

Flick, C., Owoseni, A., Fisk, M., & Firth, R. M. (2021). Visualising home technologies of the future: A report from Leicester's diverse communities. Proceedings of the ETHICOMP 2021.

Iatridis, K., & Schroeder, D. (2016). *Responsible Research and Innovation in industry: The case for corporate responsibility tools*. Springer International Publishing.

Ivanova, S., Reichetzer, C., Martinuzzi, A., Findler, F. & Miko-Schefzig, K. (2023) Frames, interests, and incentives: A typology of institutionalizing RRI in the business sector derived from ten pioneering projects, *Journal of Responsible Innovation*, *10*(1), DOI: 10.1080/23299460.2023.2267736.

Owen, R., von Schomberg, R., & Macnaghten, P. (2021). An unfinished journey? Reflections on a decade of responsible research and innovation. *Journal of Responsible Innovation*, 1–17. https://doi.org/10.1080/23299460.2021.1948789

Schönherr, N., Martinuzzi, A., & Jarmai, K. (2020). Towards a business case for Responsible Innovation. *Responsible Innovation*, 85–97.

Steen, M., Nauta, J., & Gaasterland, S. (2018). Institutionalizing Responsible Research and Innovation: Case studies, ISPIM Innovation Conference Proceedings, Stockholm.

Stilgoe, J., Owen, R., & Macnaghten, Ph. (2013). Developing a framework for Responsible Innovation. *Research Policy*, *42*(9), 1568–1580. doi:10.1016/j.respol.2013.05.008.

C2

Co-creating innovations

How to engage with users and citizens in Responsible Innovation

Florian Findler, Anja Grüll, Wilfried Konrad, Rainer Kuhn, Sarah-Kristina Wist, and Bianca Witzel

2.1 INTRODUCTION

Modern economies are characterized by rapid change that occurs through innovations. The exponential growth in technological innovations and scientific breakthroughs as well as the increased connection to the environment through digitalization have opened numerous opportunities for businesses. Even though these developments have fostered the creation of many new products and services, a significant number of innovations fail to reach a successful market uptake (Alessi, 2020). To counteract this phenomenon, businesses have moved toward more user-centric design processes (Wilkinson & De Angeli, 2014). It has become vital for companies to understand their customers' expectations and needs in order to be economically successful. In addition to the traditional business logic concerns of economic prosperity and growth, civil society is increasingly demanding that businesses take responsibility for their impact on the environment and society. In this regard, creating products and services solely for customers is not sufficient anymore, as businesses must also address the challenges faced by society today.

Responsible Research and Innovation (RRI) offers companies a conceptual framework that enables them to identify new opportunities for developing technologies, products, services, and business models that are socially desirable and that contribute to tackling current societal challenges. RRI requires business to innovate for and with society (Owen *et al.*, 2020). Therefore, businesses have to open up their innovation processes to users in order to take a broader range of perspectives, wishes, and needs into account. In this way, the risk of unwanted outcomes of innovation processes can be minimized, thereby leading to more innovations that align social and public values with business practices (Fisher, 2020). However, in order to successfully implement RRI in companies and open up innovation processes, approaches that systematically involve users are required (García *et al.*, 2016).

DOI: 10.4324/9781003319481-24

Co-creation is an approach that allows for the translation of RRI into business practices by enabling users to take an active role in the innovation processes. By involving a variety of stakeholders from different disciplines in this participatory design process, a multitude of needs and wishes are identified and common value is created. These so-called individual external contributors can range from customers and users of the firms' products or services as well as experts, students, or hobbyists (Deserti & Rizzo, 2022; Tekic & Willoughby, 2019). The underlying premise of this approach is users obtaining specific knowledge about the ways in which certain technologies, products, and services can contribute to their daily lives.

Business practitioners often struggle with co-creation processes despite the increasing popularity of this approach in recent years (Lee *et al.*, 2018). Conducting a co-creation process requires careful planning and conscious decision-making that start with preparing the process, defining the scope and objectives, and determining specific workshop designs. Business practitioners must manage the complexity that arises from these requirements. However, these practitioners often do not understand quality criteria and are not aware of appropriate methods for achieving these goals.

This chapter addresses this lack of understanding and introduces important quality criteria and methods that facilitate co-creation processes. It aims to serve as a guide for business practitioners who wish to conduct high-quality co-creation processes. This chapter builds on the experience of the European Union-funded LIVING INNOVATION project, which sought to create innovations in the emerging areas of smart home and smart health technologies and services. As part of the LIVING INNOVATION project, six co-creation labs were conducted in 2019 and 2020 in order to explore how business entrepreneurs and users can work together to develop new products and services that provide new business opportunities, satisfy user needs, and tackle societal challenges. The co-creation labs were conducted by Siemens, Telefonica, ATOS, Ottobock, Stichting Smart Homes, and the De Montfort University. Each lab consisted of a series of workshops that were accompanied by scientific evaluations. Overall, 19 workshops were held on-site at the participating organizations' headquarters in 2019 as well as online due to the restrictions resulting from the COVID-19 pandemic in 2020. The workshops were accompanied by scientific evaluations, including surveys and interviews with the representatives of the organizations and the users.

Section 2.2 provides insights into the co-creation approach. After this, the quality criteria necessary for preparing and conducting a co-creation process and organizing workshops are discussed, followed by the presentation of a set of methods that can be used to facilitate co-creation processes. The chapter is then concluded and recommendations for the future are provided.

2.2 INCORPORATING RRI INTO BUSINESS PRACTICES THROUGH CO-CREATION PROCESSES

A key approach to involving users in innovation processes is related to RRI. This practice requires businesses to innovate for and with society, and it aims to align companies' innovation strategies with societal needs and current sustainable development challenges (Owen *et al.*, 2020). In the last few years, the EU has been a strong driving force in the implementation of RRI via co-creation approaches through funding programs, such as Horizon 2020. The aim is to combine different areas of expertise and knowledge in order to tackle the challenges faced by society. In general, co-creation is understood as "any act of collective creativity, i.e., creativity that is shared by two or more people" (Sanders & Stappers, 2008, p. 6). It is a promising way to address major societal challenges through collaboratively designing sustainable solutions (Robinson *et al.*, 2021). In a business context, co-creation is the creation of common value between businesses and society (Prahalad & Ramaswamy, 2004). Thus, a company's goal is not limited to satisfying customers, but it is also centered around enabling the customer to co-shape the service experience to suit their needs and context. This requires businesses and users to actively work together and share an understanding of creating innovations that clearly differ from current industrial innovation practices in which users are mainly regarded as future customers. Co-creation can be applied in several stages of the innovation process, ranging from the planning and research phase and the pre-design phase to the post-design phase (Deserti & Rizzo, 2022; Hoffmann, 2012; Lee *et al.*, 2018).

From a company's perspective, the insights gained from co-creation processes allow for innovations that align with users' wishes while contributing to societal needs. By engaging in co-creation activities, businesses can develop and sustainably maintain a competitive advantage in the market and reduce the environment's complexity (Adamik *et al.*, 2018). The interactive experience also leads to an increase in customer satisfaction and customer trust (Iglesias *et al.*, 2020). Therefore, the economic, functional, and social dimensions are included in the added value obtained by businesses (Deserti & Rizzo, 2022; Piligrimienė *et al.*, 2015).

Even though businesses can access numerous benefits by engaging in co-creation activities, there is still a lack of proper direction in terms of setting scope, forming a strategy, and determining the design processes when engaging in co-creation activities. Therefore, in order to support business practitioners in this regard and to operationalize RRI through co-creation, appropriate guidelines and methods are required (Rizzo & Deserti, 2022). The following two sections address this lack of methods and the aim to support business practitioners in conducting sound co-creation processes in collaboration with users in order to create more socially meaningful innovations.

2.3 PREPARING THE CO-CREATION PROCESS

This section presents the most important quality criteria for preparing and running the co-creation process and organizing the workshops, which were determined in the LIVING INNOVATION project's labs.

2.3.1 Setting the objectives

Before planning workshops, it is important to understand the overall purpose and the expected results of the co-creation process. One method includes starting with a key question that frames and structures the process and workshop. Feasible solutions can also be determined by considering the possible outcomes in the beginning of the process.

Co-creation processes can serve different objectives, ranging from collecting information and ideas, opinion polling, and advice seeking to jointly developing solutions. In the beginning of the co-creation process, the objective that is being pursued and the type of participants (e.g., lay people, lead users) that would best suit this specific objective should be determined. Required user types, facilitation methods, timelines, and the like may differ significantly according to the specific objective. Therefore, matching a workshop's scope with its participants is essential for a successful co-creation process.

2.3.2 Recruiting the participants

Successful co-creation processes in a RRI context significantly depend on involving participants who represent the social groups who will most likely be affected by the outcomes of the innovation process, which can also include more parties than just the future users of the innovations. Representativity is necessary for considering different opinions, and it ensures legitimacy in the process. The need for representativity strongly depends on the context as highly specialized topics that only affect few parties will lead to the selective choosing of participants, which is in contrast to topics with a broad scope that affect a diverse range of people. If many parties are affected, representativity can be ensured by identifying all relevant parties and inviting representatives for each of them, which is referred as contextual representativity.

To ensure representativity in co-creation processes, qualitative and quantitative approaches can be applied. Quantitative approaches allow for statistical representativity, whereas qualitative representativity aims to represent all relevant arguments (Alcántara *et al.*, 2015). Most participation processes follow the latter approach, which states that comprehensive representativity in participation processes is achieved when the participants in a process represent all the social groups impacted by a specific issue (Nanz & Fritsche, 2012). Thus, before deciding on the method of recruitment, the relevant actors have to be identified according to the overall purpose and objectives of the co-creation process.

When inviting the participants, transparent information must be provided in order to build trust. Thus, an invitation's tone can vary between those addressed to experts and those addressed to lead users. While the tone should be more formal for the experts, lay users could be deterred from attending due to language that is too sophisticated. It is also helpful to focus on the potential benefits and the incentives provided when inviting participants. These incentives could be monetary, but they do not have to be as the participants could also benefit from the special insights, knowledge, or the experience. However, monetary incentives allow organizers to involve people who are not intrinsically motivated but who have a lot of knowledge that is needed, but they should not participate solely for the money. A rule of thumb for the monetary incentive is €50 for a three-hour workshop. Even more incentives could be included, like vouchers, a free meal, or more. Additionally, if there is a specific target group in mind, such as single mothers, childcare could be provided for the duration of the workshop. It is important to remember that the participants' time and knowledge are being requested, which should be valued accordingly.

2.3.3 Composing the participant groups

Depending on the purpose of the co-creation process and workshops, the different compositions of participants must be considered. In an early stage of innovation processes, where the goal is to obtain a better understanding of what is required, it may be enough to conduct workshops with lead users. Expert knowledge becomes increasingly important the further into the co-creation process one moves. The role of the experts can vary, but it should be kept in mind that lay users are also experts in their own right: They can provide a broad range of information, from everyday to empirical knowledge. When mixing the different participant types, it must be ensured that all of them have a common understanding. Bringing experts and lay users together can generate a mutual understanding and learning effects as well as ensure transparency. Although several people might be interested in observing the workshop, it is important that there are not too many of them as too many would make the participants feel as though they are more under investigation rather than being in a trusting and creative environment. Additionally, to ensure a productive atmosphere, the group should not consist of more than 15 participants. If there are more people involved, it would be more effective to build different groups and design a process that includes a switch between plenary and workgroup sessions.

2.3.4 Defining the participants' decision-making scope

The participants' decision-making scope must be well communicated in the invitations. Otherwise, the risk of misleading or disappointing the users is highly likely. There are two basic approaches that characterize participants' decision-making competencies: consultation and co-decision. Consultation is described as an exchange of views between the company and the participants, and the decision-making power exclusively lies with the company. In contrast, co-decision endows participants with decision-making competencies and actively involves them in the decision-making process.

2.3.5 Training the staff

Employees do not usually deal with lay users when developing new products or services. To facilitate the co-creation process, employees need to be trained on how to deal with lay users and familiarized with the process. Communication barriers or knowledge gaps between staff and participants are to be expected. To overcome these barriers or gaps, the staff must be open to contributions from users, and they must be willing to engage in collaborative discussions with them. To enable a broad diffusion of user inputs into the company's innovation processes, all relevant departments of the company can be included (e.g., corporate strategy, research and development, sales, marketing). In addition, the handling of participants' possible patent rights should be clarified before the start of the co-creation process.

2.3.6 Setting up the timeline and budget

A back-casting approach is recommended for determining the timeline, which means planning the co-creation process "from the end." It is important to allow sufficient time for the individual steps of the process as some steps require substantial preparation time, such as creating the materials for inviting participants.

The budget for the co-creation process and the individual workshops must be fixed prior to the start of the process. The total costs of the process comprise direct costs, such as facilitation, renting space, technical equipment, incentives, and food and beverages, as well as indirect costs, such as paying staff.

2.4 RUNNING THE CO-CREATION PROCESS

2.4.1 Facilitating the participants' involvement

There are several ways to strengthen participant involvement in the co-creation process. Particularly, emphasis should be placed on ensuring seriousness, transparency, fairness, and sustainable involvement.

- *Seriousness* is one of the most crucial quality criteria. It denotes all people involved taking the co-creation process seriously and participating with a curious, constructive, respectful, and honest attitude, which will allow viable solutions to be found. The facilitator can contribute to this by keeping the participants well informed and ensuring that they respect the co-creation process. In addition, when the participants will decide, how their contributions will be considered, and what type of feedback they will receive should be clearly communicated to them.
- *Transparency* must be ensured so that everybody can communicate and be treated as equals. For this, all participants need to be provided with clear and barrier-free information. This should be done not only at the beginning but also during the process or workshops. For example, visualizations in the workshops

can help to keep everybody on track, or important aspects can be written down on flipcharts, cards, or screens. In addition, it is helpful to provide protocols to the participants after each workshop.

- *Fairness* must be fostered. It is important that each participant has the same chance to have their say. To achieve this, the process must be designed in a way that everybody – irrespective of age, sex, income, or other factors – can participate equally. It is the facilitator's task to ensure that this aspect is properly implemented. Additionally, patent rights must be clarified in advance.
- *Sustainable involvement* needs to be facilitated so that users are involved throughout the entire innovation process. All participants need to be informed about new developments and the process's outcomes. Involvement can also be strengthened through providing participants with learning options and opportunities in order to build competencies. A well-defined relationship between organizers and participants as well as clear rules that ensure the quality of deliberative formats and methods are helpful in this regard.

2.4.2 Fostering accessibility and inclusiveness while meeting ethical requirements

Accessibility refers not only to the location of the workshop but also to working materials. Moreover, all information and materials have to meet the participants' requirements. The information should be understandable, actionable, and perceivable. Ensuring inclusiveness can become particularly challenging when vulnerable groups or people with special needs are involved in the co-creation process.

The participants' personal data also need to be protected. Justification for collecting and processing sensitive data must be included in a document that is presented to the participants before the actual process. A plan must be discussed for each workshop, which must consider the following:

- the relevant data protection regulations, such as the General Data Protection Regulation (GDPR);
- a guide for the conceptual design and facilitation of methods for protecting vulnerable people during and after the workshops;
- consent forms that address all special needs and topics, which must be signed by participants before data collection.

2.4.3 Facilitating consensual decision-making

There are different ways to facilitate consensual decision-making for those involved in this process. It is helpful for the facilitator to keep track of the diverse opinions and suggestions, such as by simple voting, for example. Methods for solving individual issues and differences can be discussed separately from the overall topic.

2.4.4 Processing and communicating the results to the participants

Participants are strongly interested in what will happen with their contributions. To avoid the participants' frustration and loss of trust, the results must be used, and the participants must be informed of this. And, if the results are not be used, the participants must be informed of this and be provided with a proper justification as to why.

2.4.5 Organizing the workshops

Each workshop can be divided into four phases (see Figure C2.1). The warm-up phase aims to foster curiosity and create a good working atmosphere. The participants become familiar with the topic, the workshop's agenda, and each other. In the orientation phase, the topic is discussed in depth, and the participants then start working on the topic in the working phase. Finally, the results are summed up and the participants have time to reflect and give feedback to the organizers in the conclusion phase (Straub *et al.*, 2009).

It takes time to achieve good and tangible results. Before the working phase, the participants have to be well informed about the agenda, the concept of RRI, and the workshop's aims. During the working phase, time is needed to create a constructive culture of engagement. Sufficient time should also be allocated to the reflection that occurs during the conclusion phase. Flexibility and room for adjustments should also be included in the workshop's design and the whole co-creation process in order to account for the participants' changing needs.

Figure C2.1

The typical structure of a co-creation workshop

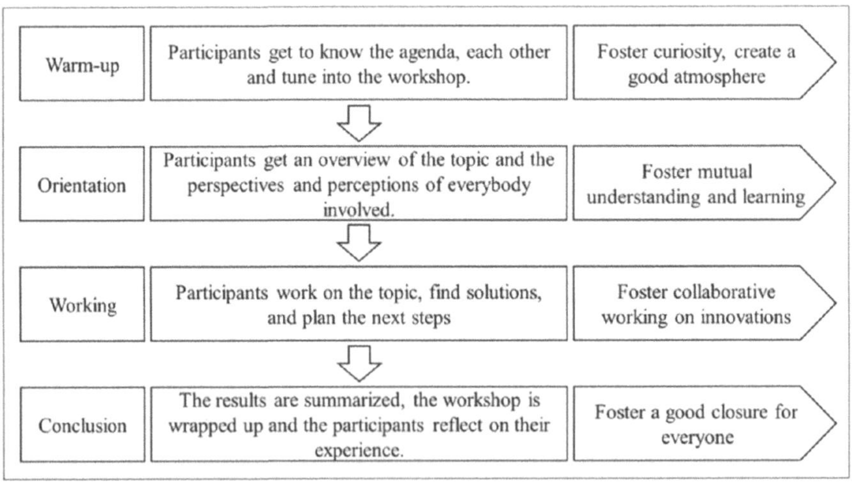

Source: adapted from Straub *et al.* (2009).

The facilitators play an important role in any workshop: They pave the way for an effective discussion and a fair group atmosphere, and they provide guidance and context to the audience. A trained facilitator can ask the right questions so as to provide a constructive and creative work flow, and they ensure that every participant is treated fairly and equally, regardless of their function or status. A facilitator can also help in designing the workshop and can ensure a target-oriented and effective structure. It is important that the facilitator is impartial and does not follow their own agenda. An external facilitator who is not involved in the company or the innovation project is ideal for this.

2.5 METHODS FOR ENRICHING CO-CREATION PROCESSES

This section details the methods that can be used to put co-creation into practice and enrich RRI processes. The methods serve different purposes: collecting ideas, structuring information, learning about needs, finding solutions, assessing impacts, and fostering empathy. Therefore, the selection of a method should be aligned with the co-creation process's goals and objectives. Especially when involving lay users, methods that promote creativity and help to build a common understanding and vision should be applied. Figure C2.2 provides an overview of the methods that facilitate co-creation processes.

Figure C2.2

Overview of methods for co-creating processes

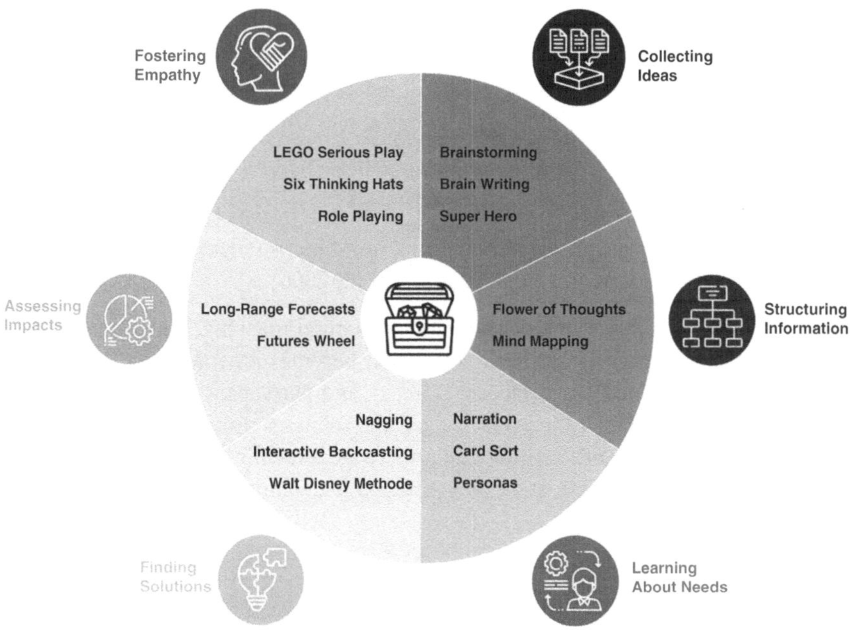

2.5.1 Collecting ideas

- *Structured brainstorming* allows for the collection of a large number of different ideas in a structured round-based framework. This approach is particularly suitable for starting a creative problem-solving process as a large number of ideas are collected. It is less suitable for very specific topics in which no expertise is available. It should also be noted that ideas mentioned at the beginning can influence the downstream process and hinder creativity. Mutual trust is the minimum requirement between participants as it allows for open exchanges (Wilson, 2013).
- *The superhero approach* allows participants to choose a famous superhero and explore the superhero's skills and special talents so as to put themselves in the superhero's place, asking themselves the question, "How would I, as superhero X, solve this problem?" This method especially helps to identify highly unconventional approaches that can contribute to sparking creative and new thinking processes (Cruickshank *et al.*, 2017).
- *Brain writing* is similar to structured brainstorming, but the collection of ideas is done in written form and individually. The written papers are exchanged, and new ideas are added. Its advantage over oral brainstorming is that the participants do not influence each other and thinking processes are not disturbed by noise. Like all brainstorming methods, it is not very helpful if expertise is necessary but not available. Variants of brain writing include the "collective notebook" and the "6-3-5 method" (Heslin, 2009).

2.5.2 Structuring information

- *Mind mapping* enables the collection of key concepts and the identification of their relationships with previously defined topics through a drawn tree or map that includes the core topic in the center. This approach helps structure information and knowledge while providing an overview of the topic's common knowledge base. It is particularly suitable for complex topics as this method helps to reduce complexity. It should be noted that mind maps reflect subjective impressions, which can vary greatly (Buzan & Buzan, 2006).
- *The flower of thoughts approach* is similar to mind mapping, but this method is usually used in group work. Each association becomes a petal of the flower, and some of the most unusual petals are selected, and participants are asked to think about the ways in which the petal matches the solutions provided. This method is useful for structuring information and knowledge, providing an overview, creating a common knowledge base, and developing possible solutions (Konrad *et al.*, 2019).

2.5.3 Learning about needs

- *The think-aloud approach* asks participants to describe aloud what they are thinking while performing a specific task related to a product. This method provides useful insights into users' motivations, concerns, perceptions, and reflections (Nielsen *et al.*, 2002).

- *The card sort approach* asks participants to name potential features, functions, or design attributes on separate cards and spatially arrange them in a way that makes sense to them. Thus, the participants' "mental models" about the innovation are revealed along with their expectations and priorities for intended features (Hayes, 2012).
- *The personas approach* enables imaginary participation. Participants create several character profiles or personas of different users whose needs are addressed by the respective product. The creation of a persona includes both textual descriptions and images. The profiles provide a clear picture of the different types of users that are the focus of the development activities. In addition, the profiles can be used for other workshop methods such as role-playing (Chasanidou *et al.*, 2015).

2.5.4 Finding solutions

- *The nagging group approach* motivates participants to complain about existing products and solutions, after which they present solutions for the criticized features. The method is suitable for determining the product's most pressing weaknesses from the user's point of view (Buzan & Buzan, 2006).
- *Interactive back-casting* allows users to select one or more futures for their analysis. By working backwards from the present situation, they interactively explore what obstacles need to be overcome and the interventions that are needed to make a certain future a reality. The method is suitable for addressing the diversity between the future and the present but also between the lead users' different views and perceptions (Buzan & Buzan, 2006).
- *The Walt Disney method* discusses a topic from three successive perspectives: Individual participants or teams take on the roles of dreamers, realists, and critics. Each participant should take each role at least once in order to allow a change of perspectives. The main goal of this method is to develop ideas that are ambitious but also achievable as determined by the spokespersons (Zec, 2022b).

2.5.5 Assessing impacts

- *The futures wheel method* is a method for structured brainstorming. The trend or event is written in the center of a piece of paper, and small spokes are drawn from the center. Primary impacts are written at the end of each spoke, and secondary impacts form the second ring of the wheel. This method is useful for collecting and visualizing the full range of possible impacts of future developments. Like all brainstorming methods, it is only suitable for specific topics and if there is a high level of expertise among participants (Buzan & Buzan, 2006).

- *Long-range forecasts* allow participants to develop scenarios that describe how social or technological trends might affect people's behavior, their use of a particular product and service, and the environment in which they live. Predictions and considerations of future changes in behavior, industry, or technology can help participants understand the implications of design decisions during the development process (Buzan & Buzan, 2006).

2.5.6 Fostering empathy

- *The LEGO® Serious Play® approach* allows participants to answer questions related to an ongoing project, task, or strategy by building symbolic and metaphorical models of their findings using LEGO® bricks, which are then presented to each other. It was developed as a sophisticated means for groups to share ideas, assumptions, and insights, engage in dialogue, and generate solutions to real-world problems (Frick *et al.*, 2013).
- *The Six Thinking Hats approach* is an approach that comprises a group of six people, each of whom argues a specific way of thinking that is symbolized by a colored hat they wear. The basic perspectives are: (1) facts, (2) emotions, (3) judgment or caution, (4) logic, (5) creativity, and (6) control. Each participant must take every role at least once. This method allows ideas to be evaluated or improved upon from different perspectives, and controversial ideas can be voiced without risk of personal offense due to the role-playing in this approach. In addition, individual contributions can be strategically arranged or excluded in order to achieve a specific goal (Zec, 2022a).
- *Role playing* allows participants to role-play a hypothetical service experience. The prerequisite is that they believe the service really exists and then take a journey through some of its functionalities. This method is used to determine how different users would behave in the same situation and which functionalities of the product are needed or missing, especially when the same scene is played several times with different personas (Simsarian, 2003).

2.6 CONCLUSION AND RECOMMENDATIONS

Innovations can make an important contribution to tackling current sustainability challenges. To develop products and services that provide new business opportunities and address societal needs, methods are required that facilitate collaboration between businesses and users. This chapter is based on the experience of six co-creation labs that were conducted as part of the LIVING INNOVATION project. The findings from this project introduce co-creation as an approach that translates the concept of RRI into practice by enabling users to take an active role in the innovation processes. It illustrates how business practitioners can involve users in their innovation processes in order to develop marketable products and services that are oriented toward societal needs.

The LIVING INNOVATION labs have shown the importance of careful planning and preparation for facilitating successful co-creation process: (1) the process should include a clear definition of the workshop's scope and its objectives, as well as a strategy on how to reach them; (2) the process for recruiting relevant users must be based on the workshop's scope and objectives because the participant types significantly influence co-creation workshops' outcomes; (3) seriousness, transparency, fairness, and sustainable involvement of users are helpful in increasing the participants' engagement; (4) the workshop design also has a significant influence on participants' motivations and outcomes. The design chosen within the LIVING INNOVATION labs comprised four phases, which resonated positively with the participants while also contributing to reaching the workshop's objectives; and (5) the labs helped to identify a range of methods that can be used by business practitioners to conduct successful co-creation processes.

The chapter is intended to serve as a guide and source for ideas. It does not provide a comprehensive framework that specifies how co-creation processes should be designed. Conceptual underpinnings, guidelines, and best practices for conducting an RRI-oriented co-creation approach are needed so as to provide a fruitful avenue for future work.

REFERENCES

Adamik, A., Nowicki, M., & Szymańska, K. (2018). Openness to co-creation as a method of reducing the complexity of the environment and dynamizing companies' competitive advantages. *Management & Marketing, 13*(2).

Alcántara, S., Bach, N., Kuhn, R., & Ullrich, P. (2015). *Demokratietheorie und Partizipationspraxis: Analyse und Anwendungspotentiale deliberativer Verfahren*. Springer-Verlag.

Alessi, C. (2020). Why do so many innovative products fail? Medium. Retrieved from https://uxdesign.cc/why-do-so-many-innovative-products-fail-1446ba33f4e6

Buzan, T., & Buzan, B. (2006). *The mind map book*. Pearson Education. Lead Innovation 2022. Available at: https://www.lead-innovation.com/insights/blog/ablauf-lead-user-methode

Chasanidou, D., Gasparini, A. A., & Lee, E. (2015). Design thinking methods and tools for innovation. In *Design, user experience, and usability: Design discourse, 4th International Conference Proceedings, DUXU, 2015* (pp. 12–23). Springer.

Cruickshank, L., Whitham, R., Rice, G., & Alter, H. (2017). Designing, adapting and selecting tools for creative engagement: A generative framework. *Swedish Design Research Journal, 15*, 42–51.

Deserti, A., & Rizzo, F. (2022). Between science, technology and society. In A. Deserti, M. Real, & F. Schmittinger (Eds.), *Co-creation for Responsible Research and Innovation* (pp. 1–9). Springer.

Fisher, E. (2020). Reinventing responsible innovation. *Journal of Responsible Innovation, 7*(1), 1–5.

Frick, E., Tardini, S., & Cantoni, L. (2013). LEGO® SERIOUS PLAY®: A state of the art of its applications in Europe. White Paper. Università della Svizzera Italiana.

García, D., Lóp, I., Perat, B., & Zuazua, E. (2016). A practical guide to Responsible Research and Innovation: Key lessons from RRI tools. RRI Tools. Retrieved from https://rri-tools.eu/documents/10184/16301/RRI+Tools.+A+practical+guide+to+Responsible+Research+and+Innovation.+Key+Lessons+from+RRI+Tools

Hayes, G. (2012). IDEO method cards. Retrieved from http://www.gillianhayes.com/Inf231F12/wp-content/uploads/2012/10/IDEOMethodCards.pdf

Heslin, P. A. (2009). Better than brainstorming? Potential contextual boundary conditions to brainwriting for idea generation in organizations. *Journal of Occupational and Organizational Psychology, 82*(1), 129–145.

Hoffmann, E. (2012). *User integration in sustainable product development. Organisational learning through boundary-spanning processes.* Greenleaf.

Iglesias, O., Markovic, S., Bagherzadeh, M., & Singh, J. J. (2020). Co-creation: A key link between corporate social responsibility, customer trust, and customer loyalty. *Journal of Business Ethics, 163*(1), 151–166.

Konrad, W., Kuhn, R., Wehner, S., & Wist, S. K. (2019). Designing the co-creation workshops: Deliverable D4. 1, "Workshop Design and Implementation Plan."

Lee, J. J., Jaatinen, M., Salmi, A., Mattelmäki, T., Smeds, R., & Holopainen, M. (2018). Design choices framework for co-creation projects. *International Journal of Design, 12*(2), 15–31.

Nanz, P., & Fritsche, M. (2012). *Handbuch Bürgerbeteiligung – Verfahren und Akteure, Chancen und Grenzen.* Bundeszentrale für politische Bildung.

Nielsen, J., Clemmensen, T., & Yssing, C. (2002, October). Getting access to what goes on in people's heads? Reflections on the think-aloud technique. In *Proceedings of the second Nordic conference on human-computer interaction* (pp. 101–110).

Owen, R., Macnaghten, P., & Stilgoe, J. (2020). Responsible research and innovation: From science in society to science for society, with society. In *Emerging technologies: Ethics, law and governance* (pp. 117–126). Routledge.

Piligrimienė, Ž., Dovalienė, A., & Virvilaitė, R. (2015). Consumer engagement in value co-creation: What kind of value it creates for a company? *Inžinerinė ekonomika*, 452–460.

Prahalad, C. K., & Ramaswamy, V. (2004). *The future of competition: Co-creating unique value with customers.* Harvard Business Press.

Rizzo, F., & Deserti, A. (2022). Assessing co-creation in relation to context for RRI operationalisation. *Co-creation for Responsible Research and Innovation, 139.*

Robinson, D. K., Simone, A., & Mazzonetto, M. (2021). RRI legacies: Co-creation for responsible, equitable and fair innovation in Horizon Europe. *Journal of Responsible Innovation, 8*(2), 209–216.

Sanders, E. B. N., & Stappers, P. J. (2008). Co-creation and the new landscapes of design. *Co-design, 4*(1), 5–18.

Simsarian, K. T. (2003, April). Take it to the next stage: The roles of role playing in the design process. In *CHI'03 extended abstracts on human factors in computing systems* (pp. 1012–1013).

Straub, H., Brachinger-Franke, L., & Haupt, T. (2009). *Gruppenprozesse in die Hand nehmen. Workshop-Abläufe und Methoden für Prozessberater, Führungskräfte, Moderatoren und Change-Manager.* ComTeam.

Tekic, A., & Willoughby, K. (2019). Co-creation–child, sibling or adopted cousin of open innovation? *Innovation, 21*(2), 274–297.

Wilkinson, C. R., & De Angeli, A. (2014). Applying user centred and participatory design approaches to commercial product development. *Design Studies, 35*(6), 614–631.

Wilson, C. (2013). *Brainstorming and beyond: A user-centered design method.* Newnes.

Zec, M. (2022a). Die 6 Denkhüte von De Bono: Kreativitätstechniken.info. Retrieved from https://xn--kreativittstechniken-jzb.info/die-6-denkhute-von-de-bono/

Zec, M. (2022b). Walt-Disney-Methode: Kreativitätstechniken.info. Retrieved from, https://xn--kreativittstechniken-jzb.info/ideen-generieren/walt-disney-methode/

C3

Responsible Design Thinking

How to integrate responsibility and sustainability into Design Thinking processes

Ursula Kopp and André Martinuzzi

3.1 INTRODUCTION

Over the past two decades, the business sector has increasingly addressed issues of responsibility and sustainability (Bugdol *et al.*, 2020; Heras-Saizarbitoria *et al.*, 2022; Mio *et al.*, 2020). While marketing, operations, finance, auditing, and reporting have integrated responsibility and sustainability into their areas, innovation management and product or service development are still at the beginning. While only a few companies explore how their innovation could be more responsive to stakeholder needs, most companies hardly examine whether desirable implications are missed by an innovation, or whether it has negative implications (Lubberink *et al.*, 2017). One of the reasons is the lack of well-established and broadly used methods to consider responsibility and sustainability in designing new products, services, and solutions.

Over the course of the EU project LIVING INNOVATION, we identified key aspects of responsibility and sustainability and integrated them into a Design Thinking process. We identified several tools that can be applied, as well as tested our concept in a series of workshops. This chapter first describes what Design Thinking is and how it works. Then we identify key aspects of responsibility and sustainability and highlight how and where they can be integrated into a standard Design Thinking process. We emphasize how to consider societal needs, how to follow a systemic approach, and how to assess future impacts. For practical implementation, we present three tools for each of these three aspects.

3.2 WHAT IS DESIGN THINKING?

Innovation is often driven by groundbreaking research and new technologies. Many of the products we use today would not be possible without this technology push. However, there is also another perspective on innovation that put the needs of people

DOI: 10.4324/9781003319481-25

into the center and tries to fulfill this demand. Companies that serve the needs of users best design globally successful products and services.

Design Thinking is a well-established method on how to better understand user needs, on how to develop innovative ideas and then rapidly prototype and test them. Its success story starts in the early twenty-first century based on the profound knowledge of how designers work and provides a step-by-step guide for innovation managers in companies. Among the best-known Design Thinking schools and practitioners are IDEO (Tim Brown), the Stanford School (David Kelley), The Hasso Plattner Institute, and IBM.

Design Thinking is a human-centered approach to innovation that equally integrates the needs of people, the technological possibilities, and the requirements of businesses. Design Thinking is considered a supportive approach for a range of business challenges and can be viewed as "the application of design methods by multidisciplinary teams to a broad range of innovation challenges" (Seidel & Fixson, 2013, p. 19). Methodologically, Design Thinking it is a productive mix of analytical and intuitive thinking, drawn from a designer's toolkit (Brown, 2008; Martin, 2009).

Nowadays, Design Thinking is a well-described innovation model able to be used by both designers and non-designers. (Seidel & Fixson, 2013) Although slightly different models of Design Thinking have been developed, they all follow some main principles (e.g., Micheli *et al.*, 2018; Schallmo *et al.*, 2018; Shapira *et al.*, 2017):

- Human needs are the starting point.
- Core attitudes are creativity, open-mindedness, and optimism.
- Multidisciplinary teams.
- Experimentation elements in an iterative, non-linear process.
- Visualization and abductive reasoning.

A Design Thinking process consists of six iterative phases[1] (Plattner *et al.*, 2009) configured in two main spaces: the problem space and the solution space (Figure C3.1).

3.2.1 The problem space

The problem space focuses on a better and deeper understanding of user needs and consists of the following three phases:

- *Understand* aims at generating a common view or picture of the problem situation among all members of the innovation team by collecting and/or visualizing as many aspects as possible.
- *Empathize* focuses on collecting detailed insights into the views and needs of the different user groups.

Figure C3.1
Standard Design Thinking model

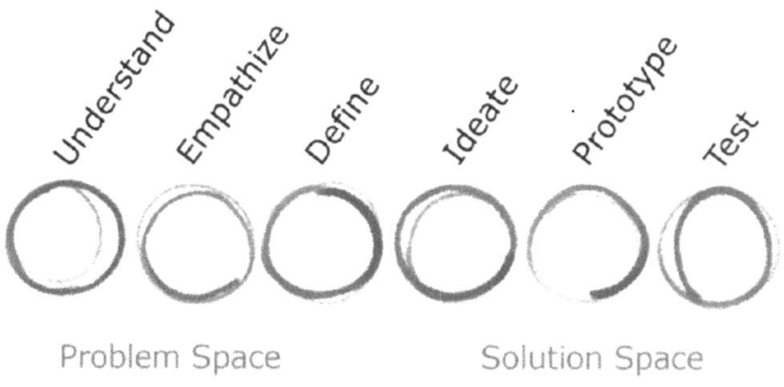

- In the *Define* phase, all inputs and lessons from before are processed and the real problem is defined in the form of a question to be answered in the following phases – this new question can differ from the original question/problem at the beginning of the DT process, as new insights were generated.

3.2.2 The solution space

The solution space aims at developing new products or services based on the insights from the previous phases and consists of:

- To *ideate* means to develop as many new ideas as possible to solve the problem with the help of creativity techniques ("the more, the better"). Then the most promising ideas are selected and developed further.
- *Prototypes* are produced by using materials, such as paper, cardboard, Lego, etc., rather simple and rapidly.
- *Test*: The most promising prototypes are then tested with different user groups and are developed further.

Design Thinking is an iterative process. In any phase, it can be useful to go one or several steps back if the innovation process turns out to be moving in the wrong direction or new insights offer new ideas and possibilities.

Within each phase, several tools can be used depending on the type of problem, on the team, on the progress, as well as on the experience and abilities of the person guiding the process (examples are customer journey, personas, stakeholder map, business model canvas, for further details, see Micheli *et al.*, 2018).

Over the past 15 years, Design Thinking has been successfully used not only by large companies, such as AirBNB, Bayer, BMW, Bosch, Otto, Pinterest, SAP, Siemens,

Swisscom, Volkswagen, but also in urban and regional planning (e.g., Ge & Maisch, 2016; Lalicic *et al.*, 2021; Lewis *et al.*, 2020; Lewrick & Link, 2015).

Benefits of Design Thinking result from the involvement of users throughout the whole process of developing new solutions, products, or services. Design Thinking teams are often more diverse, show higher trust in their abilities to design change as well as more productive ways of dealing with failures. Altogether, this leads to higher creativity and better fitting solutions, on the one hand, and faster innovation processes, on the other (Alexandrakis, 2021; Cankurtaran & Beverland, 2020; Liedtka, 2017; Plattner *et al.*, 2009).

Possible limitations can be found in the selection and motivation of participants of a Design Thinking process, as going through all the steps as a team can be complex and time-consuming. In addition, although the basic structure of Design Thinking seems easy, implementing Design Thinking requires trained and open facilitators to guide the process.

3.3 HOW DO WE INTEGRATE "RESPONSIBILITY" AND "SUSTAINABILITY" INTO DESIGN THINKING?

In a first step, we derived three key concepts of responsibility and sustainability from the related scientific discourses:

1. By *considering societal needs* it is meant that when authors highlight that innovations should be "socially desirable" (von Schomberg, 2013), they should "tackle societal challenges" (McGahan *et al.*, 2021) or should be "oriented towards Sustainable Development Goals" (von Geibler *et al.*, 2019). In all of these cases, not only potential users or individual beneficiaries of an innovation are put into focus, but the perspective is also broadened toward grand societal challenges and a global and long-term perspective.
2. *Following a systemic approach* was key for analysing unsustainable trends from the very beginning (e.g., the famous *Limits to Growth* publication; Meadows *et al.*, 1972, was based on a systems model). Sustainability challenges were perceived as wicked problems (Pryshlakivsky & Searcy, 2013) and systems thinking was suggested as an alternative to linear and mechanistic thinking (Hjorth & Bagheri, 2006). In recent times, systems thinking reached innovation management, where the perspective on innovation eco-systems was enriched by insights from system dynamics and a systemic design practice was suggested (Colvin *et al.*, 2014).
3. *Assessing future impacts* is referred to as "anticipation" in the debate about Responsible Innovation (Stilgoe *et al.*, 2013), as "responsibility for impacts" as a key element of Corporate Social Responsibility (Martinuzzi *et al.*, 2015), and as precautionary principle in sustainability management and policy (Fisher *et al.*, 2006). Technology assessment (Tran & Daim, 2008) and foresight (Van der Duin, 2016) are well-established tools for stakeholder dialogues (e.g., on stem cell research, nano-technology, and Artificial Intelligence) or for developing business strategies, but rarely implemented in single innovation processes.

In a second step, we explored how and where these three principles can be integrated into the Design Thinking phases in a way that the resulting model offers innovation managers and facilitators a useful, adequately complex, but still easy to use, extension of the Design Thinking model.

As many important decisions about aims, scope, and implementation are taken even before the very start of a Design Thinking process, we take a close look at an explicit setup phase prior to the six standard Design Thinking phases. There, the systemic approach, the societal needs, and the assessment should be introduced in addition to the team building and diversity and the setup of rooms and materials, which are normally discussed (e.g., Uebernickel *et al.*, 2019).

We discussed the above issues with innovation managers of leading companies in the digital sector, carried out interviews with Design Thinking experts, and organized a virtual sounding board. In a third step, we explored which methods and tools can be applied in order to consider *societal needs*, a *systemic approach*, and the *future impacts* of innovations in each Design Thinking process, as well as where in the process they are most useful (see Figure C3.2).

3.3.1 Considering societal needs

Responsible Innovation means focusing not only on the novelty of a product, but also on the benefits to the users and the potential profits it might generate. Responsible Design Thinking needs to take a broader view on people's needs and grand societal

Figure C3.2
Responsible Design Thinking model

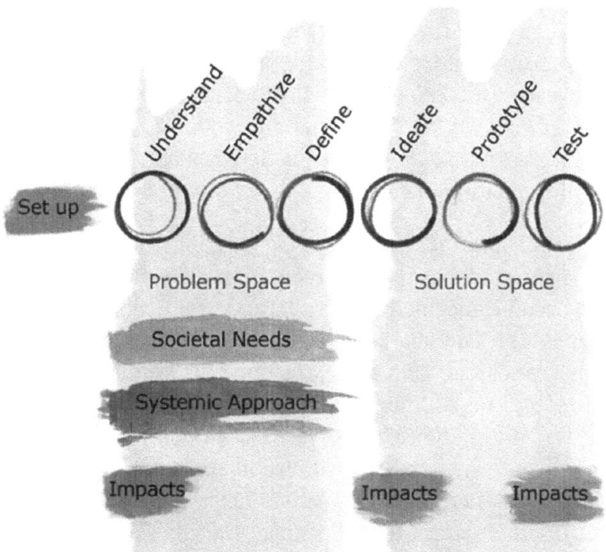

challenges, as they are addressed, for example, in the UN Sustainable Development Goals, as well as in the main societal trends, such as demographic change. Vulnerable and marginalized groups, but also natural resources such as water, air, earth, etc., need to have a stake in the innovation process from the very beginning.

At this point, it is also important to determine ecological and societal aims already, as well as according measurement criteria, as they will then serve as a reference framework for the whole Design Thinking process. It is also necessary to mention that trade-offs between the ecological, economic, and social dimensions, or between the needs of different societal groups, require a proper negotiation process.

The societal needs should be integrated into the first part of each Design Thinking process in the so-called *problem space* (see Figure C3.2). The authors suggest involving real people, representing those needs already from the very beginning, or use representative participation, or the appropriate personas in the empathize phase to support the problem definition:

- *Direct participation* means involving people directly in an innovation process (Jones & Kijima, 2018). It is essential to include people or representatives, covering a broad spectrum of societal needs and representing environmental concerns, to ensure the societal acceptance of the outcomes of an innovation process. Participants should be of different ages, genders, sociocultural, and professional backgrounds. To promote creativity, it is also advisable to include people with a creative professional background, such as artists, writers, animators, or musicians. The preparation can be challenging, as the participants must be identified, must have an interest in the content and sufficient time to participate.
- *Representative participation* means that societal interests and needs are represented by representatives of the particular groups. This can take place, for example, through the participation of members of NGOs or other specific interest groups in co-creation processes (Kazadi *et al.*, 2016). Representative participation is often easier to achieve than direct participation, because many NGOs and interest groups working on social and environmental issues are eager to participate in developing innovations that contribute to sustainable development or improve the situation of the people they are representing.
- *Imaginary participation through personas:* Sometimes it is not possible to involve real people or the right representatives. Personas is a common tool for designers to become informed about users and to empathize with them (Miaskiewicz & Kozar, 2011; Nielsen, 2013; Pruitt & Adlin, 2006) Personas are a hypothetical archetype of real users, an abstraction of consumer groups with common characteristics and needs, they are fictitious, but specific, concrete representations (Pruitt & Adlin, 2006). Persona descriptions include demographic and socio-economic information, occupations, likenesses, possessions, etc. They are given a name and a personal story, which helps to empathize with a character rather than discrete factual data. Personas work because people tend to build

internal models based on broad dispositions that predict or explain much of people's behavior. This ability helps designers to envision how users will respond to their design. Working with personas can be as realistic as working with real users, as well as with models of fictional people (Grudin, 2006).

3.3.2 Following a systemic approach

In order to create responsible innovations, it is necessary to better understand the contexts and interrelations in which a technology and product are embedded, which means fully considering and designing whole systems. Therefore, one must inevitably recognize and understand the interdependencies, dynamics, and boundaries of the systems in which people's needs are embedded. Systems thinking helps to understand the underlying interrelationships of its elements, the dynamics within the system, and to identify patterns of change (Meadows, 2008; Senge, 2006).

Within the define phase, a very close look should also be taken at whether a need is really a need or rather a symptom of an underlying need. This reframing allows looking beyond the surface to aim at systemic and, therefore, more powerful solutions. In order to develop true systemic solutions, the involvement of a broad range of stakeholders in the collaborative Design Thinking process is crucial.

Systemic visualizing techniques, such as participatory system mapping, or representations methods, such as systemic constellation, or a systemic canvas can be helpful to include the systemic view in the *problem space* of the innovation project (see Figure C3.2):

- *Systemic constellation*[2] work is the observation and analysis of the interactions and relationships between parts of a whole system, using a transverbal language (Sparrer, 2009). This is done by visualizing and externalizing the internal picture someone has of the relationships, orders, hierarchies, dependencies, and communication patterns of a system (Grochowiak & Castella, 2002) by arranging either persons, figurines, or symbols as representations of parts of a system intuitively in a room or on a table. The distances between them and the directions in which they are facing provide important information on the underlying system dynamics, as well as the feedback representatives give about the feelings, perceptions, and views that they have at the particular position (Kopp & Martinuzzi, 2013). Systemic constellations allow a view from the outside on the whole system, thus supporting system thinking and problem solving. The dialogue-oriented and open setting fosters communication, supports mutual understanding, and boosts creativity. The method is rather fast and easy to apply by a trained facilitator (e.g., Weber, 2000; Weinhold *et al.*, 2014).
- *Participatory systems mapping* is based on the principle that the behavior of a system results from the structure of its elements and provides a standardized "language" for visualizing a system and its relationships (Martinuzzi *et al.*, 2015). The central tool of participatory systems mapping are causal loop diagrams, a

formal language originating in system dynamics and cybernetics, which can be developed by a team in a workshop setting with professional facilitation (Sedlacko *et al.*, 2014). The basic idea of causal loop diagrams is to identify the whole system, understand the relationships between system components and to capture the dynamics within the system (Meadows, 2008). Selected variables and their relationships and interdependencies are the primary building blocks of causal loop diagrams. The causal relationships between the variables, as positive or negative loops, as well as longer time delays are marked accordingly.

- *Systemic canvases* link canvas approaches with system thinking in order to visualize, design, and re-design projects, products, or services by drawing a "bigger picture" and developing a shared vision among participants (Kalbach, 2016). Canvases outline all the important components, such as client information, intended results, activities, time perspective, or resources, and highlight key questions and success factors for each component. Canvases can be easily adapted to include a systemic perspective (Elia *et al.*, 2021) as direct and indirect impacts on the economy, the natural environment, and society can be addressed.

3.3.3 Assessing future impacts

Responsible Innovation also means considering the medium- and long-term impacts an innovation will have on the environment, our societies, and on our future. This includes all direct, indirect, all positive and negative, as well as all intended and unintended impacts of an innovation. The overall aim is to increase positive impacts and to reduce negative impacts wherever possible.

The consideration of future impacts happens in two distinct phases of the Responsible Design Thinking process (see Figure C3.2). At the end of the *ideate* phase, the ecological and social impacts of the ideas that were developed are being assessed. Judging them against the criteria defined earlier helps to choose the best and most sustainable and responsible solutions. In the *test* phase, user benefits and societal impacts should be considered equally by conducting materiality assessments, using scenario techniques and/or implementing technology assessment:

- *Materiality assessment* has its roots in financial reporting, auditing, and accounting. In the context of sustainability management, materiality assessment has been introduced as a promising method for determining the relevance of sustainability issues to the company and stakeholders (Taubken & Feld, 2018). The method aims to reduce the complexity that arises from the multifarious impacts of business activities, including impacts across the entire value chain (e.g., product life cycle, supply chain; Findler, 2019). In this way, decision-makers can better address the needs of society, create economic and social value, and contribute to sustainable development. Materiality assessments have been promoted by a number of widely used sustainability standards, such as the Global Reporting Initiative (GRI) and the Sustainability Accounting Standards Board (SASB). Consequently, they have found their way into corporate practice (Wu *et al.*, 2018).

- *Scenario techniques* are foresight methods that help mitigate uncertainty and complexity in the long-term. They outline multiple future scenarios that promote strategic thinking and push the boundaries of thinking (Amer *et al.*, 2013). Scenario techniques help to understand complexities of situations better by creating narratives that describe how things might unfold. There is no single approach to scenario techniques, but rather a variety of methods for creating scenarios (Varum & Melo, 2010). However, all of these methods share the same focus on defining the issues, systemically identifying key drivers, trends, constraints, stakeholders, and ranking these items by uncertainty and importance (Amer *et al.*, 2013).
- *Technology assessments* aim to identify and assess eventual impacts of technological changes and applications as early as possible. They seek to anticipate future developments of technologies, their relations to markets, and eventual impacts on society and the natural environment. As a response to the risks associated with the development of new technologies, technology assessments were first mainly used in the public domain and later adopted by the corporate sector. Recent developments include public participation and involvement in innovation processes (Rip, 2015). Technology assessments can be carried out by (or for) business firms, but also as a social or environmental impact assessment (Rip, 2015). Approaches of how to conduct technology assessments range from qualitative to quantitative methods (see Tran & Daim, 2008).

3.3.4 Adding a "setup phase" in the very beginning

In order to integrate sustainability and responsibility into Design Thinking, the setup phase is particularly important, as many decisions regarding context, scope, orientation, and purpose need to be taken before a Design Thinking process starts. Existing literature mostly refers to the setup of a schedule, space, and room, as well as materials and supporting infrastructure to work with (Uebernickel *et al.*, 2019; von Thienen *et al.*, 2012). Some authors mention team building and team composition regarding diversity, motivation, and background (e.g., Chasanidou *et al.*, 2015; Uebernickel *et al.*, 2019). Leifer and Steinert (2011) mention the organizational setup of a Design Thinking process, for example, regarding the freedom and flexibility of an innovation team in an organization.

Our approach goes one step further by suggesting a particular "setup phase" before the Design Thinking process starts. By doing so, we put special emphasis on the decisions that are taken in the very beginning and that have a substantial impact on the later phases, as well as on the whole process. During this dedicated phase, we suggest discussing and deciding about:

- context, scope, and purpose of the innovation, in general, and the Design Thinking process, in particular;
- system boundaries, stakeholders, and their interrelations;
- identification and selection of participants as well as the facilitator.

Societal needs, the systemic approach, and the consideration of impacts need to be introduced in the setup phase, in order to ensure their proper consideration during the entire process. In the best case scenario, the setup phase is supported by a professional facilitator, who is experienced in Design Thinking, sustainability, and responsibility. Team members need to be selected who are willing and able to represent and consider sustainability and responsibility issues in the later phases. During the setup phase, the participants need to develop a common understanding of how sustainability and responsibility issues will be considered. This can be achieved by formulating common sustainability and responsibility goals or minimum requirements for the outcomes of the Design Thinking process.

3.4 CONCLUSION AND RECOMMENDATIONS

The business sector can contribute significantly to solving grand societal challenges by considering sustainability and responsibility in its innovation processes. An effective strategy to disseminate these issues is to adapt and extend existing methods and frameworks and, therefore, orient innovation processes toward responsibility and sustainability. Adapting Design Thinking seems promising, but previous attempts were either rather complex or only selective.

This chapter shows a smart adaptation of the Design Thinking process that is well founded in the frameworks and theories of Responsible Innovation. It comprises three extensions: (1) considering societal needs, (2) following a systemic approach, and (3) assessing future impacts. These extensions were carefully chosen, do not hamper the creativity and agility of Design Thinking, and neither overload nor slow it down.

In order to support the practical implementation of responsible Design Thinking, we identified a number of well-established tools. Potential challenges may be the need for experienced facilitators (from the very beginning) and that team members need to be open-minded, willing, and able to consider and critically reflect upon responsibility and sustainability issues. However, we are convinced that our approach provides a valuable framework to integrate responsibility and sustainability into Design Thinking.

NOTES

1. Different schools give slightly different names to the phases, such as inspiration, ideation, and implementation (IDEO), define, ideate, prototype and test (Stanford Design School), or understand, explore, prototype, and evaluate (IBM).
2. Based on Family Constellations (Hellinger, 1994), Systemic Constellations for organizations and other systems became available in the late 1990s (Grochowiak & Castella, 2002; Weber, 2000). A recent form, the Systemic Structural Constellations, also includes abstract elements, for example, the problem, the aims, or values (Sparrer, 2009). Systemic Constellations have been used in systemic organizational consulting, policy-making, administration, regional development, adult education, etc. (e.g., Senoner & Rosselet, 2013).

REFERENCES

Alexandrakis, J. (2021). Cycling towards sustainability: The transformative potential of urban design thinking in a sustainable living lab. *Transportation Research Interdisciplinary Perspectives*, *9*, 100269. https://doi.org/10.1016/j.trip.2020.100269

Amer, M., Daim, T. U., & Jetter, A. (2013). A review of scenario planning. *Futures*, *46*, 23–40. https://doi.org/10.1016/j.futures.2012.10.003

Brown, T. (2008). Design Thinking. *Harvard Business Review*, June, 84–92.

Bugdol, M., Puciato, D., & Borys, T. (2020). Environmental management systems in the context of sustainable development: The identification of open problems. *Problemy Ekorozwoju*, *15*(2), 131–142.

Cankurtaran, P., & Beverland, M.B. (2020). Using design thinking to respond to crises: B2B lessons from the 2020 COVID-19 pandemic. *Industrial Marketing Management*, *88*, 255–260. https://doi.org/10.1016/j.indmarman.2020.05.030

Chasanidou, D., Gasparini, A. A., & Lee, E. (2015). Design Thinking methods and tools for innovation. In A. Marcus (Ed.), *Design, user experience, and usability: Design discourse*. Lecture Notes in Computer Science. 9186. Springer. https://doi.org/10.1007/978-3-319-20886-2_2

Colvin, J., Blackmore, C., Chimbuya, S., Collins, K., Dent, M., Gross, J., Ison, P., Roggero, P., & Seddaiu, G. (2014). In search of systemic innovation for sustainable development: A design praxis emerging from a decade of social learning inquiry. *Research Policy*, *43*(4), 760–771. https://doi.org/10.1016/j.respol.2013.12.010

Elia, G., Margherita, A., & Secundo, G. (2021). Project management canvas: A systems thinking framework to address project complexity. *International Journal of Managing Projects in Business*, *14*(4), 809–835. https://doi.org/10.1108/IJMPB-04-2020-0128

Findler, F. (2019). Scoping what matters: An introduction to impact mapping. In N. Schönherr & A. Martinuzzi (Eds.), *Business and the sustainable development goals: Measuring and managing corporate impacts* (pp. 55–74). Palgrave Macmillan.

Fisher, E. C., Jones, J. S., & von Schomberg, R. (Eds.) (2006). *Implementing the precautionary principle: Perspectives and prospects*. Edgar Elgar.

Ge, X., & Maisch, B. (2016). Industrial Design Thinking at Siemens Corporate Technology, China. In W. Brenner & F. Uebernickel (Eds.), *Design Thinking for innovation*. Springer. https://doi.org/10.1007/978-3-319-26100-3_12

Grochowiak, K., & Castella, J. (2002). *Systemdynamische Organisationsberatung: Die Übertragung der Methode Hellingers auf Organisationen und Unternehmen* (2nd ed.). Carl-Auer.

Grudin, J. (2006). Why personas work: The psychological evidence. In J.S. Pruitt & T. Adlin (Eds.), *The persona lifecycle* (pp. 642–664). Elsevier.

Hellinger, B. (1994). *Ordnungen der Liebe. Ein Kursbuch*. Carl-Auer.

Heras-Saizarbitoria, I., Urbieta, L., & Boiral, O. (2022). Organizations' engagement with sustainable development goals: From cherry-picking to SDG-washing? *Corporate Social Responsibility and Environmental Management*, *29*(2), 316–328. https://doi.org/10.1002/csr.2202

Hjorth, P., & Bagheri, A. (2006). Navigating towards sustainable development: A system dynamics approach. *Futures*, *38*(1), 74–92.

Jones, P., & Kijima, K. (Eds.) (2018). *Systemic design: Theory, methods, and practice*. SpringerLink: Vol. 8. Springer Japan. https://doi.org/10.1007/978-4-431-55639-8

Kalbach, J. (2016). *Mapping experiences: A guide to creating value through journeys, blueprints, and diagrams* (1st ed.). O´Reilly.

Kazadi, K., Lievens, A., & Mahr, D. (2016). Stakeholder co-creation during the innovation process: Identifying capabilities for knowledge creation among multiple stakeholders. *Journal of Business Research*, *69*(2), 525–540. https://doi.org/10.1016/j.jbusres.2015.05.009

Kopp, U., & Martinuzzi, A. (2013). Teaching sustainability leaders in systems thinking. *Business Systems Review, 2*(2), 191–215.

Lalicic, L., Marine-Roig, E., Ferrer-Rosell, B., & Martin-Fuentes, E. (2021). Destination image analytics for tourism design: An approach through Airbnb reviews. *Annals of Tourism Research, 86*, 103100. https://doi.org/10.1016/j.annals.2020.103100

Leifer, L. J. & Steinert, M. (2011). Dancing with ambiguity: Causality behavior, design thinking, and triple-loop-learning. *Information Knowledge Systems Management, 10*, 151–173.

Lewis, J. M., McGann, M., & Blomkamp, E. (2020). When design meets power: Design Thinking, public sector innovation and the politics of policymaking. *Policy & Politics, 48*(1), 111–130. Retrieved July 30, 2022, from https://bristoluniversitypressdigital.com/view/journals/pp/48/1/article-p111.xml

Lewrick, M. & Link, P. (2015). Design Thinking tools: Early insights accelerate marketers' success. *Market Review St. Gallen, 32*, 40–51. https://doi.org/10.1007/s11621-015-0507-7

Liedtka, J. (2017). Evaluating the impact of Design Thinking in action. *Academy of Management*, Proceedings. https://doi.org/10.5465/ambpp.2017.177

Lubberink, R., Blok, V., Van Ophem, J., & Omta, O. (2017). Lessons for Responsible Innovation in the business context: A systematic literature review of responsible, social and sustainable innovation practices. *Sustainability, 9*(5), 721–752. https://doi.org/10.3390/su9050721

Martin, R. (2009). *The design of business: Why design thinking is the next competitive advantage.* Harvard Business School Press.

Martinuzzi, A., Szocs, I., Krumay, B., & Kudlak, R. (2015). CSR at the crossroads: From voluntary activities to responsibility for impacts. *Academy of Management Proceedings, 1*, 16532. https://doi.org/10.1016/j.jclepro.2018.02.119

McGahan, A. M., Bogers, M. L., Chesbrough, H., & Holgersson, M. (2021). Tackling societal challenges with open innovation. *California Management Review, 63*(2), 49–61. https://doi.org/10.1177/0008125620973713

Meadows, D. H. (2008). *Thinking in systems: A primer.* Chelsea Green Publishing Co.

Meadows, D. H., Meadows, D. L., Randers, J., & Behrens, W. W. (1972). *The limits to growth. A report for the Club of Rome's project on the predicament of mankind.* Universe Books.

Miaskiewicz, T., & Kozar, K. A. (2011). Personas and user-centered design: How can personas benefit product design processes? *Design Studies, 32*(5), 417–430.

Micheli, P., Wilner, S. J. S., Bhatti, S. H., Mura, M., & Beverland, M. B. (2018). Doing Design Thinking: Conceptual review, synthesis, and research agenda. *Journal of Product Innovation Management, 36*(201802), 124–148. https://doi.org/10.1111/jpim.12466

Mio, C., Panfilo, S., & Blundo, B. (2020). Sustainable development goals and the strategic role of business: A systematic literature review. *Business Strategy and the Environment, 29*, 3220– 3245. https://doi.org/10.1002/bse.2568

Nielsen, L. (2013). *Personas: User focused design.* Springer.

Plattner, H., Meinel, C., & Weinberg, U. (2009). *Design Thinking. Innovation lernen, Ideenwelten öffnen.* mi Wirtschaftsbuch.

Pruitt, J. S., & Adlin, T. (2006). *The persona lifecycle* (pp. 46–65). Elsevier.

Pryshlakivsky, J., & Searcy, C. (2013). Sustainable development as a wicked problem. In S. Kovacic & A. Sousa-Poza (Eds.), *Managing and engineering in complex situations. Topics in safety, risk, reliability and quality* (vol. 21, pp. 109–128). Springer. https://doi.org/10.1007/978-94-007-5515-4_6

Rip, A. (2015). Technology assessment. In *International encyclopedia of the social & behavioral sciences* (pp. 125–128). Elsevier. https://doi.org/10.1016/B978-0-08-097086-8.85036-9

Schallmo, D., Williams, C. A., & Lang, K. (2018). An integrated Design Thinking approach: Literature review, basic principles and roadmap for Design Thinking. In *Proceedings of the)*

XXIX ISPIM Innovation Conference "Innovation, The name of the game," June, 17–20, Stockholm, Sweden.
Sedlacko, M., Martinuzzi, A., Røpke, I., Videira, N., & Antunes, P. (2014). Participatory systems mapping for sustainable consumption: Discussion of a method promoting systemic insights. *Ecological Economics, 106*, 33–43. https://doi.org/10.1016/j.ecolecon.2014.07.002
Seidel, V. P., & Fixson, S. K. (2013). Adopting design thinking in novice multidisciplinary teams: The application and limits of design methods and reflexive practices. *Journal of Product Innovation Management, 30*(1), 19–33. https://doi.org/10.1111/jpim.12061
Senge, P.M. (2006). *The fifth discipline: The art and practice of the learning organization* (2nd ed.). Random House Business.
Senoner, G., & Rosselet, C. (2013). *Enacting solutions: Management constellations, an innovative approach to problem-solving and decision-making in organizations.* Ledizioni.
Shapira, H., Ketchie, A., & Nehe, M. (2017). The integration of Design Thinking and strategic sustainable development. *Journal of Cleaner Production, 140*(1), 277–287. https://doi.org/10.1016/j.jclepro.2015.10.092
Sparrer, I. (2009). *Systemische Strukturaufstellungen. Theorie und Praxis* (2nd ed.). Carl-Auer.
Stilgoe, J., Owen, R., & Macnaghten, P. (2013). Developing a framework for responsible innovation. *Research Policy, 42*(9), 1568–1580. https://doi.org/10.1016/j.respol.2013.05.008
Taubken, N., & Feld, T. Y. (2018). Impact measurement and the concept of materiality: New requirements and approaches for materiality assessments. *Sustainability Management Forum, 26*(1–4), 87–100. https://doi.org/10.1007/s00550-018-0483-x
Tran, T. A., & Daim, T. (2008). A taxonomic review of methods and tools applied in technology assessment. *Technological Forecasting and Social Change, 75*(9), 1396–1405.
Uebernickel, F., Brenner, W., Pukall, B., Naef, T., & Schindlholzer, B. (Eds.) (2019). *Design Thinking: The handbook.* World Scientific.
Van der Duin, P. (2016). *Foresight in organizations: methods and tools.* Routledge.
Varum, C.A., & Melo, C. (2010). Directions in scenario planning literature – A review of the past decades. *Futures, 42*(4), 355–369. https://doi.org/10.1016/j.futures.2009.11.021
von Geibler, J., Piwowar, J., & Greven, A. (2019). The SDG-check: Guiding open innovation towards sustainable development goals. *Technology Innovation Management Review, 9*(3), 20–37.
von Schomberg, R. (2013). A vision of responsible innovation. In R. Owen, M. Heintz, & J. Bessant (Eds.), *Responsible Innovation.* John Wiley.
von Thienen, J., Noweski, C., Rauth, I., Meinel, C., & Sabine Lang, S. (2012). If you want to know who you are, tell me where you are: The importance of places.In H. Plattner, C. Meinel, & L. Leifer (Eds.) *Design Thinking research. Studying co-creation in practice* (pp. 53–74). Springer.
Weber, G. (2000). Organisationsaufstellungen: Basics und Besonderheiten. In G. Weber(Ed.), *Praxis der Organisationsaufstellungen* (pp. 34–90). Carl-Auer.
Weinhold, J., Bornhäuser, A., Hunger, C., & Schweitzer, J. (2014). *Dreierlei Wirksamkeit. Die Heidelberger Studie zu Systemaufstellungen.* Carl-Auer.
Wu, S., Shao, C., & Chen, J. (2018). Approaches on the screening methods for materiality in sustainability reporting. *Sustainability, 10*(9), 3233. https://doi.org/10.3390/su10093233

C4

Real-life inclusion

How to innovate with low socio-economic status families

Adebowale Owoseni, Catherine Flick, Roxana Firth, and Malcolm Fisk

4.1 INTRODUCTION

Innovation, what does it really entail? Innovation can mean different things to different people in different situations, but it is largely a process, rather than an outcome. Understanding the process of innovation without taking into account the role of imagination, ideation, and value proposition is difficult (Anderson *et al.*, 2014; Schuessler *et al.*, 2021), in particular, how the innovation process engages people responsibly in order to creatively generate new ideas, new perspectives, new methods, products, or services that solve real-world problems and add value. Innovation does not imply creating something from nothing; rather, it involves combining things that already exist in novel ways. It begins with creative imaginations that challenge established ways of seeing and doing things; it entails defining problems, as well as solving them in unconventional ways (Shenkar, 2010).

Against this backdrop, this chapter describes the process of innovation with low-income families in Leicester, United Kingdom, through a series of collaborative, asynchronous workshops. The workshops form an integral aspect of the EU-funded LIVING INNOVATION (LIV_IN) project. As emerging technologies continue to influence how we live, these workshops sought to create a picture of a home in 2030 by defining the problems currently being faced in homes and subsequently exploring technology-driven ideas for solving the problems. In retrospect, and for the benefit of the business community, this chapter opens up product development mechanisms that responsibly co-create solutions with socially marginalized people.

The choice of engaging low-income and economically disadvantaged homes in Leicester aligns with the core concept of Responsible Innovation, which "seeks to

DOI: 10.4324/9781003319481-26

bring issues related to innovation into the open, to anticipate their consequences, and to involve society in discussing how science and technology can help create the kind of world and society we want for generations to come."[1] Responsible Innovation in this context suggests a blueprint for framing a socially responsive and responsible innovation process; a process that considers diversity and inclusion in its approach (Groves, 2017; Robinson *et al.*, 2021). According to a report by the UK government on the multiple deprivation index, 20% of Leicester neighborhoods make up 10% of the UK's most deprived areas (Office of National Statistics, 2019). In essence, this report suggests that deprived people in Leicester are more likely to be excluded from technology-related conversations, collaborations, and innovations. In a departure from the norm, this study involved families in deprived areas of Leicester, including parents and children, in innovation processes, which identified problems in the homes and proposed digital technology-enabled solutions to the problems.

This chapter is structured as follows: First, a background to the co-creation context and objectives is provided. Next, in Section 4.2, we describe the methodology, which entails recruitment and data collection through the workshops, interviews, and observation. Following that, in Section 4.3, we present the synopsis in terms of ideas, problems and solutions generated from the workshop. In the concluding sections, we reflect on the co-creation workshops and itemize key learning points – what works, what does not work, as well as concluding remarks. The experience documented in this chapter will help businesses rethink *Design Thinking* and *co-creation* procedures in a new light. It also contributes to innovation practice in a family context, as it revealed a unique and novel approach to innovation in a family setting, through a technique that not only responsibly included the minors and the vulnerable, but also involved them in a way that demonstrated inclusion and diversity.

4.2 THE INNOVATION TECHNIQUE

This section provides a background and describes the asynchronous workshops that involved families in Leicester. It focuses on the recruitment and delivery of the workshops.

4.2.1 Background

The workshops were originally scheduled to take place on-site and in-person at three different locations (community centers) in Leicester. Each venue was located close to the homes of the target participants (families) and was expected to host three 5-hour workshop sessions. These arrangements were made in collaboration with the local partnership team at De Montfort University (DMU). However, the plans were thwarted by the UK Prime Minister's announcement on March 23 ordering people in the UK to "stay at home," which essentially signaled the start of lockdown and restrictions measures to manage the COVID-19 pandemic. These measures eventually lasted for more than two years. This was the context that necessitated a review of the research plan, and the only alternative was to consider a new approach that was flexible, remote, and online. The innovative research implemented was born out of the need to adapt the workshops to the realities of the COVID-19 pandemic. However, it appears to have turned out to be a novel technique for innovating in a family setting.

4.2.2 Recruitment

The overall objective of the study remained to explore visions of the technologies that will help solve problems in the home innovatively, especially with regard to what the home of the future (in 2030 and beyond) may look like. While keeping this objective in mind, the reality of conducting this study during a pandemic meant participants (families) would have to be recruited in a manner that is compatible with the rules of lockdown and self-isolation. Nevertheless, it was recognized, that the recruitment and workshop experience might be distorted by the context of the pandemic.

The study set out to recruit 15 families. A family should typically be comprised of a parent and one or two children between the ages of 6 to 12. This is in view of the assumption that children within the 6–12 years-old age group will have some experience with using digital technologies, both at home and in school, in Leicester, notwithstanding their socio-economic background. They are also still young enough to want to work collaboratively with their parents on specific tasks. Several methods of recruitment were explored, namely through (1) the local mothers' WhatsApp group, (2) an artist who is experienced in leading locals and children in creative artwork events, (3) a \short talk on the local BBC radio station, and (4) a website that provided a briefing about the workshops and an online registration form.

The most successful method was a combination of a snowball approach on the WhatsApp group, the website, or registration form. Information about the workshops, including the website and registration form, were shared with the mothers and they were encouraged to pass it on to friends and colleagues who might be interested. After three weeks, 14 families with at least one adult and one child aged 6–12 had been recruited; two of the families were involved in the pilot while the remaining 12 successfully completed the main workshops that lasted for four weeks, four months after lockdown was announced in March 2020. Although the original objective of physically recruiting participants from three relatively deprived areas of Leicester was somewhat out of control due to the snowball convenient sampling approach, the final cohort was approximately 70% from lower socio-economic groups, judging from the participants' postcodes.

4.2.3 Workshop procedure

In response to the pandemic and lockdown situation, the "new" set of workshops addressed emerging and future technologies for domestic settings, as well as asking the participants to imagine the home of the future. It used a creative approach, where the participants had the opportunity to crystallize their thoughts and ideas on the topic through art making, such as drawing, sketching, and collage. It involved a set of virtual workshops, where art making was employed alongside Design Thinking principles. Design Thinking encapsulates the process of first understanding human needs in a specific problem context, then framing the needs and problems in a way that appeals to people in that context, and finally developing testable and scalable solutions through imagination and hands-on prototyping (Brown, 2008; Foster, 2021).

The focus throughout the workshops gave special attention to children and their creative abilities. Participants interacted with facilitators remotely through online meeting applications, such as Zoom, supported with friendly emails. Specifically, following the recruitment of families, the workshops unfolded in five stages; it was a remote engagement primarily facilitated by two researchers from DMU and professional support from a local artist as follows:

1. Families were briefed about the tasks and the expectations. First, they were told the workshops would last for four weeks, with weekly touchpoints through emails; second, they are required to make artworks that depict a problem or a solution to a problem. Third, the workshops at the end of the fourth week will be finalized through interview sessions with the facilitators. The briefing was delivered to the parents via email. A typical week for the workshop started on Wednesdays and ended on Tuesdays. The motivation for this approach was to allow parents to work with the children over the weekend, in particular, for parents who are working from home during the lockdown, and essential workers who may have to be at work physically.
2. In the first week, families were asked to think about their home setting and identify a technology-related challenge they are currently facing, as well as the potential impact of the problem on their home and the way they live in 2030. Based on their reflections of the problems and the impacts, they should (within the family) create an artwork to illustrate the selected problem or challenge. On completion, they should exchange the artwork with another family by emailing the picture(s) with a brief description of the challenge and the artwork to the facilitator.
3. For the second week, facilitators randomly mapped the "problem" pictures and descriptions received to other families while taking note of the mapping. The "receiving" families were asked to create an artwork that depicted a solution to another family's problem thatthey just received. Upon completion, the picture of the solution artwork was returned to the originating family for further consideration. This marked the activities for the second week.
4. In the third week, the workshop continued. This time, the problem-originating families received pictures of artwork that demonstrated technology-driven solutions to the challenge they had identified and illustrated in drawing. The task of this week was to create a new or improved solution to the same problem. Like previous weeks, the pictures of the newly created or extended artwork and

a brief description should be emailed to the facilitators. We considered week two and three activities the "co-creation" and "Responsible Innovation" aspects of workshops and it was fascinating to see and reflect on how this *co-creatively Responsible Innovation* played out in a remote, asynchronous setting involving families from socio-economically deprived areas in Leicester.

5. The set of workshops ended with an online interview with the families, each family at a time, to discuss the problem or challenge. They were asked to talk about their artwork and how they found inspiration, the approach taken in creating a solution, and their views on the co-creation and Design Thinking process within and across the families.

Enquiries about the workshops, either through the website, email, telephone, or WhatsApp channels for more explanations about or prompts for activities associated with the workshops, were moderated by two of the DMU research team who were appointed as "facilitators" for the individual families for the whole duration of the workshop. Moreover, in order to help align and streamline the thoughts of each family to the goal of the workshop, the weekly activities, as highlighted above, were supported by a series of short, illustrative videos clips produced by the engaged local artist, who was a professional at leading creative artwork events. The final video was generic and encouraged families to continue making art during the lockdown despite the fact that the workshops had ended. Also, participants (parents and children) received a certificate of co-creation and a gift voucher at the end of the workshops. Figure C4.1 depicts the innovative process and the series of workshops.

4.3 THEMES ARISING FROM THE WORKSHOPS

This section describes the outcome of the workshops along with the artworks created by the families and their thematic groups. A wide range of technology-related problems and solutions were generated by the families. They attempted to address issues relating to mental health, security, safety, and waste management/recycling. Specifically, the problems identified are presented as captioned by the families and discussed.

4.3.1 Mess

A family illustrated the concept of a mess in a drawing. It was evident that the children involved were delighted to have the task of illustrating the drawing of discarded clothes, toys on the floor, and an unfinished board game. More fascinating were the comments in the drawing that demonstrated dialogue such as "I can't find anything!"; "I can't concentrate"; "Time to tidy up"; and "Cleaning is boring." The family who received the problem had a good time brainstorming ways to solve mess problems using technology. At least for 6- to 8-year-olds, their modification and final solution sound innovative. They imagined an app with a point-based reward system, in which points were awarded for cleaning tasks completed within a specified time frame,

Figure C4.1
The Virtual Workshop model

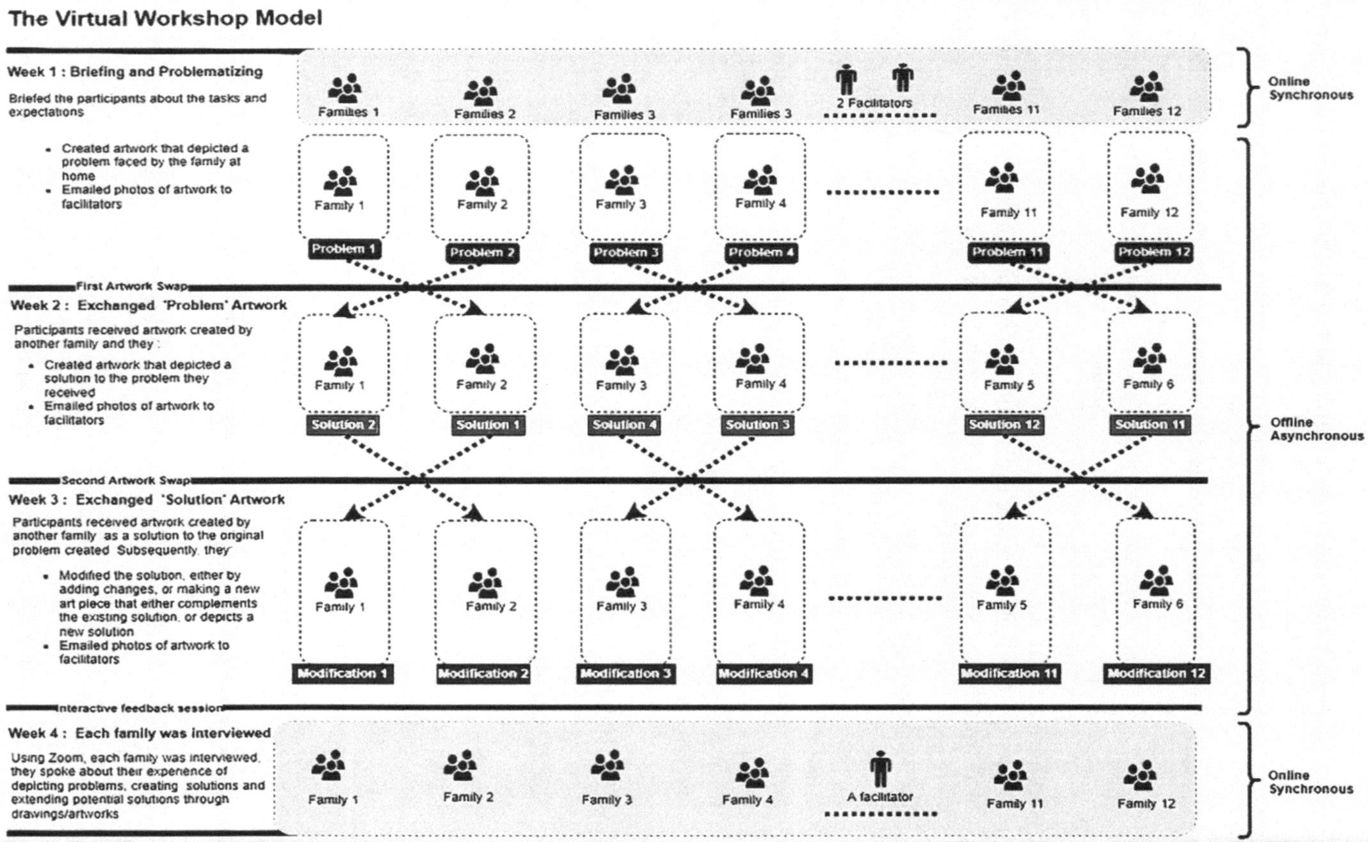

Figure C4.2
The mess problem and proposed solutions

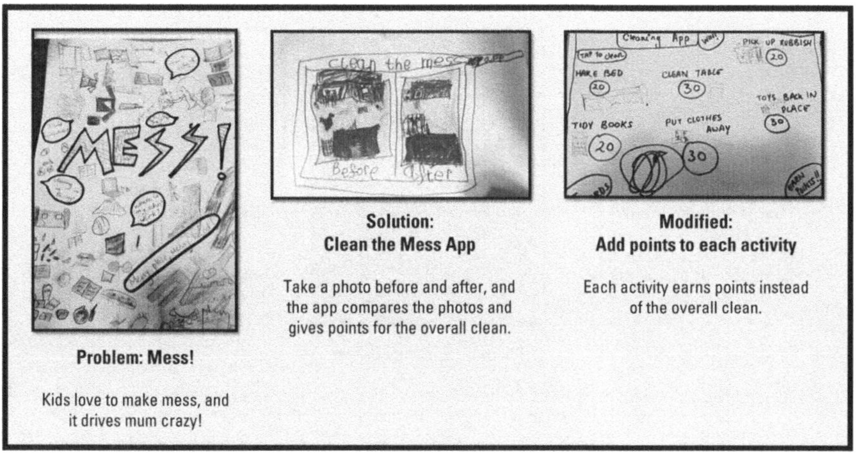

which could be weekly or daily. The number of points awarded would be proportional to the difficulty of the task. For example, "make bed" (20), "clean table" (30), "put clothes away" (30), "put toys back in place" (30), "tidy books" (20), and "pick up trash" (20). Figure C4.2 depicts the problem, as well as proposed and modified solutions.

4.3.2 Bored during lockdown

This challenge of boredom would have resonated with all the families involved in the workshops. Nonetheless, this drawing illustrates a child's solitude with his/her garden in what appears to be an imaginary tree-house – real; the bedroom and other parts of the house having become their new and limited world. The added text reads "This TV program is boring"; "I hate lockdown"; "Mummy, I am bored"; and Mummy's reply – "I am busy." The drawing includes (in large letters) "Help!." The responding family then took the idea further with the idea of a "Boredom Buster" machine with which children could interact. The machine asks (though it is not clear if there is an automated voice that speaks) "Are you bored?" and offers alternative options, namely "creative stuff," "sports," "educational," "science experiment," or "something else." Additional choices, with colored icons, were noted at the foot of the drawing as "play-do," "arts and crafts," "badminton," "baking," and "learn Chinese"! The solution/drawing extended the "Boredom Buster" machine idea into a robot – capable of more intuitive interactions (see Figure C4.3).

4.3.3 Lockdown 2020

Lockdown 2020 viewed the boredom problem from another perspective. It is interesting to note that the drawing of the problem includes a link to the school, the

Figure C4.3
The "boredom" problem and proposed solutions

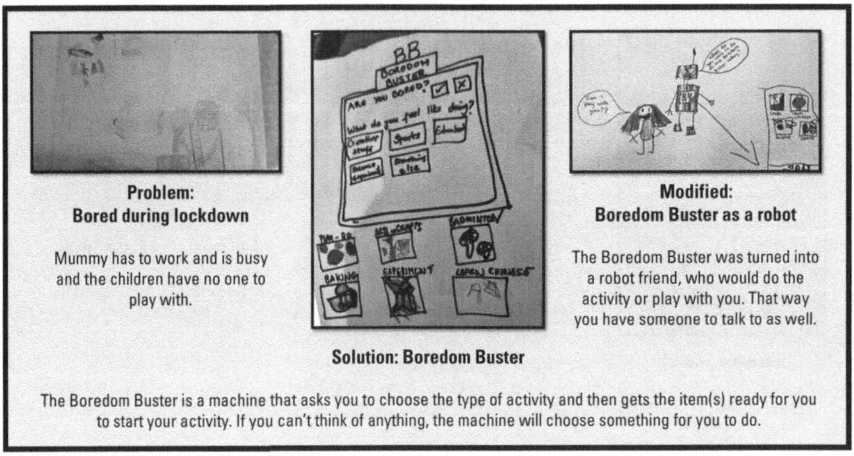

illustration appears as within a strongly fenced perimeter labeled "No School." There is no link to a park (distinctly green with flowers), the illustration of which (like the school) carries a seemingly firm perimeter. Black clouds hover over the house, albeit accompanied by a rainbow (this being the commonplace symbol in the UK during lockdown of support for the NHS staff who continued to care for many people with COVID-19). A hospital (labeled as such) is at the edge of the drawing. The responding family in their drawing focused on the ways in which the home environment could, through technologies, offer the means of escape through virtual or augmented reality. The drawing illustrated a "virtual park," and "virtual holidays" among other virtual possibilities. The original family, while noting the virtual options, took a very different perspective, and proposed a "COVID-free zone"– with a "flying house" seemingly linked to some kind of transporter machine or rocket – carrying the message "away we go" and seemingly moving away from the dark clouds of the "COVID-19 pandemic" and associated "Restrictions" (see Figure C4.4).

4.3.4 Communication under lockdown

The problem illustrated related to the challenge of communication under lockdown in family settings where their first language might not be English and/or their knowledge of English might be poor. A delightful "solution" was offered by the responding family that took the form of a "Butterfly Translator," "The butterfly sits on the edge of your computer and translates when a person is speaking a different language." It appears that the butterfly ("Le butterfly") would come in a box. The instruction (appearing on an iPad device) states, "On the box there should be a code. After you found it, type it in the box below," adding "then press enter" (an Enter icon is offered) "and setting for butterfly should appear. And you just select the language you want

Figure C4.4
The "lockdown 2020" problem and proposed solutions

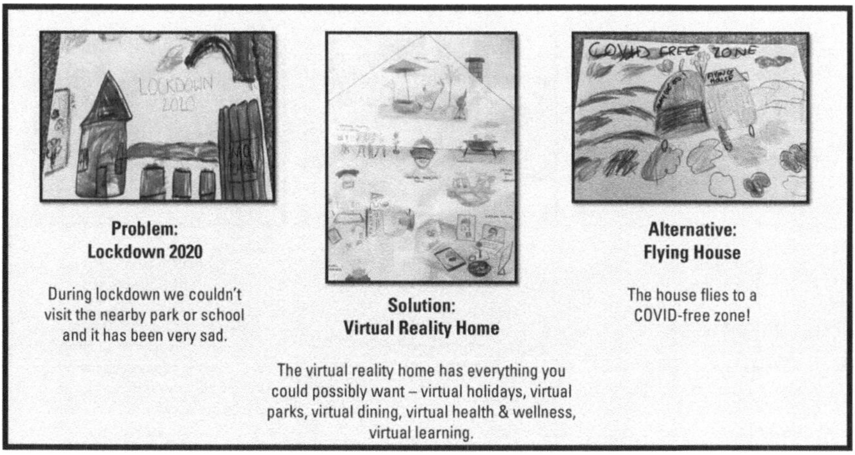

Figure C4.5
The "communication under lockdown" problem and proposed solutions

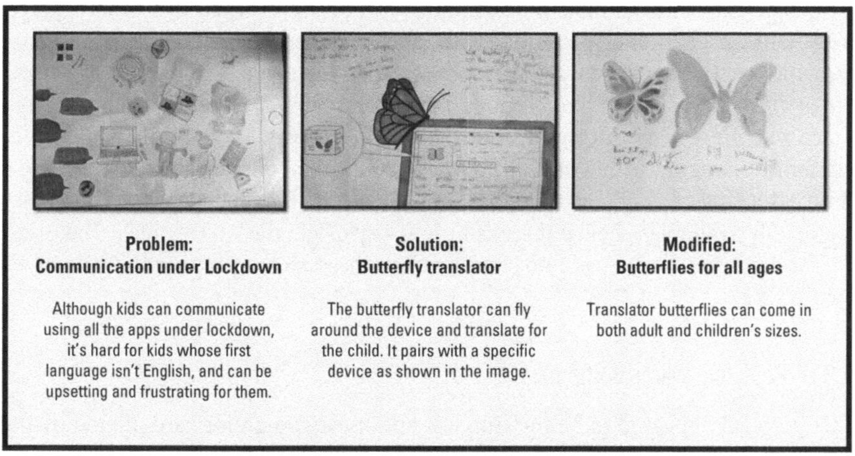

it to translate." In the final iteration, the solution was accepted and enjoyed by the original family with no significant added functionality (see Figure C4.5).

4.3.5 Home security

The problem identified by this family appeared to be related to a traumatic experience of having their house burgled or their car stolen. The choice of topic appears to have been made by a parent and, though it is not clear the extent to which this was a "team"

Figure C4.6
The "home security" problem and proposed solutions

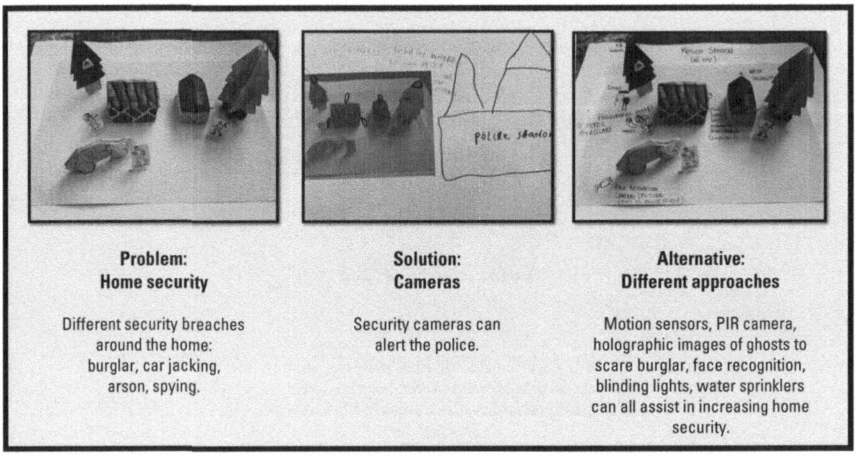

decision, the trauma of their home being violated will have been equally felt by the children. In addressing the problem, the family went further than two-dimensional "drawing." They built and illustrated simple cardboard constructs of a house, garage, trees, and car (a "model") together with labeled "stand-up" intruders (a "burglar" carrying away stolen goods; a "car jacker" stealing the car; and an "arsonist" setting fire to the garage). Part of the solution to their "problem" is, in fact, signaled through a face with binoculars in a tree overlooking the house, garage, and car. The responding family came up with a straightforward solution involving cameras – adding a simple drawing of a police station that stood alongside the model. Such technologies are readily available – hence there is little if any originality to this idea. The original family in response made no significant addition to the proposed solution (see Figure C4.6).

4.3.6 Reusable water-bottle filler

This problem appeared to be the simplest and most straightforward offered by the families. The recycling issue is, nevertheless, important, given the attention now being given world-wide to the problem of plastic pollution. The drawing, clearly done by a child, shows a plastic bottle and explains (in text) that "a watbotl was empty and somwon fild it up"; and (in respect of the necessary solution) "because it is not wasting trash." The recycling challenge indicated was taken up by the responding family who illustrated a "bottle recycler home appliance" that anyone might have in their home – thus potentially obviating the need to send such plastics to a recycling plant. A detailed drawing shows how bottles would be fed into a kind of hopper (with a "compactor" and "grinder") that reduces the matter to granules. A "melting pot" then feeds the matter into "3D printer heads" that produces "different shapes and styles

Figure C4.7
The "reusable water-bottle filler" problem and proposed solutions

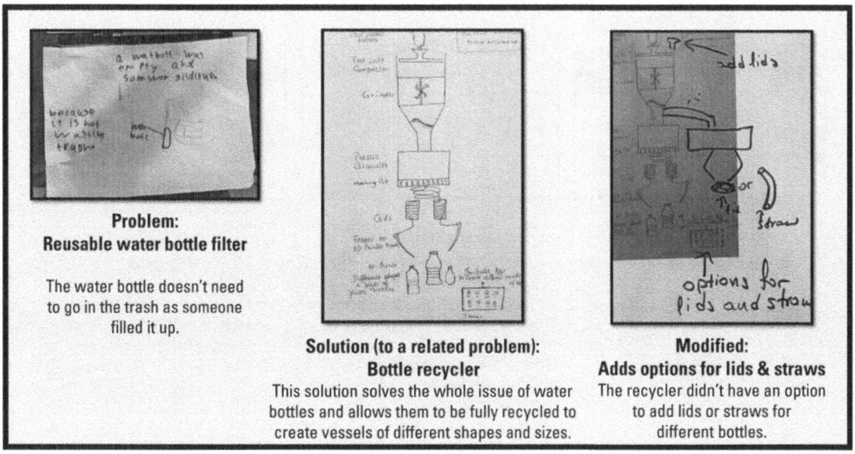

of plastic bottle" for re-use. In the final response, the original family then simply expanded the scope of the innovation with pointers to optional inclusion of other recyclable items, such as straws and lids (see Figure C4.7).

4.3.7 Wires around the home

The problem identified by this family related to a safety issue "at home" that, perhaps, would have come into greater focus because of the lockdown. The problem (as became clear in the interview) related not just to any electrical or trip hazard, but also to the extra nuisance that arises by virtue of the home having ever more electrical devices including mobile phones, etc. No "drawing" of the problem was produced, rather it was a collage with photos of selected items in different rooms. A "central" message was offered about "too many charge points around the home – safety hazards, gadgets lying around and looks messy." An adult influence was apparent in the choice of topic though the parent affirmed that it followed a family brainstorming session. In the interview, the father stated that he did the visuals, mum then chipping in with "we did it as a team" with the children going around and taking the photos that were used in the collage (see Figure C4.8).

The responding family saw a solution to the challenge as having a socket protector linking to a "rubber wall shelf so no clutter wires on floor" that tidies up otherwise trailing wires. The original family extended the solution and suggested an "eCharge" unit with instructions on how the device works. For instance, it was described as "a platform to charge your gadgets," "download gadget on app and platform for compatibility," "Bluetooth enabled," "aesthetically pleasing," "charge in one area – so not messy" and open to hazards.

Figure C4.8

The “wires around the house” problem and proposed solutions

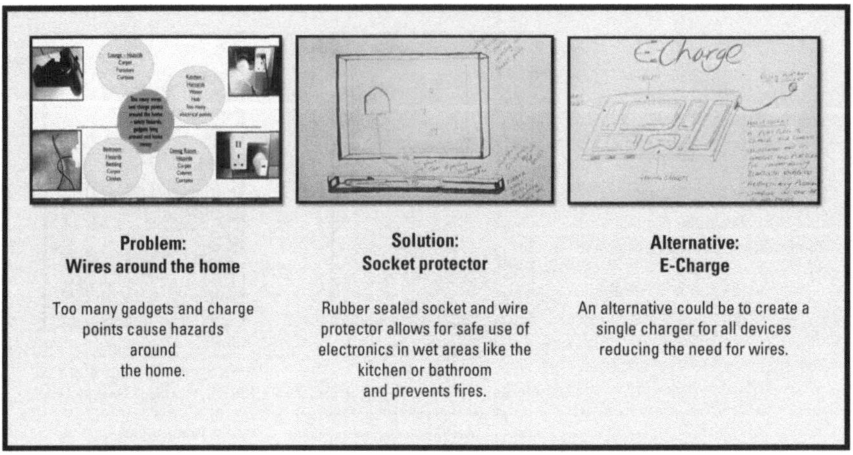

4.3.8 Lockdown affecting mental health

The family explored different problems, but the mother explained that she was sad about lockdown – and the topic of mental health was something her child could relate to. In a drawing that illustrated this challenge, the viewer is confronted with a large face that seems to offer an emotion somewhere between fear and surprise. This affirms that “people’s” mental health is being tested during lockdown more than usual. Feelings and emotions that affected people’s mental health were shown in the bubbles namely – “no control,” “no routine,” “trapped feeling,” “illness,” “money worries,” “missing friends,” “feeling lonely,”; “eating disorder,” “bullying,” “feeling scared,” “insomnia,” “disappointed” (see Figure C4.9). The responding family gave pointers to the benefits of exercise alongside a smart TV with icons carrying the labels “holiday,” “holographic,” “calendar,” “camera,” “message,” “call,” and “power” and the affirmation that this is “combining” features of current technology with bonus features. The original family then took the smart TV idea further and added an alternative or complementary device – “a watch to sense your mood. For instance, if you are sad, the watch can ask if you are OK or need help.” Buttons on the watch relate to “health,” “diet,” “blood sugar / medicine” (with a “remind” facility), “exercise,” “sleep,” “mood / emotion” with one extra “choose what you want the button to do.” Notable is that the “watch could change color depending on your mood.” And yet more activities are signaled that might combat low mood, namely “watch TV together,” “holographic features to send and save messages to loved ones,” “calendar / weather feature to help focus on activities in the day” and “holiday button allows you to virtually travel to a destination.”

Figure C4.9
The "lockdown and mental health" problem and proposed solutions

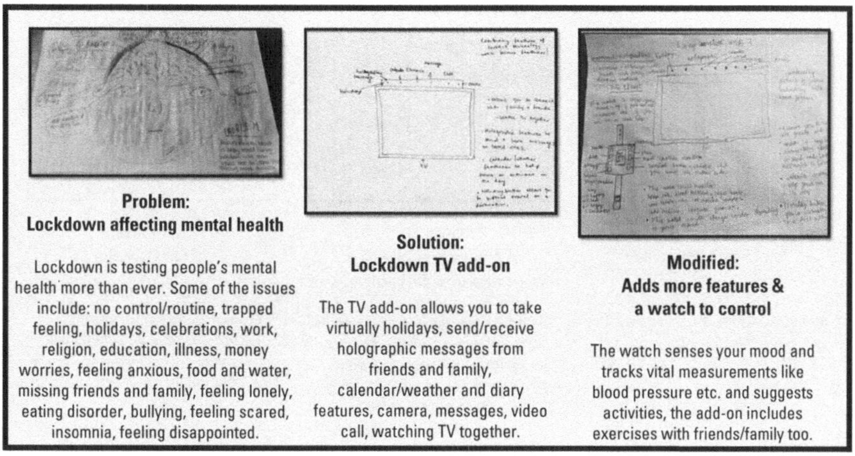

4.3.9 Ants in the bedroom

The problem identified by this family is neatly illustrated in the drawing done, in its entirety, by a daughter. The problem of scale (the large size of the family home and the tiny size of the ants) was cleverly overcome by including a magnifying glass. By this means, the ants were shown heading to or from the corner of a bedroom. The garden adjoins – this being the potential origin of the insects. The solution idea of the responding family is clear from their drawing of the "Ant Detector App" supported by a "Peppermint and White Vinegar" spray bottle – with this particular mixture deemed to be harmless (the family had done some research online about this) but having the necessary deterrent effect. The spray bottle carries the message "Ants no longer" and a yellow "Warning Ants" triangular sign is added for good effect. The original family, on receiving this "solution" then came up with "The Official Country Cloud Riding Ant," which is described as Artificial Intelligence enabled (Robotic) ant that could lead other ants in a convoy to a new destination of choice (see Figure C4.10).

4.3.10 Spiders in the house

For this family, the problem was spiders in the home. The drawing was created by the daughter, with extra inputs from a nephew. Illustrated in a line drawing of a house with three (two very large) spiders. The responding family came up with a humane approach to catching spiders based on a folding paper "spider mat." The mat would be placed on the floor and, on sensing a spider, would gently fold around it. The written details explained the approach – "Place sensory mat in place you usually see spider … leave overnight"; "sensors on the mat detect when spider walks on the mat. Once the

Figure C4.10
The "ants in the bedroom" problem and proposed solutions

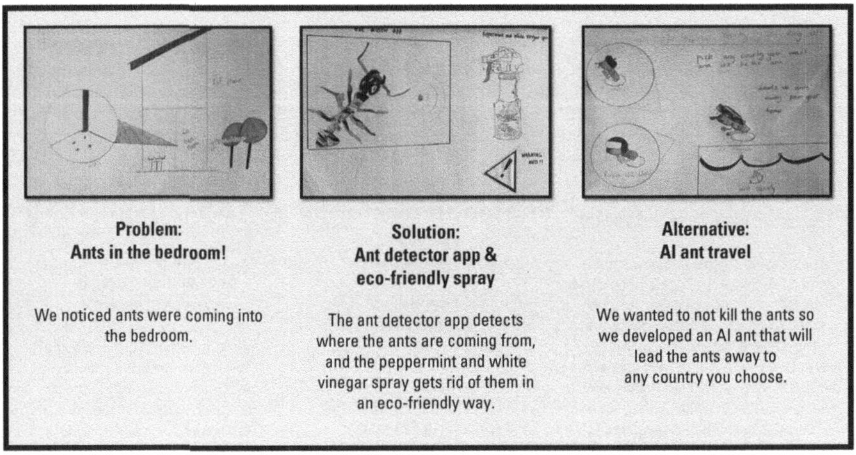

Figure C4.11
The "spiders in the house" problem and proposed solutions

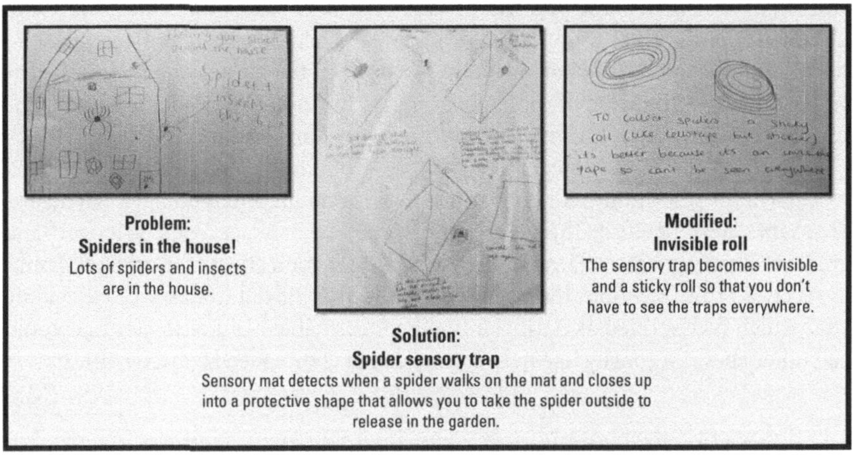

mat senses 8 legs it immediately closes into a pyramid shape enclosing the spider. Tiny pinprick holes allow the spider to breathe"; "In the morning take the pyramid outside, unstick one side and release into garden"; "unroll the mat and use again." When asked to explain the solution, the original family offered the idea to trap spiders in the form of "a sticky roll" (like Sellotape but stickier) – "it's better because it's an invisible tape and can't be seen everywhere" (see Figure C4.11).

4.3.11 Self-sufficiency in a COVID-19 world

The original family adopted self-sufficiency as their "problem." Their artwork illustrates different ways in which they might meet the challenge both in the home (e.g., washing and ironing clothes), outdoors (growing vegetables) and for the family members (through helmets to protect against the virus). Added to this (boldly colored) is the "idea" of "1 fruit tree for every house" and a label that suggests "community sharing of fruit and veg." The helmet (worn by three people in the drawing) is labeled "plastic, washable" and advises "micro virus filter shield allows air." A shower head is indicated to permit washing (clearly with the virus in mind) before entering the home; with a washing machine and shower room being immediately available. A machine is present into which "washed clothes" are placed. An "automatic sensor" is activated, and the clothes then emerge "ironed and folded"! In the garden there is a "self-sufficient greenhouse with veg all year round." Healthy green plants are evident, nurtured by "rainwater collecting (water-saving tanks)" (see Figure C4.12).

The responding family replied with an artwork that was part drawing, part collage. They retained the theme that embraced indoors and outdoors. Getting clothes to the washing and ironing machine is illustrated as helped by a chute that goes directly from the upstairs bedroom or bathroom, the label advising that "it helps the people who cannot carry heavy loads downstairs"; and outdoors (the collage of pictures) it affirms the idea of "gardens to have manageable greenhouse – compulsory in new homes built" and, for the wider community (in parks) to have trees with "edible fruits for all to share." The original family took positively to the idea of greenhouses for all (new) homes, stating the need for "government help to build green house in any house garden" with "free fruit and veg garden learning tools and resources online," for example, on growing techniques to be available – and an indication of the desirability of local council involvement.

Figure C4.12

The "self-sufficiency in a COVID-19 world" problem and proposed solutions

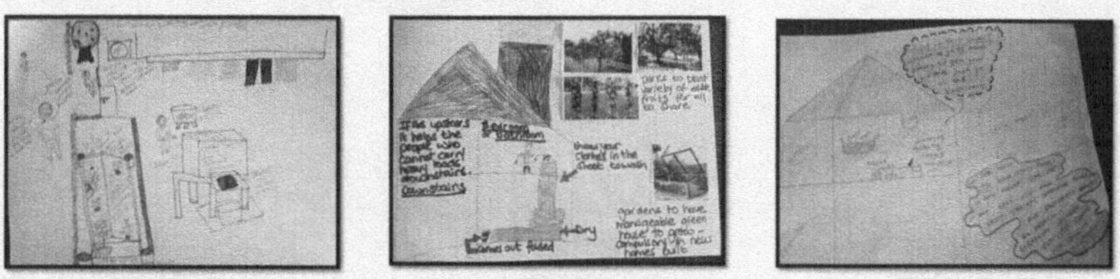

Problem:
Self sufficiency in a COVID-19 world

A few different ideas are captured here: safety, self-sufficiency, water saving, community sharing, making things easier at home, protection from the virus.

Solution:
Community Food & Laundry Machine

The laundry machine is brought into the house and folds laundry. Parks have community fruit trees and new build homes are required to have gardens with greenhouses for growing food.

Modified:
Community Food & Laundry Machine evolved

Laundry machine now works entirely in one room so no needing to go up/down stairs. Existing houses get grants to build greenhouses & assistance with learning how to grow food.

4.3.12 Mess and chaos

The original family (similar to one of the others in the workshops) took "mess" in the home as their problem. It can be surmised that the extent of mess had become a special concern in a context where children were necessarily (due to lockdown) spending more time in the home. The carefully colored artwork illustrates this well, with the family living room being festooned with all kinds of toys, games, etc. with the sense of "disruption" enhanced by the crooked picture hanging on the wall, and a cupboard door being left open. The living room door is also open – giving a glimpse of footwear being left there and (symptomatic of the times) a discarded face mask. In the room itself, as well as including the standard kind of furnishings, there are board games (scattered on the floor), Lego bricks (emptied onto the carpet), an opened book, a mobile phone, unplugged headphones, doll's clothes, a football, and more (see Figure C4.13).

The challenge for the responding family could not have been clearer. Their solution was one that would, indeed, have resolved much of the mess – but as a somewhat generic solution. The original family took the idea forward. The "space hoover" was given in detail and illustrated as many would imagine a spaceship. On the underside of the spaceship are four "grabbers" that, it can be presumed, would extend and pick up the items that constituted the "mess." The multiple toys illustrated (a board games, "Monopoly," "Snakes and Ladders," and "Scrabble," "toy cars and a train," a "racket," "dolls," and a "rabbit"), neatly colored, would be picked up (rather than sucked up) and assigned to categories labeled at the top of the artwork as. "Lego," "cars," "dolls," "sports" and "board games."

Figure C4.13

The "mess and chaos" problem and proposed solutions

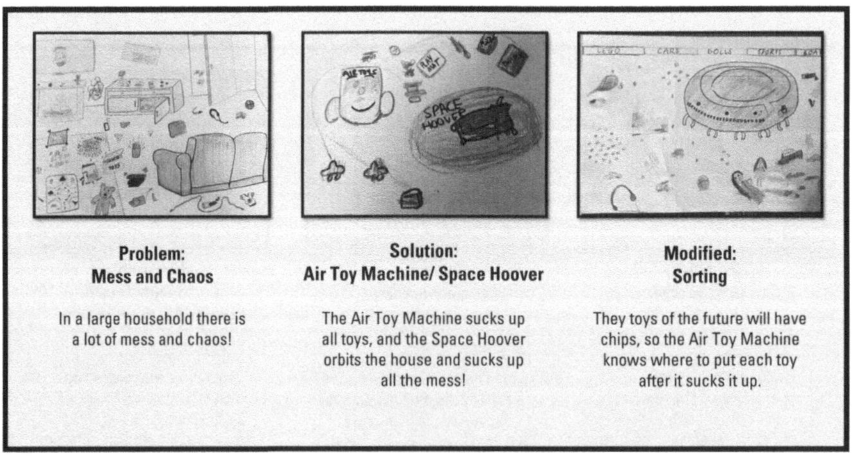

4.4 WHAT BUSINESSES CAN LEARN FROM THE WORKSHOP

The aim of the workshop was to engage families in the economically deprived areas of Leicester in creative activities that identified challenges in the homes and generate technology-driven ideas that could potentially solve the challenge. The ideas generated could potentially produce digital products in the form of tangible tools or services. In doing so, the principles of design thinking, co-creating, and responsible innovation were demonstrated. The online virtual workshop narratives and the workshop outputs sufficiently demonstrated the novelty of the innovation process in ideation and product development. However, beyond the fascinating artworks and innovative ideas put forward by the children and their parents, what are the implications for business practitioners?

1. The workshop methodology made innovation enjoyable. The families reported that they had enjoyed the activities – this perspective was expressed strongly by parents and children, because of the backdrop of the COVID-19 lockdown (and the fact that they were severely restricted in their social activities). Some quotes from the interviews bear testimony to this. Furthermore, the families appear to be "unaware" that they are performing tasks for "research" and "innovation" purposes. The methodology struck a chord with the families, and they eagerly anticipated getting together as a family to brainstorm and design solutions with little or no guidance from the DMU facilitators. This perception reflected in the quality of the generated ideas, as well as the strength of collaboration. The key lesson learned is the importance of developing innovation workshops that align with participants' social context, especially in ways that appeal to their social needs. If this is done, the experience (of participants and facilitators) promises to be memorable, on one hand, and, on the other, generates viable business products, tools, and services.
2. The asynchronous approach to the responsible innovation demonstrated by these workshops extends the possibilities of innovation-driven product development practices. First, it implies that ideation and co-creation could involve a diverse group of people from various demographics, and geographical locations at various times for up to four weeks. Second, it suggests that participants in ideation process could be inspired to take ownership of the ideation process while innovation experts simply provide cues when necessary. The families involved in the Leicester workshops took ownership of the activities; they organized themselves as a team and sustained the required energy levels from the start of the workshops until the end, as well as for weeks afterwards.
3. The way the drawings were co-created within and between the families sees the artworks as spanning from the simple and imprecise to the complex and more precise. Notable is the fact that responses to the interview questions attested to the fact that the families worked in "teams." Also, the sense of "positive progress" toward a "solution" came through in the interviews – where there was frequently

an element of anticipation that might be related to the question, such as "could this idea or proposed innovation really work?" Of course, the answer in several cases, was "no, it can't," simply because current technologies to allow them to happen were not known, or were perceived to be expensive and, therefore, it would be unrealistic to consider them as being accessible and usable by the families engaged in the project; but most, if not all, of today's high technologies started as "impossible" ideas. This implies that business practitioners should not be too quick to discard seemingly impracticable ideas or outcomes of innovation processes

4. One of the apparent drawbacks of the workshops was the difficulty in clearly seeing how each member of the families influenced the innovative process and the creative outcome (artwork). Although interviews indicated that some problem or solution ideas were heavily influenced by parents and, in some cases, children, granular analysis of individual influence and contributions was unavailable. As a result, the implicit factors that influenced innovation in this family setting were not well understood – this could have better informed how to manage and organize similar workshops in the future. Furthermore, the workshop's innovation process appears inconclusive. Yes, the participants enjoyed the process, but they were also curious about what would become of their artworks in the future. The lesson in this instance is to design innovative workshops in such a way that each team member's influence in a co-creative innovation activity is clearly "identifiable"; as well, the contributions of participant should be acknowledged and rewarded if possible.

Regardless of the lessons learned and limitations of the co-creation and Responsible Innovation workshops with families in Leicester, one key factor that was obvious was that the participants and families enjoyed and appreciated the workshops. According to the survey administered to families after the workshops, there was 100% satisfaction with the workshop itself, and the methods used were generally well received.

4.5 CONCLUSION AND RECOMMENDATIONS

So far, the narrative has been that of asynchronous virtual workshops involving families from the socially deprived areas of Leicester. The workshops demonstrated the application of Responsible Innovation and co-creation in product development. Fourteen families, including parents and children, created artwork that illustrate problems and solutions to challenges faced by low-income household in Leicester. The learning from the workshops suggests how co-creation and Design Thinking concepts, in light of Responsible Innovation, can improve participation and produce impressive outcomes, in particular, when the innovation process is designed and delivered within the social frame of participants. In this context, relevant digital technology-driven techniques can be leveraged to maximize participation.

However, it is important that researchers, as well as business practitioners responsible for managing product innovation, align innovation activities with participants' social contexts, particularly in ways that appeal to their social needs. Furthermore, the experience from the virtual workshops demonstrated the benefits of embedding co-creation and teamwork activities in innovation sessions or events, as it helps drive innovative outcomes incrementally, depending on the rounds of co-creations. For instance, we saw instances where three families worked as a team, they created a problem and solutions to the problem, yet the families did not know one another, they existed in their different worlds, but the problems and solutions brought them together. As a result, this resonates with solution-driven organizations, since, at the end of the day, the solution is the converging point for all stakeholders, and business practitioners must build strategies that bring people together to generate ideas on how their problems can be solved responsibly.

This chapter contributes to innovation practice by revealing a unique and novel approach to innovation in a family setting, as well as proposing and demonstrating a technique that not only responsibly involves children in innovation, but also encourages inclusion and diversity. Several aspects of the narratives presented in this chapter are adaptable and applicable to product innovation procedures across business domains.

NOTE

1. "RRI in a nutshell" developed by the EU project RRI Tool, at https://rri-tools.eu/about-rri

REFERENCES

Anderson, N., Potočnik, K., & Zhou, J. (2014). Innovation and creativity in organizations. *Journal of Management*, *40*(5), 1297–1333. https://doi.org/10.1177/0149206314527128

Brown, T (2008). Design Thinking. *Harvard Business Review*, Available at https://hbr.org/2008/06/design-thinking (accessed 22 April 2022)

Foster, M. K. (2021). Design Thinking: A creative approach to problem solving. *Management Teaching Review*, *6*(2), 123–140. DOI:10.1177/2379298119871468.

Groves, C. (2017). Review of RRI tools project, http://www.rri-tools.eu. *Journal of Responsible Innovation*, *4*(3), 371–374, DOI: 10.1080/23299460.2017.1359482.

Office of National Statistics (2019). English indices of deprivation 2019. Available at https://assets.publishing.service.gov.uk/government/uploads/system/uploads/attachment_data/file/835115/IoD2019_Statistical_Release.pdf (accessed April 22, 2022).

Robinson, D. K. R., Simone, A., & Mazzonetto, M (2021). RRI legacies: co-creation for responsible, equitable and fair innovation in Horizon Europe. *Journal of Responsible Innovation*, *8*(2), 209–216, DOI: 10.1080/23299460.2020.1842633.

Schuessler, E., Svejenova, S., & Cohendet, P. (2021). Organizing creativity for innovation: situated practices and process perspectives. In E. Schuessler, P. Cohendet, & S. Svejenova.(Eds.) *Organizing creativity in the innovation journey* (vol. 75, pp. 1–16), Emerald Publishing Limited. https://doi.org/10.1108/S0733-558X20210000075002

Shenkar, O. (2010). Defend your research: Imitation is more valuable than innovation. *Harvard Business Review*, *88*(4). https://doi.org/Article

C5

Inclusive workshops

How to facilitate workshops with blind and visually impaired participants

Anja Grüll, Klaus-Peter Wegge, and Bianca Laue

5.1 INTRODUCTION

Innovation is crucial for maintaining an organization's position in the market and ensuring businesses' survival. In the last few decades, business practitioners have increasingly recognized the importance of including users in the early product design stages in order to appropriately address their requirements. This user-centered design approach is positively related to a product's market uptake, customer adoption, and a business's competitiveness (Gray *et al.*, 2014; Magnusson *et al.*, 2018). When it comes to innovating new products or reinventing existing ones, workshops are a popular method for gathering ideas and insights. Based on the required outcomes, there are numerous workshop designs, such as user experience workshops, co-design workshops, product development workshops, and many more. All of these workshops have one thing in common: The dominant tools for enabling knowledge exchange and fostering creativity are visual. Brainstorming cards, story boarding, or using stimulating images are just a few examples of the wide range of available visual methods. The difficulty with these practices is that these tools are not accessible to all end-users, leading to the exclusion of these groups' needs and wishes in the innovation process. According to the World Health Organization, there are more than one billion people worldwide who are visually impaired or blind (World Health Organization, 2021). By excluding their perspectives, businesses not only ignore their responsibility for inclusive societal development but also fail to address this significant portion of potential customers. Consequently, there has been a growing demand to include people with visual impairment or blindness not only when it comes to assistive technologies but also in the design of everyday products (Bittenbinder *et al.*, 2021).

While there is a vast number of guides available on general moderation techniques and tools, there is only sparse information available on the ways in which to conduct workshops with blind or visually impaired people. Previous research has attempted

DOI: 10.4324/9781003319481-27

to address this issue by providing strategies on how to integrate the perspectives of blind or visually impaired people through more accessible design processes, but no overview of the techniques and tools uncovered in this research has been provided (Bennett, 2018; Bittenbinder *et al.*, 2021).

The aim of this chapter is to equip workshop facilitators with tools and guidelines that can be used to push for the implementation of RRI practices in inclusive innovation processes while simultaneously addressing the users' needs as defined in the European Accessibility Act (European Union, 2019). The described toolkit provides an easy-to-use guide for an inclusive workshop design in order to enable the co-creation processes of multiple stakeholders within the product innovation process. It provides key points and questions the workshop conductors should consider, as well as practical tools that can be used for the facilitation of such an accessible workshop.

There are numerous benefits to using this toolkit. First, it provides a comprehensive guide to the aspects that need to be considered when conducting an accessible workshop, which reduces the time allocated to planning and helps to avoid mistakes. Second, the individual tools are flexible and specific, allowing them to align with the specific requirements of the workshop. Moreover, the theories and instruments have a scientific underpinning and have been tested, providing a reliable foundation. This toolkit is intuitive and easy to use, adaptable to different contexts, and provides comprehensive access to materials and knowledge. Therefore, it is an intuitive solution that can be used by both experienced and novice users.

5.2 THE TOOLKIT

Before providing a detailed description of the toolkit, it is important to note the difference between people who are blind and those with visual impairment. Blind people cannot perceive any meaningful visual information at all, and they replace the visual information with other sensory information (e.g., touch, smell). On the other hand, people with visual impairment have reduced eyesight, with a visual acuity of less than 0.3 and a restricted field of vision. Visually impaired people still use sight as their primary source of information. People with visual impairments are 40 to 50 times more prevalent in the population than blind people. This distinction is crucial for the workshop design as the groups require different setups and frameworks.

The toolkit consists of three sections: (1) a discussion of the guidelines and considerations that need to be made in the planning phase of the workshop; (2) a description of the practical tools and instruments that can be used within the workshops; and (3) a presentation of the solutions for technical and organizational challenges when conducting online workshops (see Figure C5.1).

5.2.1 Group composition

The group make-up is a strategic decision that is very important for the output of the innovation process and should therefore be the first consideration when

Figure C5.1

The toolkit

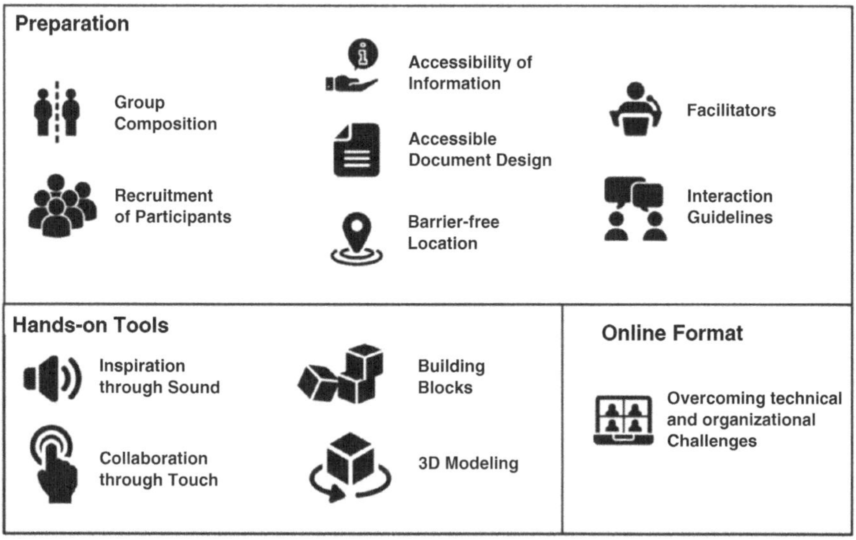

Source: made using Flaticon.com.

planning the workshop. To date, the dominant approach has been working with homogeneous groups of either sighted people or persons with visual impairment and blindness. This approach has led to the exclusion of relevant stakeholders in the design process and has fostered the creation of products that do not adequately address all users' needs. Therefore, before starting the design process, it is important to reflect on who the end-users of the product are going to be. Careful consideration in the pre-design stage can help to avoid difficulties later in the product development process.

In general, mixed groups are crucial in the process of designing devices that should be accessible for everyone. These products include any kind of public infrastructure, such as ATMs, ticket machines, or packing stations. Another example of a product category that falls into the mixed group design is home appliances. Producers tend to ignore the fact that people live in mixed households, which necessitates these devices being usable by anyone, including those with and without eyesight. These products include kitchen devices such as ovens, microwaves, and stoves. In this case, bringing diverse people together helps to address people's different interests and needs in the design, thereby promoting accessibility through the design-for-all approach.

Conducting workshops with homogeneous groups is advisable for products that are designed for the users' specific needs. Focus groups can be used in these product innovation processes so as to identify the relevant features in order to ensure accessibility for all. While visually impaired people might require monitors with large text, these would be useless for people with no vision as they prefer different tactile or audio features. This is especially the case for assistive technologies.

5.2.2 Recruiting participants

One challenge in conducting a workshop with blind or visually impaired people is recruiting suitable participants. As such, when recruiting participants, it is advisable to draw on already existing structures of established institutions, such as associations for blind and visually impaired people, as these organizations can easily distribute information and invitations to their members through their network and can directly target people who are suitable candidates for the workshop, due to their specific expertise. In order to increase motivation among potential candidates, an incentive for participation should be provided. In addition, people wish to know how the workshop's results will be incorporated into further product development beforehand. Therefore, it is important to include information regarding the workshop's context and intentions.

5.2.3 Accessibility of information

For the purpose of time efficiency in the workshop, it is highly recommended to make important information available beforehand in order to provide the participants with the opportunity to prepare for what is awaiting them. This information can include a description of the general formalities, organizational aspects, the workshop's procedure, the location, and supporting materials.

During the workshop, the facilitators should ensure that everything that is presented visually is also explained verbally so as to ensure that the content is also comprehensible for people without vision. Moreover, all written information should be read aloud to all participants. Visual information such as images or videos must also be accessible through other mediums, including tactile prints or audio descriptions. For instance, when showing a video in which relevant information is not included in the audio track, the facilitators should pause the video and explain what was shown. According to the Web Content Accessibility Guidelines 2.1 (2018), special care ought to be taken regarding the image colors or font sizes so that people with visual impairment can also understand the shared information. This is especially important when using PowerPoint slides. Presentation content should also be provided in Braille for blind people.

5.2.4 Accessible document design

There are various guides available on the internet that contain information on the right format, fonts, and colors to use in documents. The focus in this section lies on the techniques used to create documents that are accessible to visually impaired, blind, and sighted people simultaneously. There are several means for creating these documents, including both plain text and Braille texts, which can be created using specialized printers. These mechanical printers are connected to a computer, and a plain text file is printed in a large font, after which the printer punches dots onto the paper. It is important that the process follows this order as, otherwise, the printer would flatten the dots. Since these kinds of prints are costly, an alternative is outsourcing the task to professional printing services. Another option is do-it-yourself Braille printing. There are fonts for computers that represent Braille in graphics. A grid of points is automatically provided on the screen, which can then be printed on special paper, such as swell paper, and heated in the oven, causing black dots to rise. This technique is also useful for creating tangible graphics.

It is often assumed that all blind people can read Braille when, in fact, only about 25% are able to read it. The main reason is that, with increasing age, the sense of touch decreases and learning becomes significantly more difficult. These tactile letters and numbers are called pyramid fonts, which can be used to mark certain positions, and cutting off the top right corner (of a business card, for example) allows the object to be correctly oriented. Siemens developed an innovative questionnaire combining large print and Braille as well as normal tactile letters that were used to order the questions. In order to also make the information accessible to blind people who could not read Braille, the questionnaire was also read aloud. Instead of ticking a box, the people could select their answers by pressing the element flat or marking it with a pen. Thus, everyone answered the questions without any help and a certain anonymity was ensured. This questionnaire was not limited to "yes" or "no" questions as a visual and tactile scale from 0–9 was provided. Even people without knowledge of Braille were able to count the assessment bars and mark their choice using standard pens or by scratching out points, and only the open-ended questions required assistance.

5.2.5 Barrier-free location

When choosing the location for a workshop, special care should be taken to ensure that it is barrier-free. The infrastructure should allow for persons with blindness or visual impairment to orient themselves independently without additional support. This includes several aspects, such as marking the rooms in a recognizable manner and providing tactile floor guide systems. It is also advisable to send out information on the workshop's location and the building plan in advance. Moreover, it is important that the rooms are spacious enough for people to bring their guide dogs, and the rooms should be equipped with sufficient power connections for assistive technologies. Additionally, there should be no disturbing sounds since a quiet environment helps to increase speech intelligibility (e.g., silent projector, quiet air conditioning). Another important aspect is the room's lighting as people with visual impairment still have vision to some extent, which can be enhanced through appropriate illumination. In addition, tripping hazards such as cables, luggage, cupboards, or open windows need to be avoided as people could injure themselves. If a buffet or drinks are offered, there should be at least one person providing support if needed.

5.2.6 Facilitators

A popular method for generating ideas in workshops is discussions and creative brainstorming in small groups. After the brainstorming phase, the groups often present their outcomes to the plenary for discussion. However, there is a risk of forgetting ideas if they are not noted during the brainstorming phase. To prevent this from happening when working with visually impaired or blind people, each group should be provided with an assistant during the brainstorming phase.

Previous research has shown that lack of knowledge on how to interact with the participants can significantly hinder the workshop's process (Bittenbinder *et al.*, 2021). Therefore, the assistants need to be properly briefed on interaction with the participants and the kind of support they should provide beforehand (see interaction guidelines below). For instance, the wording should come mostly from the participants themselves and not be implied by the assistants. The assistant's job is to note everything down, listen, and ask questions like, "What should I write down?" and "How should I formulate this?"

When the ideas are presented to the plenary, there are three main roles the assistant can take to be of support:

1. *The prompter*: Assistants taking the role of the prompter only support the presentation by stating which points have not yet been mentioned. They provide keywords and say nothing about the content itself. This is the best method because the participants work mostly independently.
2. *The interviewer*: If the first method is not feasible, then the assistant should increase the amount of assistance provided by reading the contents of the cards and asking the group how they came up with it or whether the group wants to say something else.
3. *The presenter*: If the above options do not work well enough, the assistant could share the results for the group.

The approach that is the most suitable significantly depends on the group itself. It is recommended to try the prompter approach first and then steadily increase the amount of support if necessary. It is very important that the assistant influences the process and results as little as possible.

5.2.7 Interaction guidelines

There are some important considerations when meeting people with visual impairment or blindness. These tips are helpful for both workshops and everyday life.

- Blind people recognize others by their voices, which is why it is more than just polite to present yourself with your name before you speak. For example, at web meetings, you can start your speech by providing your name.
- Address the blind person directly and not only their companion. When a blind person goes to a public place like a restaurant, the accompanying person is often

asked what the blind person wants. This is uncomfortable and discriminatory for a blind person.

- Blind people sometimes need help. If you want to help, approach the person and verbally offer help first. Do not simply touch the person.
- Use normal language. Terms like "See you again" are not a problem. Avoid disability-specific or discriminatory language, such as "Hear you."
- Never touch or distract a guide dog from their job while they are on duty.
- When giving a presentation, verbalize all of the important information.
- Describe the position of important facilities in unfamiliar environments, such as table arrangements, the lectern, emergency exits, or the routes to the toilets. Describe the positions precisely and, if possible, place yourself at the given position during the description to ensure acoustical orientation.
- Do not make assumptions about what the blind person is not capable of doing. Nowadays many blind people use smartphones or "watch" television.

5.2.8 Inspiration through sound

When it comes to sparking creativity among participants in a workshop, facilitators often use visual cues, such as abstract images or ink paintings. There are several alternatives to these visual stimuli that can be used to stimulate the participants' imagination. One possible approach is providing the participants with acoustic impulses. Noises and tones trigger associations in people, especially if they cannot be clearly recognized. Acoustic impulses can be stimulating for visually impaired, blind, and sighted people. One possibility is using what are called "audicons." These are short acoustic elements recorded in everyday life that are often not clearly identifiable, so the experience of determining what it is or where it comes from becomes even more exciting. The participants' imaginations are particularly challenged if the tones are not immediately recognized. Numerous websites offer such noises. Alternatively, you can record them yourself by throwing crumpled paper into a trashcan, for example. It is highly important that the sound has a good quality. Therefore, if it is possible, stereo or surround recordings should be made. The spatial acoustic arrangement can also trigger emotions, especially in people who rely exclusively on hearing. Furthermore, when choosing the sounds, it is important to rely not on films, music, or well-known acoustic elements from companies as these triggers already have strong and clear associations.

5.2.9 Collaboration through touch

In workshops, participants often engage in collaborative exercises to enhance their "out-of-the-box" thinking. There are several tools to enable this knowledge exchange and to foster creativity. However, they include mostly visual elements, such as visualizing or mind mapping. These prominent techniques do not have to be abandoned altogether; they just need to undergo some re-thinking and possibly some re-designing. For instance, cards are a popular tool in workshops in the context of brainstorming or mind mapping, but this brainstorming process does not necessarily need to undergo radical change. For example, by using strong and contrasting colors such as bright yellow, red, and dark blue, visually impaired people will find it easier to separate the cards. For blind people, the corners could contain embossed characters, and an edge could be cut on cards that have text on them in order to signal which side is on top.

When talking about ideas, drawings sometimes show more than a thousand cards could. This problem can be overcome by using a tactile foil through which quick sketches can be easily created. A tactile foil is a plastic film that is placed on a rubber mat. If one draws on it with a ballpoint pen and applies strong pressure on the fleece, the lines are curled and therefore easy to feel. Thus, participants can easily pass sketches back and forth.

5.2.10 Building blocks

The previously described methods for gathering ideas could serve as a basis for low-fidelity prototyping. The following tools could either be based on the gathered ideas or used independently. Using building blocks is one method of building models or prototypes of products, such as technical devices. One advantage of this approach compared to hand drawings is that these models can be easily assembled and reassembled. One of the benefits of using building blocks is the playful and interactive aspect of this activity, which results in a positive and stimulating experience for the participants.

There are some important considerations when using building blocks in an innovation workshop setting:

- The stones should be pre-sorted according to their respective importance in preparation for the workshop. In order to reduce the time the participants spend searching for the stones they want, a handout that details the sorting is helpful. This handout can be distributed among the participants before the workshop takes place.
- The building blocks should allow for turning and folding or have certain shapes that are easily recognizable. Thus, LEGO® building blocks with imprints such as faces or figures are unsuitable as it must be possible to derive the blocks' function from their forms.
- At the beginning of the process, the meaning of each stone needs to be defined for all participants. As an example, within the LIVING INNOVATION project, blind and visually impaired participants designed a radio device model. Within the workshop, the facilitators defined the flat stones without knobs at the top as buttons, stones that looked like a roof as switches, and round stones as dials.

- The construction of the models must take place on a large grid plate in order to allow for the free design of dimensions.
- It is important to note that such a co-creation activity can be time-consuming. When planning the workshop, at least one to two hours should be allocated to the building block activity as the participants have to first understand the concept, learn the meanings of the stones, and get used to the tools.

5.2.11 3D modeling

Visually impaired and blind people often have difficulties in comprehending spatial arrangements or defining them themselves. Tactile three-dimensional (3D) models can help these groups understand the world better by providing orientation through touch. For instance, if buildings need to be discussed in terms of how to redesign a floor or plan it, a 3D model is ideally suited for this activity.

As with building blocks, 3D models can also be based on the participants' initial sketches. However, the creation of such a model takes a lot of time, and the model itself cannot be changed, unlike the building blocks technique. This eliminates the possibility of flexible conversion of printed 3D models during the workshop as a way of discussing variants.

When creating 3D models, the required accuracy plays an essential role. Model houses are too filigree-structured and too complicated. Compared to building blocks, 3D-printed models have the advantage of representing objects more precisely in three dimensions.

Apart from buildings, 3D models are have numerous applications. For instance, maps can be printed with interesting features or even different figures being shown, and Braille descriptions can also be included. 3D models can also assist in the interoperability with assistive technology.

5.2.12 Online format

Web participation is a challenge particularly for participants with disabilities. The LIVING INNOVATION project's switch to a web-based workshop had a positive impact on participants' willingness to take part in the complete series of workshops, due to time saved, reduced traveling costs, and barrier-free traveling. The considerations below are based on the experiences of the LIVING INNOVATION project's online workshops.

How to overcome technical challenges:

- Identify an accessible meeting tool. Configure and test the accessibility of the tool before the workshop. Provide support to the participants when they are installing and configuring the tool.
- Provide special guidance for screen reader or screen magnifier users.

- Test the microphone, headset, and camera. Provide keyboard shortcuts for main functions (e.g., mute).
- Improve the sound quality.
- Ensure alternative telephone access as a fallback strategy.
- Provide technical assistance before and during the web meetings.
- Simplify the login procedure as much as possible by, for example, providing codes or passwords in the invitation link.
- Avoid unnecessary or misleading information in the invitation, such as costly American dial-in numbers.

How to overcome organizational challenges:

- Split the workshop into shorter meetings with fewer participants.
- Focus on one clearly defined topic at each web meeting.
- Reserve more time and consider the breaks needed.
- Remember that using tactile materials or ad-hoc tactile drawings is not possible;
- Verbalize everything on the screen and repeat the information several times if necessary.
- Split into breakout sessions sparingly as this always costs time and participants are often lost.

5.3 TESTING THE TOOLKIT

In order to test the toolkit we organized a workshop in Saulgrub, Germany. This workshop was geared toward identifying and solving the everyday problems of people with blindness or visual impairment. It was facilitated by employees from the Siemens Accessibility Center, the Institute for Managing Sustainability, and Dialogik as part of the LIVING INNOVATION project in 2019. There were three overarching topics comprising the framework of the workshop:

- How will we live in 2030?
- How do blind or persons with low vision want to live in 2030?
- How can new technologies enhance their lives?

The workshop's overall intention was to co-create solutions that are non-intrusive, non-stigmatizing, affordable, and, in the best-case scenario, disruptive. While the first phases aimed to identify general problems through open discussions and assessments of the participants' experiences, innovation on a product level took place in the last phase of the workshop.

According to the inquiry at the end of the workshop, the participants found the toolkit's methods highly stimulating, and the overall feedback was predominantly positive. The participants were asked to evaluate the facilitation techniques and moderation methods as well as provide their general assessment of this workshop framework in a questionnaire. Participants emphasized the importance of addressing the societal aspect in future technologies, and they were convinced that the toolkit fostered the co-creation process and resulted in the collaborative identification of fruitful solutions. The building blocks experience particularly triggered positive associations as one participant said, "I used to play with LEGO® when I was a kid, and I didn't expect it in this context. That was a true surprise." They feel that, especially when it comes to people with blindness or visual impairment, rapid technological development has resulted in their needs and wishes being neglected. As one person stated,

> You should also look at what people actually need and act accordingly. Always keep in mind that what is good for people with disabilities will probably also be good for everyone else. For instance, cooks regard a stove with touch controls as highly impractical because it constantly turns off when the water boils over. For me as a blind person, it means this stove is hot, sticky, and... no longer work[s].

The participants called for manufacturers and designers to create accessible products from the start and produce devices or equipment that can be used by anybody.

Through only this one workshop, a multitude of ideas and insights were collected regarding users' needs and wishes for future products and specific attributes that should be included in product design. In general, products' user interfaces should provide at least two different modes of operation: one for beginners and a more complex one that contains more features and settings for experts. Manuals should be designed with accessibility in mind and include information on special accessibility features. This need also extends to product descriptions in online stores. One approach to increasing the accessibility for visually impaired or blind people is converting an optical environment into an acoustic experience in which the surface texture is also reproduced.

Apart from general needs, the participants also identified concrete attributes that should be included in specific products. For example, there is a need for sustainable and reliable accessibility features in smart TV sets, including incorporating partial support for speech input and output for some functions. The participants also required a platform that has independent speech modules for consumer products and household appliances. There were also new product development ideas, such as a digital camera with voice guidance and voice assistance. The participants also expressed some discontent about current practices. People who have no affinity for the internet are often excluded from new technological developments. Numerous mobile applications are not accessible to people with blindness or visual impairment. These concerns should be taken into consideration for future innovations and product development.

5.4 INNOVATIONS DEVELOPED USING THE TOOLKIT

The toolkit has already enabled the development of various inclusive and accessible products, and some of them are already available on the market. These include:

- *PadaSprinter-App:* This application enables passengers with restricted mobility to use local public transport more independently. The application is barrier-free and particularly helpful for blind and visually impaired people as they can use the operating aids in any smartphone as it is voice output-supported. The application supports its users in various ways: incoming buses are recognized via Bluetooth and displayed or announced along with the route number and destination; information on upcoming stops, transfers, or exits is provided; and, through acoustic signals, blind passengers can locate the entrance door. The app is currently available for taxis, elevators, traffic lights, and other public transport utilities.
- *Cookit:* Food processors with cooking functions are a modern digital trend that are catered toward assisting those who are not experienced in cooking. While modern hobs are no longer accessible to blind or visually impaired persons due to touch controls, an all-in-one cooking machine is a promising alternative if it can be operated by these user groups. But these machines also require operation via a touch display. This problem can be solved by having the cooking machine controlled by a mobile application via the internet. A small group of technically enthusiastic blind persons tried this approach by using a Bosch Cookit connected to the Home Connect service while using the Home Connect application on their personal iPhones with assistive functions turned on. The most interesting function of "guided cooking" is that it is accessible, while automatic or basic cooking functions could not be controlled by blind users yet. The result will be not only a cooking machine accessible to blind users, but the modifications will also allow remote control of all the many household appliances that are compatible with the Home Connect services.
- *E-Scooter*: E-scooters are extremely dangerous for persons who cannot see or hear them. This problem may be partially solved by an idea that was intensively discussed at an online workshop with blind users who are trained to use a white cane for their mobility: When a blind person comes into the Bluetooth range of an e-scooter, it automatically emits a warning signal, which helps the blind person locate the vehicle, whether it is parked or in operation. The blind user installs an application on their personal smartphone for this function. However, this idea has not been thoroughly evaluated yet. Moreover, it is currently not clear if this idea is feasible because e-scooter companies need to agree on a standard for the Bluetooth communication in order to prohibit misuse by other persons, and what happens when a bunch of e-scooters are nearby is not predictable.
- *Digital twins for navigation support*: The digitalization of buildings is a modern technique supporting, for example, the. maintenance and construction of

buildings. The digital twin can be used to navigate through a complex building by taking pictures with a smartphone. Experts and blind employees from Siemens have long discussed how this established solution for indoor navigation can be used for blind persons. It took a long time to identify the detailed user requirements, set up a complex test site, and conduct field tests. Through this work, it was determined that the required accuracy for blind persons can be achieved by the image processing software in real time. The special software for the indoor navigation, based on digital twins, moved to a small Dutch company, which has named it EZwalkZ and will be rolling it out shortly. The first locations with this publicly accessible feature will include museums and stations in the Netherlands.

- *Low-cost amateur radio*: Within a product innovation workshop, 15 visually impaired and blind participants designed an amateur radio device's user interface, which fully supports the needs of blind people. All functions of the device are easily operable without vision. The functions and features of brand-new digital radio devices are mainly defined by the software, which is a replacement of the manufacturer's original software with another piece of software that supports the requirements of blind operators by, for example, providing text to speech output. This is an intelligent method for adapting existing software into low-cost devices. However, doing so requires profound technical knowledge. Therefore, the findings of the workshop were carried over to an open-source community already experimenting with software patches. Meanwhile, the worldwide open-source activity separated into different branches that supported various hardware. Thus, this workshop was at least a trigger for these unexpected activities, which has led to more than five different low-cost amateur radio sets being produced for blind operators.

5.5 CONCLUSION AND RECOMMENDATIONS

There is a growing requirement from the perspectives of both the user and policies to re-think the ways in which innovation processes and product designs are designed. Through widening the approach by including more perspectives, businesses can attain numerous benefits, such as gaining additional customers, understanding their potential users' needs more clearly, and establishing their position in new markets. The described toolkit provides an easy-to-use guide for the facilitation of co-creation with people with visual impairment or blindness within the product innovation process. It provides important considerations for planning and conducting such a workshop as well as practical tools.

The design-for-all approach is not only a trend but also a systemic transition in how innovations and their role in society are perceived. As such, this chapter represents the starting point for potentially inclusive frameworks by focusing on blind and visually impaired people. In order to achieve an inclusive society, future work should focus on how to include the needs and wishes of people with different disabilities.

REFERENCES

Bennett, C. L. (2018). A toolkit for facilitating accessible design with blind people. *ACM SIGACCESS Accessibility and Computing*, (*120*), 16–19.

Bittenbinder, S., Pinatti de Carvalho, A. F., Krapp, E., Müller, C., & Wulf, V. (2021). Planning for inclusive design workshops: Fostering collaboration between people with and without visual impairment. In *Proceedings of 19th European Conference on Computer-Supported Cooperative Work*. European Society for Socially Embedded Technologies (EUSSET).

European Union (2019). Directive 2019/882. On the accessibility requirements for products and services. European Parliament, Council of the European Union. Retrieved May 12, 2022, from https://eur-lex.europa.eu/legal-content/EN/TXT/?uri=CELEX%3A32019L0882

Gray, M., Mangyoku, M., Serra, A., Sánchez, L., & Aragall, F. (2014). Integrating design for all in living labs. *Technology Innovation Management Review*, *4*(5).

Magnusson, C., Hedvall, P. O., & Caltenco, H. (2018). Co-designing together with persons with visual impairments. In E. Pissaloux & R. Velazquez (Eds.), *Mobility of visually impaired people* (pp. 411–434). Springer.

Web Content Accessibility Guidelines (WCAG) 2.1. (2018). Retrieved July 16, 2022, from https://www.w3.org/TR/WCAG21/

World Health Organization. (2021). Vision impairment and blindness. Retrieved May 29, 2022, from https://www.who.int/news-room/fact-sheets/detail/blindness-and-visual-impairment

A strategic approach to Responsible Innovation in the business sector

Conclusion and outlook

André Martinuzzi and Svetlana Ivanova

1 WHERE WE STARTED OUR JOURNEY

The debate about the responsibility of companies beyond making profits can be traced back to the 1920s (Berle, 1931; Dodd, 1932; Donham, 1927). It gained momentum after World War II (Abrams, 1951; Bowen, 1953) and has remained a contested field ever since. While several influential scholars have highlighted that the responsibility of the business sector should be limited to profits, growth, or market shares only (Friedman, 1962; 1970), there is an emerging debate about a broader view of companies' responsibility that takes into account ethical, societal, environmental, and sustainable development issues (e.g., Carroll, 1979, 1999; Dahlsrud, 2008; Matten & Crane, 2005; Porter & Kramer, 2006, 2011; Rodriguez-Gomez *et al.*, 2020). Moreover, several thousand empirical studies have shown positive correlations between corporate social, environmental, and financial performance (Friede *et al.*, 2015; Hirsch *et al.*, 2022). Today, many companies have successfully integrated responsibility and sustainability into their operation management, controlling, reporting, marketing, and communication. However, the integration of these aspects into corporate research, innovation, and development is still in its initial stages (Jarmai *et al.*, 2020).

The discourse concerning the societal responsibility of research and innovation is notably diverse and relatively recent. While scholars have discussed various aspects of the responsibility of research and innovation since the 1970s (Owen & Pansera, 2019), it was only around a decade ago that the concept of Responsible Research and Innovation (RRI) was put forward by EU programs for research and innovation (von Schomberg, 2012). Initially, RRI primarily targeted public research-funding organizations, such as national science funds, and research-performing organizations, like universities and other higher education institutions (Owen *et al.*, 2021). Although the business sector, with its specific logics of profits and competition, became of interest to scholars (Martinuzzi *et al.*, 2018), the concepts, methods, and tools developed in the public sector have rarely been taken up on a large scale by companies (Schönherr *et al.*, 2020).

DOI: 10.4324/9781003319481-28

This book therefore intends to spread awareness of the strategies and tools for Responsible Innovation among the business sector and to demonstrate how responsibility and sustainability can be considered in the highly competitive area of innovation. Instead of solely addressing societal concerns and ethical challenges posed by emerging technologies, the book places a spotlight on business opportunities and illustrates how Responsible Innovation can be successfully implemented in daily practice. In this concluding chapter, we summarize the key points from the proceeding chapters and draw conclusions for researchers, policy-makers, and business leaders. We present a strategic approach to Responsible Innovation in the business sector, grounded in the foundational concepts of RRI, aligned with the prevailing framings and narratives in the business world and informed by the various contributions of this book.

2 INSIGHTS AND CHALLENGES

Part A of this book provided valuable insights into the mindsets, experiences, and expectations of industry leaders, policy-makers, renowned researchers, and a top-selling science fiction author. The interviews spanned a wide range of innovation-related topics, including AI, extended reality, our future daily lives, as well as the grand challenges of sustainable development. Despite the diversity of backgrounds among our interviewees, several common themes emerged:

- *Responsible Innovation strategies are firmly grounded in values.* While our interview partners referred to various types of values – such as ubiquitous values, European values, corporate values, and individual values – they all emphasized that these values extend beyond the profit- and competitiveness-driven logics of markets. In the short term, giving priority to responsibility and sustainability may lead to competitive disadvantages, particularly if competitors from other parts of the world do not share these values. However, in the medium and long term, considering values becomes a fundamental necessity for effective innovation management and innovation policy. In this context, it is crucial to note that values and innovations are interconnected: innovations are tangible manifestations of values, and, therefore, values must be taken into account when implementing innovation processes. Simultaneously, the dissemination of values necessitates technological sovereignty. Consequently, global competition can be viewed as both an economic phenomenon – a race to develop the next ground-breaking innovation – and a competition of value systems that manifest themselves in technologies and products.
- *Responsible Innovation strategies are typically oriented to the long term.* However, both the policy-making arena and the business sector often grapple with shortened cycles and limited attention spans, which tend to favor incremental improvements. This short-term focus can overshadow the urgent economic, societal, and environmental challenges that demand greater consideration. Many of our interview partners emphasized the importance of adopting a

responsible and sustainable perspective that considers medium- to long-term societal and technological trends. They emphasized the significance of conducting thorough research on the potential impacts of innovation on both current and future generations and the natural environment. Although they acknowledged the inherent challenges in dealing with "unknown unknowns," they shared the belief that preventing potential negative impacts is superior, more effective, and more efficient than merely mitigating risks and damages. Particularly when innovations have a direct impact on the way we live, concepts like co-creation, stakeholder involvement, and deliberative innovation become paramount. It is evident that these practices can increase complexity, delay time to market, and, consequently, result in certain competitive disadvantages. However, the benefits of reducing risks, safeguarding the social license to operate, and addressing societal needs can outweigh such disadvantages.

- *Responsible Innovation strategies are geared toward collaboration.* Perspectives on this aspect varied, depending on the background and experience of our interview partners. For policy-makers, the emphasis was on fostering global research partnerships, encouraging interdisciplinary and cross-sectoral collaboration in research programs and projects, and nurturing regional innovation ecosystems. On the other hand, business leaders stressed the importance of collaboration with business partners, stakeholders, consumers, and lead users. The collaborative nature of Responsible Innovation becomes particularly evident when addressing shared objectives or common issues, such as those within a specific region or in relation to the UN SDGs. It is also pronounced in precompetitive collaboration, as seen in fundamental research. Challenges arise, however, in relation to competition for technologies, access to strategic resources, or market share. A strategic approach to Responsible Innovation acknowledges these tensions and follows the principle of "co-opetition," which involves flexible and reflective engagement with actors who are both collaborators and competitors.
- *Responsible Innovation strategies consider sustainable development.* The UN SDGs have gained widespread acceptance as a comprehensive framework for both policy-makers and business leaders, providing a contextual framework for Responsible Innovation strategies. While responsibility can be seen as a process-oriented aspect, the SDGs provide substantive guidance on the outcomes and impacts of innovations. Responsible Innovation strategies are therefore infused with meaningful content and purpose, as they seek to improve people's actual living conditions or, at the very least, ensure that these conditions do not deteriorate. This perspective is shared by leading scientists in the field of Responsible Research and Innovation (RRI), who place significant importance on addressing grand societal challenges, such as climate change and biodiversity loss. Consequently, they advocate for the integration of sustainability as an additional element in their RRI frameworks. For businesses, this presents both a challenge and an opportunity: to better align sustainability management with innovation

management, an alignment has the potential to make innovation management more responsible and sustainability management more innovative.

- *Responsible Innovation strategies seek systemic change.* Prior discussions regarding RRI have often revolved around high-risk technologies (such as AI, nanotechnology, or biotechnology) or the incorporation of new components into innovation processes (such as technology impact assessment or deliberative and participative innovation). However, several of our interview partners highlighted a third aspect of Responsible Innovation strategies: the design and transformation of entire systems. This extension significantly broadens the range of participating stakeholders and increases the complexity of the innovation process. Co-creating and co-designing combine elements of collaborative innovation, on the one hand, while aligning innovation with the SDGs, on the other. However, this encompasses various other aspects of systems thinking, including the consideration of feedback loops, system dynamics, and tipping points. Systemic innovation policies should therefore focus on fostering innovation ecosystems and promoting a systemic approach within research and innovation programs. As for innovation management, orienting toward systemic change entails a stronger emphasis on embedding technologies, products, and services within larger systems and recognizing the diverse and systemic interactions between a company and its stakeholders.

The Responsible Innovation strategies outlined above are not to be seen in isolation; rather, they are interconnected. They are not intended to extend or replace existing RRI frameworks but can serve as strategic guidance for decision-makers at various levels and across different organizations. They offer valuable orientation for policy-makers, corporate innovation managers, and top-level executives within organizations.

3 PROJECTS AND EXPERIENCES

The eight projects presented in Part B of this book aimed at implementing RRI in companies by addressing a particular level of the business sector:

3.1 Corporate level

Four projects focused on individual companies: RESPONSIBLE-INDUSTRY was a pilot project in RRI for business, PRISMA and COMPASS focused on different sectors and sizes of companies, from SMEs and startups to large multinational enterprises, while I AM RRI concentrated on value chains of additive manufacturing.

All corporate-level projects highlighted the *potential benefits of RRI for companies*: COMPASS emphasized the strategic value of RRI for high-tech startups; RESPONSIBLE-INDUSTRY collected case studies on the corporate benefits of RRI; PRISMA linked RRI to the concept of business value; and I AM RRI addressed the interfaces between companies in complex webs of value chains.

All the projects deeply incorporated *CSR* in their conceptual work, project implementation, and dissemination. To do this, they drew upon certain similarities between CSR and RRI, as both approaches address societal needs and concerns and hold companies responsible for their impacts. While this aspect is relatively broad in CSR, particularly as defined by the most widely accepted version, where CSR encompasses a company's responsibility for its impacts, it takes on a more specific dimension within the context of RRI and technology assessment. Also, aspects of participation show similarities between CSR and RRI, although CSR addresses it in a rather limited form (e.g., in stakeholder dialogues or during materiality assessments), whereas RRI follows a broader approach (e.g., through deliberative engagement). In addition, while CSR and RRI are both perceived as societal responsibilities, it should be noted that companies also view them as strategic opportunities (e.g., by safeguarding their license to operate, reducing sunken costs, and improving their corporate image).

Open innovation, another well-established concept in the business sector, was addressed by many projects, sometimes referring to related concepts (such as Design Thinking, Social Innovation, UX Design, Lead User Innovation, etc.), sometimes with slightly different meanings, and often in different contexts. As openness is a core element of RRI, the projects considered it to be a perfect link to Open Innovation as a well-established discursive frame in companies, for which a broad variety of tools are already available.

All corporate-level projects interpreted RRI following the process-oriented *ARRI framework*[1](Stilgoe *et al.*, 2013), with a special emphasis on participation and anticipation. While reflexivity and responsiveness were not as frequently highlighted, two projects (PRISMA and RESPONSIBLE-INDUSTRY) added sustainability as a fifth dimension to the ARRI framework.

All projects utilized *information-oriented incentive mechanisms* to disseminate RRI in the business sector: well-documented case studies (which show the benefits of RRI for companies and address their self-interest) and hands-on tools (which allow other companies to follow these cases). In addition, two projects (RESPONSIBLE-INDUSTRY and COMPASS) developed benchmarking tools that enable companies to assess their RRI maturity and compare themselves to the anonymized data of other companies. One project (PRISMA) used international standards as an incentive mechanism and collaborated with the European Committee for Standardization (CEN) and several national standard organizations to integrate RRI into a technical document by the CEN.

Most projects attempted to establish *user groups and online communities* beyond the consortium partners and hoped that being a member of such groups would serve as a network-based incentive mechanism for disseminating RRI in the business sector. However, the long-term effects of these networks were limited, and, in some cases, the project websites are no longer online. These findings underscore the challenges that individual projects encounter when trying to establish incentive mechanisms independently due to constraints in budget, outreach, and time.

3.2 Process level

One project (SISCODE) placed its focus on individual innovation processes, experimented in ten co-creation labs with a broad variety of topics, and delivered a virtual learning hub using a wide range of tools and an interactive guidebook for practitioners. The project implemented a detailed and sophisticated exploitation strategy and established a platform to share and learn about co-creation, and they strongly relied on the dissemination and uptake of research findings.

SISCODE based its work on the concept of *co-creation*, which can be understood as a non-linear process that involves multiple actors and stakeholders in the ideation, implementation, and assessment of product services, policies, and systems. By doing so, the project aimed to establish co-creation as a new, independent, and unique frame that is only loosely linked to and supported by RRI and does not explicitly refer to other framings of responsibility or sustainability. While elements of reflexivity were occasionally considered, they were generally addressed in more general terms and not in the specific context of the ARRI framework. Furthermore, the project did not prioritize examining the impacts of innovations.

The project addressed various *challenges of co-creation*, such as power imbalances among the actors involved, resource limitations (especially by citizens), alignment of goals and values, coordination issues, and limited trust when actors have different views on what constitutes success. These potential tensions were intended to be resolved through the development of a shared language and method for reflection during the process, fostering a common understanding that drives innovative thought processes for positive societal impact. However, beyond these aspects, the SISCODE did not highlight any tensions prior to a co-creation process (whether it be regarding an innovation agenda or the focus of a co-creation process), or after a co-creation process had finished (regarding the share of profits that an innovative solution, product, or service might generate).

3.3 Territorial level

Three projects (DigiTeRRI, SeeRRI, and RRI2SCALE) set out to integrate RRI into their regional development and therefore actively involved local and regional authorities as well as businesses covering multiple regions in Europe. They all included public authorities as well as businesses as consortium partners, focused on integrating RRI principles into regional smart specialization strategies, developed roadmaps, and designed implementation processes beyond the pilot regions.

All three projects interpreted RRI following the *RRI keys of the European Commission* and referred to developmental and society-oriented policy goals, such as wealth, wellbeing, and regional economic development, and used policy-driven monetary benefits as incentive mechanisms to disseminate RRI in their target regions and beyond.

All territorial-level projects referred to the *quadruple helix* of innovation as a fundamental principle of the consortium composition. In implementing the projects, the quadruple helix served as an inclusive strategy for involving a broad range of actors in workshops and was referred to in multiple project outcomes. In this view, the complementarity of assets, interests, and actors stands in the foreground, while competitive elements are regarded as less important or only relevant to local competition with other regions. As a result, the predominant focus was on societal goals and shared interests, overshadowing potential conflicts, with the expectation being for policy, business, and research sectors to collaborate and work together to achieve these common aims.

The most important incentive mechanism for integrating RRI into regional development strategies and businesses stems from the European Union: while the *European Structural Funds* provide (co-)funding for regional development programs and projects, they also require regions to develop "smart specialization strategies," identifying strategic areas for innovation and development with wide stakeholder involvement. All three regional projects took these well-established incentive mechanisms as their main anchor points for integrating RRI into regional development. This approach was driven by the perception that the principles of RRI align with existing policies, processes, and strategies, making them compatible and conducive to regional development.

3.4 Institutionalizing RRI in the business sector

On the one hand, the very broad understanding of institutional theory suggests that most of the project deliverables potentially support the institutionalization of RRI in the business sector, particularly as all of them are open access. On the other hand, it is difficult to determine the extent to which an individual deliverable has actually driven institutional change. This is because most of the projects did not track the impacts of their deliverables, either because they lacked tracking data or because it was too early to provide evidence of impact. Therefore, we can only report on the different types of deliverables and the institutional changes they sought:

- *Roadmaps*: Most projects developed roadmaps and published them as project deliverables, but a closer look revealed a certain degree of variation in these documents. Some contained a number of recommendations drafted by one or several consortium partners, while others were developed in the course of stakeholder dialogues involving key players in their implementation, making these roadmaps more of a commitment for practical adoption. The latter can therefore be perceived as the first step of institutionalizing RRI in the business sector.
- *Integration of RRI into smart specialization strategies*: Regional-level projects integrated RRI into their well-established governance procedures, documents, and institutions. These institutions were not new, but they were open to such an integration, and the projects led to changes in their operation. This is a specific form of institutionalization.

- *Integration of RRI into tools of innovation management*: Process-level projects integrate RRI into well-established methods (e.g., Design Thinking, innovation canvas) and develop guidelines and toolkits for co-creation. In these types of projects, institutionalization can occur through the introduction of tools, the training of experts who apply them, and the quality control of their application (e.g., through professional associations).
- *Integration of RRI into CEN standards*: One corporate-level project succeeded in integrating RRI into a newly developed innovation management standard of the European Committee for Standardization (CEN), which has vast potential for institutionalizing RRI across a broad range of companies.
- *Policy briefs*: Several projects published policy briefs, such as on co-creation and on implementing RRI in health and aging. The impacts of these documents on policy and on institutionalizing RRI remain unclear, as there is no available evidence of their uptake.
- *Events*: All projects organized outreach events, such as workshops, dialogues, webinars, training, and other interactions, at which industry representatives, policy-makers, researchers, and members of civil society were brought together. While these events exhibited some degree of continuity during the project's duration, they were rarely sustained once the project concluded.

3.5 Experiences and conclusions

- *Responsible Innovation strategies speak the language of the business sector.* Although most of the projects referred to the RRI keys of the European Union and/or the ARRI framework, their primary aim was to adapt these concepts for the business sector, for example, by using business-oriented language, demonstrating the benefits of RRI for business, showing that certain elements of RRI are already in place, and illustrating how to integrate the missing components. In this way, they moved beyond RRI as a list of binding criteria, instead emphasizing the deeper meaning of RRI for the business sector.
- *Responsible Innovation strategies require resources and tools.* Nearly all projects attempted to showcase their RRI approach and developed new tools to explain it. The term "tool" can refer to a broad range of deliverables, ranging from downloadable how-to guidelines and checklists, to online self-check tools that enable data input and generate benchmarking results based on the data of a peer group of other companies. However, implementing the key elements of RRI requires the use of additional resources and cannot be done as simply another part-time job of busy innovation managers or CSR managers.
- *Responsible Innovation strategies address the truly important issues.* Several projects addressed new transformative technologies such as nanotechnology, biotechnology, the Internet of Things, autonomous vehicles, or AI. These

technologies are the foundation of competitive advantage, and any irresponsible business conduct can risk the acceptance of these technologies and the operational license of the companies involved. However, these potential costs of inaction still require more precise quantification to be fully considered in management decision-making processes.

- *Responsible Innovation strategies build up trust among stakeholders.* Innovation bears the risk of potential conflicts between profit and growth, on the one hand, and environmental sustainability and societal wellbeing, on the other. To work with such potential conflicts, the projects demonstrated how to create a space for building trust and how such a collaborative culture can explore desired futures, for example, by using foresight, shared visions, or joint roadmaps.

4 TOOLS AND METHODS

Part C of this book presented four distinct tools that were developed as part of the EU project, LIVING INNOVATION. All these tools focus on inclusion, participation, and deliberative innovation – key aspects of RRI. Other aspects, such as anticipation, reflexivity, and responsiveness, were considered when developing and implementing these tools but are not their focus.

- *Co-creation* supports the translation of RRI into business practices by enabling users, citizens, and other stakeholders to take an active role in innovation processes so as to better identify needs and wishes. As business practitioners often struggle with co-creation processes, Chapter C2 explores how to ensure high-quality co-creation processes through careful planning and conscious decision-making from the very beginning, by defining scope and objectives, and by applying specific designs. By considering these aspects, business practitioners can manage the complexity of co-creation processes, better consider quality criteria, and apply appropriate methods.
- *Responsible Design Thinking* is a targeted, smart, and efficient extension of the Design Thinking model, a well-established method on how to better understand user needs, develop innovative ideas, and then rapidly prototype and test them. It comprises four extensions: considering societal needs, following a systemic approach, assessing future impacts, and adding a setup phase in the very beginning. These extensions were carefully chosen, do not hamper the creativity and agility of design thinking, and neither overload nor slow it down. Chapter C3 provides suggestions for several methods that can be applied for each of these extensions.
- *Real-life inclusion* provides comprehensive insights into a case study that involved 14 families, including parents and children, residing in three relatively deprived areas of Leicester, in the UK. The study in Chapter C4 focused on how these families identified innovative digital technology ideas that might impact future homes. The workshops reflect important aspects of Responsible

Innovation and have developed and tested a unique methodology through which socially disadvantaged persons could be involved in systems or product development responsibly. It provides business practitioners with a novel approach to co-creation involving marginalized groups.

- *Inclusive workshops* necessitate the use of tools designed to (better) include blind or visually impaired people in innovation processes. These tools encompass various considerations, including participant recruitment, the workshop setting, accessibility of information, and interaction guidelines for facilitators. Additionally, the tools include hands-on, practical methods for providing creative inspiration, fostering collaboration among the participants, and facilitating the design process for specific products. At the end, Chapter C5 showcases several inclusive products that were already developed using the toolkit.

5 A COMPELLING BUSINESS CASE FOR RESPONSIBLE INNOVATION

The aim of this book is to transform RRI from a vague societal aspiration to a compelling business case. The book seeks to broaden the perspective beyond profit and competitiveness by emphasizing the value of co-creating responsible and sustainable innovation for the future we want. It also elucidates the strategic advantages of Responsible Innovation and provides practical tools for its implementation. Furthermore, it demonstrates the tangible benefits that RRI can have for innovation managers, consultants, and facilitators working on Responsible Innovation and sustainability management.

To integrate the diverse findings from the preceding chapters and offer a business-oriented and opportunity-driven perspective on Responsible Innovation, this final chapter outlines a strategic approach to Responsible Innovation. To do this: (1) it draws from state-of-the-art concepts of Responsible Innovation to provide a sound scientific basis; (2) it covers a concise set of core elements that can be effectively communicated; (3) it explains the associated business opportunities and societal benefits; and (4) it proposes tools for its practical implementation (Figure 1).

5.1 Managing impacts of innovations

The first key element underscores the importance of considering the long-term societal, environmental, and economic impacts of innovations. It requires that businesses extend their responsibility beyond markets and innovate in order to achieve a positive impact. The notion of taking responsibility for impacts comes from the discourse on CSR and sustainability management, aligning with the well-established narrative of responsibility within the business sector (Vogel-Pöschl *et al.*, 2020). Contemporary CSR frameworks seek to maximize a company's positive impacts and minimize its negative impacts on the social and environmental systems in which it operates. This orientation toward corporate impacts had already been put forward by the European Union back in 2011 (European Commission, 2011) and has been integrated into sustainability

Figure 1

A strategic approach to Responsible Innovation in the business sector

	Impacts of Innovation	Co-Creating Innovations	Systemic Perspective
Responsibility	... beyond markets	... to put societal needs central	... to future-oriented solutions
Innovate	... for positive impact	... in a truly inclusive manner	... by understanding interrelationships
Business Case	... to increase value and reduce risks	... to develop more and better ideas	... to become an industry game-changer
Societal Benefits	... to contribute to prosperity and wellbeing	... to tackle grand societal challenges	... to increase societal resilience and sustainability
Methods	1. Materiality assessment 2. Foresight 3. Technology assessment	1. Imaginary participation 2. Representative participation 3. Direct participation	1. Systemic Canvases 2. Causal Loop Diagrams 3. Systemic Constellation

standards since then. For example, the Global Reporting Initiative (GRI) standards, which form the basis for most companies' sustainability reports, require businesses to assess the materiality of their direct and indirect, planned and unplanned, ecological, economic, and social impacts (Adams *et al.*, 2021). Furthermore, this emphasis on impacts has become central to the Greenhouse Gas Protocol, which incorporates the indirect impacts of purchased goods and services as well as the impacts of sold products and investments (i.e., Scope 3 emissions) into its framework (Russell, 2019).

- *Business case*: Actively managing the impacts of innovations enhances a company's value and mitigates risks. This proactive approach secures the social license to operate for technologies and products while also reducing the likelihood of incurring sunk costs (Edwards *et al.*, 2021).
- *Societal benefits*: At the societal level, giving due consideration to impacts contributes to prosperity and wellbeing. It also helps to prevent high social follow-up costs of innovations, as exemplified by historical cases such as Thalidomide, asbestos, and nuclear power (Bessant, 2013; Hohmeyer, 2012). This approach aligns with the ongoing discourse on anticipation as a core element of RRI (Stilgoe *et al.*, 2013).
- *Methods*: A variety of sustainability management techniques can be used to manage impacts: materiality assessments (which are relatively straightforward to implement), foresight methods, scenario techniques, and technology assessments (which demand a more substantial investment of time and effort):

- *Materiality assessment* originates from financial reporting, auditing, and accounting. It has been introduced into sustainability management as a method for determining the significance of sustainability-related matters to a company and its stakeholders (Taubken & Feld, 2018). Materiality assessments have gained traction through endorsement by prominent sustainability standards, such as the GRI standards or the standards laid out by the Sustainability Accounting Standards Board, and have subsequently been applied in corporate practice (Wu *et al.*, 2018).
- *Foresight methods and scenario techniques* are valuable tools for mitigating long-term uncertainty and complexity. They enable the development of multiple future scenarios by fostering strategic thinking and pushing the boundaries of conventional thinking (Amer *et al.*, 2013). These methods, which were first applied for social forecasting and public policy analysis in the 1960s, have since been widely adopted in the corporate sector for strategic planning (Turner, 2022). While there is no single approach to foresight and scenario techniques (Varum & Melo, 2010), all these methods share a common emphasis on defining the issues, systemically identifying key drivers, trends, constraints, and stakeholders, and ranking these factors according to their level of uncertainty and importance (Amer *et al.*, 2013).
- *Technology assessment* focuses on the early identification and evaluation of the potential impacts of technological advances and applications. Initially employed in the public domain (Rip, 2015), this method has since been embraced by the business sector as well. Technology assessments play a crucial role in anticipating the future developments of technologies, their interplay with markets, and their potential impacts on society and the natural environment. In corporate or project-level technology assessments, a wide array of tools is employed, encompassing both qualitative and quantitative methodologies (Tran & Daim, 2008).

5.2 Co-creating innovations

The second key element necessitates that businesses place societal needs at the center of their innovation processes, thus enabling them to innovate in a truly inclusive manner. This approach expands the stakeholder circle far more than established approaches like open innovation (West & Bogers, 2014), lead user innovation (Franke *et al.*, 2006), and Design Thinking (Brown, 2008). These more established methods typically involve only lead users, employees, and their families, and are strongly oriented toward the preferences of highly educated, wealthy, tech-savvy, young, and predominantly male individuals. In contrast, co-creation prioritizes societal needs in innovation processes, involves a broader range of stakeholders, and designs innovation processes in a truly inclusive manner (Voorberg *et al.*, 2015).

- *Business case:* The business case of innovating with and for the people provides several compelling advantages, including the generation of a greater number of ideas that better align with user needs (Lindberg, 2018), enhanced user experience (Kraft, 2012), and improved reputation and trust (Iglesias *et al.*, 2020).
- *Societal benefits:* At the societal level, co-creation directs a company's innovation capacities toward grand societal challenges (Voegtlin *et al.*, 2022). This approach also aligns with the ongoing RRI-related discourse on participatory and deliberative innovation (Brand & Blok, 2019).
- *Methods:* A wide array of co-creation methods are available: imaginary participation using the personas method; representative participation by politicians, members of NGOs, or other specific interest groups; and direct participation involving people directly in co-creation processes.
    - *Imaginary participation*, using the personas method, originally emerged from IT development before being applied in marketing and product development within the context of co-creation (Nielsen, 2011). Personas are highly detailed virtual representations of people who belong to specific target user groups, capturing typical "real-world" characteristics in an abstract manner (Dennerlein *et al.*, 2018). When developing a persona's profile, the following aspects need to be taken into account: age, gender, profession, residence, marital status, educational background, career trajectory, hobbies, current personal and professional situation, lifestyle, values, attitudes, aspirations, and needs. In the development of personas, major societal trends, such as those identified in the European Commission Global Trend Report (European Commission, 2019), should be considered.
    - *Representative participation* requires societal interests and needs to be conveyed through representatives. This can involve the participation of politicians, members of NGOs, or other specific interest groups in co-creation processes (Kazadi *et al.*, 2016). Representative participation is easier to implement than direct participation, as NGOs and interest groups working on social and environmental issues are often enthusiastic about engaging in the development of innovations that enhance the wellbeing of the individuals they represent.
    - *Direct participation* involves engaging individuals directly in co-creation processes (Jones & Kijima, 2018). It is essential to include people from diverse age groups, genders, sociocultural backgrounds, and professional fields, encompassing a wide range of societal needs and concerns. This inclusivity is vital to ensuring the societal acceptance of the outcomes resulting from co-creation processes. Identifying and involving a varied participant group can be a challenge, as selected individuals must possess a genuine interest in the respective innovation project and have sufficient time to participate. To enhance creativity, it is advisable to include additional participants with a creative professional background, such as designers, artists, or architects.

5.3 A systemic perspective

The third key element places a strong emphasis on the collective responsibility of businesses and other stakeholders in developing future-oriented solutions. It roots innovation in a deeper understanding of interrelations and systems dynamics with the aim of achieving the following: (1) integrating systems thinking into innovation processes (Galanakis, 2006), (2) expanding the perspective from innovating individual technologies, products, and services to consider the broader systems in which they are embedded, and (3) focusing on entire systems as objects of innovation processes. A systemic perspective, stemming from the discourse on systems thinking, emphasizes that a system is more than the sum of its parts (Elia *et al.*, 2021). It seeks to understand underlying interrelationships among its elements, the dynamics within the system, and the identification of patterns of change (Meadows, 2008; Senge, 2006). It also aids in understanding the relationships between system components, the dynamics at play, and the identification and reinforcement of positive feedback loops (Aramo-Immonen & Vanharanta, 2009). Furthermore, a systemic perspective offers flexibility, which is necessary in dealing with the uncertainty and complexity that can result from considering sustainability aspects in innovation processes (Kapsali, 2011).

- *Business case*: Embracing a systemic perspective empowers businesses to co-design entire systems, providing them with greater flexibility and relieving constraints imposed by regulation, market forces, and competition. This approach not only fosters radical innovation but also enables companies to become industry "game-changers," leading the transformation of sectors, value chains, and technology landscapes (Geels & Schot, 2007).
- *Societal benefits*: At the societal level, a systemic perspective helps to realize the innovation potential for sustainable and more resilient solutions. This is particularly valuable in addressing systemic challenges, such as climate change and biodiversity loss. Additionally, a systemic perspective aligns with the ongoing discourse about system innovation and the transition toward sustainability (Elzen *et al.*, 2004).
- *Methods*: Various methods can be employed to nurture a systemic perspective. Systemic innovation canvases represent the simplest approach and are relatively easy to apply. Causal loop diagrams are more demanding as they require a comprehensive understanding of their specific "language." Lastly, systemic constellations are the most complex to put into practice, typically requiring the aid of trained facilitators. All three methods share the common objective of providing a holistic perspective, focusing on interrelationships within and between systems, considering system dynamics and feedback loops, emphasizing resilience, and enabling the incorporation of multiple perspectives.
    - *Systemic canvases* link canvas approaches – a visualization method to depict a "big picture" and establish a shared vision (Kalbach, 2016) – with system-thinking (Elia *et al.*, 2021). In this method, the final adopters, users, and

stakeholders of innovations are considered, enabling the examination of direct and indirect impacts on the economy, the natural environment, and society as well as their interrelations. The use of flowcharts provides a dynamic view on the relationships between the various components. Additionally, the incorporation of systems archetypes, which describe behavioral patterns in systems, can further enhance a systemic perspective and aid in managing complexity.

- *Causal loop diagrams* have their roots in the feedback concepts of cybernetics and the theory of servomechanics (Sedlacko *et al.*, 2014). They aim to identify the whole system, understand the relationships between system components, and capture the dynamics within the system (Meadows, 2008). Participatory systems mapping provides a standardized "language" for visualizing a system and its interrelations (Martinuzzi *et al.*, 2015; Sedlacko *et al.*, 2014) and enables innovation managers to gain an understanding of the individual and collective behavior of system elements. However, working with causal loop diagrams requires proficiency in the method's "language," which often requires comprehensive training and mentoring (Ackermann & Alexander, 2016).
- *Systemic constellations*, originally developed in the field of family therapy and psychology in the 1980s (Kopp & Martinuzzi, 2013), have been adapted for organizational contexts to address dynamics and complexity (Königswieser & Hillebrand, 2016). In this method, abstract elements, like problems, aims, or values can be incorporated, focusing on the concerns, explanations, interpretations, and ideas of stakeholders (Sparrer, 2016). Systemic constellations offer an outside view of the entire system by making implicit knowledge explicit and through visual representation. This aids in enhancing cognitive perception, systemic thinking, and problem-solving (Weinhold *et al.*, 2014).

The strategic approach to Responsible Innovation outlined above connects the fundamental principles of Responsible Innovation with both business opportunities and societal benefits. It combines frames and narratives from the scientific and policy discourse regarding responsibility and sustainability with the business-focused concepts of CSR, Open Innovation, and systemic change. This outline will serve as the foundation for a cohesive narrative of Responsible Innovation in our forthcoming research endeavors.

6 OUTLOOK

In recent years, the ideas, principles, and methods of RRI have been successfully transferred from the public sector to the business arena (Ivanova *et al.*, 2023). Initially, societal needs and concerns were often perceived as an additional burden by companies, but the competitive advantages of Responsible Innovation have started to become more recognized and valued. This book sought to contribute to this evolving perspective, positioning Responsible Innovation as a strategic business opportunity. Nevertheless, there are several further steps that could be taken to foster the dissemination of Strategic Responsible Innovation in the business sector:

- *Future research and innovation programs*, such as Horizon Europe, could ensure greater continuity of activities and streamline the alignment and integration of project outcomes. Individual projects often invest significant efforts into developing tools and strategies, yet they frequently lack outreach and struggle to integrate their results into a bigger picture. Thus, this book sought to foster collaboration, expand outreach, and construct a model for the integration, demonstration, and dissemination of successful projects.
- *Future research endeavors* should dive deeper into the analysis of potentially conflicting interests of business and society and provide an even more nuanced understanding of both synergies and trade-offs. Building upon these insights, RRI-related policy instruments could provide stronger incentives than showcases, tools, and networking activities and consider the specificities of Responsible Innovation in a globalized economy.
- *Future business strategies* should leverage Responsible Innovation as a competitive advantage by strengthening the connections between innovation management, on the one hand, and responsibility and sustainability management, on the other. They should also focus on assessing the future impacts of innovations, promote co-creation, and adopt a systems thinking perspective on innovation. This book has outlined these key concepts as elements of Responsible Innovation strategies. Future research, though, will play a crucial role in further enhancing our comprehension of the business case of Responsible Innovation.

NOTE

1. The ARRI framework operationalizes RRI through four dimensions: anticipation, reflexivity, inclusion, and responsiveness.

REFERENCES

Abrams, F. W. (1951). Management's responsibilities in a complex world. *Harvard Business Review*, *29*, 29–34.

Ackermann, F., & Alexander, J. (2016). Researching complex projects: Using causal mapping to take a systems perspective. *International Journal of Project Management*, *34*(6), 891–901. https://doi.org/10.1016/j.ijproman.2016.04.001

Adams, C. A., Alhamood, A., He, X., Tian, J., Wang, L., & Wang, Y. (2021). The double-materiality concept: Application and issues. Global Reporting Initiative. Available at: https://www.globalreporting.org/media/jrbntbyv/griwhitepaper-publications.pdf

Amer, M., Daim, T. U., & Jetter, A. (2013). A review of scenario planning. *Futures*, *46*, 23–40. https://doi.org/10.1016/j.futures.2012.10.003

Aramo-Immonen, H., & Vanharanta, H. (2009). Project management: The task of holistic systems thinking. *Human Factors and Ergonomics in Manufacturing, 19*(6), 582–600. https://doi.org/10.1002/hfm.20185

Berle, A. A. (1931). Corporate powers as powers in trust. *Harvard Law Review, 44*(7), 1049–1073. https://doi:10.2307/1331341

Bessant, J. (2013). Innovation in the twenty-first century. In R. Owen, J., Bessant, & M. Heintz (Eds.), *Responsible innovation* (pp. 1–25). Wiley.

Bowen, H. R. (1953). Social responsibilities of the businessman (1st ed.). Harper and Brothers.

Brand, T., & Blok, V. (2019). Responsible innovation in business: A critical reflection on deliberative engagement as a central governance mechanism. *Journal of Responsible Innovation, 6*(1), 4–24. https://doi.org/10.1080/23299460.2019.1575681

Brown, T. (2008). Design thinking. *Harvard Business Review, 86*(6), 84.

Carroll, A. B. (1979). A three-dimensional conceptual model of corporate performance. *The Academy of Management Review, 4*(4), 497–505.

Carroll, A. B. (1999). Corporate social responsibility: Evolution of a definitional construct. *Business & Society, 38*(3), 268–295.

Dahlsrud, A. (2008). How corporate social responsibility is defined: An analysis of 37 definitions, *Corporate Social Responsibility and Environmental Management, 15*(1),1–13. https://doi:10.1002/csr.132

Dennerlein, S., Kowald, D., Pammer-Schindler, V., Lex, E., & Ley, T. (2018). Simulation-based co-creation of algorithms. In *CEUR Workshop Proceedings, 2190.*

Dodd, E. M. (1932). For whom are corporate managers trustees?, *The Harvard Law Review, 45*(7), 1145–1163.

Donham, W. B (1927). The social significance of business. *Harvard Business Review*, 4(4), 406–419.

Edler, J., Blind, K., Kroll, H., & Schubert, T. (2023) Technology sovereignty as an emerging frame for innovation policy. Defining rationales, ends and means. *Research Policy*, 52(6), 104765.

Edwards, P., Fleming, A., & Kelly, R. (2021). Responsible research and innovation and social licence to operate: Aligning concepts for advancing marine innovation and development governance. *Current Opinion in Environmental Sustainability, 49*, 12–17.

Elia, G., Margherita, A., & Secundo, G. (2021). Project management canvas: A systems thinking framework to address project complexity. *International Journal of Managing Projects in Business, 14*(4), 809–835. https://doi.org/10.1108/IJMPB-04-2020-0128

Elzen, B., Geels, F., & Green, K. (Eds.) (2004). *System innovation and the transition to sustainability: Theory, evidence and policy*. Edward Elgar Publishing

European Commission (2011). A renewed EU strategy 2011–14 for Corporate Social Responsibility. COM(2011) 681 fin, Communication from the Commission to the European Parliament, the Council, the European Economic and Social Committee and the Committee of the Regions. Brussels: European Commission.

European Commission (2019). Global trends to 2030: Challenges and choices for Europe, Publications Office. https://data.europa.eu/doi/10.2872/074526

Franke, N., Von Hippel, E., & Schreier, M. (2006). Finding commercially attractive user innovations: A test of lead-user theory. *Journal of Product Innovation Management, 23*(4), 301–315.

Friede, G., Busch, T., & Bassen, A. (2015). ESG and financial performance: Aggregated evidence from more than 2000 empirical studies. *Journal of Sustainable Finance & Investment, 5*(4), 210–233. https://doi:10.1080/20430795.2015.1118917

Friedman, M. (1962). *Capitalism and freedom*. University of Chicago Press.

Friedman, M. (1970). The social responsibility of business is to increase its profits. *New York Times Magazine*, September 13, pp. 32–33.

Galanakis, K. (2006). Innovation process. Make sense using systems thinking. *Technovation, 26*(11), 1222–1232.

Geels, F. W., & Schot, J. (2007). Typology of sociotechnical transition pathways. *Research Policy, 36*(3), 399–417.

Hirsch, S., Petersen, T., Koppenberg, M., & Hartmann, M. (2022). CSR and firm profitability: Evidence from a meta-regression analysis. *Journal of Economic Surveys*. doi:10.1111/joes.12523.

Hohmeyer, O. (2012). *Social costs of energy consumption: External effects of electricity generation in the Federal Republic of Germany*. Springer Science & Business Media.

Iglesias, O., Markovic, S., Bagherzadeh, M., & Singh, J. J. (2020). Co-creation: A key link between corporate social responsibility, customer trust, and customer loyalty. *Journal of Business Ethics, 163*, 151–166.

Ivanova, S.; Reichetzer, C., Martinuzzi, A., Findler, F., & Miko-Schefzig, K. (2023). Frames, interests, and incentives: A typology for institutionalizing RRI in the business sector derived from ten pioneering projects. *Journal of Responsible Innovation, 10*(1). https://doi.org/10.1080/23299460.2023.2267736

Jarmai, K., Tharani, A., & Nwafor, C. (2020). Responsible innovation in business. In K. Jarmai (Ed.), *Responsible innovation: Business opportunities and strategies for implementation* (pp. 7–17). Springer.

Jones, P., & Kijima, K. (Eds.). (2018). *Systemic design: Theory, methods, and practice*. Springer Japan. https://doi.org/10.1007/978-4-431-55639-8

Kalbach, J. (2016). *Mapping experiences: A guide to creating value through journeys, blueprints, and diagrams* (1st ed.). O'Reilly.

Kapsali, M. (2011). Systems thinking in innovation project management: A match that works. *International Journal of Project Management, 29*(4), 396–407. https://doi.org/10.1016/j.ijproman.2011.01.003

Kazadi, K., Lievens, A., & Mahr, D. (2016). Stakeholder co-creation during the innovation process: Identifying capabilities for knowledge creation among multiple stakeholders. *Journal of Business Research, 69*(2), 525–540. https://doi.org/10.1016/j.jbusres.2015.05.009

Königswieser, R., & Hillebrand, M. (2016). *Systemic consultancy in organisations: Concepts – tools – innovations* (1st ed.). Carl Auer Verlag. https://ebookcentral.proquest.com/lib/gbv/detail.action?docID=5471756

Kopp, U., & Martinuzzi, A. (2013). Teaching sustainability leaders in systems thinking. *Business Systems Review, 2*(2), 191–215.

Kraft, C. (2012). *User experience innovation: User centered design that works*. Spinger.

Lindberg, M. (2018). Relating inclusiveness and innovativeness in inclusive innovation. *International Journal of Innovation and Regional Development, 8*(2), 103–119.

Martinuzzi, A, Blok, V., Brem, A., Stahl, B., & Schönherr, N. (2018). Responsible research and innovation in industry: Challenges, insights and perspectives. *Sustainability, 10*(3), 702.

Martinuzzi, A., Sedlacko, M., & Jaeger, J. (2015). Responder: Linking sustainable consumption and growth debates following a systems-thinking approach. In A. Martinuzzi & M. Sedlacko (Eds.), *Knowledge brokerage for sustainable development: Innovative tools for increasing research impact and evidence-based policy-making* (1st ed., pp. 275–288). Taylor and Francis.

Matten, D., & Crane, A. (2005). Corporate citizenship: Toward an extended theoretical conceptualization. *Academy of Management Review, 30*(1), 166–179. doi:10.5465/amr.2005.15281448.

Meadows, D. H. (2008). *Thinking in systems: A primer*. Chelsea Green Publishing Co.

Nielsen, L. (2011). Personas in co-creation and co-design. Paper presented at Eleventh Danish HCI Research Symposium.

Owen, R., & Pansera, M. (2019). Responsible innovation and responsible research and innovation. In R. Owen & M. Pansera (Eds.), *Handbook on science and public policy*. Edward Elgar.

Owen, R., von Schomberg, R., & Macnaghten, Ph (2021). An unfinished journey? Reflections on a decade of Responsible Research and Innovation. *Journal of Responsible Innovation*, *8*(2), 217–233. https://doi:10.1080/23299460.2021.1948789

Porter, M. E., & Kramer, M.R. (2006). Strategy and society: The link between competitive advantage and corporate social responsibility. *Harvard Business Review*, *84*(12), 78–92.

Porter, M. E., & Kramer, M.R. (2011). Creating shared value. *Harvard Business Review*, *89*(1–2), 62–77.

Rip, A. (2015). Technology assessment. In *International encyclopedia of the social & behavioral Sciences* (pp. 125–128). Elsevier. https://doi.org/10.1016/B978-0-08-097086-8.85036-9

Rodriguez-Gomez, S., Arco-Castro, M. L., Lopez-Perez, M. V., & Rodríguez-Ariza, L. (2020). Where does CSR come from and where does it go? A review of the state of the art. *Administrative Sciences*, *10*(3). https://doi:10.3390/admsci10030060

Russell, S. (2019). Estimating and reporting the comparative emissions impacts of products. https://ghgprotocol.org/sites/default/files/standards/18_WP_Comparative-Emissions_final.pdf

Schönherr, N., Martinuzzi, A., & Jarmai, K. (2020). Towards a business case for Responsible Innovation. In K. Jarmai (Ed.), *Responsible Innovation* (pp. 85–97). Springer.

Sedlacko, M., Martinuzzi, A., Røpke, I., Videira, N., & Antunes, P. (2014). Participatory systems mapping for sustainable consumption: Discussion of a method promoting systemic insights. *Ecological Economics*, *106*, 33–43. https://doi.org/10.1016/j.ecolecon.2014.07.002

Senge, P. M. (2006). *The fifth discipline: The art and practice of the learning organization* (2nd ed.). Random House Business.

Sparrer, I. (2016). *Systemische Strukturaufstellungen: Theorie und Praxis* (3rd ed.). Carl-Auer Verlag GmbH.

Stilgoe, J., Owen, R., & Macnaghten, P. (2013). Developing a framework for responsible innovation. *Research Policy*, *42*(9), 1568–1580. https://doi.org/10.1016/j.respol.2013.05.008

Taubken, N., & Feld, T. Y. (2018). Impact measurement and the concept of materiality: New requirements and approaches for materiality assessments. *NachhaltigkeitsManagementForum | Sustainability Management Forum*, *26*(1–4), 87–100. https://doi.org/10.1007/s00550-018-0483-x

Tran, T. A., & Daim, T. (2008). A taxonomic review of methods and tools applied in technology assessment. *Technological Forecasting and Social Change*, *75*(9), 1396–1405. https://doi.org/10.1016/j.techfore.2008.04.004

Turner, J. (2022). Using principal–steward contracting and scenario planning to manage megaprojects. *Project Management Journal*, *53*(1), 8–16. https://doi.org/10.1177/87569728211061836

Varum, C. A., & Melo, C. (2010). Directions in scenario planning literature: A review of the past decades. *Futures*, *42*(4), 355–369. https://doi.org/10.1016/j.futures.2009.11.021

Voegtlin, C., Scherer, A. G., Stahl, G. K., & Hawn, O. (2022). Grand societal challenges and responsible innovation. *Journal of Management Studies*, *59*(1), 1–28.

Vogel-Pöschl, H., Martinuzzi, A., & Schönherr, N. (2020). Evaluating corporate impacts on the SDGs: Tools, cases, and future challenges. *Zeitschrift für Evaluation*, *2020*(02), 261–290. https://doi.org/10.31244/zfe.2020.02.04

von Schomberg, R. (2012). Prospects for technology assessment in a framework of responsible research and innovation. In M. Dusseldorp & R. Beecroft (Eds.), *Technikfolgen abschätzen lehren: Bildungspotenziale transdisziplinärer Methoden* (pp. 39–61). Verlag für Sozialwissenschafte.

Voorberg, W. H., Bekkers, V. J., & Tummers, L. G. (2015). A systematic review of co-creation and co-production: Embarking on the social innovation journey. *Public Management Review, 17*(9), 1333–1357

Weinhold, J., Bornhäuser, A., Hunger, C., & Schweitzer, J. (2014). *Dreierlei Wirksamkeit: Die Heidelberger Studie zu Systemaufstellungen* (1st ed.).Carl-Auer Verlag GmbH.

West, J., & Bogers, M. (2014). Leveraging external sources of innovation: A review of research on open innovation. *Journal of Product Innovation Management, 31*(4), 814–831

Wu, S., Shao, C., & Chen, J. (2018). Approaches on the screening methods for materiality in sustainability reporting. *Sustainability, 10*(9), 3233. https://doi.org/10.3390/su10093233

Index

Note: **Bold** page numbers refer to tables; *italic* page numbers refer to figures.